D0876125

Small Business Management Fundamentals

Small Business Management Fundamentals

FIRST CANADIAN EDITION

ANDREW J. SZONYI
Ph. D., P. Eng., M.B.A.
Toronto, Ontario
DAN STEINHOFF
D.S.Sc.
Professor of Business Management
University of Miami

McGRAW-HILL RYERSON LIMITED
Montreal Toronto

To W.F.G.

Canadian Cataloguing in Publication Data

Szonyi, Andrew.
Small business management fundamentals

Based on the 2d American ed. by D. Steinhoff.
Includes bibliographies and index.

ISBN 0-07-082916-0

1. Small business — Management. 2. Self-employed.
3. Small business — Canada — Management.
4. Self-employed — Canada. I. Steinhoff, Dan.
II. Title.

HD69.S6S96 658'.022 C79-094268-2

1 2 3 4 5 6 7 8 9 10 D 8 7 6 5 4 3 2 1 0 9

Printed and bound in Canada

Small Business Management Fundamentals

Preface

The first Canadian edition of *Small Business Management Fundamentals* builds on the strength of the American text. Because of my great respect and admiration for Dan Steinhoff and his work, none of the revisions tampered with his original concepts. Moreover, I have done my best to present the Canadian material in a manner consistent with Dr. Steinhoff's style and approach to the teaching of this subject. Of course, I accept full responsibility for the alterations and additions.

The objective of this textbook is to present a straightforward, fundamental approach to managing a small firm in the Canadian milieu. The reader will benefit from the clear, logical presentation of the necessary steps in planning, operating, and evaluating a small business concern in Canada. As such, the text is suitable for community colleges and universities, as well as for practising small business planners and managers.

Both approach and format are shaped primarily by Dr. Steinhoff's and my experience in managing small firms, in consulting for small businesses, and in serving as officers for several banking and financial institutions in the United States and Canada. We have had the opportunity to observe the general lack of comprehension of the most basic management fundamentals among owners and operators of many of the firms involved. Although many fine books exist on the subject, there is still a need for a simple, concise, how-to-do-it text. This is the first small business management textbook designed to answer this need in Canada.

Another motivation for this book is our experience in teaching small business courses for many years. The need for a basic approach which outlines steps in planning and operation and then explains how each step can best be accomplished has been made clear. The plan of the book is first to describe the small business scene and then to proceed, in short, digestible chapters, with examinations of a series of planning and operational areas for a contemplated firm. Special management areas and problems are discussed in later chapters. The book concludes with a management consultant's checklist.

The text is flexible in that the format allows for study of operational problems, either in sequence or isolation. The emphasis on basic accounting principles and statements in the early chapters reflects Dr. Steinhoff's and my conviction that managers of small firms need this knowledge for more effective decision making.

Questions for discussion and illustrative problems are included at the end of each chapter. Both are confined to the subject matter of the chapter. References for further reading are provided at the end of the chapters for readers interested in pursuing the subject in more detail.

March 1979, Toronto *Andrew J. Szonyi*

To the Instructor

An instructor's manual has been prepared in conjunction with the text. It contains suggested answers to the end-of-chapter questions and problems. The objective of the exercises is to stimulate ideas and discussion. Any repetition of basic points is intentional and based on observed value in repeating key management principles.

To aid busy instructors, suggested examinations and/or short quiz questions are included at the end of each chapter in the instructor's manual. Use of the case studies in Part 7 will vary with each instructor.

The Late Learner is a fictional character created as a source of assumed quotations at the beginning of each chapter, although many of the quotes are actual ones from our experiences with small firm owners. We hope their inclusion will prove stimulating and at least bring an occasional smile to students as they dig into still another area of study.

Beginning with Chapter 1 and extending through Chapter 20, a continuous problem has been included for student assignment. Students may develop a complete analysis of a firm by combining all the assignments throughout these chapters, or the problem may be used for class discussion if the instructor prefers.

Dan Steinhoff and Andrew J. Szonyi

CONTENTS

Part 7 CASE STUDIES

Appendix 1 MANAGEMENT CONSULTANT'S CHECKLIST

Appendix 2 **GOVERNMENT PUBLICATIONS TO AID SMALL BUSINESS**

Part 1

INTRODUCTION

CHAPTER 1

The Small Business Scene

I have had the impression for a long time that small business firms were on the way out. Possible exceptions would be the Mom and Pop stores and an occasional gasoline station. I am happy to learn that this is not true.

The Late Learner

It is currently estimated that there are over 1 million business firms of all sizes in Canada, excluding small, independent farmers. All studies of these statistics show that at least 95 percent of these firms are "small," regardless of which measure of "smallness" is applied. We will investigate these measures of size in this chapter. Meanwhile, we can recognize that the small business scene in this country comprises about 800 thousand individual firms.

These small firms have been established to manufacture, distribute, and retail innumerable goods and services for our population at home and to export products as well. The vast majority of these firms concentrate on selling material products, but many firms provide a service. Although most service firms operate for local markets, services, too, are exported. Recent years have seen a great increase in the export of management consulting, medical, and technological services.

The truth of these statements often comes as a surprise to those who have the impression that the world of business consists chiefly, or only, of business giants. It is true that we do have many giant corporations in our country and that they are essential in making economies possible through mass production and mass distribution. Without these mass facilities, the present standard of living in Canada could not have been reached. Many small firms are dependent on larger firms for raw materials or finished products, which would be much more costly without the economies of mass production or not even available without the larger business firms which produce and distribute them.

But large firms are likewise dependent upon small firms. Mass-production industries recognize that they could not distribute their goods and services without the hundreds of small firms which do that job. It has been estimated that an average of 500 small suppliers and 3,000 retailers support every major manufacturing firm in the country.

To understand the small business scene, we must recognize that of the more than million business firms in Canada, fewer than ½ of 1 percent employ as many as 2,500 people. Among manufacturing firms, more than 90 percent employ fewer than 100 people, and 66 percent employ fewer than 20 people. When we look at distributors, retailers, and service firms, these percentages are even more surprising in demonstrating the numerical preponderance of small firms.

The great majority of Canadian business firms are small and independently owned and operated by small business proprietors. Numerical evidence is abundantly available to support this fact, both in Canada and in most other countries of the Western world. Study of this evidence makes it clear that small business firms actually constitute the backbone of the free enterprise economies.

In 1977 there were some 35 small business firms for every 1,000 persons in our total population. Small firms employ about 1.8 million people and produce almost 20 percent of the total gross national product. They employ one-third of the total work force and produce goods and services with a value of about $77 billion each year. Despite the importance of our large corporations—which play an essential role in our total economy—in terms of the number of business units, the volume of business, and the percentage of paid employment, the small firm remains a significant factor in Canada and most of the Western world.

WHAT IS A SMALL BUSINESS?

A small business is one which possesses at least two of the following four characteristics:

1 Management of the firm is independent. Usually the managers are also the owners.

2 Capital is supplied and the ownership is held by an individual or a small group.

3 The area of operations is mainly local, with the workers and owners living in one home community. However, the markets need not be local.

4 The relative size of the firm within its industry must be small when compared with the biggest units in its field. This measure can be in terms of sales volume, number of employees, or other significant comparisons.

This definition of a small business was developed years ago by the Committee for Economic Development (CED), based upon a cross-section of characteristics. It is this CED definition of the small business we will have in mind throughout the text. Of the four characteristics just cited, however, the authors believe that the fourth (relative size) is probably the most important. Any firm can be considered small when its sales volume, total employees, capital investment, and so forth are much smaller than the corresponding figures for the largest firms in its field. Under this relative size concept, American Motors has been considered small in government circles because it is only a fraction of the size of General Motors or Ford Motor Company. Similarly, a chain of food markets might still be considered small if compared to the Loblaws Company chain of grocery stores.

It will be obvious that our definition of a small business encompasses a wide gamut of firms, from Mom and Pop stores to substantial manufacturing plants, distributors, retailers, and service firms. Our emphasis will be on the small firms which desire to grow. Management principles are common to all types and sizes of businesses, as we shall see.

The subject of what a small business is can receive an unwarranted amount of space, time, and discussion, which is not appropriate to the objectives of this text. Nevertheless, some facts bear mentioning here because the definitions are often important in connection with legislation which has been passed to provide assistance to small firms.

Definitions of a small firm, for these purposes, demand some measurement of its size compared with that of large firms. Various measures, including the number of employees, the volume of sales, the nature of firm ownership, and the area of operations, have been used. Within these measures of size, differences are often noted when comparing manufacturing, wholesaling, and retailing firms.

The somewhat time-honoured dollar measures of a small firm,

which originated with the U.S. Small Business Administration, were as follows in 1977:

In retailing a firm is considered small if its annual sales do not exceed $2 million.

Among service firms a firm is considered small if its annual receipts do not exceed $2 million.

In wholesaling a firm is considered small if its total annual sales do not exceed $9½ million.

In manufacturing a firm is considered small if it does not have more than 250 employees.

In transportation and warehousing a firm is considered small until its annual receipts exceed $1 million.

In construction a firm is considered small unless its income exceeds $5 million for the immediately preceding three years.

Special circumstances may justify variations from these limits.

It should be hurriedly added, however, that these measures are subject to frequent changes. They do not, for example, fully reflect the inflationary trends of the decade of the seventies. Each year the size limits for eligibility for SBA services may change several times.

An excellent definition of a small business is contained in the Small Business Act passed by the United States Congress in 1953. That definition says a small business is "one which is independently owned and operated and not dominant in its field of operations." The feature of "dominance in its field" has come to be of greatest importance in most attempts to specifically define a small business.

It should be noted, however, that due to the much smaller scale of the Canadian economy, as well as the relatively greater importance of world competition, it is possible that many firms could be dominant in their field in Canada and yet should still be considered small because the volume of their sales, assets employed, and the number of employees in these firms is small relative to world competition.

The Canadian Government has no overall definition of small business, however, major federal programmes do indeed specify various measures of eligibility. For example, the Small Business Loans Act, passed in 1960, sets $1 million annual gross revenue as the upper limit for consideration. In the area of management counselling, firms are eligible to use the Counselling Assistance to Small Enterprises (CASE) programme if they have no more than seventy-five full-time employees.

In recent publications by the Minister of State (Small Business), small business is referred to as manufacturing firms employing fewer than 100 workers, and firms in other sectors employing fewer than 50 people.

A very important definition of eligibility exists in the Canadian

Income Tax Act passed by Parliament in 1971. Under Section 125, all Canadian controlled private corporations (of any size) qualify for a "small business deduction" and pay a lower tax rate of 25% on the first $150,000 of active business income per year. A firm can claim the "small business deduction" over several years up to a maximum cumulative total of $750,000.

Every small business owner and every student of small business management has a very clear conception of what is considered to be a small business. Their interest in volumes such as this is to get into the "nitty-gritty" of planning and operating a small firm, of developing devices to solve specific problems, and of learning ways to bring all phases of management into a cohesive whole.

ADAPTING VERSUS ADOPTING MANAGEMENT PRINCIPLES

An important observation can be made with regard to this matter of size. The same principles of business management apply to the largest firms in the country as well as to the smallest. This does not mean that a principle should be *adopted* uniformly in all cases, but that principles should be *adapted* to the particular needs of the firm. Nevertheless, the fundamental truths of business management must be recognized regardless of size. Division of labour and ability to delegate responsibility are cases in point.

TYPES OF ACTIVITY OF SMALL BUSINESS

The areas of activity for most small firms can be classified as follows:

Manufacturing
Mining
Wholesaling
Retailing
Service

Manufacturing Manufacturing firms engage in the gathering of raw materials necessary for the creation of consumer and industrial products and in giving them useful form through their manufacturing processes. Most small manufacturing firms then pass their finished products on to wholesalers or other distributors (jobbers, sales agents, brokers, commission merchants, or manufacturers' agents) who handle their further distribution to the eventual users of these products. The use of manufacturers' agents to represent small factories in this process seems to be on the increase in the 1970s. This is particularly true in the machinery and heavy industrial goods industries. Very few small manufacturers of home-consumer products engage in the distribution process beyond normal wholesale channels.

Primary manufacturing is the processing of basic raw materials such as nickel ore, uranium, petroleum, beef, and milk; a smelter would be a good typical example. Secondary manufacturing is the production of fabricated parts, materials, finished goods utilized by industry (for example, a milling machine or a conveyor belt) or by the final consumers (a toaster or a dress). Canadian primary manufacturing industries have been long established with substantial exports to the United States and to overseas markets; secondary manufacturing industry relies heavily on the domestic market for the sale of its output.

Service industries that directly support the manufacturing sector, such as computer services, engineering services, and scientific services are sometimes classified as tertiary manufacturing industry. Canada has always been considered at a disadvantage in the area of secondary manufacturing; the economies of scale (size of production runs), limited domestic market, and long delivery lines all have adverse effects and influences. On the other hand, the tertiary industries are far less vulnerable to these factors. With their high content of sophistication, they are decidedly skill and management intensive.

Mining Mining firms engage in gathering raw materials from the bowels of the earth, from the sea, or from the air. They either process the raw materials into consumer goods as part of their normal operation or sell them to other firms which convert them into usable form. An example of the former is the small salt mine where the salt is gathered and packaged in its own operation. The latter is exemplified by the small oil-well operator who drills for a product but sells it to a refinery.

Wholesaling Wholesaling for the distribution of both consumer and industrial goods is a large part of the small business scene. For most consumer goods, marketing experience in business has demonstrated the economic benefits of using established wholesale channels of distribution. Let us consider a pork-and-beans cannery attempting to distribute its product to all the individual stores that would like to have it on their shelves. By using wholesalers, the costs of distribution are greatly reduced. In addition, one wholesaler handles many other products in his particular area of activity—in this case, groceries—providing further benefits to the individual stores, which can obtain other products at the same time from the same source.

Retailing Retailing represents a large percentage of all small firms. Small retailers are to be found in every area of products and services we can imagine. Perhaps this is because more people feel competent to attempt independent firm ownership in this field. All retail firms buy their products from wholesalers, jobbers, or other distributors in final form for use by the consumer. The function of retailers is to give these products *place utility,* that is, to make them available to the consumer where he desires them. Creation of this place utility and provision of other services to the consumer are the economic justification of the retailers' profits.

Service Service firms are numerous and varied. They are engaged in rendering an essential service to their customers. Pure services are not tangible products which may be inventoried, but they are in great demand by many people in many areas. Doctors and dentists provide services. Consultants and accountants provide services. Many common types of services are supplied by firms which do work on products that are owned by their customers, for example, repairing TV sets or washing machines, or dry-cleaning clothing for customers. Other service firms perform such services as barbering or obtaining tickets to the current hit play in town. The essential characteristic of all service firms is that they do not provide a consumable product for their customers, but a special, nonmaterial service.

THE FEDERAL GOVERNMENT AND SMALL BUSINESS

The federal government has a major and long-standing commitment to small business; its present level of financial support of this segment of our economy is estimated at well in excess of $500 million per year. The provinces, as well, are providing financial assistance to the small business community through a variety of support programs administered by provincial development corporations.

Since its inception in 1944, the Industrial Development Bank (IDB) provided debt capital (term loans) to small firms and served as an important source of financing for new and expanding small business. In 1975, it was replaced by a new Crown corporation, the Federal Business Development Bank (FBDB), with a greatly expanded mandate: converting it from a somewhat conservative term lender into a supplier of everything from education through equity capital to the independent business community, more branch offices, faster turnaround time in loan applications, and improved attitude to risk taking. During fiscal 1978 the FBDB authorized 9908 loans for a total amount of over $479 million and made 69 equity investments, mostly in high technology undertakings. For a nominal fee, management assistance is also made available (Figure 1-1).

The Small Business Loans Act (SBLA) is another federal program to help small firms: it actually utilizes private sector (banks, trust companies) funds by guaranteeing loans made by these institutions

SMALL BUSINESS NEWS

Winter 1978/79

Recommendations to help Canadian Manufacturers

IMPORTS: CANADIAN MANUFACTURING MUST COMPETE

In February 1978, representatives from Canadian firms, unions, and universities got together to form 23 Task Forces. These Task Forces had a mandate of making recommendations to the Federal and Provincial Ministers of Industry on ways Canada's manufacturing industries could increase their activities for the 1980's, especially in view of the growing conditions of international competition.

The recommendations of the Task Forces were analyzed, reviewed and then presented at two Federal-Provincial conferences of Ministers of Industry in November. While many of the recommendations are to be further examined by the Federal and Provincial governments, and while many of the recommendations pertain to large manufacturers, the importance of small business was recognized.

Some of the actions, under way or in the planning stages, as a result of the Task Forces will be of help to the smaller manufacturer. These include an industry-based Critical Trade Skill Training Program; a relaxing of certain commercial criteria applied by the Export Development Corporation so as to favour smaller enterprises; a reduction in statistical reporting requirements for small business; and, an increased transfer of technology from government laboratories to industry.

Marketing initiatives, that may help the smaller Canadian firm, include a $5 million per year grant program to share industries' costs of identifying new products, product user research, and product and market testing. A number of unique promotional projects will be undertaken annually to increase the range of Canadian products introduced to export markets. As well, there will be a computerized listing of Canadian suppliers and their capabilities distributed across government offices in Canada and posts abroad. This is to assist Canadian industry, consumers, and foreign buyers to purchase their requirements from Canadian firms.

During early 1979, various government departments will be announcing details of these and other programs to assist Canada's manufacturing industries.

Family Business Succession

A recent US published study* on management succession in the family business may have parallels for Canadian small business. Management succession in the family-owned business is reported as involving a lengthy, almost lifelong period of development. The study divided the succession process into seven stages:

- The pre-business stage is where the successor may be aware of some facets of the organization. The orientation of the successor by family members is unplanned or passive.
- The introductory stage is when the successor is exposed by family members to the jargon, staff and environment of the business prior to part-time employment in the firm.
- The next stage is introductory-functional where the successor works as a part-time employee. Gradually, the tasks become more difficult and complex.
- The functional stage is when the successor enters the organization as a full-time employee and is involved in non-managerial jobs.
- The advanced functional stage is when the successor assumes a managerial position. This includes all supervisory positions prior to becoming "president" of the firm.
- Early succession is when the successor assumes the presidency but must have time to become the leader of the organization.
- Mature succession is when the successor has (1) assumed the leadership role in the organization as well as the leadership position and (2) is relatively autonomous in that role, particularly in terms of relationship to his or her predecessor.

* Justin G. Longenecker and John E. Schoen, "Management Succession in the Family Business", *Journal of Small Business Management*, Vol. 16, No. 3 (1978) pp. 1-6.

Figure 1-1 *Government supports small business.*

for small business start-ups and expansions. In 1976 some $80 million was made available to small firms under the SBLA.

The Enterprise Development Program (EDP) is a recent federal program, inaugurated in 1977. It is operated by the Department of Industry, Trade, and Commerce on a decentralized, regional basis. Under EDP, small manufacturers in all areas of the country may apply for grants and loan guarantees for specific projects: to produce and market new products and to implement innovative production techniques.

Small business now has a political voice in the federal cabinet through the recently created post of Minister of State for Small Business. This is an important development in the relationship between the small business community and the federal government which, hopefully, will lead through reorganization (and not by expansion!) to a strong permanent departmental-level civil service to protect and to further the interests of the small businesses.

The value of good, healthy competition is recognized in our society. Competition is deemed essential for keeping a strong free enterprise system. If we recognize that more than 80 percent of the more than 1 million firms in Canada employ fewer than 50 people, we can appreciate the statement that thousands of small firms act both as suppliers of materials and products to our large firms and as distributors of products for these firms.

From this review of the small business scene, the reader can probably appreciate that the big firm is the exception and not the rule in our business community.

THE INDIVIDUAL SMALL FIRM AND THE TOTAL BUSINESS SCENE

ADVANTAGES OF SMALL FIRMS

The fact that small firms are such an important part of our economy is not an historical accident. It is not only the result of government programs to aid small firms or a benevolent policy by large firms. Competition in our type of society is recognized as desirable in order to serve the population better. Small firms actually have advantages over large firms in many cases. All large firms were once small. They grew because they were well managed with dynamic leadership. Many of today's small firms will become giants in tomorrow's business world.

Some of the situations in which small firms have distinct advantages are the following:

1 *When new products or ideas are being tried out.* The freedom to attempt new types of business ventures is one of our cherished rights, and when one is engaging in such a business, it is much better to start with a small firm. Growth can always come with success. The acceptability of the new product or idea may need market testing. It is often better to check market reaction before investing too much money in a new product or idea. Management requirements may be uncertain and financial needs unknown in the starting period of the new firm.

2 *When the personal attention of the owner is essential to daily operations.* The owner of a fine restaurant is an example. If the owner's presence, as host or as executive, is important to the growth of the business, it will be more successful if it is small enough for one person to supervise.

3 *Where personal services, either professional or skilled, are dominant.* Firms which offer the professional or nonprofessional services of their employees in offering their product or service to the public usually have a distinct advantage if they are small. Examples include the beauty parlor, the real estate office, interior-decorating firms, TV repair shops, and major heavy-equipment repair firms. Any possible advantages of large size in these areas are usually offset by greatly enlarged overhead, less efficiency on the job, and loss of the personal touch of the smaller firm. Medical and dental services are usually rendered by small firms.

4 *When the market for the product or service is mainly local.* In some types of firms, it just is not economical to attempt a scale of operation which exceeds the local market demand. The making of bricks or concrete blocks for the construction industry is an example. Transportation costs are prohibitive for moving such products. The independent real estate firm specializing in residence sales usually falls in the category of firms which do better on a smaller, local scale.

5 *When the firm deals in perishable materials or products.* Small florists may join together to have their "by wire" services, but still the greatest volume of business is done through local orders. Dairy products are now sold in wider markets, but the local firms have distinct advantages in dealing with these perishable products. Local canneries still do much of the canning of fruits and vegetables in closely supervised small firms.

6 *When only a limited market is available or sought.* One example is custom tailoring. And neighbourhood groceries with alert managements have successfully competed with the trend toward large supermarkets.

7 *When the industry is characterized by wide variations in demand or in styles.* Examples include ladies' dress lines, ornamental candlemakers, and custom-made chandeliers and lamp shades. These circumstances just do not invite large firm development in most cases. Large production plants need stable markets and the ability to plan production quantities of products in economical lot sizes. The small, flexible firm usually can adjust to the necessary variations much more easily.

8 *When close rapport with personnel is essential.* Small firm owners usually have the valuable advantage of being close to employees. They do not have to receive grievances through a committee or hold formal hearings on them. They know problems from daily conversations and can adjust employment to abilities better because of this close association. As a result, they are usually able to maintain better morale and efficiency in the firm, which can be most important in any business.

The individual firm has benefited from having these and other advantages. In addition to the types of firms cited, small firms in such fields as construction, wholesaling, retailing, and the service industries have faced up well to their larger firm competition. Insurance and smaller finance firms have also been very successful. The profitable firms have not relied upon the inherent advantages of small firms as such, but have combined these advantages with alert and competent management to achieve their success.

Real and Alleged Disadvantages of Small Firms

It is very easy for persons who have failed in a small business to explain the disadvantages of being small. In too many such cases, however, their failures were likely due to lack of management ability, lack of proper planning, or simply the fact that the type of firm established did not have a chance in the first place.

Small firms are often said to labour under such disadvantages as inability to secure competent employees, tax burdens, inability to finance expansion which has been proved to be practicable, limited vendor goodwill, inability to cope with monopolistic practices, lack of support by "vested interests," discriminatory practices by large shopping-centre developers, lack of time for the small proprietor to handle multiple assignments, lack of research facilities, and the problems of making a new firm or product known in its market.

While it cannot be denied that there is substance to some of these alleged disadvantages (such as shopping-centre developers desiring chain stores instead of small local firms for tenants), it can also be contended that many of these problems are a direct result of improper planning and operation, as will be outlined in succeeding chapters. Large firms share many of the problems that small firms have. The adage that "an ounce of prevention is worth a pound of cure" was never more aptly demonstrated than in the planning stage of a new firm. So many of the business failures that occur every year could have been avoided had the firm been properly planned. Many would likely not have been established. (See Figure 1-2)

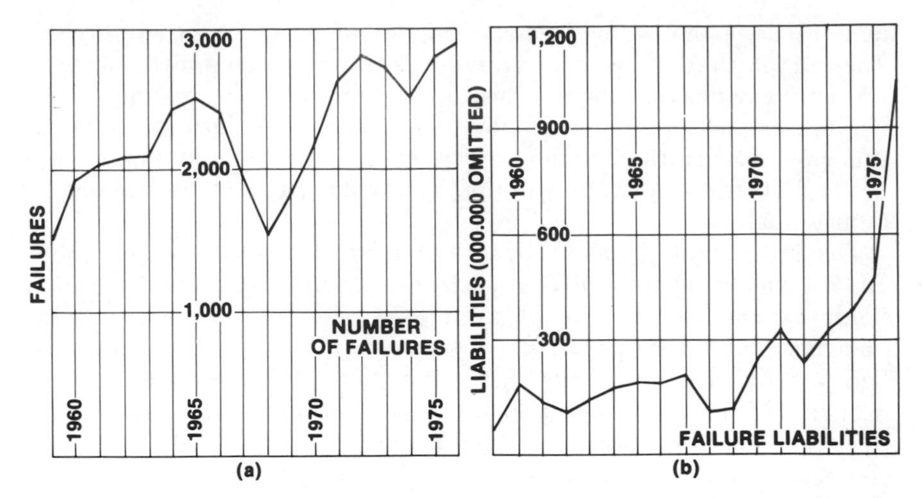

Figure 1-2 *(a) The number of business failures have been mostly on the rise since 1968. (b) For firms that do fail, the average liabilities have been increasing substantially during the past few years. (From Dun & Bradstreet Canada Limited/Limitée)*

We have cherished the right of all citizens to go into business for themselves. We have probably given more attention to preserving this right than to the matter of helping those starting new firms prepare to be successful.

Fortunately, not all Canadians believe that they would be successful managers of their own firms. Respect for the responsibilities of ownership and management of a business is a first requirement for success. When this respect exists, the person contemplating setting up a new firm will recognize the need for education in management as the first step in planning.

PREPARATION FOR SMALL FIRM OWNERSHIP

There is no better way to prepare for a successful business operation than by learning the ingredients of good planning, having some experience in the particular line, and knowing the essentials of good management. This truth is aptly demonstrated by the fact that the most popular causes of small firm failures are incompetence, improper experience, and lack of management training. It is also shown in the fact that businesses which survive the early years of their existence have a much better success record. In a recent study by Dun & Bradstreet, Inc., results showed that firms in existence for less than 3 years accounted for 37 percent of total failures, those in existence for 4 to 5 years accounted for 26 percent of the failures, those in existence for 6 to 10 years accounted for approximately 22 percent of the failures, and those in existence for over 10 years represented approximately 15 percent of the failures.[1]

PERSONAL CHARACTERISTICS OF SUCCESSFUL SMALL FIRM OWNERS

Many studies have been made in search of the definitive list of personal characteristics that an individual should have in order to succeed in small firm ownership. No generally agreed-upon total of characteristics has resulted, which is to be expected when one is dealing with human beings. Different characteristics appear to greater or lesser degrees in different people. Offsetting features may be more dominant in one person than in another. These facts, however, should not deter an attempt to list characteristics which have been found generally applicable in studies of successful small firm owners. Some of these follow.

Especially prominent features of successful managers of small firms include:

Energy
Initiative
Ability to organize
Personality
Technical competence
Administrative ability
Good judgment
Restraint
Communication ability
Leadership qualities
Patience
Preownership experience

Experienced small firm owners will agree with any list of success characteristics such as the above. They hurriedly point out, however, that they believe the chief characteristic for success is *willingness to work hard*. Being one's own boss means that you do not punch a clock, your hours are not 9 to 5, but instead you must do what is necessary

[1]These facts represent findings from detailed studies made by the Business Economics department of Dun & Bradstreet Canada Limited, Toronto. This fine research firm serves business, government, and educational institutions with many reports on operational phases of the business community. (Quoted by permission.)

in the total management of the firm. That usually means long hours and hard work, often hours beyond those when the firm is open for business, at least in the early years of the firm.

THE REWARDS OF SUCCESSFUL SMALL FIRM OWNERS

The rewards of success in operating one's own business are seen differently by different people. The retired couple who wish only to maintain a small income and have something to do in their senior years will measure rewards quite differently from the young college graduate who opens his new firm with big ideas for expansion and growth. The entire approach of this text is toward the new small firm which will be able to grow. The discussion of rewards is accordingly directed to such firms.

All proprietors seek the reward of *good profits*. Many small firms realize excellent profits. Most small firm owners find a great reward in the *satisfying nature of their work*. The ability to *be one's own boss* is an important reward to many. The *status in the community* which attaches to being a successful firm owner ranks high in the list of rewards for most proprietors.

While these rewards are the chief ones that most owners seek, other owners may gain satisfactions of a quite different nature. *Family pride, ability to educate children well, preservation of family tradition,* and an *outlet for creativeness* are only some of these.

Regardless of individual rewards sought, it is clear that successful ownership of one's own business can be a most satisfying and profitable experience. Furthermore, the right to start your own firm is always available in our country. If it is coupled with competence in planning and operating the firm, the individual's desire for reward can be achieved. The creation of more such success stories is the objective of this book.

SUMMARY

Small business firms are an integral part of the total business scene in Canada and in most countries of the Western world. In all major areas of business activity—manufacturing, mining, wholesaling, retailing, and service businesses—small firms account for a large part of the total dollar sales.

The preservation and development of a healthy small business community is an avowed policy of our governments. The Department of Industry, Trade and Commerce and the Minister of State (Small Business) are charged with specific activities to aid small firms. Their support ranges from management and financial assistance to help in securing government contracts.

Big business recognizes its dependence on small firms and gives more than lip service to help preserve their strength and profitability. Many suppliers of parts and materials to large corporations are very small firms. Mass-production factories could not distribute their output without the services of thousands of small retailers. Purchasing policies of many of our largest industries specify special consideration for buying from small firms.

There are many circumstances in business where the small firm has distinct advantages over the larger firm. These include the introduction of new products or ideas, when personal attention of the owner is necessary for success, where personal services are dominant, when markets are mainly local, where perishable materials or products are handled, where only limited markets are sought or available, and when close rapport with employees is essential.

Many of the alleged disadvantages of small firms could be overcome with better planning. An ill-conceived business, be it large or small, has little chance of success if its planning has not been properly done. Good research in the planning stage can reveal opportunities for success. It can also indicate when a contemplated business should not be undertaken.

Small business and large business are completely intertwined in our economic society. Together they have produced the highest standard of living enjoyed by any nation in the history of the world.

Men and women who properly plan for small firm ownership and who have the right personal qualities for successful management will find rich and varied rewards from their efforts.

QUESTIONS FOR CLASS DISCUSSION

Q1-1 How many small businesses are there in Canada per 1,000 population?

Q1-2 How does the Committee for Economic Development measure a small business?

Q1-3 Do large business firms which employ more than 2,500 people represent 30 percent, 20 percent, 10 percent, or less than ½ of 1 percent of the total firms in the country?

Q1-4 Does the Government of Canada support small business firms? How?

Q1-5 Can you name an example of a manufacturing firm? A mining firm? A wholesaling firm? A retailing firm? A service firm?

Q1-6 What is meant by saying principles of management are adaptable even though not always adoptable?

Q1-7 Can you name three service firms whose services you have used?

Q1-8 Are more small firms engaged in retailing than in manufacturing? Why do you think this is so?

Q1-9 Why would large companies be interested in the welfare of healthy small companies?

PROBLEMS AND QUESTIONS FOR WRITTEN ASSIGNMENT

P1-1 There are approximately 35 small business firms in Canada per 1,000 population.

- **a** Does this mean that a small town of 1,000 people would support 35 different small firms? Explain.
- **b** Prepare a list of 35 firms which would serve a cross section of 1,000 people in a large city.

P1-2 Prepare a written evaluation of the definitions of small business given in the U.S.A. Small Business Act, by the Committee for Economic Development, and by the various Canadian Government programs and legislations. Which definition do you prefer? Why?

P1-3 Write a brief essay demonstrating the difference between adaptability and adoptability of a particular principle of management.

CONTINUING PROBLEM:
THE SUCCESS HARDWARE STORE

Part 1. Introduction

At the end of each of the first 20 chapters of this text, our continuing problem will give students an opportunity to prepare a detailed planning report on a proposed small business. Actual writing assignments are included in Chapters 2 through 20. Each assignment applies the planning details covered in the chapter just studied. By the time we have finished the continuing problem, each student will have prepared a cohesive report on all aspects of good planning.

Each assignment wil be related to all the previous assignments as we prepare the various reports on all aspects of planning. Research facts are provided in condensed form where appropriate, to minimize the time required for gathering the basic data.

Our study is built around your assumed desire to establish a new hardware store in Edmonton, Alberta. You have already decided to call it the Success Hardware Store.

Your instructor may prefer that you write your continuing analysis on another type of firm. Perhaps you are seriously thinking of a business you plan to establish after graduation. Some students may wish to write on their family's business.

The type of analysis throughout our continuing problem can be applied to almost any kind of retail, wholesale, or manufacturing business. Service firms will not utilize as many of the details of the analysis we propose to make. Some students may write on many different types of business firms, if the instructor approves. Students who gather current facts for the business they are writing about may, of course, substitute those facts for the condensed data given in the various assignments.

Assignment for Part 1

Spend some time thinking about what type of business you would like to analyze with a thorough planning report. (Written assignments will not be required until Chapter 2.)

REFERENCES FOR FURTHER READING

Archer, M., *An Introduction to Canadian Business,* 3d ed., McGraw-Hill Ryerson Ltd., Toronto, 1978, chap. 28.

Broom, H. N., and J. G. Longenecker, *Small Business Management,* 2d ed., South-Western Publishing Co., Inc., Cincinnati, 1966, chap. 1.

Glos, Raymond E., and Harold A. Baker, *Business: Its Nature and Environment,* 7th ed., South-Western Publishing Co., Inc., Cincinnati, 1972, chap. 1.

Kelley, Pearce C., Kenneth Lawyer, and Clifford M. Baumback. *How to Organize and Operate a Small Business,* 5th ed., Prentice-Hall, Inc., Englewood Cliffs, N.J., 1973, chap. 1.

Musselman, Vernon A., and Eugene H. Hughes, *Introduction to Modern Business,* 6th ed., Prentice-Hall, Inc., Englewood Cliffs, N.J., 1973, chap. 1.

Peterson, Rein, *Small Business—Building a Balanced Economy,* Press Porcépic Limited, Erin, Ontario, 1977.

Preshing, W. A., *Business Management in Canada,* Wiley Publishers of Canada Ltd., Toronto, 1974, chaps. 4, 5.

Part 2

ESSENTIALS FOR PLANNING

CHAPTER 2

Steps in Planning a New Business: A Comprehensive Business Plan

---

Do you mean I should have planned all those things when I started this business? I didn't even know what the terms meant. Today I realize that if I had planned better, I would have avoided many headaches in this business.

The Late Learner

A completed business plan is designed to provide a visualization of the firm before operations are started. When financial assistance from bankers, trade creditors, or investors is necessary, their first request is to see the total business plan. With it they can visualize the credit-worthiness of the business. In this chapter we will investigate the key parts of such a total business plan.

Because there are so many areas in total management, so many decisions to be made in proper overall planning, we must recognize at the beginning that there is no one sequence of steps in planning which is agreed upon by all authorities in the field. The most important thing in planning a new small firm is that all phases of its operation be considered in the planning stage. The person planning a new firm should have very definite ideas about profits, financing, accounting records, merchandising plans, location, market and customers, general method of operation, policies, advertising and promotion, amount and type of expenses, break-even point, legal form of organization, depreciation policies, and inventory valuation methods, among other factors. As previously stated, there is no better application of the adage about an ounce of prevention versus a pound of cure. Mistakes in the planning stage of a new firm, or lack of proper attention to planning, can cause severe handicaps from which a new firm may never recover.

Based upon years of experience, the authors subscribe to what is known as the *desired income approach* to the entire planning process. In the most basic language, this approach suggests that the planner's first question should be, "How much profit do I expect to receive from this business in return for my time and investment in it?" This approach is based upon a conviction that this question has been neglected much too often by new firm planners. No commitments, contracts, or obligations relative to a new business should be undertaken without a clear plan of profit possibilities for at least one year of operation.

FOURTEEN BASIC STEPS IN A COMPREHENSIVE BUSINESS PLAN

Using the desired income approach, there are 14 major steps in planning. They will be discussed briefly here; then follow some additional items that may be appropriate in some cases.

Step 1 *Determine what profit you want from this business, recognizing the time you will give and the investment you will have. Then complete a projected income statement based upon your decision.*

With the profit figure clearly in mind, it is possible, using business statistics now abundantly available, to calculate the sales volume that is necessary to produce that particular profit. The planner should complete a projected income statement for a typical first year of operation, and standard statistics will help in doing this. This statement, when it achieves its final form (a budgeted income statement) in the planning process, can serve as a budget during the coming year. How to prepare a projected income statement is discussed in Chapter 4.

Step 2 *Survey the market you plan to serve to ascertain if the necessary sales volume required to produce the profit called for in step 1 is obtainable.*

The basic objective of step 2 is to find out what can reasonably be expected in sales if the business is established within the intended market area. Market surveys are very important to business success. If the market survey shows that the necessary sales volume to produce the profit called for in step 1 is not available, the planner can prevent a waste of time and money by canceling plans at this point. Good market surveys would probably have prevented many business failures for firms which never had a chance in their area of operations. The techniques for making market surveys have been vastly improved in recent years. Specific market data information is essential in coming up with a dependable or attainable sales potential. The process of making a market survey is covered in Chapter 5. With its results known, we will also refine our projected income statement into a budgeted income statement covering the first year of operations.

It is always good news in the second step to find that the reasonably attainable sales volume exceeds the minimum required to produce the profit desired. In the majority of market surveys the authors have participated in over many years, the results have shown sales volume attainable to be in excess of that required in step 1. It must be hurriedly added, however, that about one case in three has demonstrated that the business being considered should not be established. These facts demonstrate the importance of step 2. When adequate sales and profits appear likely, we proceed to step 3.

Step 3 *Prepare a statement of assets to be used.*

A statement of assets to be used is merely a list of the assets which are essential to the operation of the business. Values in dollar amounts should be attached to each asset needed by the business. This step has the value of giving students and business people an appreciation of the workings of the business economy as they later determine how these assets are to be provided for the new firm.

For example, if the business needs machinery, equipment, tools, dies, delivery trucks, merchandise and raw material inventory, land and buildings, store equipment, office equipment, and cash, specific dollar amounts must be attached to each. This step requires careful thinking by the planner to be sure that all needs are thoroughly considered. This step can also involve policy decisions on such matters as whether or not you plan to carry your own accounts receivable or even sell on credit.

If credit sales are contemplated and you plan to finance your own accounts receivable, an added investment will be needed by the firm. This must be planned in a later step. The procedure for developing a statement of assets to be used will be further explained and illustrated in detail in Chapter 6.

Step 4 *Prepare an opening day balance sheet.*

Step 4 involves close study of the asset needs of the business as determined in step 3 and decisions on how they are to be met. Here we decide whether to rent or buy the business building; whether to buy or lease the equipment; whether to buy delivery trucks, on what terms, or whether to hire a delivery service or even eliminate such service; and how we will finance the inventory from choices available. Every asset to be used, every liability to be incurred, and the resulting necessary investment by the proprietor must be clarified in this step. This will involve knowing the various types of financing available in providing each asset and how much we can safely use. Basic information relative to the nature of a balance sheet and of an income statement is necessary to do this task well. These statements will be reviewed in Chapter 3. Details of building the opening day balance sheet will be further discussed and illustrated in Chapter 7. Sources of financial aid are covered in Chapter 8.

Step 5 *Study the location and the specific site chosen in relation to specific characteristics.*

Too many small firms are located in space which "just happened" to be available, without any analysis of that space as a suitable location for the specific type of firm planned.

General location and specific site can be large factors in the success or failure of many businesses. This matter merits close study by the small firm planner. Details of measuring good versus poor locations and sites will be explained in detail in Chapter 9.

Step 6 *Prepare a layout for the entire space to be used for business activity.*

Have you ever wondered why the dessert section in a cafeteria is usually first in line? Have you observed where the prescription counter is located in a drugstore? Have you commented that some stores "seem like a jungle" without pattern or purpose in the way merchandise is presented to customers? The reasons for each location are to be found in a study of the good and bad things in layout. Reasons of a very positive nature explain the first two locations. Lack of recognition of good layout principles accounts for the third situation.

Every planner should create an actual floor-plan drawing of the operation which will reflect good layout principles. The rules of layout for different kinds of small firms will be reviewed in Chapter 10.

Step 7 *Choose your legal form of organization.*

The fact that most small firms are proprietorships, as contrasted with partnerships or corporations, does not assure that proprietorship is the best legal form of organization. The authors believe that many small firms should be using the other legal forms. Planners should study not only the characteristics of the three major legal forms of organization but should seek out the true management advantages of each. The idea that the corporate form of organization is designed only for large firms can be seriously questioned. Different circumstances in different firms may call for advantages of one legal form rather than another. These considerations will be detailed in Chapter 11.

Step 8 *Review all aspects of your merchandising or marketing plan.*
"Merchandising" is a broad term as generally used in business circles. It covers plans for presenting products to customers, the various channels of distribution that a firm may use to get its products to consumers, inventories in terms of dollar amount and lines of goods, sales promotion plans, advertising plans, pricing policy, public relations, markups, markdowns, seasonal variations in business, planned special sales, and many associated things. It will take five chapters (12 through 16) to cover these items in our continuing study throughout this book. It is in the study of these factors that many previous convictions or impressions of new business planners are seriously jarred or adjusted.

Step 9 *Analyze your estimated expenses in terms of their fixed or variable nature.*
When the budgeted income statement has been completed, it will show all operating expenses in detail. Of great value to the owner in making management decisions for the firm will be close scrutiny of these expenses in terms of their fixed or variable nature. The relation of risk to expenses should be known. This subject will be developed and illustrated in Chapter 17.

Step 10 *Determine the firm's break-even point.*
In simplest terms or in a more sophisticated formula, the old concept of a break-even chart is just as important to the small firm as to the large one. Most students know the concept in broad terms but cannot actually make a break-even chart from an income statement for a specific business. We will do that for a contemplated firm in Chapter 17.

Step 11 *If you are even considering sales on account, review the advantages and administrative decisions involved. Then establish a credit policy.*
The process of selling to customers on credit has many more implications than generally assumed. There are various types of credit plans available. Most are used by large firms. Small firms can do the same. Investment capital is necessary to carry your own

receivables. Credit-card sales cost money. Open accounts risk uncollectibility. This subject, too, is a large one for small firm planners. Its many ramifications are discussed in detail in Chapter 18.

Step 12 *Review the risks to which you are subject and how you plan to cope with them.*

We all face risks in everything we do daily. Small business firms are subject to many risks every day. The more we know about the risks around us, the better we can prepare the firm to protect itself against them. Such terms as "insurable interest" and "incidence of risk" should become a part of all small firm owners' vocabularies. We will look at details in this regard in Chapter 19.

Step 13 *Establish a personnel policy at the outset.*

Small business has been accused of not being able to keep good employees. Everyone recognizes that good workers are the most valuable asset any business organization can have. Their importance may be even greater to small firms than to their large competitors. What will your policy be in this regard? How will you attract and keep good employees? Will you understand employee desires? How will you establish policies regarding them? This whole matter will be covered in Chapter 20.

Step 14 *Establish an adequate system of accounting records.*

Good accounting records are essential to making decisions for any business. They are necessary for government reports, tax returns, and operations analysis. Every new firm should provide for an adequate system of accounting records in the planning stage. Details of the makeup and use of the basic financial statements are covered in Chapter 3. Establishing a basic system of records is illustrated with actual transactions in Chapters 23 and 24.

OTHER ITEMS TO CONSIDER

The preceding 14 steps in planning are deemed appropriate to almost every new small firm. Depending upon the size of the operation undertaken, other items may be considered in the planning stage. Larger firms may need to consider machine accounting, computer terminal services, use of quantitative techniques, or special financial reports such as cash flow statements or source and application of funds statements. Cash flow statements are explained and illustrated on pages 310-313. The average small firm can have good management control if the first 14 steps outlined are followed conscientiously. As the firm grows, investigation of these additional areas will become appropriate. For the average owner of the existing small firm and for student introduction to the subject of small firm management, we will confine our basic discussions to the 14 steps listed here.

Well-managed firms can grow quickly. This manufacturer of transportable industrial and residential structures had sales of less than $250,000 about twenty-five years ago. In 1978 this Canadian-owned multinational corporation had sales of over $250,000,000, earning excellent profits.
Courtesy of Atco Industries Ltd.

Whether the reader's objective is academic study of small firm management, preparation of a contemplated new firm, or analysis of an existing firm in line with established principles, competence in the field will be enhanced by studying each of the steps outlined in sequence or in isolation.

QUESTIONS FOR CLASS DISCUSSION

Q2-1 Do you think it is advisable for someone planning a new firm to think about what profit it will produce before beginning operations? Why?

Q2-2 What is the objective of a market survey?

Q2-3 Are people who operate their own small business entitled to both a salary and a profit on their investment?

Q2-4 What is "a statement of assets to be used"?

Q2-5 What do we mean by "planning a new business"?

Q2-6 Do you agree with the steps in a comprehensive business plan as outlined in this chapter? How would you change them?
Q2-7 Could a neighbourhood grocery store justify the expense of a computer? Why?
Q2-8 What is a legal form of organization?
Q2-9 Do you believe that all small business firms should sell on credit? Why?
Q2-10 What do you like about the small firms you do business with?

PROBLEMS AND QUESTIONS FOR WRITTEN ASSIGNMENT

P2-1 What is meant by "the desired income approach" to business planning? Do you agree with the steps in this process as outlined in Chapter 2? Can you suggest any other approach to new firm planning?
P2-2 If you were starting your own business, how would you determine the amount you would expect as profit on your investment and payment for your time?
P2-3 How can the steps outlined in Chapter 2 help someone make an analysis of his or her present business?
P2-4 When one is starting a new business, why is it desirable to have some idea of the sales volume expected and profits that should be made?

CONTINUING PROBLEM: *THE SUCCESS HARDWARE STORE*

Part 2: Steps in Planning

Assignment for Part 2

Prepare a title page and a table of contents for your report. The title page should indicate that this is a study of a proposed new hardware store in Edmonton, Alberta. Include your name as the author. The table of contents should have a separate, double-spaced line for each step you will cover in your analysis. A suggested list of subjects in your report would be:

Present visualization of the firm
A projected income statement
The market survey

A budgeted income statement
Statement of assets to be used
The opening day balance sheet
Location analysis
Site analysis
Legal form of organization
Merchandising and sales promotion plans
Fixed and variable expense analysis—a break-even chart
Credit selling plans
Risk analysis
Personnel policies

Other headings or subheadings may be added during the course of your study as directed by your instructor.

REFERENCES FOR FURTHER READING

Broom, H. N., and J. G. Longenecker, *Small Business Management,* 2d ed., South-Western Publishing Company, Inc., Cincinnati, 1966, chap. 13.

Kelley, Pearce C., Kenneth Lawyer, and Clifford M. Baumback, *How to Organize and Operate a Small Business,* 5th ed., Prentice-Hall, Inc., Englewood Cliffs, N.J., 1973, chap. 6.

McQuillan, Peter, and Howard Taylor, *Sources of Venture Capital in Canada,* 2d ed., Department of Industry, Trade and Commerce, Ottawa, 1977, Section 3.

Musselman, Vernon A., and Eugene H. Hughes, *Introduction to Modern Business,* 6th ed., Prentice-Hall, Inc., Englewood Cliffs, N.J., 1973, chap. 6.

CHAPTER 3

Understanding the Basic Financial Statements from a Management Viewpoint

I never believed that understanding balance sheets and income statements would make me a better business owner. I thought it was enough to sell lots of merchandise and let the accountant tell me how much I made.

The Late Learner

Competence in managing any business demands an understanding of the basic accounting statements, which necessarily reflect the results of operations and the present financial position. Management decisions must be weighed in terms of their effect on these statements. This matter is so important that we will preface our entire investigation of management fundamentals by clarifying for the nonaccounting student and the new business proprietor the relationships of the basic statements and their meaning and composition.

The two basic financial statements are (1) the balance sheet, and (2) the income statement.

1 The Balance Sheet The balance sheet shows the assets, liabilities, and owner's net worth in a business *as of a given date.* Assets are the things owned by the business, including both physical things and claims against others. Liabilities are the amounts owed to others, the creditors of the firm. Net worth is the owner's claim to the assets after liabilities are accounted for. Accounting has a basic equation which says *assets minus liabilities equals net worth.* In simplest terms, this means that what the business owns, less what it owes to creditors, equals its net worth. If liabilities exceed the assets, the net worth is a minus quantity. Profits made in each fiscal period add to this net worth as they are carried from the income statement to the balance sheet.

2 The Income Statement The income statement shows the income received and the expenses incurred *over a period of time.* Income statements are usually issued for a year's operations, but interim statements may be made for a month, a quarter, or a half-year as well. Some firms have daily or weekly income statements. Even though formal income statements may be issued only once a year, the proprietor should know, for shorter periods, whether the income has exceeded the expenses and by how much.

Income received (sales) comes essentially from the sales of the basic merchandise or service which the business is formed to sell. Expenses incurred are the expired costs which have been incurred during the same period of time. The income statement for firms with an inventory to sell have three basic parts: the *income received,* the *cost of the goods sold* during the period, and the *operating expenses* incurred during the same period. The difference between sales income and cost of goods sold is known as the *gross margin.* When the operating expenses are subtracted from the gross margin, we arrive at net profit from operations.

Service firms, such as banks, insurance companies, laundries, consultants, ticket agencies, or repair services, which do not carry an inventory of merchandise for sale, will not have a cost of goods sold section on their income statement. Their statements will show total income from all sources and then deduct operating expenses, which may be classified as desired. See Table 3-3 (p. 40) for an example of an income statement for a service firm.

All accounts which record income and expenses during the fiscal period are summarized at the end of each period. The income and expense accounts are then closed and the resulting profit or loss is transferred to the owner's net worth account. This is in contrast to balance sheet accounts, which remain open in the ledger until the particular asset is disposed of, liability paid off, or change made in the ownership.

Let us first study the example of the balance sheet statement shown in Table 3-1.

TABLE 3-1
ABC COMPANY
BALANCE SHEET
DECEMBER 31, 1978

ASSETS

Current assets:			
Cash			$1,780
Accounts receivable			3,100
Merchandise inventory			4,550
Prepaid expenses			760
Total current assets			$10,190
Fixed assets:			
Store equipment	$4,200		
Less accumulated depreciation	900	$3,300	
Office equipment	$2,000		
Less accumulated depreciation	500	1,500	
Delivery truck	$3,000		
Less accumulated depreciation	1,000	2,000	
Total fixed assets			6,800
Total assets			$16,990

LIABILITIES

Current liabilities:			
Accounts payable		$1,500	
Notes payable		1,000	
Contracts payable		2,000	
Total current liabilities		$4,500	
Fixed liabilities:			
Contracts payable	$2,000		
Long-term note payable	1,000		
Total fixed liabilities		$3,000	
Total liabilities			$7,500
NET WORTH			
J. Jones, proprietorship			9,490
Total liabilities plus net worth			$16,990

RELATIONSHIPS WITHIN THE BALANCE SHEET

First note that the total assets ($16,990) minus the total liabilities ($7,500) equal the owner's net worth or proprietorship ($9,490). This is the fundamental accounting equation:

Assets - liabilities = proprietorship (net worth)

Every asset, liability, and net worth account is presented on the balance sheet.

Ratio Analysis

Current Ratio Note that the assets are divided into current assets and fixed assets. This distinction is not necessary to make the books balance but is made for management reasons. The relationship between current assets and current liabilities is a prime measure of liquidity of any firm. Liquidity is the measure of ability to pay debts as they become due.

Current assets are those which are in the form of cash or will convert into *cash within one year*. Current liabilities are those debts which will be *due within one year*. The relationship between current assets and current liabilities is called the current ratio. Standards for a satisfactory ratio will vary between industries and companies. A general rule of thumb demands that this ratio be at least 2 to 1. The current ratio is found by dividing the current assets by the current liabilities:

$$\text{Current ratio} = \frac{\text{current assets}}{\text{current liabilities}} = \frac{\$10,190}{\$4,500} = 2.26$$

The ABC Company, therefore, has a current ratio of 2.26 to 1 and is safely within the sound rule of a 2 to 1 current ratio.

Quick Ratio The quick ratio is also known as the acid test of liquidity. It is the relationship between only the most liquid assets (cash and accounts receivable) and the total of the current liabilities. The conservative rule in this regard is that *this ratio should be at least 1 to 1*. In other words, the cash plus receivables should equal or exceed the current liabilities.

$$\text{Quick ratio} = \frac{\text{cash plus receivables}}{\text{current liabilities}} = \frac{\$1,780+\$3,100}{\$4,500} =$$

$$\frac{\$4,880}{\$4,500} = 1.08$$

Thus the ABC Company meets this test of liquidity because the company's quick ratio of 1.08 exceeds the minimum of the conservative rule. The quick ratio combined with the current ratio of 2.26 indicates that the present liquidity of the company is good.

Working Capital Working capital is the difference between the current assets and the current liabilities expressed in dollars. On the balance sheet of the ABC Company we see total current assets of $10,190 and current liabilities of $4,500. Working capital is therefore $5,690 ($10,190 - $4,500). In normal operations involving daily sales receipts, buying more merchandise, meeting payrolls and other expenses, and making payments due on current liabilities, it is the net working capital which provides the ability to meet all obligations as they become due. The measurement of adequate cash on hand, as discussed later, is a valuable supplement in determining the adequacy of working capital.

The Proprietorship Ratio There are many other ratios utilized in the analysis of business firm operations. Most small firms which maintain adequate current ratios, quick ratios, and working capital, proper inventories, and a 50 percent proprietorship ratio will maintain soundness in their financial structures.

The proprietorship ratio is the relationship between the owner's investment in the firm and the total assets being used in the business. It is computed by dividing the owner's investment by total assets. For the ABC Company we see the owner's investment (the equity in the assets) is $9,490. Total assets used in the business are valued at $16,990.

$$\text{Proprietorship ratio} = \frac{\text{owner's investment}}{\text{total assets}} = \frac{\$9{,}490}{\$16{,}990} = .56$$

The proprietorship ratio can be expressed as a ratio of owner investment to total assets or as a percentage of those total assets. In this case, proprietorship is 56 percent of total investment in the firm or a ratio of .56 to 1.00. This proprietorship ratio is safely above the conservative minimum of 50 percent.

TRADING ON EQUITY

In connection with owner investment, we should become familiar with the phrase *trading on equity.* This phrase refers to the relationship between creditor capital (liabilities) in the business and the owner capital. *Trading on too thin an equity* is a term used to describe owners who have too little of their own money invested compared with the creditor capital (liabilities) used to finance the business. A proprietorship ratio of 50 percent indicates that the owner or owners have invested half the value of the total assets used in the business. When this ratio falls below 50 percent, the outside creditors are supplying more of the firm's total capital needs than the owners are. This indicates, in most cases, that further credit will be more difficult to obtain either from current loans, sale of securities, or other investors. Such owners are truly trading on too thin an equity and probably need more investment capital of their own.

An example of trading on too thin an equity would be the owner of a dress shop which needs $60,000 in total assets. The owner raises $50,000 of that total with credit from merchandise suppliers, short term loans from friends, and a 90-day bank loan. All these debts are current liabilities. The owner's investment on the opening day balance sheet is only $10,000. That balance sheet shows total assets of $60,000, current liabilities of $50,000, and proprietorship of $10,000. The resulting proprietorship ratio is 16 2/3 percent ($10,000 divided by $60,000) which is far short of the recommended 50 percent. It will be most difficult to obtain further credit of any kind. The pressing debts make the business less able to weather any kind of a serious drop in profits.

The reason that creditors look to the proprietorship ratio is to see how much of the total risks are being borne by the owners of the firm. The owners' incentive to stick with the firm in less prosperous times is often influenced by the extent of their investment. When they have only a small part of the total investment, the temptation to "leave a sinking ship" is great. If that happens the creditors stand to incur serious losses.

We should also note here that *all shareholders are owners*. Both preference and common shareholder investments count as owner capital in computing the proprietorship ratio. *Bondholders are creditors*. Their investment is listed on the balance sheet as fixed liabilities. The total face value of all bonds outstanding is counted as creditor capital in computing the proprietorship ratio. We will look at this matter more closely in Chapter 8 when we discuss financing sources for small firms.

It is recognized, of course, that there are special types of business firms in which variations from the ideal ratio rules advocated here can be justified. Public utilities are a notable example. Unless positive evidence is available to justify exceptions, however, the new firm planner will do well to abide by these conservative rules of financial soundness in making plans for the new firm.

In summary, our analysis of the ABC Company's balance sheet shows a healthy financial structure. Its current ratio, quick ratio, and proprietorship ratio all exceed the minimums dictated by sound financing principles. Its working capital seems to be adequate. Before sitting back, however, the owner should check these ratios against the available statistics for the most efficient firms in the same line of business. Sources of such data are discussed in Chapter 4.

Let us now turn to an analysis of the income statement, an example of which is shown in Table 3-2.

TABLE 3-2
ABC COMPANY
INCOME STATEMENT
JANUARY 1—DECEMBER 31, 1978

Sales		$100,000
Cost of goods sold:		
Beginning inventory Jan. 1	$10,000	
Purchases during year	40,000	
Goods available for sale	$50,000	
Less ending inventory Dec. 31	10,000	
Cost of goods sold		40,000
Gross margin		$ 60,000
Operating expenses:		
Rent	$ 6,000	
Salaries to employees	17,000	
Supplies used	2,000	
Advertising and promotion	1,000	
Insurance expense	1,000	
Delivery expense	2,000	
Depreciation expense	1,700	
Bad debts	1,000	
Local taxes paid	1,000	
Utilities expense	300	
Miscellaneous expenses	2,000	
Total operating expenses		35,000
Net profit from operations		$ 25,000

ANALYSIS OF THE INCOME STATEMENT

Note first that the period of the ABC Company income statement is one year, ending December 31, 1978. As a period-of-time statement, a proper title necessitates that two dates be stated or determinable. "Year ended December 31, 1978" denotes two dates would be an acceptable title for the statement. Parenthetically, let us note here that the calendar year is not necessarily the best fiscal period (annual accounting period) for all businesses. More and more firms are now using the date of actually starting the business as the beginning of an annual fiscal period, or some other date in the year which more closely represents a complete cycle in annual operations. This is particularly applicable to firms which have a high degree of seasonal variation in their income.

The ABC Company income statement emphasizes the basic parts previously described. The firm earned $25,000 profit from operations. It had net sales of $100,000, of which $40,000 was paid for merchandise sold and $60,000 was its gross margin. It paid out $35,000 in operating expenses, and thus had $25,000 profit from operations remaining in the business. The experienced student or business person will judge this a highly successful business on the basis of these facts. They will recognize that not many firms operate on a markup of 60 percent of sales price. Two qualifying factors must be kept in mind, however. First, the $25,000 represents both salary and return on investment for Mr. Jones, the owner. Second, this $25,000 profit from operations is before income taxes on profits have been paid. The shocking truths in this regard will be discussed later. We can be sure at this point that the proprietor with three children will not be living in great luxury if this firm is the family's sole source of income.

An appealing profit does not mean that the income statement should not have regular analysis by the proprietors. As they review their year's operation, they should ask themselves at least the following questions:

1 Is our markup high or low compared with successful firms in this type of business?

2 Is our consequent cost of goods sold high or low?

3 Is our inventory adequate for the sales volume which the business produced? Did we lose sales because of stockouts? Can we justify all parts of the inventory on the basis of sales of the items carried?

4 Is our total overhead in line with the most efficient firms of this type? Is our occupancy charge (rent) the proper percentage of sales? How about our other expenses?

As we shall see in Chapter 4, the availability of abundant trade statistics will give the proprietors comparative data with which to find answers to these questions. Studying their operations will usually reveal special strengths in their firm and areas which need improvement. For example, they may find that their merchandise turnover was four times per year, but the most successful firms operate with a turnover of five times per year while maintaining the same margins. They should satisfy themselves as to why the other firms have this turnover and pursue the possibilities of improving their own operation. They may find that successful firms operate with a smaller loss on bad debts. If so, this should cause them to question their whole credit-account policy. Similar analysis should be made of all key items on the balance sheet and the income statement. When so used, the basic accounting statements become tools for management to use for decision making and not merely dreary accounts of what happened in the last fiscal period.

Income statements for service firms which do not carry an inventory of merchandise for sale will not have a cost of goods sold section. They will show total income from services or fees and then deduct the operating expenses to arrive at net profit from operations. See Table 3-3 for illustration.

TABLE 3-3
INCOME STATEMENT*
BILL'S HOME LAUNDRY & DRY CLEANING
YEAR ENDED FEBRUARY 28, 1978

Income:			
From laundry operations		$125,000	
From dry cleaning		65,000	
From repairs and miscellaneous		10,000	
Total income			$200,000
Operating expenses:			
Variable expenses:			
Employee wages	$98,000		
Delivery expenses	4,000		
Operating supplies	18,000		
Repairs and maintenance	3,000		
Administrative and legal	1,000		
Advertising	1,500		
Bad debt expense	300		
Miscellaneous expenses	4,200		
Total variable expenses		$130,000	
Fixed expenses:			
Rent	$ 6,000		
Utilities	8,500		
Insurance	4,000		
Taxes and licenses	2,500		
Depreciation	9,000		
Total fixed expenses		30,000	
Total operating expenses			160,000
Net profit from operations			$ 40,000

**Typical income statement for a service type business which does not carry an inventory of merchandise for sale. Note that this income statement does not have a cost of goods sold section.*

TABLE 3-4
THE FIVE KINDS OF ACCOUNTS: THEIR DEFINITION AND STATEMENT APPEARANCE

These accounts appear on the balance sheet (a point-of-time statement)	**1** Assets—things owned **2** Liabilities—amounts owed **3** Net worth—owner's investment
These accounts appear on the income statement (a period-of-time statement)	**4** Income—sales revenue **5** Expense—expired costs

TABLE 3-5
THE FIVE KINDS OF ACCOUNTS: HOW INCREASES AND DECREASES ARE MADE FOR EACH

ACCOUNTS	INCREASES	DECREASES
1 Assets	Debits	Credits
2 Liabilities	Credits	Debits
3 Net worth	Credits	Debits
4 Income	Credits	Debits
5 Expense	Debits	Credits

Tables 3-4 and 3-5 summarize much of what has been discussed. They will serve as a useful guide for students having their first introduction to the preparation and use of accounting statements and their value to management. For people who are already proprietors, they will be a useful refresher.

Table 3-4 shows that there are only five different kinds of accounts used in the most sophisticated accounting systems. It defines the accounts and shows on which of the two basic statements they appear. Students should note again the difference between a *point-of-time* and a *period-of-time* statement. Table 3-5 shows how each of these accounts increased or decreased in the operation of a double-entry bookkeeping system. Most new students are surprised to learn that there is nothing sacred in the terms *debit* and *credit*. They could equally be called left and right, port and starboard, or gee and haw. In Chapter 23 we will study how to install a simplified journal-ledger accounting system which will adequately serve most small firms.

QUESTIONS FOR CLASS DISCUSSION

Q3-1 What is the chief difference between a balance sheet and an income statement? Explain.

Q3-2 How is the profit for a fiscal period transferred from the income statement accounts to the owner's net worth account?

Q3-3 Do the terms "debit" and "credit" mean anything different from "left" and "right"?

Q3-4 Are all accounts increased with debits?

Q3-5 What are the five different kinds of accounts?

Q3-6 What does each of the five kinds of accounts represent?

Q3-7 What is the difference between current assets and fixed assets?

Q3-8 What is the current ratio? What is the conservative rule as to a minimum limit on this ratio?

Q3-9 Is the quick ratio different from the current ratio? How?

Q3-10 When a business is said to be trading on too thin an equity, what is meant?

Q3-11 Do you agree that total assets represent the total capital employed in the business? If so, how is this capital provided?

Q3-12 What is the working capital of any business?

Q3-13 When business owners analyze their income statement, what facts and comparisons should they consider?

Q3-14 What do we mean when we say that the net worth, or proprietorship account, represents the owner's claim to the assets?

Q3-15 When a firm sells merchandise for cash, what account is credited and what account is debited?

PROBLEMS AND QUESTIONS FOR WRITTEN ASSIGNMENT

P3-1 Prepare a typical balance sheet for a wholesale grocery business which will illustrate the various kinds of asset, liability, and net worth accounts.

P3-2 For the same wholesale grocery business, prepare a typical income statement for one year's operations. Use the ABC Company income statement in Chapter 3 as your guide.

P3-3 Can you prepare the current assets and current liabilities sections of a balance sheet so that the firm would have a current ratio of at least 2 to 1 and still be unable to pay its current bills?

P3-4 Jones TV Repair Service is strictly a service firm. Prepare a possible income statement for the firm, emphasizing the expected accounts that would appear on it.

P3-5 Write a short essay explaining what depreciation of a fixed asset is, how it is charged as business expense, and the importance of making the depreciation charge.

CONTINUING PROBLEM:
THE SUCCESS HARDWARE STORE

Part 3. Present Visualization of the Business

Assignment for Part 3

Write a brief description of the Success Hardware Store as you now visualize it. Details are not needed at this time. The objective is to write down general ideas about the business you have in mind. Will it be on a main street or a side street? Will it be downtown or in a shopping centre? About what size do you plan for a store building? What lines of merchandise will the store carry? How many employees do you now think will be necessary? What kind of store hours will you plan? What type of lighting? What service for deliveries? Will you sell on credit? Two or three double-spaced pages should provide a clear picture of how you now see the firm in your mind. Present thoughts are not binding upon later findings. This is only the starting point for detailed work to follow.

REFERENCES FOR FURTHER READING

Archer, M., *An Introduction to Canadian Business,* 3d ed, McGraw-Hill Ryerson Ltd., Toronto, 1978, chap. 13.

"Financial Reporting and Analysis—the Independent Business Way," *Your Business Matters,* No. 5, The Royal Bank of Canada, 1976.

"How to Read Financial Statements," The Canadian Securities Institute, Toronto, 1977.

Langhout, J., *Analysis and Interpretation of Canadian Financial Statements,* University Press of Canada, St. John's, Newfoundland, 1972.

Meigs *et al., Accounting: The Basis for Business Decisions,* 2d. Canadian ed., McGraw-Hill Ryerson Ltd., Toronto, 1976, chap. 1.

Musselman, Vernon A., and Eugene H. Hughes, *Introduction to Modern Business,* 6th ed., Prentice-Hall, Inc., Englewood Cliffs, N.J., 1973, chap. 6.

Preshing, W.A., *Business Management in Canada,* Wiley Publishers of Canada Ltd., 1974, chaps. 31, 32, 33, 34.

CHAPTER 4

The Desired Income Approach to Business Planning: Making a Projected Income Statement

---

Desired income? Heck, when I took over this firm I only hoped to be able to feed my family. And that wasn't easy for some time. Today, I would plan each step and know what profit I could make if I maintained the planned sales volume.

The Late Learner

As we discussed in Chapter 2, small business owners must recieve both a return for their time spent in operating the business and a return on their investment. For example, if it is determined that they should receive $15,000 in profit the first year, they should consider whether this is only for time spent in running the business or if it also includes what they desire as a return on the money they must invest. Alternatives must be kept in mind. They can take another job and earn a salary while working for someone else, or they can invest their money in other ways to earn a return on it.

Once the small business owners determine their desired income, continuing planning is made easier today by the abundant statistics available, which were not in existence when our grandparents were merchants. All potential new firm owners should become familiar with the statistics for the types of firms they plan to have. Previous employment in the type of firm planned is recommended for all prospective proprietors. This experience should enable them to gain valuable information about the statistics and operation of the type of business at first hand. But even without this experience, planners have many sources for gathering basic facts about their type of firm. Trade associations, chambers of commerce, government departments, Canadian Census, Annual Census of Manufacturers, Federal Business Development Bank, Statistics Canada, and business service organizations like Dun & Bradstreet Canada Limited are some sources readily available. Many publications of the government agencies are free of charge. Most are available in local libraries. Other agencies make only a minor charge for specific data reports.

Dun & Bradstreet regularly issues a publication which provides specific ratios and other financial data for 166 different lines of business. This publication covers firms in retailing, wholesaling, manufacturing, and construction. Comprehensive data ranging from the current ratio to the relationship of sales to fixed assets are presented. The figures are averages for hundreds of different firms in each line and include both profitable and unprofitable concerns. (See Figure 4-1.)

Among the other excellent sources of data on operating statistics for all types of business firms we should note at least the following:

For Canadian firms:

Derived from actual financial statements filed with Revenue Canada by incorporated businesses of different classifications, informative aggregated balance sheet and income statement details are published annually by Statistics Canada (Catalogue No. 61-207). Another valuable quarterly by Statistics Canada (Catalogue No. 61-003) worthy of note focuses on corporations operating in Canada and provides comparisons and trends by broad groupings of the financial transactions reflected on the balance sheet, statement of retained earnings, and statement of income, together with other selected items and a brief financial overview. The report covers the total industrial corporation sector of the Canadian economy.

The Economics Division of the Canadian Imperial Bank of Commerce publishes annually "Capital at Work," which provides selected corporate ratios such as current ratio, inventories to sales, cost of sales to sales, debt to equity, etc., for major industrial groupings, wholesale and retail trade, construction, and services.

For USA firms:

Annual Statements Studies, published by Robert Morris Associates, Philadelphia National Bank Building, Philadelphia, PA 19107.

Barometer of Small Business, published by the Accounting Corporation of America, 1929 First Avenue, San Diego, CA 92112.

Annual Statement Studies covers manufacturing, wholesaling, retailing, service, and construction firms in each area. Both balance

LINE OF BUSINESS (and number of concerns reporting) TYPE D'ENTREPRISE (et nombre d'entreprises étudiées)	Cost of Goods Sold Coût des marchandises vendues	Gross Margin Marge bénéficiaire brute	Current Assets to Current Debt Coefficient du fonds de roulement	Profits on Sales Coefficient du profit sur les ventes	Profits on Tangible Net Worth Coefficient du profit sur la valeur nette tangible	Sales to Tangible Net Worth Coefficient des ventes sur la valeur nette tangible	Collection Period Période de recouvrement	Sales to Inventory Coefficient des ventes sur les stocks	Fixed Assets to Tangible Net Worth Coefficient des immobilisations sur la valeur nette tangible	Current Debt to Tangible Net Worth Coefficient des exigibilités sur la valeur nette tangible	Total Debt to Tangible Net Worth Coefficient des dettes totales sur la valeur nette tangible
	Per Cent Pour cent	Per Cent Pour cent	Times Fois	Per Cent Pour cent	Per Cent Pour cent	Times Fois	Days Jours	Times Fois	Per Cent Pour cent	Per Cent Pour cent	Per Cent Pour cent
Non-Met. Min. Products, Other (218) Produits miniers non métalliques, autres	74.3	25.7	1.96	7.51	15.24	2.03	51	6.1	62.1	43.0	67.6
Orn. Iron Works (433) Fer forgé	76.8	23.2	1.36	4.83	24.12	5.00	68	5.6	59.3	155.1	215.6
Paint & Varnish (120) Peintures et vernis	69.6	30.4	1.81	4.71	16.72	3.55	54	4.4	46.8	78.9	113.4
Paper Boxes & Bags (221) Boîtes et sacs de papier	76.6	23.4	1.56	6.98	30.67	4.39	50	6.2	80.9	97.4	187.3
Paper Products, Other (182) Produits de papier, autres	70.9	29.1	1.81	8.85	24.48	2.77	50	5.2	51.6	64.8	87.5
Pet. & Coal Products, Other (18) Produits du pétrole et du charbon, autres	53.0	47.0	1.60	8.29	15.38	1.85	41	17.4	32.1	30.8	59.8
Pet. Refineries (36) Raffineries de pétrole	68.1	31.9	1.53	8.50	16.83	1.98	63	7.4	70.9	52.9	97.7
Pharmaceuticals (156) Produits pharmaceutiques	55.9	44.1	1.89	6.60	15.71	2.38	65	3.8	47.2	67.0	84.6
Planing Mills (700)	76.5	23.5	1.36	3.73	17.71	4.75	48	5.6	71.3	129.3	195.2
Publishing Only (558) Edition	46.5	53.5	1.50	4.71	20.03	4.25	67	7.8	36.7	125.3	182.7
Publishing & Printing (476) Edition et imprimerie	3.7	96.3	1.59	9.44	18.75	1.99	51	—	43.9	32.5	67.5
Pulp & Paper Mills (120) Moulins de pulpe et papier	74.4	25.6	1.59	10.52	17.97	1.71	27	6.0	94.4	47.6	121.4
Radio & TV Receivers (25) Récepteurs radio/TV	77.3	22.7	1.35	0.25	1.19	4.73	64	3.5	40.0	197.8	234.9
Refrigeration, Coml. (39) Réfrigération, secteur commercial	81.9	18.1	1.77	3.16	14.73	4.66	76	4.2	43.4	138.5	196.4
Rubber Products (117) Produits de caoutchouc	77.7	22.3	1.74	2.15	6.65	3.10	61	4.3	99.4	76.0	146.7

Sawmills (973)	81.8	18.2	1.12	1.88	7.22	3.84	26	5.3	154.8	114.2	221.5
Scientific&Professional Equipment (334) Equipement scientifique et professionnel	67.5	32.5	1.87	4.75	11.18	2.35	62	4.1	51.9	60.3	86.1
Smltg & Ref., Rolling (214) Affinage et raffinage, laminage	80.6	19.4	1.83	6.97	16.86	2.42	31	4.6	103.6	56.6	160.3
Soap & Cleaning Compds (83) Savons et nettoyeurs	58.6	41.4	1.64	4.83	13.56	2.81	28	5.6	81.0	55.4	130.3
Soft Drinks (347) Boissons gazeuses	64.7	35.3	1.37	3.16	12.49	3.95	31	9.8	76.2	73.1	113.0
Sporting Gds & Toys (189) Articles de sport et jouets	72.5	27.5	1.30	0.80	4.17	5.20	64	2.9	61.5	246.1	319.7
Structural Steel (173) Acier de structure	79.4	20.6	1.32	6.29	19.94	3.17	79	2.3	57.5	165.9	217.0
Textile Products, Other (366) Produits textiles, autres	75.7	24.3	1.48	3.90	16.71	4.29	54	3.9	54.3	129.6	164.8
Textiles, Synthetic (74) Textiles, synthétiques	81.5	18.5	1.59	5.14	12.79	2.49	46	5.2	92.7	64.2	114.0
Tobacco Products (21) Tabac	80.1	19.9	1.29	4.51	10.01	2.22	15	3.6	17.7	69.6	93.8
Toilet Preparations (81) Produits pour la toilette	54.4	45.6	1.95	4.79	11.28	2.35	53	4.1	30.6	67.5	79.5
Transportation, Misc. (361) Transport, divers,	78.1	21.9	1.17	3.47	10.74	3.10	46	2.9	96.5	160.4	235.6
Truck Bodies (273) Carrosseries de camions	82.9	17.1	1.38	4.15	21.89	5.27	53	4.6	54.9	149.8	196.0
Veneer & Plywood (63) Bois de placage et contre-plaqué	81.6	18.4	1.70	2.80	7.89	2.82	33	6.2	73.1	54.5	136.8
Wineries (25) Vins	64.5	35.5	1.42	4.17	5.44	1.30	52	1.4	65.7	94.2	131.3
Wire & Wire Products (232) Fils métalliques et produits connexes	74.6	25.4	1.62	8.62	24.87	2.88	47	4.1	62.8	82.0	121.5
Wood Products, Miscellaneous (327) Produits du bois, divers	79.6	20.4	1.07	3.27	12.03	3.68	38	5.8	128.4	116.7	184.0

Figure 4-1 *Sample of Dun & Bradstreet's financial statistics for manufacturing. Similar information is available for wholesaling, retailing, and construction. (From Dun & Bradstreet Canada Limited/ Limitée, Key Business Ratios, 1977)*

sheet and income statement data are included. *Barometer of Small Business* is a semiannual publication which concentrates on retail firms of many types. Complete income statements are presented with percentages of sales for each item instead of dollar amounts. The data is classified for firms of different sales volume. Even trends, geographical variances, and seasonal data are provided. Complete balance sheets are presented in detail for each of the various types of firms reviewed.

A visit to the closest Federal Business Development Bank office and the provincial government department agency dealing with industry, trade, or commerce should be made by all who plan to open a new firm. Small business owners can also benefit from such visits by finding data by which to compare their specific situation with the principles set forth in the available reports. Many searchers will be surprised to find the information available for most lines of business. They may even find a pamphlet on their particular type of business. Often it will contain additional information that can be of value in planning or checking the status of an existing firm.

With the desired income known, only three statistics are necessary to enable the planner to make a complete projected income statement. These three statistics are:

1 The average merchandise (inventory) turnover for this type of business

2 The average markup (gross margin)

3 Profits as a percentage of sales

These terms may need clarification. *Merchandise turnover* is the number of times the average inventory is sold each year. If a firm carries an inventory of $15,000 and has a cost of goods sold of $60,000, the merchandise turnover is four times per year. Cost of goods sold (as remembered from our review of accounting statements in Chapter 3) is the price paid for the merchandise purchased and sold. Merchandise turnover is computed by dividing the cost of goods sold by the average inventory carried in stock. For this example, the computation is as follows:

$$\frac{\text{Cost of goods sold}}{\text{Average inventory}} = \frac{\$60{,}000}{\$15{,}000} = 4 \text{ (the merchandise turnover)}$$

Inventories carried and their adequacy and inadequacy are one of the truly dynamic subjects in management. They will be referred to many times throughout this text and discussed in detail in a later chapter.

The *average markup* is the dollar difference between the cost of goods sold and sales, expressed as a percentage of sales. In dollar amounts, the markup provides the gross margin. If sales are $100,000 and cost of goods sold is $60,000, the gross margin is $40,000. Expressed as a percentage of sales, we observe that the markup is 40 percent. It is computed by dividing gross margin by sales. In this example, the computation is as follows:

$$\frac{\text{Gross margin}}{\text{Sales}} = \frac{\$40{,}000}{\$100{,}000} \times 100 = 40\% \text{ (markup)}$$

Profits as a percentage of sales means just that. New firm planners want to find out what percentage of the sales dollar remains in the company as profits in their line of business. Existing operators want this figure to compare their firm's average with the averages of other similar firms. The arithmetical computation is to divide average profits by the sales volume, as follows:

$$\frac{\text{Net profits}}{\text{Sales}} = \frac{\$15{,}000}{\$100{,}000} \times 100 = 15\% \text{ (profits as a percentage of sales)}$$

This percentage can be figured on the basis of profits either before federal income taxes or after applicable income taxes have been deducted. It is important to planners to know which basis they are using.

The more searching we do for figures, the better our planning will be. Local or regional averages are generally more applicable than national averages. We may find three figures from three different sources for average merchandise turnover. We must then decide which are most applicable to our area. Without specific factors to support one or the other, it may be best to average the three for planning purposes. Similar considerations should be applied to the markup and profits as a percentage of sales figures.

BUILDING A PROJECTED INCOME STATEMENT

With only these three statistics and our desired profit, we may now proceed to construct a projected income statement for a planned retail firm. The new student should follow each step and each calculation carefully.

For our illustration of this process, let us assume that the carefully gathered and adopted figures for these three items are as follows:

Profits as a percentage of sales: 12 percent

Merchandise turnover: Four times per year
Markup: 35 percent of sales
Desired profit: $15,000 (includes salary and return on investment)

From Chapter 3 it will be recalled that the key parts of an income statement are as shown in Table 4-1. Actual figures for the above situation have been inserted with each entry numbered in parentheses (1), (2), etc., so that the explanatory comments following the table may be traced.

All the figures on this projected income statement have been computed from only the four facts previously determined. The statement has been completed from the bottom up and not from the top down. The numbers in parentheses indicate the order in which they were inserted. Their explanation follows:

1 The desired profit is $15,000. This is the goal desired by the planner. We therefore insert this figure first on the last line.

2 We have found that profits average 12 percent of sales, so we must find the amount of which $15,000 (profits) is 12 percent. We divide $15,000 by 12 to find 1 percent ($1,250) and multiply by 100 to find 100 percent of sales. We can now insert $125,000, our necessary sales volume, as item (2).

3 We have determined in our search of statistics that markup averages 35 percent of sales. Accordingly, we find 35 percent of our $125,000 sales and insert this figure as our gross margin ($43,750), as item (3).

TABLE 4-1
JONES HARDWARE COMPANY
PROJECTED INCOME STATEMENT
YEAR BEGINNING JANUARY 1, 1978

Sales			$125,000.00	(2)
Cost of goods sold				
Beginning inventory, Jan. 1	$ 20,312.50	(5)		
Purchases during the year	81,250.00	(7)		
Goods available for sale	$101,562.50	(6)		
Less ending inventory, Dec. 31	20,312.50	(5)		
Costs of goods sold			81,250.00	(4)
Gross Margin			$ 43,750.00	(3)
Operating expenses			28,750.00	(8)
Net profit from operations			$ 15,000.00	(1)

4 Gross margin is the difference between what we paid for the merchandise (our cost) and what we sold it for. Therefore, if we subtract the gross margin ($43,750) from the sales ($125,000), it must tell us the cost of goods sold. Accordingly, we insert this figure on the projected income statement as item (4) ($81,250).

5 We have determined that the desired merchandise turnover is four times per year. This means that if the cost of goods sold is $81,250, it represents four times the average inventory which must be carried in stock to produce the sales volume we have indicated. Therefore, $81,250 divided by 4 gives us $20,312.50 as the average inventory necessary to support our sales volume. This figure is inserted on the statement for both our beginning and ending inventory as item (5). If enlarged inventories are contemplated, adjustments can be made. For present purposes, we will assume that the inventory will remain at the same level.

6 The cost of goods sold plus the inventory on hand at the end of the year must total the value of all the merchandise which has been available for sale during the year. Therefore, we add the cost of goods sold ($81,250) and the ending inventory ($20,312.50) to arrive at goods available for sale ($101,562.50), item (6).

7 If $101,562.50 of goods were available during the year but only $20,312.50 were on hand in the beginning inventory, the difference must represent the merchandise purchased during the year. Therefore, we subtract the beginning inventory of $20,312.50 from goods available of $101,562.50 to arrive at purchases of $81,250. This is item (7).

8 If gross margin is $43,750 and net profit from operations is $15,000, the difference must be the total of the operating expenses during the year. By subtracting the net profit from the gross margin, we have the total operating expenses of $28,750. (Item 8.)

We have now completed a first-phase projected income statement. Operating expenses will have to be detailed at a later date. They will again be based upon available statistics on how much should be paid for rent, salaries, supplies, and other expenses. These amounts will again all be computed as a percentage of sales. The comparable figures are easily available from the same source we have previously noted. Most reports will express these expenses as a percentage of sales.

This projected income statement tells the planners that if they are to realize the objective of $15,000 net profit, they will have to produce a sales volume of $125,000, maintain a merchandise inventory of $20,312.50, turn that inventory over four times during the year, and maintain an average markup of 35 percent on their entire sales volume.

SPECIAL ASPECTS OF SERVICE FIRM PLANNING

We have previously noted that a purely service firm which does not carry an inventory of merchandise for resale to its customers will not have a cost of goods sold section on its income statement. (See Table 3-3.) The income section of the statement will reflect the total dollars derived from sales of a service rather than from sales of a physical product. The operating expense section of the statement will include all expenses incurred, including any supplies used in the rendering of the firm's service.

Some service firms may also have sales of products — such as a TV repair shop which also sells new television sets. In such cases they should preferably separate sales income into service fees and product sales, have a special cost of goods sold section for the new product sales, and assign operating expenses to each phase of the operations as possible. Most helpful for proprietors of such firms is to develop income statements in separate columns, one for retail sales and one for service operations, and then total the two across the sheet for a summary of total operations. Each phase of the business can then be closely analyzed to determine its profitability.

SPECIAL ASPECTS OF MANUFACTURING FIRM PLANNING

The same type of statistics to which we have previously referred are also abundantly available for planners of new factory operations which produce their final products from raw materials. Financial statements for factory firms, however, have distinct features which are not part of retail firm statements. Some of these are:

1 The merchandise inventory figure on the balance sheet of a factory is not one figure representing total inventory on hand. Instead, it is broken down into raw materials, goods in process, and finished goods. (See Table 4-2.)

This means that when one is planning a factory operation, provision must be made not only for buying the original raw materials but also for carrying the investment in goods in process (half-finished goods) and the finished goods until they are sold. That is why the total inventory investment of a small factory is usually a higher percentage of total current assets than in most other types of firms. Average statistics are available to help the new factory planner determine the required investment.

Accounting is a bit more involved for factory operations because of the necessity of keeping track of the value of goods in process and total cost of the finished goods. This involves cost accounting procedures to add the labour expenses and overhead costs to raw

TABLE 4-2
BALANCE SHEET
GOMEZ AUTO BODY MANUFACTURING COMPANY
JANUARY 1, 1978

ASSETS			LIABILITIES		
Current assets:			Current liabilities:		
Cash		$ 6,000	Accounts payable	$ 40,000	
Notes receivable		4,200	Notes payable	20,000	
Marketable securities		15,800	Accrued taxes payable	5,000	
Inventories:			Total current liabilities		$ 65,000
Raw materials	$ 25,000				
Goods in process	40,000		Fixed liabilities:		
Finished goods	48,000	113,000	Contracts payable		35,000
Prepaid assets		1,000			
Total current assets		$140,000	Total liabilities		$100,000
			SHAREHOLDERS' EQUITY		
Fixed assets:			Capital shares outstanding:		
Land		$ 45,000	Preference share	$ 80,000	
Plant buildings	$165,000		Common stock	100,000	
Machinery and equipment	80,000		Retained earnings	45,000	
	$245,000		Total shareholders' equity		$225,000
Less depreciation	105,000	140,000			
Total fixed assets		185,000	Total liabilities and shareholders'		
Total assets		$325,000	equity		$325,000

materials placed in production to find the value of the unfinished products and the value of the products finished in the factory and placed in inventory for sale.

2 The income statement for a factory will show the cost of goods manufactured and sold, rather than merely a beginning inventory, plus purchases, less ending inventory, to find cost of goods sold, as is done for a retailing firm. The total cost of goods manufactured is preferably shown as a separate statement. See Tables 4-3 and 4-4 for illustrations of these statements.

This is again because the factory uses raw materials, expends labour and overhead on them, has products in all stages of manufacture in its inventories at a given time, and must calculate the total costs of its completed products.

Some factories produce products to order only, rather than producing for inventory stock on hand. This enables them to minimize the investment in materials and assures that all goods finished are sold as soon as they are ready for delivery.

The examples of a balance sheet, an income statement, and a statement of cost of goods manufactured for a small factory shown in Tables 4-2, 4-3, and 4-4 illustrate the preceding comments.

In our desired income approach to planning, we can now turn to the market survey — step 2 in Chapter 2 — to find out if the necessary sales can reasonably be achieved in the market we plan to serve. It is useless to further refine our financial planning unless that volume of sales can be achieved. When we know the results of our market survey are favourable, we will proceed to determining the assets required for the business and how they will be provided.

QUESTIONS FOR CLASS DISCUSSION

Q4-1 What does "the desired income approach to planning" mean to you? Do you agree with it? Why?

Q4-2 What advantages do small firm planners have today which were not so abundantly available when our grandparents started their business firms?

Q4-3 Where can people who plan new firms find some statistics to guide their planning?

Q4-4 What are the key items of statistics needed to make a projected income statement?

Q4-5 What is the merchandise turnover? How is it computed?

Q4-6 What is average markup? Can it be expressed both in dollars and as a percentage of sales? Give examples.

Q4-7 Why is it important to know whether profits as a percentage of sales is computed on profits before or after income taxes?

TABLE 4-3
THE KELLY MANUFACTURING COMPANY
INCOME STATEMENT
FOR YEAR ENDED DECEMBER 31, 1978

Sales		$2,150,000
Less cost of goods manufactured and sold		1,450,000
Gross margin on sales		$ 700,000
Operating expenses:		
Marketing Expenses (listed in detail)	$350,000	
Administrative expenses (listed in detail)	175,000	
Total operating expenses		525,000
Profit from operations before taxes		$ 175,000

TABLE 4-4
SMUCKER MANUFACTURING COMPANY
STATEMENT OF COST OF GOODS MANUFACTURED
YEAR ENDED DECEMBER 31,1978

Direct materials:		
Raw materials inventory January 1	$100,000	
Plus purchases during year	65,000	
Materials available during year	$165,000	
Less inventory December 31	40,000	
Direct materials used during year		$125,000
Direct labour expenses for year		265,000
Factory overhead (All factory overhead expenses would be listed in detail: indirect labour; power, heat, and light; salaries; factory supplies; depreciation; repairs and maintenance; patent expenses and insurance; and so on.)		80,000
Total manufacturing costs		$470,000
Add work in process January 1		45,000
		515,000
Less work in process December 31		65,000
Cost of goods manufactured during the year		$450,000

Q4-8 If we know goods available for sale and the beginning inventory, how do we find purchases?

Q4-9 If we know cost of goods sold and merchandise turnover, how do we find the average inventory?

PROBLEMS AND QUESTIONS FOR WRITTEN ASSIGNMENT

P4-1 Mr. Smith is planning to enter a new business. He has found that the average markup in this line of business is 40 percent, profits average 8 percent of sales, and the merchandise turnover is six times per year. He wishes to make $20,000 before income taxes. Prepare a projected income statement for Mr. Smith.

P4-2 Write a brief essay explaining the nature and value of a projected income statement for people planning to start a new business.

P4-3 Explain the difference between markup as a dollar figure and markup as a percentage of sales. Does either of these markups have any association with the gross margin? Why?

CONTINUING PROBLEM: *THE SUCCESS HARDWARE STORE*

Part 4. Developing a Projected Income Statement

We now know that only four things are necessary to construct a projected income statement. These are the desired profit, profits as a percentage of sales, average markup in this line of business, and the average merchandise turnover for independent stores of this type.

Assume that you have gathered data on these items from independent merchants, the trade association, Dun & Bradstreet, Statistics Canada, and the CIBC publication "Capital at Work." You have studied the variations in the figures gathered and decide to plan on an average markup of 30 percent, a merchandise turnover of four times per year, and profits of $15,000 for the first year, which should represent 10 percent of net sales.

Assignment for Part 4

Prepare a projected income statement for the first year of operations based on the data you have developed.

REFERENCES FOR FURTHER READING

Davidson, William R., and Alton F. Doody, *Retailing Management,* 3d ed., The Ronald Press Co., New York, 1966, chap. 4.

"Forecasting for a New Business," Pamphlet No. 5, Minding Your Own Business Series, *Federal Business Development Bank.*

Kelley, Pearce C., Kenneth Lawyer, and Clifford M. Baumback, *How to Organize and Operate a Small Business,* 5th ed., Prentice-Hall, Inc., Englewood Cliffs, N.J., 1973, chap. 10.

CHAPTER 5

Surveying the Market to Be Served

Do you really mean that I should have known before I started this business approximately how much my sales would be the first year? You must be kidding.

The Late Learner

The person who starts a new business without a fairly accurate idea of the total sales volume it will have is a poor planner. Such neglect places the fate of the business in jeopardy from the beginning. If the proprietor is lucky, the business may still succeed. It is much better judgment to first survey the market to be served and then to build the business to fit that market.

The techniques of making market surveys have been vastly improved in recent years. Many planners contemplating a new firm in a specific location employ an outside firm to make a survey of that market for them. Advertising firms often offer this service. Market research firms specialize in making such surveys. The cost of having such a survey made for a newly planned business varies in most cities from $500 to $2,000, depending upon the degree of detail requested.

If the planners cannot undertake the survey, any expenditure to have it done by an outside firm may be the best investment they can make. If the survey shows that the desired or required sales volume does not exist in the market, their expenditure for the survey will protect them from losing their investment in a firm which cannot produce profitable results. If the survey shows that they can exceed desired sales results, they can rearrange their planning to support this larger sales volume and larger profits.

THE OBJECTIVE OF A MARKET SURVEY

Stated most simply, the objective of a market survey is to determine a reasonably attainable sales volume in a specific market area for a specific type of business. This means finding out how many potential consumers of the planned merchandise or service there are in this market and how many of them can reasonably be expected to become customers of the firm under consideration.

The thoroughness of a market survey will vary under different conditions. The survey is essential to stores which plan to develop much of their own customer traffic. If sales are to depend on the firm's merchandising policies, its sales promotion efforts, its special services, or its uniqueness, a very thorough market survey should be made in advance. Firms which plan to rely on the established customer flow already generated by other businesses in the area may follow less thorough procedures. The latter types of firms have often been described as "parasite stores," meaning that their location has been dictated by the existing firms in the area that have attracted a substantial traffic flow, which the new firm will tap for its own sales. Examples of small firms in this category are a restaurant in a skyscraper lobby, a medium-priced dress shop next to a large department store, an office-building tobacco shop, or a drugstore in an airline terminal. In these cases, the amount and nature of the traffic and its sales potential are pretty well established. Such firms may still, however, exert various types of sales promotion activities to increase total income within that traffic.

Our chief concern here is for the types of firms which must rely heavily on a market survey to help them build much of their customer traffic.

WHAT IS A MARKET?

The market, or trading area for a particular firm, is the area which it seeks to serve with its products or services. From the buyer's point of view, it is the area within which the buyer knows he or she can find desired goods and services at desired prices. The definition of a market, or trading area, from the buyer's and the seller's view may not be the same. Sellers may desire to expand their markets beyond the limits which are normally recognized by buyers. Experience will tell merchants the proper limits of their trading areas if they have the means of measuring the sources of sales. Market areas may change with the development of new shopping centres in adjacent areas. At any given time, a market has its limits set by the area within which the firm can economically sell its goods or services.

PROCEDURE FOR MAKING A MARKET SURVEY

We know that the objective of the market is to determine a reasonable sales forecast. How is this accomplished? The procedure will vary from factory to wholesaler to retailer. In all cases, however, it will seek to determine the number of customers in the market area who may become customers for the planned business. For retailing, the steps should include the following:

1 Determine the limits of the market or trading area.
2 Study the population within this area to determine its potential sales characteristics.
3 Determine the purchasing power of the area.
4 Determine the present sales volume of the type of goods or services you propose to offer.
5 Estimate what proportion of the total sales volume you can reasonably obtain.

Each of these steps involves special considerations which deserve discussion here.

1 Determining Limits of the Marketing Area Firms in downtown locations, especially those in the central business districts of large cities, tend to draw customers from a wider market area than those in suburban or small city locations. This is so because customers come from wider areas to shop at the larger department stores or widely publicized shops, and they also come into the urban area for specialized services such as medical care. Downtown locations therefore often face much more competition than suburban or small-city locations. The decline of public transportation systems in most cities has been accompanied, in many areas, by an increase in the number of freeways and express highways, so that potential customers still go downtown despite increased surburban and small-city shopping centres. But partly because of decreasing public transportation, the number of suburban shopping centres has increased. The conclusion is, however, that for small firms, the market limits in urban locations are generally the same as for larger firms.

Interestingly, even a large department store reports that it measures its market area in terms of ease of access. This access is measured in 5-minute, 10-minute, 15- and 20-minute drives from its location in the central business district. Whenever travel obstacles, such as bridges, narrow streets, or congested areas, are encountered, the area beyond is considered less significant as part of the market area to be served. Cities bordering on a river, such as Winnipeg, find that their market area may be limited by that factor. Railroad yards, cemeteries, and other traffic obstacles can have similar effects on a given market area.

In suburban and small-city locations, the market area is determined more by neighbouring population and its characteristics, the nature of other stores in the area, and parking facilities. Ease of access and location, size, and quality characteristics of the firm are also important. Although many shoppers visit various shopping centres, they generally tend to patronize the nearest centre if it is otherwise satisfactory for their needs.

A popular method of measuring market areas for small firms in suburban and small-city areas is, therefore, to draw a map of their area and plot the location of competitors. By measuring the distance in each direction from closest competitors, small firm proprietors may establish an area in which, other things being equal, they should be thought of first by most shoppers. This assumes, of course, that the firm's existence is well known.

Adequacy of market area for a new small firm can be measured by knowing approximately how many people are necessary to support an average firm in this line of business. A composite of some of the best market research in this area shows, for example, that 600 people are needed to support one grocery store. See Table 9-1 for population requirements estimated to support one store in several other types of business. If a town of 10,000 population has 10 grocery stores, or an average of one grocery for every 1,000 people, the figures would suggest that the local population could support another grocery. Grocery retailers normally serve only their immediate neighbourhoods and the limits of their market area are almost determined by that neighbourhood.

The factor of economical limits to a market area is most applicable when such elements as delivery expense are involved. It just does not pay to deliver in remote areas when the time and expense required are prohibitive.

Recognition of primary areas (where the firm has distinct advantages) as against secondary areas (where some trade is still possible) has less significance for the typical small firm than for larger ones.

2 Studying the Population within the Market Area What does the market researcher look for in studying population to make a market survey? Its *size* is important—but size does not guarantee that the population has sufficient numbers of the type of customers sought. The *trend* of the total population is important. Growing populations are usually better markets than stable or declining populations. For many market surveys, the population should be translated into *number of households* in order to make a more meaningful survey. The *part-time* nature of the population is very significant, especially in resort towns.

After the size of the population is determined, a study of its characteristics may be even more important to the new firm planner.

A first classification of vital statistics relative to the population would include determining its composition by sex, age, income, occupation, marital status, average family size, race, religion, and average educational level. These characteristics vary sharply from city to city. Victoria, B.C., is not a likely market for too many baby-clothes stores. College towns are usually good markets for men's clothing. Bookstores do better when average education is high. A market survey for a particular type of business looks for those characteristics which make demand for its products or services.

Behavioural characteristics of the population are also very important. Do people buy the subject products weekly, monthly, on impulse or after shopping, in certain seasons or regularly? Is the usual objective in buying these products their obvious usefulness or their ability to satisfy psychological desires, or do they have special uses of significant quantity? Who makes the purchasing decision? Who makes the purchase? Who uses the product? Are the people brand-conscious or price-conscious? Is the population responsive to good promotion and advertising?

It should be obvious that the more planners know about the population and its characteristics, the better sales forecast they can make.

3 Determining Total Purchasing Power of the Market Area The next step in a thorough market survey is to determine the total purchasing power of the market area. The average income, found in studying population characteristics, is most helpful here. Occupations carry certain income ranges and can assist in determining total purchasing power. Other sources of key data are listed later in this chapter.

4 Determining Present Sales Volume in the Line of Business Students may be amazed to find that even statistics for the present sales volume can be obtained. The market surveyor not only wants to know the total sales in his line, but he also desires to estimate how the present sales volume is divided among the local firms engaged in this line. Average consumer expenditures in this line are available. See the sources listed later in this chapter.

5 Determining What Proportion of Sales Volume You Can Obtain It should be recognized in approaching this final objective of the survey that one new firm has little effect either on the total purchasing power in a market area or on the distribution of consumer expenditures. Until the new firm becomes better established, it must rely upon capturing a portion of the existing sales volume in that market area. Its initial merchandising and promotional activities will be directed toward that objective. Important attention, however, may be given to what additional demand may be created by promotion. This is especially important for new products.

This initial sales forecast will be governed by whether or not the market area is saturated with similar stores or has less than the normal number of competitors. Substantial knowledge on this matter will have been gathered in step 4.

Barring special circumstances, a market survey will determine whether the new firm can obtain a proportionate share of the total sales in this line in the market surveyed. This means that if five competitors are now dividing $500,000 of sales in this market, entrance of the new firm should make it six firms dividing $500,000 of sales. Anticipated growth in population can be reflected in the forecast. Merchandising policies should be directed to the set objective. Promotion activities of all types should be consistent with this objective. The new small firm has in its favour the fact that it is closer to customers within a certain area, the discontent of potential customers with existing firms, the promotion of its opening, and the accompanying opportunity to make permanent customers of the first visitors; and it can have a set of services which have been planned to meet the competition. New small firms may have other advantages, such as established contacts or contracts for substantial sales, exclusive distributorships for highly desired merchandise, well-known persons in their employ who bring customers, handier parking facilities, or price lines or lines of merchandise not offered by the competition. All these factors should be taken into account as the final sales forecast is determined.

This forecast of potential sales can then be used as the foundation of a budgeted income statement for the coming year. It is this statement which provides the basis for all budgeting and policy making.

It must be quickly recognized here that neglect of good market surveys has been a feature of too many newly planned small firms. This is probably due to lack of familiarity with the proper sources of market data, which are easily available, and/or lack of knowledge of how to use analytical procedures. For these reasons, the next section of this chapter is devoted to sources of data for making market surveys.

SOURCES OF DATA FOR MAKING MARKET SURVEYS

In market research data, collection tends to consume the most time and effort. There are two principal kinds of sources:
(a) primary sources—data which are gathered for the first time, typically collected by the researcher himself; and
(b) secondary sources—data that are already assembled and reported on.

It is most important for managers of small businesses, whose budgets are usually limited, to be aware of the availability of the vast array of secondary data sources:

1. Canadian Census. An excellent source of geographical market and population data is the Canadian census conducted by Statistics Canada (formerly the Dominion Bureau of Statistics) for the years ending in 1 and 6. Much of the desired information about population breakdown statistics with respect to age, sex, race, income, educational level, occupation, etc., can be found in census reports.

The two basic geographical units of census data that offer the highest potential for market analysis and the development of marketing strategy are those related to census tracts and enumeration areas.

Enumeration areas (EA) are the building blocks of the whole census. An EA is the section of a city or town or of the rural countryside covered by a single enumerator, or census taker. It represents an average of 150 households or 500 persons. Census tracts are sections of a large city, embracing from three to twelve or more enumeration areas. Census tracts are not created by simply aggregating a number of EAs into a larger package; the boundaries are established to include groups of adjacent EAs which have common or similar economic and social characteristics.

It should be noted that the Data Dissemination Section of Statistics Canada can provide a service of unlimited flexibility—one not available anywhere else in the world—called geocoding, and utilizing a geographically referenced data storage and retrieval system (GRDSR). All one needs to do is to take a map of a given city and with a pen outline the exact area to be covered. Then, in a letter, list the specific data needed from the area in question to determine the best prospects. The census people will translate the outline map into a numerical code that instructs the computer to pull out only the data which have been requested for only the area designated. The cost is most reasonable, well within the capacity of even a small retailer.

2. Statistics Canada Publications cover a wide array of data and analyses. (See Figures 5-1 and 5-2 for samples.) Statistics Canada maintains regional offices at St. John's, Halifax, Montreal, Toronto, Winnipeg, Edmonton, Regina, and Vancouver, where one can find complete files of current publications. In addition, certain libraries located in major cities in every province are designated as "full depository" and receive one copy of all publications.

3. Annual Census of Manufacturers. In addition to census data referred to above, Statistics Canada also provides yearly data on such topics as size of establishment, operating costs, wages, locations, etc., as well as studies on particular industries. It includes total shipments of most commodities produced in Canada.

4. The Financial Post Survey of Markets. This annual publication by Maclean-Hunter is considered indispensable by professional market research people. It is an excellent handbook of marketing facts; it contains consumer market data, a national industrial survey, and a bibliography of published market research studies. It has an exclusive guide to buying power and gives area ratings by income, by retail sales, and by market growth rates. (Samples are shown in Figures 5-3 and 5-4.)

5. Sales & Marketing Management Magazine. Once each year it publishes its "Survey of Buying Power" issue, which contains information on total population, households, breakdown of retail sales, and total purchasing dollars represented in each city and county in every province in the country. (An illustration is shown in Figure 5-5.)

6. Trade Sources. Many business, trade, and professional associations issue regular reports on total sales volume, costs, operating data, and other relative data in their particular fields, which can assist the new firm planner. Numerous trade and technical periodicals devote one issue per year to a listing of products and suppliers as a guide to buyers. The bulletins and newsletters issued by several Canadian banks and financial institutions can provide useful information on current economic and financial trends and developments. Handbooks, Industrial Directories, City Cross-Reference Directories, and Media Directories usually supply a wealth of information.

TABLE 7-2. Residential Construction, Starts, Completions and Under Construction, by Type of Dwelling, 1971, 1974, 1975 and 1976 – Continued

TABLEAU 7-2. Construction domiciliaire, mises en chantier, achèvements et logement en construction, par genre de logement, 1971, 1974, 1975 et 1976 – suite

Residential construction – Construction domiciliaire	1971	1974	1975	1976	Percentage change 1976/1975 Variation en pourcentage	Metropolitan area as a percentage of province – Région métropolitaine en pourcentage de la province			
						1971	1974	1975	1976
	number – nombre								
	7-2-14. Saint John, N.B. – N.-B.								
Starts – Mises en chantier									
Total	1,048	1,139	2,283	1,732	– 24.1	21.3	19.4	32.7	25.6
Single detached – Individuels non attenants	382	621	861	781	– 9.3	12.5	14.9	18.1	16.1
Two family – Bifamiliaux	62	60	180	118	– 34.4	19.0	27.0	72.3	67.8
Row – En rangée	60	72	109	42	– 61.5	26.1	64.3	84.5	31.1
Apartment and other – Appartements et autres	544	386	1,133	791	– 30.2	41.2	28.5	61.1	49.3
Completions – Achèvements									
Total	622	1,230	1,436	1,866	+ 29.9	17.0	18.1	24.7	26.1
Single detached – Individuels non attenants	344	565	726	764	+ 5.2	14.8	11.9	17.7	14.8
Two family – Bifamiliaux	76	62	96	149	+ 55.2	21.7	17.0	59.6	64.8
Row – En rangée	10	70	154	87	– 43.5	5.6	48.6	60.2	89.7
Apartment and other – Appartements et autres	192	533	460	866	+ 88.3	23.9	34.2	35.9	52.5
Under construction – Logement en construction									
Total	715	817	1,663	1,552	– 6.7	21.7	23.0	37.3	40.1
Single detached – Individuels non attenants	159	317	445	454	+ 2.0	8.0	17.8	19.3	22.0
Two family – Bifamiliaux	24	36	128	102	– 20.3	15.4	52.9	74.0	81.0
Row – En rangée	50	100	55	10	– 81.8	24.8	54.6	98.2	33.3
Apartment and other – Appartements et autres	482	364	1,035	986	– 4.7	50.6	23.9	53.6	59.6

	7-2-15. Saskatoon, Sask.								
Starts – Mises en chantier									
Total	498	1,232	2,486	2,965	+ 19.3	14.0	16.0	23.7	22.6
Single detached – Individuels non attenants	498	1,172	1,512	1,535	+ 1.5	17.0	18.3	20.4	20.2
Two family – Bifamiliaux	–	18	20	112	+ 460.0	–	6.0	4.7	14.9
Row – En rangée	–	–	–	188	...	–	–	...	31.1
Apartment and other – Appartements et autres	–	42	954	1,130	+ 18.4	–	4.8	43.6	27.0
Completions – Achèvements									
Total	487	1,274	1,316	2,575	+ 95.7	17.6	19.6	17.1	23.3
Single detached – Individuels non attenants	457	1,017	1,217	1,688	+ 38.7	20.1	19.8	19.0	20.7
Two family – Bifamiliaux	2	14	10	26	+ 160.0	2.0	7.7	3.6	5.6
Row – En rangée	28	–	–	–	–	35.4	–	–	–
Apartment and other – Appartements et autres	–	243	89	861	+ 867.4	–	26.4	10.6	40.9
Under construction – Logement en construction									
Total	177	611	1,751	2,084	+ 19.0	8.8	12.2	22.7	22.4
Single detached – Individuels non attenants	177	583	848	665	– 21.6	12.1	15.8	18.3	17.4
Two family – Bifamiliaux	–	10	20	108	+ 440.0	–	4.6	5.4	18.5
Row – En rangée	–	–	117	305	+ 160.7	–	–	19.8	34.3
Apartment and other – Appartements et autres	–	18	766	1,006	+ 31.3	–	1.9	35.8	25.0
	7-2-16. Sudbury, Ont.								
Starts – Mises en chantier									
Total	3,761	449	922	1,058	+ 14.8	4.2	0.5	1.2	1.2
Single detached – Individuels non attenants	1,268	374	687	718	+ 4.5	4.1	0.4	2.0	2.2
Two family – Bifamiliaux	226	28	90	184	+ 104.4	3.1	0.5	1.1	2.2
Row – En rangée	242	–	–	–	–	3.2	–	–	–
Apartment and other – Appartements et autres	2,025	47	145	156	+ 7.6	4.6	0.1	0.6	0.6
Completions – Achèvements									
Total	2,522	786	925	980	+ 5.9	3.4	0.8	1.1	1.2
Single detached – Individuels non attenants	1,199	372	580	699	+ 20.5	4.7	1.0	1.8	2.2
Two family – Bifamiliaux	216	28	38	136	+ 257.9	3.7	0.4	0.5	1.6
Row – En rangée	341	42	25	–	...	4.8	0.3	0.3	–
Apartment and other – Appartements et autres	766	344	282	145	– 48.6	2.2	0.7	0.8	0.5
Under construction – Logement en construction									
Total	2,426	458	433	434	+ 0.2	2.9	0.6	0.6	0.6
Single detached – Individuels non attenants	425	138	224	198	– 11.6	2.8	0.9	1.3	1.1
Two family – Bifamiliaux	78	20	69	80	+ 15.9	1.7	0.6	1.3	1.5
Row – En rangée	145	23	–	–	–	2.3	0.3	–	–
Apartment and other – Appartements et autres	1,778	277	140	156	+ 11.4	3.1	0.5	0.3	0.4

Figure 5-1 *Source: Statistics Canada,* Market Research Handbook, 1977-1978, *Cat. No. 63-224.*

TABLE 19. Detailed Average Expenditure, by City, All Families and Unattached Individuals

Canada, 1974

		City – Ville													
		St. John's (Nfld.) – St-Jean (T.-N.)		Halifax		Saint John (N.B.) – Saint-Jean (N.-B.)		Quebec		Montreal		Ottawa		Toronto	
		Av. per fam. – Moy. par fam.	% rptg. – % décl.	Av. per fam. – Moy. par fam.	% rptg. – % décl.	Av. per fam. – Moy. par fam.	% rptg. – % décl.	Av. per fam. – Moy. par fam.	% rptg. – % décl.	Av. per fam. – Moy. par fam.	% rptg. – % décl.	Av. per fam. – Moy. par fam.	% rptg. – % décl.	Av. per fam. – Moy. par fam.	% rptg. – % décl.
	Furnishings and equipment – continued														
	Furniture, concluded														
187	Other metal– shelving, bunks, cots, etc.	.6	2.1	3.7	5.8	.7	1.1	2.5	2.3	1.3	2.0	4.3	6.9	3.5	3.3
188	Mattresses and box springs	7.3	5.7	21.7	13.9	8.7	7.0	13.6	8.6	20.8	12.9	23.9	15.5	12.0	8.0
189	Upholstered chesterfields, sofas, chairs	55.9	13.5	71.4	15.1	38.7	7.8	41.4	9.3	54.4	11.9	72.2	15.5	59.2	11.6
190	Occasional upholstered chairs, recliners	10.2	7.2	14.7	10.4	8.6	6.1	5.7	4.3	11.3	5.4	12.5	8.5	8.7	4.4
191	Upholstered dual purpose living room	5.0	3.6	3.1	1.3	3.9	.9	5.2	1.2	7.0	1.5	9.4	3.1	3.7	1.2
192	Benches, footstools and hassocks	1.3	3.8	1.2	3.9	.3	1.2	1.9	3.8	.6	2.0	1.0	3.7	.6	1.0
193	High chair, baby crib, other nursery	3.6	4.2	1.9	4.1	2.5	4.0	4.5	3.3	3.7	3.8	4.1	3.8	3.2	3.6
194	Wall mirrors	1.0	3.9	2.0	7.5	1.9	3.8	1.4	3.9	1.9	4.4	4.7	8.4	2.2	3.9
195	Lamps and lamp shades	6.5	11.8	11.5	19.5	4.4	9.7	11.0	14.2	11.6	14.4	21.4	29.3	13.4	13.6
196	Art objects, paintings, prints, sculptures	4.7	7.3	12.9	15.2	1.9	2.9	3.7	5.0	13.1	6.2	23.0	18.1	12.2	8.7
197	Other	4.7	3.1	3.2	3.0	1.6	2.0	6.4	2.6	7.4	2.5	2.7	2.7	4.0	2.2
200-203	Floor covering	68.3	31.8	72.6	27.8	47.6	27.1	46.7	23.6	64.4	24.7	108.8	30.2	81.9	28.2
200	Rugs, broadloom and carpeting	62.5	27.6	65.2	24.0	37.0	19.6	38.5	20.4	56.3	20.3	96.6	29.4	79.3	26.2
201	Underpadding	.4	1.0	3.0	2.9	1.4	.5	.2	.8	1.3	1.6	6.4	2.8	.7	1.2
203	Hard surface floor covering, sheeting	5.3	6.4	4.4	6.5	9.2	9.1	8.0	6.2	6.8	6.2	5.8	3.8	1.9	3.0
210-214	Non-electric kitchen equipment	11.3	42.8	16.9	49.2	7.9	34.0	13.5	33.4	11.4	28.9	18.9	52.8	13.6	35.2
210	Metal cooking utensils	5.4	18.5	7.7	25.0	3.3	13.6	6.9	15.3	4.8	12.0	9.0	23.9	6.2	17.4
211	Kitchen crockery and glassware	2.6	14.7	3.0	14.6	2.1	10.0	2.4	9.2	2.3	9.6	3.6	17.6	3.5	13.4
212	Plastic kitchen utensils	1.3	12.4	2.9	22.0	1.1	11.0	1.2	7.6	2.7	9.3	2.1	17.8	1.6	10.2
213	Garbage containers, metal or plastic	.6	7.6	1.3	13.6	.6	9.0	.8	8.5	.5	6.2	1.5	16.1	1.0	6.4
214	Other non-electric kitchen equipment	1.3	9.0	2.0	16.4	.8	10.3	2.3	7.0	1.2	6.5	2.7	18.0	1.3	8.2
220-252	Household appliances	160.4	60.3	128.5	64.7	139.0	55.3	170.6	59.5	144.6	60.8	185.8	77.1	140.9	63.5
220	Vacuum cleaner	18.7	11.7	15.4	10.8	11.3	6.5	15.7	7.6	13.9	9.0	18.2	13.2	12.6	9.9
221	Electric floor polisher	1.5	.7	.3	.7	1.1	.5	1.3	1.2	.9	.6	.9	1.4	.9	.8
222	Dishwasher	10.5	3.1	6.7	1.9	3.2	.9	15.3	3.9	7.9	1.9	10.6	3.0	5.7	1.8
223-225	Refrigerator	19.8	7.3	16.1	5.8	25.5	6.0	33.4	8.4	22.0	6.2	25.8	6.5	19.3	5.3
223	Electric	19.8	7.3	16.1	5.8	25.5	6.0	33.4	8.4	22.0	6.2	25.7	6.1	18.9	5.2
225	Other	.0	.0	.0	.0	.0	.0	.0	.0	.0	.0	.0	.3	.4	.1
226	Home freezer	22.5	8.5	10.5	4.2	7.0	2.1	9.4	3.3	7.9	2.7	10.0	4.7	11.1	4.3
227-229	Cooking stove	16.4	6.5	16.1	7.5	21.1	7.1	13.9	5.1	20.0	7.4	14.4	5.0	17.6	5.6
227	Electric	13.5	5.2	15.0	6.8	19.0	6.0	13.9	5.1	19.6	7.0	14.4	5.0	15.6	4.7
228	Gas	.0	.0	1.1	.7	.0	.0	.0	.0	.3	.4	.0	.0	2.0	.9
229	Other	2.8	1.3	.0	.0	2.1	1.2	.0	.0	.0	.0	.0	.0	.0	.0
230-233	Washing machine and dryer	42.1	14.6	26.8	8.9	47.9	14.7	43.2	9.5	39.9	11.5	40.3	12.5	22.5	7.1
230	Automatic washer	19.3	6.1	11.7	4.1	28.5	8.3	26.9	7.4	20.3	6.7	21.7	6.4	14.5	5.0
231	Wringer type washer and spin dry	8.3	4.1	3.9	1.8	2.7	1.4	2.7	1.0	3.3	1.8	4.9	3.1	1.9	1.0
232	Dryer	13.6	5.9	8.1	3.8	15.1	6.4	12.2	4.9	13.5	6.1	13.7	5.7	5.7	2.7
233	Combination washer and dryer	.9	.4	3.2	1.5	1.6	.9	1.4	.3	2.8	.8	.0	.0	.4	.2
234-235	Sewing machine	7.6	2.9	4.1	3.4	2.7	1.4	11.3	4.8	5.1	2.9	8.6	4.4	10.1	4.7
234	Electric	7.6	2.9	4.1	3.4	2.7	1.4	10.2	4.8	5.1	2.9	8.6	4.4	10.1	4.7
235	Other	.0	.0	.0	.0	.0	.0	1.1	.3	.0	.0	.0	.0	.0	.0
236	Humidifier, dehumidifier – portable	1.0	1.4	6.4	5.9	1.5	1.6	5.5	6.4	3.6	5.3	5.5	5.2	3.5	4.3
237	Air conditioner (window)	.2	.3	.1	.3	.8	.5	.0	.0	2.5	.8	14.4	5.1	15.7	4.8
238	Micro-wave oven	.0	.0	.0	.0	.0	.0	.0	.0	.0	.0	1.9	.3	1.0	.1
239	Garbage compactor	.0	.0	.0	.0	.2	.5	.5	.5	.0	.0	.0	.0	.0	.0
240	Hot plate	.4	1.7	.1	1.1	.0	.5	.0	.0	.2	.7	.2	.7	.2	.7
241	Electric kettle	1.2	7.3	1.7	11.5	.6	5.0	1.5	9.3	1.3	8.8	2.3	15.6	1.4	9.7
242	Electric toaster	1.5	7.8	2.3	10.9	1.5	9.2	2.4	12.7	2.4	12.6	3.1	14.0	2.5	12.0
243	Electric frying pan	2.0	7.2	1.9	7.2	1.0	5.2	.7	2.6	.5	2.0	1.7	5.4	1.0	3.8
244	Electric mixers and blenders	2.3	5.8	3.9	11.5	3.0	6.9	2.9	6.1	2.4	6.9	3.1	8.2	2.1	7.3
245	Electric coffee makers	.3	1.4	.9	3.4	.3	1.4	.8	3.8	.6	2.4	.5	3.1	.6	2.5
246	Other electric kitchen equipment	1.0	6.1	1.8	7.8	.6	3.9	1.7	6.5	1.2	6.3	2.9	12.1	1.2	6.5
247	Irons	1.0	4.7	2.2	11.7	2.0	10.0	1.4	6.6	1.9	8.4	2.7	14.4	1.9	9.1
248	Electric heaters and fans	.3	1.4	1.0	4.4	.7	2.5	1.5	4.1	2.2	5.9	4.4	10.9	1.3	5.1
249	Hair dryers	4.1	15.1	3.1	11.5	2.3	9.5	3.1	11.4	2.8	10.4	4.6	20.3	2.6	9.9
250	Electric blankets	.3	1.0	.9	2.6	.5	1.2	.2	1.3	.4	.8	1.3	3.6	1.0	2.9
251	Electric razors	2.1	6.6	2.4	7.9	1.1	4.3	2.2	7.2	1.8	5.7	3.4	11.6	1.8	5.8
252	Other electrical equipment	3.5	12.1	3.8	16.0	2.8	10.8	2.8	10.0	3.3	10.5	5.0	20.1	3.6	15.7
260-263	Glass, china and tableware	12.6	31.0	12.3	37.0	6.1	26.2	6.7	20.4	10.8	25.1	21.4	39.8	13.2	29.9
260	Silver or stainless steel	2.8	10.1	3.8	11.5	1.1	4.7	1.5	4.6	1.5	4.4	5.9	11.6	3.4	8.2
261	Glassware for table use, crystal	2.7	19.5	2.2	19.4	1.3	16.8	1.7	8.8	3.5	13.9	5.4	24.7	3.5	18.3
262	Dinnerware, china, earthenware	6.4	9.4	5.6	14.3	3.0	8.6	2.3	6.1	4.3	9.8	8.2	13.1	5.7	11.1
263	Other– plastic or substitute dinnerware	.7	3.6	.7	3.8	.7	4.3	1.3	5.8	1.5	5.1	1.8	8.0	.7	3.8
270-283	Household textiles and plastics	71.7	80.4	70.6	80.0	52.4	67.8	78.3	72.0	71.0	66.3	85.8	80.3	75.0	70.6
270	Sheets	14.4	47.1	11.9	42.8	10.4	43.3	13.0	39.7	12.5	38.4	12.7	45.7	14.3	43.1
271	Pillowcases	3.4	34.6	2.8	34.1	2.9	34.5	2.2	22.9	3.2	30.1	3.2	34.8	3.0	27.8
272	All wool blankets	1.7	8.7	1.4	7.2	1.0	5.7	2.4	6.7	1.9	7.0	2.6	8.0	2.1	7.2
273	Other blankets	1.1	6.2	.7	3.8	.8	5.5	.7	4.0	1.1	5.6	1.5	8.5	1.8	7.4
274	Comforters, quilts, pillows, cushions	2.3	12.1	2.8	14.4	1.6	9.3	2.8	7.1	1.1	5.3	3.3	14.8	2.3	10.9

Figure 5-2 *Source: Statistics Canada, Urban Family Expenditure, 1974, Cat. No. 62544.*

7. Chambers of Commerce, Boards of Trade, or Business Development Departments. Major cities have these organizations, which have the important job of encouraging the development of new business firms in their communities. They will gladly supply all types of information regarding population studies, income characteristics of the community, trends, payrolls, industrial development, and so on. Such information is usually free for the asking. Maps showing major

TABLEAU 19. Dépenses moyennes détaillées, selon la ville,
Toutes familles et personnes seules

Canada, 1974

City – Ville															
Thunder Bay		Winnipeg		Regina		Saskatoon		Calgary		Edmonton		Vancouver			
Av. per fam. — Moy. par fam.	% rptg. — % décl.	Av. per fam. — Moy. par fam.	% rptg. — % décl.	Av. per fam. — Moy. par fam.	% rptg. — % décl.	Av. per fam. — Moy. par fam.	% rptg. — % décl.	Av. per fam. — Moy. par fam.	% rptg. — % décl.	Av. per fam. — Moy. par fam.	% rptg. — % décl.	Av. per fam. — Moy. par fam.	% rptg. — % décl.		
														Articles d'ameublement et accessoires – suite	
														Meubles, fin	
3.6	4.3	2.4	3.6	2.1	4.2	5.1	5.5	2.5	5.3	3.1	6.1	2.5	2.9	Autre mobilier en métal, lits, etc.	187
12.9	6.1	21.1	15.3	14.0	11.8	14.9	10.6	19.1	13.3	19.8	13.5	18.9	11.5	Matelas et sommiers	188
89.8	15.8	79.2	15.6	79.0	17.9	91.2	18.0	59.1	14.9	106.1	21.7	56.0	12.9	Canapés, sofas, fauteuils rembourrés	189
12.9	8.0	12.1	8.2	18.3	9.5	21.4	10.9	11.5	9.7	14.7	7.9	15.5	8.8	Fauteuils non assortis, inclinables	190
5.7	1.5	5.2	2.4	7.2	2.7	4.0	2.5	2.5	1.9	2.9	1.7	2.7	1.0	Meubles de salon, double usage	191
1.8	1.1	1.1	3.7	.2	1.0	1.3	3.4	1.1	3.1	2.8	3.8	.2	1.0	Bancs, tabourets, poufs	192
1.4	2.8	4.0	4.4	1.2	3.8	1.4	2.4	2.0	4.2	2.5	4.4	3.0	3.2	Chaises hautes, lits, autres pour bébés	193
2.1	4.2	1.0	3.2	1.8	6.9	1.5	4.9	3.1	7.1	2.1	6.0	3.0	5.9	Miroirs muraux	194
10.2	16.1	10.6	17.3	11.9	20.9	11.8	19.3	11.8	19.9	9.6	18.7	11.8	18.1	Lampes et abat-jour	195
5.3	8.7	23.3	16.6	9.1	15.7	9.8	13.4	21.0	18.6	12.2	14.0	24.7	13.2	Objets d'art, tableaux, gravures, sculptures	196
1.8	2.1	2.1	3.8	1.2	3.0	14.4	3.8	3.6	5.1	7.1	3.8	4.2	4.8	Autres objets d'art	197
100.4	26.7	66.4	27.7	55.3	26.0	101.5	30.7	104.1	31.5	78.2	26.9	71.8	27.3	Couvre-parquets	200-203
92.1	25.3	61.7	25.8	51.2	24.5	91.0	28.8	97.6	29.7	73.3	25.1	65.5	25.7	Moquettes, tapis et carpettes	200
1.7	2.3	.8	1.3	.4	1.6	5.2	5.0	3.7	4.8	3.2	2.7	1.8	2.6	Sous-tapis	201
6.5	3.8	3.8	4.9	3.7	2.8	5.3	5.2	2.8	2.4	1.8	2.0	4.5	3.5	Couvre-parquets à surface rigide	203
16.8	43.4	17.6	48.6	13.9	45.9	10.7	45.0	20.7	54.8	19.9	50.0	14.9	46.7	Accessoires de cuisine non électriques	210-214
8.0	20.3	8.7	23.7	6.1	19.0	3.7	17.6	8.7	23.2	9.9	22.9	7.1	22.2	Autoclaves, batteries de cuisine, etc.	210
3.3	13.6	2.5	15.0	1.7	11.5	1.4	11.4	5.1	19.5	4.1	17.1	3.3	15.4	Faïence et verrerie de cuisine	211
2.4	14.5	3.1	15.7	3.1	18.6	2.8	16.7	2.8	17.4	2.2	15.4	1.4	12.0	Ustensiles de cuisine en plastique	212
1.1	9.5	1.0	10.9	1.0	11.7	1.0	12.4	1.2	13.0	1.1	13.4	1.0	10.8	Poubelles en métal ou en plastique	213
2.0	15.2	2.3	18.9	2.0	15.7	1.9	15.5	2.9	23.7	2.7	19.5	2.2	17.6	Autres accessoires de cuisine non électriques	214
169.9	62.5	167.0	67.6	173.0	69.4	168.6	72.5	183.4	75.2	156.9	68.7	126.1	60.8	Appareils ménagers	220-252
23.9	11.5	20.7	13.5	14.0	10.3	15.6	10.2	17.7	10.9	24.5	15.6	16.5	11.8	Aspirateur	220
1.0	1.4	.3	1.0	.8	.6	.4	.8	.5	.5	2.4	1.7	.1	.2	Cireuse électrique	221
8.1	2.1	15.0	4.4	11.1	3.6	14.2	3.5	25.2	6.7	17.7	4.9	9.2	2.7	Lave-vaisselle	222
33.9	10.2	32.4	8.6	30.3	9.9	37.3	12.3	22.5	6.6	21.3	6.0	19.5	5.5	Réfrigérateur	223-225
32.0	9.5	32.4	8.6	30.3	9.9	37.3	12.3	22.5	6.6	21.0	5.8	19.5	5.5	Électrique	223
1.9	.7	.0	.0	.0	.0	.0	.0	.0	.0	.3	.4	.0	.0	Autre	225
7.3	3.4	13.7	5.4	14.5	6.6	10.4	4.1	14.2	5.8	12.7	5.2	12.6	4.6	Congélateur	226
16.3	6.6	23.2	8.2	24.7	10.1	11.9	6.5	11.2	3.5	12.6	4.6	15.1	4.7	Cuisinière	227-229
15.7	6.3	22.1	7.4	24.6	9.8	11.9	6.5	10.9	3.2	12.5	3.9	13.1	3.8	Électrique	227
.6	.4	.9	.5	.1	.4	.0	.0	.3	.3	.1	.7	2.0	.9	À gaz	228
.0	.0	.1	.2	.0	.0	.0	.0	.0	.0	.0	.0	.0	.0	Autre	229
49.5	14.1	27.7	9.8	34.4	11.8	37.7	11.2	41.4	10.6	24.7	6.7	22.8	7.1	Laveuse et sécheuse	230-233
32.3	9.8	12.4	3.8	17.1	6.4	21.2	6.7	26.2	7.8	11.7	3.6	12.9	4.5	Laveuse automatique	230
4.4	2.5	.5	.9	1.6	1.5	1.8	1.9	2.2	1.4	1.7	1.2	1.0	.8	Laveuse-essoreuse, etc.	231
12.8	5.3	13.1	6.3	13.6	7.0	11.9	5.0	12.6	5.1	6.8	3.1	7.5	3.5	Sécheuse	232
.0	.0	1.7	.7	2.1	.8	2.9	1.3	.5	.1	4.6	.7	1.5	.3	Laveuse-sécheuse	233
5.8	3.0	6.3	2.9	11.3	4.5	11.2	5.4	9.2	4.5	14.3	5.9	6.6	3.4	Machine à coudre	234-235
5.8	3.0	6.0	2.4	11.3	4.5	11.1	5.2	8.9	4.2	14.3	5.9	6.5	3.4	Électrique	234
.0	.0	.4	.5	.0	.0	.1	.2	.3	.3	.0	.0	.1	.2	Autre	235
1.0	1.4	1.1	2.0	3.8	4.5	3.3	3.2	3.1	4.4	2.3	3.0	.4	1.2	Humidificateur,déshumidificateur	236
.0	.0	.5	.2	2.0	.9	2.5	1.2	.0	.0	1.0	.5	.0	.0	Climatiseur (à fenêtre)	237
.0	.0	.0	.0	.0	.0	.0	.0	1.8	.5	1.4	.2	2.0	.4	Four à micro-ondes	238
.0	.0	.3	.2	.9	.4	.0	.0	.0	.0	.0	.0	.0	.0	Pulvérisateur de déchets	239
.2	1.0	.1	.5	.1	.1	.0	.0	.4	2.2	.1	.2	.3	1.4	Réchaud	240
1.7	10.7	1.6	11.4	2.1	14.5	1.7	11.9	2.0	11.9	.9	6.3	1.1	7.8	Bouilloire électrique	241
2.4	10.7	2.2	11.3	2.6	13.6	2.2	9.4	2.8	13.8	2.0	10.7	2.0	8.6	Grille-pain électrique	242
1.4	5.3	1.1	4.3	1.0	3.4	1.4	5.2	2.4	9.0	1.1	4.7	1.2	4.5	Poêle à frire électrique	243
2.1	6.3	3.0	8.7	2.7	7.7	2.7	9.3	5.0	11.8	2.4	8.0	3.4	9.7	Malaxeurs électriques	244
1.2	5.4	.8	3.2	1.8	8.4	1.2	7.7	2.3	8.8	1.5	6.5	1.1	4.3	Cafetières électriques	245
.9	5.0	1.5	7.9	2.1	10.1	1.0	5.9	2.0	8.8	1.6	8.3	1.3	6.6	Autres appareils de cuisine électriques	246
2.1	8.7	2.8	13.2	2.0	14.2	2.2	10.1	1.9	9.7	2.2	10.6	2.1	10.4	Fers à repasser	247
1.6	3.3	2.0	7.1	1.1	5.4	1.8	7.2	1.9	6.5	1.0	4.0	1.1	3.5	Chaufferettes, ventilateurs électriques	248
3.1	11.6	3.0	13.0	2.2	9.8	2.5	11.1	3.8	14.2	3.4	12.4	2.7	9.3	Séchoirs à cheveux	249
.4	.7	.6	1.7	.1	.4	.4	1.6	1.3	4.0	.8	2.3	.2	.7	Couvertures chauffantes	250
2.0	6.4	2.5	7.7	2.2	7.4	2.9	9.6	4.2	13.3	1.9	7.5	1.8	6.1	Rasoirs électriques	251
3.8	17.6	4.6	21.5	4.5	21.8	4.0	22.0	6.6	24.7	3.0	15.3	3.1	15.3	Autres appareils électro-ménagers	252
18.7	37.7	15.8	35.6	16.1	34.1	12.7	32.5	26.9	47.7	21.0	39.2	13.5	31.6	Verrerie, porcelaine et argenterie	260-263
5.0	11.8	2.5	8.2	5.8	10.0	2.5	8.1	7.7	13.3	5.7	12.8	3.3	7.6	Argent ou en acier inoxydable	260
5.6	24.6	3.3	21.5	2.9	18.4	2.9	20.8	4.0	30.2	5.1	23.0	3.3	18.8	Verrerie de table, taillée	261
6.7	8.3	9.2	12.9	6.2	12.1	6.5	9.8	13.7	18.7	8.4	11.4	6.5	13.4	Vaisselle de table, plats de faïence, etc.	262
1.4	7.6	.9	6.1	1.2	8.1	.8	5.1	1.5	10.9	1.8	8.2	.5	3.6	Vaisselle en plastique ou succédané	263
80.2	75.7	83.7	77.7	73.8	74.9	66.9	76.0	88.4	83.2	87.5	81.2	65.5	75.7	Toiles et plastiques de ménage	270-283
14.5	46.6	9.8	41.7	10.7	39.4	10.4	40.9	15.2	50.6	12.6	43.6	12.5	45.5	Draps	270
2.9	28.5	2.8	31.7	2.0	23.6	2.1	23.3	3.7	35.6	2.9	28.7	2.7	31.8	Taies d'oreiller	271
2.6	6.8	1.1	4.0	.7	3.2	.9	4.2	1.6	5.1	1.4	6.1	1.4	5.4	Couvertures tout laine	272
1.4	5.1	.9	5.7	1.0	6.0	.6	3.7	2.3	10.6	1.3	7.3	1.2	5.9	Autres couvertures	273
4.8	17.7	3.0	15.7	4.7	15.7	2.9	14.5	4.9	20.1	4.5	19.0	2.4	12.2	Douillettes, édredons, oreillers, coussins	274

trading areas are often available from these sources. Such maps indicate where the major business of the subject area is being done and thus reflect buying habits of the population. A study of the road network of any area gives information on ease of access to a particular site. We have seen that access is an important consideration in determining market area limits.

8. Provincial Government Market Surveys. These are prepared in most provinces by the appropriate departments, such as, for example,

Exclusive Buying Power Indexes

Retail Trade 1978

(Sales in $ millions)

By Class of Business

By province, economic area, county and major urban area (over 30,000 population)

	Total Sales ($000,000)		Food Stores		Motor Vehicle Dealers		Service Stations		Clothing & Shoe Stores		Hardware Stores		Furniture, Appliance, TV & Radio	
	Sales	% Total	Sales	% Total	Sales	% Total	Sales	% Total	Sales	% Total	Sales	% Total	Sales	% Total
Canada	**67,523.7**	**100.00**	**17,300.3**	**100.00**	**12,811.0**	**100.00**	**4,645.8**	**100.00**	**3,623.3**	**100.00**	**733.7**	**100.00**	**1,819.5**	**100.00**
Newfoundland	**1,266.7**	**1.88**	**302.1**	**1.75**	**212.5**	**1.66**	**119.1**	**2.56**	**59.7**	**1.65**	**2.4**	**0.33**	**32.6**	**1.79**
Labrador:														
Division No. 10	79.9	0.12	14.5	0.08	14.5	0.11	2.7	0.06	1.3	0.04	0.0	0.00	1.1	0.06
Total	79.9	0.12	14.5	0.08	14.5	0.11	2.7	0.06	1.3	0.04	0.0	0.00	1.1	0.06
Western:														
Division No. 4	46.2	0.07	12.9	0.07	3.2	0.03	7.5	0.16	4.5	0.12	0.2	0.03	1.7	0.09
Division No. 5	119.6	0.18	29.6	0.17	17.5	0.14	12.9	0.28	6.1	0.17	0.2	0.02	5.4	0.30
Division No. 9	31.8	0.05	10.2	0.06	0.8	0.01	4.1	0.09	0.6	0.02	0.2	0.02	1.0	0.06
Total	197.6	0.30	52.7	0.30	21.5	0.18	24.5	0.53	11.2	0.31	0.6	0.07	8.1	0.45
St. John's Southeastern:														
Division No. 3	42.0	0.06	9.8	0.06	0.8	0.01	2.3	0.05	2.5	0.07	0.2	0.02	1.3	0.07
Division No. 2	58.1	0.09	15.3	0.09	4.4	0.03	6.6	0.14	0.8	0.02	0.6	0.08	0.3	0.02
Division No. 1	591.2	0.88	150.6	0.87	122.3	0.95	53.1	1.14	32.5	0.90	0.6	0.08	15.8	0.87
St. John's*	492.6	0.73	107.4	0.62	122.6	0.96	38.8	0.84	29.3	0.81	0.3	0.05	14.5	0.80
Division No. 7	65.5	0.10	18.6	0.11	8.3	0.06	9.9	0.21	0.8	0.02	0.1	0.01	0.3	0.02
Total	756.8	1.13	194.3	1.13	135.8	1.05	71.9	1.54	36.6	1.01	1.5	0.19	17.7	0.98
Central:														
Division No. 6	151.1	0.22	24.9	0.14	39.1	0.30	11.6	0.25	8.3	0.23	0.3	0.04	4.4	0.24
Division No. 8	81.4	0.12	15.6	0.09	1.5	0.01	8.4	0.18	2.2	0.06	0.2	0.02	1.3	0.07
Total	232.5	0.34	40.5	0.23	40.6	0.31	20.0	0.43	10.5	0.29	0.5	0.06	5.7	0.31
Prince Edward Island	**318.0**	**0.47**	**64.0**	**0.37**	**57.3**	**0.45**	**28.8**	**0.62**	**9.8**	**0.27**	**1.0**	**0.14**	**2.2**	**0.12**
Kings	35.7	0.00	8.3	0.05	2.9	0.02	5.3	0.11	2.2	0.06	0.0	0.00	0.1	0.00
Prince	107.9	0.16	19.3	0.11	24.0	0.19	8.5	0.18	2.7	0.07	1.0	0.14	0.4	0.02
Queens	174.4	0.26	36.4	0.21	30.4	0.24	15.0	0.32	5.0	0.14	0.0	0.00	1.7	0.09
Nova Scotia	**2,110.4**	**3.13**	**511.8**	**2.96**	**381.4**	**2.98**	**193.3**	**4.16**	**115.7**	**3.19**	**17.6**	**2.40**	**53.6**	**2.95**
Halifax-South Shore:														
Digby	45.3	0.07	12.3	0.07	7.7	0.06	4.7	0.10	1.1	0.03	0.7	0.09	2.0	0.11
Yarmouth	53.3	0.08	13.1	0.08	6.2	0.05	5.2	0.11	4.2	0.12	1.3	0.18	2.2	0.12
Shelburne	32.3	0.05	5.5	0.03	6.9	0.05	3.6	0.08	1.0	0.03	0.5	0.07	0.6	0.03
Queens	29.2	0.04	6.3	0.04	5.9	0.05	3.4	0.07	1.0	0.03	0.6	0.09	1.2	0.07
Lunenburg	112.6	0.17	27.5	0.16	17.7	0.14	11.2	0.24	4.6	0.13	0.9	0.12	2.7	0.15

Figure 5-3 *Source: The Financial Post Survey of Markets, 1979.*

Cranbrook

In East Kootenay regional district, British Columbia.
Chamber of Commerce—Maurice McNair, manager, P.O. Box 84, V1C 4H6.
City Lands Manager—O.R. Newman, 40-10th Ave. S. V1C 2M8. 604-426-4211.
Government—Mayor and six aldermen elected for two years in November.

Market: 84% above national average

Retail sales, 1978	**$73,000,000**
% Canadian total	**0.11**
Per capita	**5,260**

Income: 10% above national average

Personal disposable income, 1978	**$100,900,000**
% Canadian total	**0.06**
Per capita	**$7,280**

Current Growth Rate: 23% per decade

Population, June 1, 1978	**13,900**
% Canadian total	**0.06**
% Change, '71-'78	**+15.83**

POPULATION

1976 Census:

Total		13,505
Male		6,800
Female		6,705
Age groups:	Male	Female
0-4	630	565
5-9	640	675
10-14	740	700
15-19	745	725
20-24	560	595
25-34	1,100	1,105
35-44	865	785
45-54	690	670
55-64	425	455
65-69	150	150
70+	265	285

FAMILIES

	1976
No.	3,330
Aver. no. per family	3.5

HOUSEHOLD FACILITIES

	1971 Census No.	% Total
Occupied dwellings	3,280	100.0
Dwellings with:		
Refrigerator	3,255	99.2
Home freezer	1,755	53.5
Television	3,110	94.8
Automobile	2,830	86.3
Furnace heating	2,930	89.3
Fuel:		
Oil	940	28.7
Electricity	40	1.2
Coal	5	0.1
Gas	2,215	67.5

HOUSING

	1976 Census	% Total
Occupied dwellings, no.	4,220	100
Owned	2,950	70
Rented	1,270	30
Type of Dwelling:		
Single detached	2,850	68
Double	110	3
Row	165	4
Apartment	690	16
Duplex	165	4
Mobile	230	5

HOUSEHOLDS

	1976
No.	4,221
Aver. no. per household	3.1

MOTHER TONGUE

	1976 Census	% Total
English	12,005	88.9
French	195	1.4
German	280	2.1
Italian	345	2.6

RACIAL ORIGIN

	1971 Census	% Total
British	6,990	58.3
French	575	4.8
German	1,040	8.7
Italian	860	7.2
Netherlands	195	1.6
Polish	170	1.4
Scandinavian	870	7.2
Ukrainian	405	3.4
Native Indian	80	0.7
Other	810	6.7

RELIGION

	1971 Census	% Total
Protestant	7,055	58.8
Roman Catholic	3,115	26.0

SCHOOL ATTENDANCE

	1971 Census	% Total
Population, 5 years +	10,790	100.0
Attending full-time:		
Less than Grade 5	1,185	11.0
Grades 5-8	995	9.2
Grades 9-13	955	8.8
University	115	1.1
Not attending full-time:		
Less than Grade 5	605	5.6
Grades 5-8	1,505	13.9
Grades 9-13	4,830	44.8
Some university	355	3.3
University degree	240	2.2

BANKING

Branches, no. (1978)	9

BUILDING PERMITS

	1977	1976	1975
		—$000—	
Value	17,819	20,124	9,464

HOMES BUILT

	1977	1976	1975
No.	291	†263	†181

†For 1971 area.

MANUFACTURING INDUSTRIES

	1975	1971
Plants	12	12
Employees	62	106
	—$000—	
Salaries, wages	683	729
Mfg. materials cost	1,429	1,676
Mfg. shipments, value	2,762	2,995
Total value added	1,300	1,178

RETAIL TRADE

1971 Census

Total sales, $000	32,309
Stores, no.	120
Year-end inventory, $000	4,357
Employees, no.	593
Payroll, total, $000	3,176

By kind of business group:	Stores No.	Sales $000
Food	23	8,074
General merchandise	5	3,407
Automotive	32	9.975
Apparel & access.	17	2,134
Hardware & home furnishings	15	2,082
Other	28	6,635

TAXATION STATISTICS

	1976
Total returns, no.	9,433
Total income, $000	104,938
Average income, $	11,124
Total tax, $000	17,489
Average tax, $	2,262

NEWSPAPERS

	1978
Newspaper, daily:	
Daily Townsman	
Total circulation	4,403
Newspapers, weekly:	
Courier Town & Country TV Supplement	
Total circulation	23,000
Kootenay Advertiser	
Total circulation	22,008
Portal and Ranch Review	
Total circulation	8,938

RADIO STATION

CKEK, 10,000 watts; 1,000 watts night.

Figure 5-4 *Source: The Financial Post Survey of Markets, 1979.*

Industry and Tourism in Ontario and Trade and Commerce in Manitoba. They usually cover all aspects of the provincial economy and provide comparative statistics and market data.

NEW BRUNSWICK

N.B. S&MM ESTIMATES — POPULATION 12/31/77 · RETAIL SALES—1977 · SALES/ADVERTISING INDEXES

COUNTIES CITIES	Total Pop (thousands)	% Of Canada	Households (thousands)	% Of Canada	Total Retail Sales ($000)	% Of Canada	Food ($000)	Eating & Drinking Places ($000)	General Mdse ($000)	Apparel & Accessories ($000)	Furnit.-Furnish.-Appl ($000)	Automotive ($000)	Gas Stations ($000)	Hardware ($000)	Drug ($000)	Sales Activity	Buying Power	Quality
Albert .... .513	24.5	.1044	7.3	.0969	18,814	.0290	6,997	2,258	1,535	298	730	548	3,355	0	1,001	28	.0750	72
Carleton	24.6	.1049	7.5	.0995	63,673	.0981	11,725	2,410	9,890	2,181	1,816	19,564	5,104	2,038	1,901	94	.0865	82
Charlotte	25.6	.1092	8.2	.1088	55,623	.0857	13,729	6,192	8,105	1,510	1,928	13,219	1,920	1,499	1,453	78	.0843	77
Gloucester	83.1	.3543	21.0	.2787	175,674	.2706	41,696	15,168	23,202	8,259	8,853	31,235	12,848	5,263	3,013	76	.2646	75
Kent	30.3	.1292	8.1	.1075	47,688	.0735	10,423	3,414	12,960	472	1,728	5,097	4,774	0	0	57	.0920	71
Kings .... .523	47.6	.2029	14.0	.1858	74,387	.1146	20,388	5,901	6,884	1,112	1,960	19,062	8,779	564	2,947	56	.1583	78
Madawaska	35.0	.1492	9.5	.1260	72,491	.1117	17,729	9,599	8,144	3,849	3,961	14,927	3,551	1,042	1,400	75	.1138	76
Northumberland	54.5	.2324	14.3	.1898	113,360	.1746	26,060	8,991	19,690	4,587	3,788	21,907	8,324	1,455	3,971	75	.1770	76
Queens	12.8	.0546	3.9	.0517	25,066	.0386	5,785	2,028	7,731	168	136	2,049	2,196	1,042	1,821	71	.0372	68
Restigouche	40.4	.1722	10.8	.1434	93,352	.1439	21,932	5,699	14,565	4,910	3,393	21,018	5,808	1,299	2,437	84	.1339	78
St. John .... .523	89.4	.3812	28.4	.3768	286,982	.4421	68,404	24,809	59,110	13,104	5,723	59,363	11,840	909	6,799	116	.3721	98
▲St. John	85.0	.3624	27.2	.3609	284,853	.4388	67,958	24,734	58,873	13,008	5,605	59,180	11,625	909	6,040	121	.3610	100
Sunbury	21.4	.0912	6.0	.0797	29,965	.0462	8,246	2,523	2,574	201	574	1,001	3,756	353	1,194	51	.0840	92
Victoria	21.1	.0900	6.0	.0796	50,526	.0778	11,987	2,836	8,118	1,117	3,813	11,790	2,975	1,237	1,214	86	.0713	79
Westmorland ...... .513	107.9	.4601	33.2	.4405	358,053	.5516	71,998	27,540	70,896	15,270	9,388	80,333	21,899	1,580	12,515	120	.4447	97
△Moncton	56.2	.2396	18.6	.2468	249,994	.3851	47,736	14,683	51,644	13,361	6,817	47,952	10,979	1,142	11,705	161	.2754	115
York	73.5	.3133	23.3	.3092	241,938	.3727	48,812	15,234	50,826	11,691	5,469	52,143	17,301	2,186	7,570	119	.3145	100
Fredericton	46.2	.1970	15.4	.2044	201,287	.3101	39,692	12,858	43,664	11,492	4,599	44,427	9,150	2,171	6,531	157	.2301	117
Province Totals	691.7	2.9491	201.5	2.6739	1,707,592	2.6307	385,911	134,602	304,230	68,729	53,260	353,256	114,430	20,467	49,236	89	2.5092	85

N.B. S&MM ESTIMATES — EFFECTIVE BUYING INCOME—1977 · % Of Hslds By EBI Group (A)$0–$4,999 (B)$5,000–$7,999 (C)$8,000–$9,999 (D)$10,000–$14,999 (E)$15,000 & Over

COUNTIES CITIES	Total EBI ($000)	% Of Canada	Per Capita EBI	Avg Hsld EBI	A	B	C	D	E
Albert .... .513	126,450	.0908	5,161	17,322	7.9	9.0	10.2	32.0	40.9
Carleton	100,620	.0722	4,090	13,416	12.9	23.2	16.8	37.4	9.7
Charlotte	102,572	.0737	4,007	12,509	18.6	20.6	16.1	32.8	11.9
Gloucester	313,373	.2249	3,771	14,923	12.4	15.3	12.1	37.2	23.0
Kent	122,923	.0883	4,057	15,176	7.7	14.9	11.8	49.8	15.8
Kings .... .523	232,090	.1666	4,876	16,578	10.9	14.0	10.9	31.6	32.6
Madawaska	140,570	.1009	4,016	14,797	13.9	14.6	11.9	37.0	22.6
Northumberland	217,910	.1564	3,998	15,238	10.2	16.5	13.3	39.5	20.5
Queens	41,100	.0295	3,211	10,538	15.7	13.6	11.8	46.6	12.3
Restigouche	156,491	.1124	3,874	14,490	10.9	11.6	9.5	36.4	31.6
St. John .... .523	455,129	.3267	5,091	16,026	7.8	12.3	11.7	38.6	29.6
▲St. John	437,112	.3138	5,142	16,070	7.8	12.1	11.8	38.7	29.6
Sunbury	144,472	.1037	6,751	24,079	1.2	6.1	8.1	81.3	3.3
Victoria	83,449	.0599	3,955	13,908	14.1	18.3	16.7	33.6	17.3
Westmorland ...... .513	521,483	.3744	4,833	15,707	9.3	15.4	14.5	31.8	29.0
△Moncton	311,827	.2239	5,549	16,765	7.2	13.4	13.2	33.2	33.0
York	390,269	.2801	5,310	16,750	8.5	14.0	13.2	36.8	27.5
Fredericton	272,204	.1954	5,892	17,676	6.5	14.8	14.2	35.8	28.7
Province Totals	3,148,901	2.2605	4,552	15,627	10.2	14.6	12.7	37.7	24.8

NEWFOUNDLAND

Nfld. S&MM ESTIMATES — POPULATION 12/31/77 · RETAIL SALES—1977 · SALES/ADVERTISING INDEXES

COUNTIES CITIES	Total Pop (thousands)	% Of Canada	Households (thousands)	% Of Canada	Total Retail Sales ($000)	% Of Canada	Food ($000)	Eating & Drinking Places ($000)	General Mdse ($000)	Apparel & Accessories ($000)	Furnit.-Furnish.-Appl ($000)	Automotive ($000)	Gas Stations ($000)	Hardware ($000)	Drug ($000)	Sales Activity	Buying Power	Quality
Division 1 .... .524	230.8	.9840	59.4	.7883	571,271	.8801	137,492	36,928	96,177	32,219	13,746	123,534	46,225	671	26,080	89	.8312	84
▲St. John's	85.3	.3637	23.4	.3105	368,925	.5684	75,109	19,233	72,951	27,736	11,448	69,894	33,274	568	15,867	156	.4165	115
Division 2	30.1	.1284	7.1	.0942	53,949	.0831	14,471	2,810	17,561	837	1,082	5,716	5,868	243	3,539	65	.0878	68
Division 3	26.1	.1113	5.7	.0756	40,254	.0620	9,545	1,620	18,321	2,477	1,444	856	2,229	119	1,287	56	.0750	67
Division 4	30.5	.1300	6.8	.0902	45,644	.0704	12,064	3,561	9,241	4,573	1,428	3,538	6,681	233	1,276	54	.0836	64
Division 5	46.4	.1978	11.2	.1487	108,137	.1666	27,933	5,283	22,166	6,321	3,744	17,773	11,525	111	2,531	84	.1603	81
Corner Brook	24.7	.1053	6.2	.0823	86,368	.1331	20,397	3,973	16,359	4,500	2,582	16,932	9,540	0	2,224	126	.1049	100
Division 6	43.4	.1851	10.5	.1393	144,259	.2222	23,135	7,913	30,954	8,538	4,670	41,849	10,246	376	3,741	120	.1750	95
Division 7	43.8	.1867	10.9	.1447	62,571	.0964	17,874	2,539	19,999	879	381	8,819	8,938	32	1,262	52	.1271	68
Division 8	53.5	.2281	12.3	.1632	76,536	.1179	15,490	2,836	39,486	2,425	1,063	1,931	7,903	237	2,014	52	.1357	59
Division 9	25.4	.1083	5.5	.0730	30,704	.0473	9,965	1,713	11,087	614	616	566	3,709	373	0	44	.0678	63
Division 10	34.5	.1471	8.1	.1075	95,855	.1477	13,426	23,573	26,601	1,251	937	14,755	2,503	0	4,471	100	.1400	95
Province Totals	564.5	2.4068	137.5	1.8247	1,229,180	1.8937	281,395	88,776	291,593	60,134	29,111	219,337	105,827	2,395	46,201	79	1.8835	78

Nfld. S&MM ESTIMATES — EFFECTIVE BUYING INCOME—1977 · % Of Hslds By EBI Group (A)$0–$4,999 (B)$5,000–$7,999 (C)$8,000–$9,999 (D)$10,000–$14,999 (E)$15,000 & Over

COUNTIES CITIES	Total EBI ($000)	% Of Canada	Per Capita EBI	Avg Hsld EBI	A	B	C	D	E
Division 1 .... .524	1,031,712	.7406	4,470	17,369	11.4	14.1	11.7	37.1	25.7
▲St. John's	482,530	.3464	5,657	20,621	6.6	9.9	9.9	39.1	34.5
Division 2	103,597	.0744	3,442	14,591	11.9	20.5	11.5	41.5	14.6
Division 3	95,040	.0682	3,641	16,674	11.1	16.7	13.7	48.9	9.6
Division 4	101,809	.0731	3,338	14,972	17.1	15.7	12.0	28.8	26.4
Division 5	197,125	.1415	4,248	17,600	11.5	16.7	11.8	32.1	27.9
Corner Brook	122,486	.0879	4,959	19,756	7.8	15.6	10.7	35.7	30.2
Division 6	198,788	.1427	4,580	18,932	6.7	11.5	9.3	47.5	25.0
Division 7	169,370	.1216	3,867	15,539	15.3	18.2	10.3	34.1	22.1
Division 8	152,541	.1095	2,851	12,402	18.5	24.3	12.0	24.6	20.6
Division 9	88,938	.0638	3,501	16,171	16.5	24.9	19.0	13.3	26.3
Division 10	184,625	.1326	5,351	22,793	6.6	4.8	3.3	11.8	73.5
Province Totals	2,323,545	1.6680	4,116	16,899	12.2	15.8	11.3	34.0	26.7

Figure 5-5 *Source:* Sales and Marketing Management Magazine.

9. Faculties and Departments of Business, Management, and Economic Research at Universities. These organizations are usually fortified with many market studies. Published reports are available to the public.

10. Market Research and Advertising Firms. Many of these firms offer their professional services in making complete market surveys. They also, however, have reports covering special market areas, which in many instances may be procured. Often one can obtain multi-client reports at a very reasonable cost.

READJUSTING THE PROJECTED INCOME STATEMENT TO REFLECT RESULTS OF THE MARKET SURVEY

It will be recalled that in Chapter 4 we constructed a projected income statement based upon average firm statistics and the desired profit. Our chief objective there was to find what volume of sales was necessary to produce the desired profit. In that process we found that $125,000 of sales was required if the small firm planner had the average merchandise turnover, average markup, and profits as a percentage of sales, in order to achieve the desired profit of $15,000.

If our market survey now shows that we can reasonably expect a sales volume of $200,000, for example, we can refine that projected income statement to reflect this sales volume; thus, we can convert that statement into a budgeted income statement for the first year of operation. This can be done by applying the same standard statistics to the newly determined expected sales volume. In Chapter 4 we found those statistics to show profits as 12 percent of sales, merchandise turnover four times per year, and markups as 35 percent of sales. With the increased sales volume, we would naturally expect the profits to exceed the $15,000 previously planned for. As we apply these figures against the new sales volume, the profit becomes $24,000 (12 percent of $200,000), gross margin becomes $70,000 (35 percent of $200,000), cost of goods sold becomes $130,000 ($200,000 less $70,000), and average inventory increases to $32,500 ($130,000 divided by turnover of four times per year). Operating expenses will increase from the $28,750 for a volume of $125,000 to $46,000, the difference between a gross margin of $70,000 and a net profit of $24,000. Individual expenses will increase at the same percentages of the increased sales volume.

To clarify this process, we can compare the projected income statement from Chapter 4 with the refined budgeted income statement, which now reflects the results of the market survey. This comparison is shown in adjacent columns in Table 5-1.

The right column, based on a reasonable sales forecast of $200,000, now becomes the basis of all budgeting for the new firm. It is now appropriate to detail each operating expense in dollar amounts, based on industry statistics showing what percentage of sales should be

TABLE 5-1
JONES HARDWARE COMPANY
COMPARISON OF PROJECTED AND BUDGETED INCOME STATEMENTS WHICH REFLECTS MARKET SURVEY

	PROJECTED STATEMENT BASED ON INCOME NEEDS TO MAKE DESIRED PROFIT	BUDGETED STATEMENT BASED ON SALES VOLUME AS PER MARKET SURVEY
Sales	$125,000.00	$200,000.00
Cost of goods sold:		
Beginning inventory, Jan. 1	20,312.50	32,500.00
Plus purchases during year	81,250.00	130,000.00
Goods available for sale	$101,562.50	$162,500.00
Less ending inventory, Dec. 31	20,312.50	32,500.00
Cost of goods sold	$ 81,250.00	$130,000.00
Gross margin	$ 43,750.00	$ 70,000.00
Operating expenses (total)	28,750.00	46,000.00
Net profit from operations	$ 15,000.00	$ 24,000.00

spent on each operating expense. Reference to our basic sources of statistics, cited in Chapter 4, may be necessary. These will tell us the percentage of sales that should be spent on rent, employee salaries, average owner salaries, bad-debts expense, depreciation, advertising, and miscellaneous expenses. Precise expense accounts will, of course, vary with the particular type of business being planned. We know now from our budgeted income statement that a total of $46,000 is appropriate for total operating expenses. We must divide this total into the individual expense accounts which make up this total.

DETAILING THE OPERATING EXPENSES

Our budgeted income statment was based on an average markup of 35 percent, which provided the gross margin of $70,000. Our net profit from operations was 12 percent of sales, or $24,000. The difference between these two amounts, $46,000, is listed on the statement as operating expenses. This means that 23 percent of sales (this $46,000) must cover all our operating expenses if we are to arrive at the profits of $24,000 as planned.

The same statistical sources used in Chapter 4 will provide typical breakdowns of operating expenses for our type of business. Modest variations will be found, depending upon the precise type or size of the store under consideration.

A typical set of operating expenses, expressed as a percentage of sales, for an average hardware store can be found as follows:

Rent, 4 percent
Employee salaries, 8 percent
Advertising, 1 percent
Bad debts, 1 percent
Delivery expense, 2 percent
Depreciation, 1 percent
Supplies, 1 percent
Miscellaneous expenses, 5 percent

These expenses total 23 percent of sales, as per our budgeted income statement. This is not the normal case. All new planners must study their expense structures to ascertain the appropriateness of the individual expenses to their particular firms. Perhaps in our case delivery service is not contemplated. Perhaps the owner plans a greater expense for employee salaries.

The important thing in planning in this case is that the total operating expenses not exceed 23 percent of sales if the firm is to stay on schedule, as per the budgeted income statement.

If we assume that the above percentages are acceptable to our planning for the Jones Hardware Company, we then convert the percentages into dollar amounts. These would be as follows:

Rent, $8,000
Employee salaries, $16,000
Advertising, $2,000
Bad debts, $2,000
Delivery expense, $4,000
Depreciation, $2,000
Supplies, $2,000
Miscellaneous expenses, $10,000

Since the generous amount left for miscellaneous expenses may seem excessive to the uninitiated, we should emphasize here that there are always unanticipated expenses in any business. It is usually wise to abide by the suggestions of standard statistics in this regard.

We have now contemplated every detail in planning income, margins, inventories, and expenses for the new firm. The complete budgeted income statement can now serve as a schedule against which to check our operations each month or at other periods. Conformance to that schedule will ensure that the planned results will become fact. That finalized budgeted income statement will be shown in Table 5-2.

TABLE 5.2
JONES HARDWARE COMPANY
BUDGETED INCOME STATEMENT
FIRST YEAR OF OPERATIONS

Net sales		$200,000
Cost of goods sold:		
Beginning inventory, January 1	$ 32,500	
Purchases	130,000	
Goods available for sale	$162,500	
Ending inventory, December 31	32,500	
Cost of goods sold		130,000
Gross margin		$ 70,000
Operating expenses:		
Rent	$ 8,000	
Employee salaries	16,000	
Advertising	2,000	
Bad-debts expense	2,000	
Delivery expense	4,000	
Depreciation	2,000	
Supplies	2,000	
Miscellaneous expenses	10,000	
Total operating expenses		46,000
Net profit from operations		$ 24,000

As we take a reverse look at our planning to this point, it will be recalled that we planned to have a profit of $15,000 to cover the owner's time and return on his investment. We must not assume that the $24,000 net profit from operations means that we have exceeded that goal by very much. This amount is profit before income taxes. If our business is incorporated in Ontario, it will pay a combined federal and provincial tax of 25%, or $6,000 on this amount. If the firm is a proprietorship, a net taxable income of $24,000 will currently demand an income tax of $6,400 from the owner who is unmarried. This subject will be further explored in Chapter 11.

We can be satisfied with our planning in that we have found our desired profit is attainable. Our necessary sales volume seems easily obtainable in our market. With good management we should achieve our objective.

Our attention should now turn to the next step in planning—providing a financial structure to support the firm. This is done in Chapter 6.

QUESTIONS FOR CLASS DISCUSSION

Q5-1 What is a market survey? What is its objective?

Q5-2 What kinds of firms should make especially thorough market surveys? Why?

Q5-3 What is a parasite firm?

Q5-4 How can inaccessibility limit a market area? Give examples.

Q5-5 Why is a study of population characteristics important in making a good market survey?

Q5-6 Do you agree that the urban small firm gets business from a wider area than its neighbourhood residents? Explain.

Q5-7 How can new firm planners find the total purchases in their counties for a particular line of goods?

Q5-8 What services does *Sales & Marketing Management* magazine and *The Financial Post Survey of Markets* provide for new firm planners and for established retail firms?

Q5-9 Do you think a professional market survey is worth $1,000? What advantages would such a report have, even if it shows that the planned firm should not be established?

Q5-10 How would you compare the projected income statement prepared in Chapter 4 with the budgeted income statement which is prepared after the results of the market survey are known?

PROBLEMS AND QUESTIONS FOR WRITTEN ASSIGNMENT

P5-1 Mr. Smith has made a thorough market survey of his community, where he plans to open a small department store. He finds that 70 percent of the people buy the types of goods he plans to sell from the large urban department stores. His five competitors share the remaining 30 percent of department-store sales in his market area. Total department-store sales in his market area are $7 million per year. On the basis of this information only, what sales forecast can he reasonably set for his new store?

P5-2 Ms. Hernandez is planning a new drugstore in a city of 35,000 people. She is much concerned about the number of households in her market area. How can she find such information? How can she find out total drugstore purchases in her market?

P5-3 What is a census tract? Explain how such tracts can be valuable to a new small firm planner.

P5-4 How can a chamber of commerce assist market surveys?

CONTINUING PROBLEM: *THE SUCCESS HARDWARE STORE*

Part 5. The Market Survey

Our study of the proposed market included much research in many areas. We studied census data of the county, road maps, aerial views, trading-area maps, the Canada census, *Sales & Marketing Management* magazine's special annual issue on buying power, *The Financial Post Survey of Markets,* local chamber of commerce data, and reports from the Canadian Hardware and Housewares Manufacturers Association. We clearly defined our market area and found that we could expect business from outside areas as well. We set the essential limits of the trading area and then studied the population for size, trend, households, permanence, sex, age, income, occupations, marital status, number of families and family size, race, religion, and average education. We studied the population further to learn its buying habits, the products emphasized, who makes the buying decisions, brand desires, and price preferences.

We found that the market area in which we plan to operate has a population of 120,000, is now served by 10 hardware stores, has total hardware sales now of $2,200,000, and includes 20,000 households with an average family of six. Each household spends an average of $30 in area drugstores and $120 for hardware items—all of which are not purchased in this market area. It takes 5,000 people in this type of community to support an independent hardware store. Special advantages of the site we have under consideration suggest that we should be able to obtain 10 percent of the present hardware sales in the area, plus another $10,000 in sales from surrounding areas and passing traffic. Our potential for increasing sales beyond this first-year estimate is extremely good.

We complete our market survey with a sales estimate of $230,000. This is 10 percent ($220,000) of the present area hardware sales of $2,200,000, plus $10,000 (our estimated sales advantage of location).

ASSIGNMENT FOR PART 5

Prepare a budgeted income statement based on the estimated sales figure of our market survey. Apply the same percentages for markup, merchandise turnover, and percentage of sales as profits that you used for the projected income statement in Part 4 of the continuing problem. Start with the sales estimate of $230,000 at the top of the statement. We would expect profits to exceed our original estimate because sales will exceed those on the projected income statement. When you detail the operating expenses, you will have 20 percent of sales for their total (30 percent markup less 10 percent profits). Use the percentages of sales for each expense given in the illustrative problem in Chapter 5 unless you have a better distribution of the operating expenses. Miscellaneous expenses can be only 2 percent of sales if you use the illustrative percentages for all other expenses. That is because the total operating expenses there were 23 percent, but you have 20 percent to allocate over the various operating expenses.

REFERENCES FOR FURTHER READING

Broom, H. N., and J. G. Longenecker, *Small Business Management,* 2d ed., South-Western Publishing Co., Inc., Cincinnati, 1966, chap. 19.

"Forecasting for a New Business," *Federal Business Development Bank,* Minding Your Own Business, Pamphlet No. 6.

"Market Planning," Your Business Matters, No. 14, The Royal Bank of Canada, 1978.

Markin, Rom J., Jr., *Retailing Management,* Macmillan Publishing Co., Inc., New York, 1971, chaps. 5, 6, 7.

McCarthy, E. Jerome, and Stanley J. Shapiro, *Basic Marketing,* 1st Canadian Edition, Irwin-Dorsey Ltd., Georgetown, Ontario, 1975.

Stanton, W. J., M. S., Sommers, and J. Barnes, *Fundamentals of Marketing,* 2nd Canadian Edition, McGraw-Hill Ryerson Ltd., Scarborough, Ontario, 1977.

Part 3

FINANCING THE NEW FIRM

CHAPTER 6

Statement of Assets to Be Used

I had no idea how many more assets would be needed to operate this business when I started. Almost all of the profits went to buy new assets the first few years. Next time I will know better.

The Late Learner

Every new firm needs various kinds of assets with which to begin operations. Cash assets are needed for working capital; cash funds are needed to invest in accounts receivable; inventories are a large asset which must be purchased. Buildings and land are expensive assets which must be acquired by purchase or rented. Supplies are assets which must be purchased. Prepaid insurance policies must be provided and premiums paid. Machinery, store fixtures and equipment, and office furniture and fixtures are other assets which must be provided for the firm. Perhaps delivery trucks need to be purchased.

One of the commonest causes of financial difficulty for a new firm is the owners' failure to look seriously at the total asset requirements of the firm in the planning stage. Too many new firms open their doors literally "on a wing and a prayer," only to find that they have not anticipated or provided all the various assets needed to start operations properly. The result too often is the necessity for then acquiring needed assets through expensive and dangerous financing or appropriating anticipated profits in advance to buy the assets which should have been provided from initial investment capital.

To avoid these dangers, the planner should analyze his firm by listing every asset the business will need. The result will be a *statement of assets to be used.* This statement can be compared to the left side (asset side) of a balance sheet.

PROCEDURE FOR DEVELOPING ASSET REQUIREMENTS

Preparing a list of all types of assets needed does not necessitate concern over their cost or how they will be provided. We can assume that cost is not a consideration at this point. In a later planning step (see Chapter 7), we will decide how to provide these assets or the services they render. In that process, we can learn much about how the business economy really works as it supplies credit, financial loans, or services under various circumstances.

The important thing at this point is that we listed every asset of every kind which the business will need. The new student will recall that assets were defined in Chapter 3 as "things owned." They can be in the form of cash, claims against others, inventories, supplies, buildings, fixtures and equipment, delivery trucks, and prepaid insurance policies. All require investment capital; all are basic assets the new firm will need.

Continuing our example of a newly planned firm from Chapter 5, we have produced a budgeted income statement to serve as a guide to operations for the first year. We must now develop a statement of assets to be used to list all the things (assets) which will be needed to operate the firm at the level indicated on the budgeted income statement.

As we have contemplated the firm's asset needs, let us assume that we have found the following assets to be essential:

Cash
Capital to carry accounts receivable
Merchandise inventory (the amount here is provided from our budgeted income statement)
Prepaid supplies
Prepaid insurance
Land and buildings
Store fixtures
Office furniture and fixtures
Delivery truck(s)

This listing of assets can be entitled a "Statement of Assets to Be Used."

We can now turn our attention to finding a dollar value to attach to each asset and/or to determining how much cash we should have on hand when all noncash assets have been provided. We can find out how much cash will be needed to cover our planned investment in accounts receivable. Market prices can be used to give dollar amounts to our noncash assets. Details for these calculations and conservative rules relating to them are as follows:

Cash on hand How much cash should the firm have on hand? The suggested conservative rule is: Cash should equal the out-of-pocket operating expenses for the period of one turnover of the merchandise inventory. This will seem extremely conservative for some types of firms. Unless positive reasons for relaxing the general rule are identified, however, good management demands adherence to it.

How would we find this amount for our planned firm? First we go back to our budgeted income statement (see Chapter 5) and find that total operating expenses for the first year are planned at $46,000. This figure must be divided into out-of-pocket and noncash expenditures. The out-of-pocket expenses are those which are paid in cash by the firm in the form of checks written or petty cash expenditures. Noncash expenditures are those which are recorded in the expenses but do not result in the firm's actually giving up cash — such as depreciation expenses on buildings, store equipment, or office furniture and fixtures.

If $10,000 of the total year expenses of $46,000 represents noncash expenditures, the balance of $36,000 is the total of out-of-pocket expenses for the first year. This amount represents $3,000 per month ($36,000 divided by 12). Our merchandise turnover is 4 times per year, or once every 3 months. We must therefore provide 3 months of out-of-pocket expenses as our cash requirement under our rule. Three times $3,000 is $9,000, which is our cash requirement for opening day.

The calculation of the cash requirement may be more easily understood this way. Merely divide the annual out-of-pocket expenses by the merchandise turnover. Thus, in our example here, the annual out-of-pocket expenses are $36,000. Divide this total by the merchandise turnover of 4 and we get the same $9,000 answer.

If the merchandise inventory turnover were 6 times per year, the cash requirement would be $6,000 ($36,000 divided by 6). If the turnover were once every 45 days (one-eighth of a 360-day business year), the cash requirement would be $4,500 ($36,000 divided by 8). These figures demonstrate the variable nature of the cash requirement and how our rule allows for this variance. The higher the inventory turnover, the lower is the requirement for cash on hand.

Funds to Carry Accounts Receivable New firms which decide to sell on credit to approved customers and plan to carry the accounts receivable on their books cannot neglect the fact that they will have money invested in those accounts receivable. They may, of course, decide to sell on established credit cards only. In this way the credit-card company advances the account balances to them, usually monthly, less its charge for the service. Various credit-card companies have arrangements which cost the firm from 3 to 10 percent of the amount of the sales for their service to the business firm. Such charges represent a true sales discount to the firm and must be accounted for in pricing policy. If the firm has many customers who prefer to use credit cards, this may be the most desirable method of operation. If the new firm has limited capital resources, this fact may encourage a decision to make credit sales on credit cards only. In exchange for the credit-card company's charges, the firm is protected against loss on bad debts and the expenses of administering its own credit policy. It should be noted, however, that a well-managed credit policy usually has bad-debt losses which are less than the average credit-card company charges. Another alternative available to new firms is to sell for cash only. This policy defies the basic truism that firms selling on credit will sell more merchandise to the same customers if credit is available.

If the firm is able to carry its own accounts receivable, it can usually make the credit operation pay its own way when it charges for the credit privilege, such as in installment sales contracts or interest on monthly balances. Small firms have not exercised these possibilities nearly as much as the larger firms with various credit plans available for their customers. Details of credit policies are discussed in Chapter 18.

Financial difficulties may be encountered by the small firm which decides to carry its own receivables and is not financially prepared to tie up much of its working capital in such an asset. The proprietor who believes that all credit accounts are paid in full on the first of the following month is due for a great surprise when he gets into operation. The question therefore arises, "How much investment capital should be provided to carry accounts receivable?"

The conservative rule suggested here for firms planning to carry their own receivables is: "Sufficient working capital to carry 1½ to 2 times the credit sales in the maximum credit period." Applying this rule to our planned firm, we must first determine what percentage of the planned annual sales of $200,000 will be on credit. If experience and/or available statistics show that about 30 percent of the sales are on credit, we will use $60,000. This means that credit sales average $5,000 per month. If the maximum credit period is 30 days, we should plan on 1½ to 2 times the monthly credit sales to be invested in accounts receivable by the end of the first year of operation. This means $7,500 to $10,000. The variation will be determined by the strictness of the credit-granting policy and the follow-up policies adopted on collections.

We can see from the foregoing comments why many small firms decide to absorb the credit-card company charges or to discount their sales contracts with finance companies. It is indeed sad to observe a company which has a good current ratio but is unable to pay its current bills because too much cash is tied up in delinquent accounts receivable or slow-moving inventory which has not been converted into cash according to a planned schedule.

Merchandise Inventory In our calculations for the budgeted income statement, we found that an inventory of $32,500 was necessary to support our contemplated sales. We must accept this figure for our statement of assets to be used.

Prepaid Supplies and Insurance After studying the need for supplies of various kinds and learning the insurance costs for the policies we decide we must have, we total the costs of these items. This figure becomes the dollar amount for our statement of assets to be used. We can use $1,000 for our illustration.

Land and Building Even though we do not plan even to consider buying the land and building to be used by our firm, it is good business experience to find out what they would cost if that were our plan of operation. Landlords are not philanthropists and we would not desire that they be so. There are distinct advantages to renting as against buying, and there are also advantages to owning your own building. These considerations will be discussed later. At this time, we should get a cost estimate for the type of land and building we plan for our operation. Such an expenditure, when undertaken, is usually the largest single investment for the typical small firm.

If available land in your desired area is priced at $400 per front foot for a 50-foot lot, its cost would be $20,000. If the building you want calls for 2,000 square feet and construction costs are $10 per square foot, its costs would be $20,000. Such investments can be financed after a good down payment. The mistake often made, however, is believing that the mortgage principal payments are an operating expense. Such principal repayments do not come out of operating expenses but must be paid out of the net profits from operation or some new, additional investment capital must be provided for to make such payments. Similar consideration must be given to providing all the fixed assets for the firm. When these are purchased on credit contracts (conditional sales contracts), the payments towards principal are not operating expenses but must also come out of the net profits or new investment capital. Many a potentially successful small firm has been forced to close its doors because of this mistake in financial planning.

For our purposes here, we insert $40,000 on our statement of assets to be used as the value of land and buildings. A final decision on the matter of renting or building will be made when we make our transition to an opening day balance sheet (see Chapter 7).

Store Fixtures, Office Furniture and Fixtures The important thing here is that we clearly understand our needs for these items. We can obtain prices from several suppliers and insert the appropriate one in our statement of assets. We will use $7,000 for our illustration — $5,000 for store fixtures and $2,000 for office furniture and fixtures.

Delivery Truck For purposes of this statement of assets, we assume that we will purchase a delivery truck. We do not have to make the decision now about whether we will use other methods of making deliveries. Accordingly, we insert $3,500 as the cost of the truck.

When we have obtained dollar amounts for all the items, we can refine our statement, as shown in Table 6-1.

TABLE 6-1
STATEMENT OF ASSETS TO BE USED

Cash	$ 9,000
Funds to finance accounts receivable	7,500
Merchandise inventory	32,500
Prepaid expenses (supplies and insurance)	1,000
Land and buildings	40,000
Store fixtures	5,000
Office furniture and fixtures	2,000
Delivery truck	3,500
Total assets required	$100,500

The new firm planners who have approximately $20,000 to invest may easily get discouraged when they see that the firm will use more than $100,000 of assets. They should not. It is good to realize that the firm will actually use this dollar amount of assets if things go as planned. It is good to appreciate how business institutions are interwoven, what credit means to the total business economy, and what alternatives there are in providing these assets for the firm. We will demonstrate that the firm can be started with the $20,000 and provide a capital structure which is sound when we proceed to an opening day balance sheet.

For early relief of discouragement, we can point out several very obvious factors. First, the amount we provided for investment in accounts receivable does not have to be available on opening day. The whole consideration here was to warn the new planners that they will have capital invested in these accounts during the first year. Second, new planners may quickly determine that they will rent a store space rather than build and thus eliminate a $40,000 investment. Third, we must consider credit available in providing the other assets. Good management should always take advantage of available free credit. We will look again at all these items in Chapter 7.

QUESTIONS FOR CLASS DISCUSSION

Q6-1 If a person invests in a delivery truck for a business as part of the total investment, is that truck an asset of the firm?

Q6-2 Is it possible to accurately determine in advance all the assets a business will need when it starts operations? Explain.

Q6-3 What is the conservative rule for determining how much cash a firm should have on hand? Explain the rule with an example.

Q6-4 Why is it necessary to consider whether or not sales will be made on account when evaluating total asset needs?

Q6-5 If credit sales are to be made, how much investment to carry the accounts receivable should be planned?

Q6-6 What are the pros and cons of making credit sales only on the basis of credit cards held by customers?

Q6-7 Should small business owners know the costs of the land and building even though they plan to rent? Why?

Q6-8 Can someone with only $20,000 to invest establish and control a business which requires $97,000 of assets? What are some of the alternatives?

Q6-9 What are the pros and cons of doing business with family members who help finance your new firm?

Q6-10 "Good management takes advantage of any free credit available." Do you agree? Why?

PROBLEMS AND QUESTIONS FOR WRITTEN ASSIGNMENT

P6-1 Prepare a statement of assets to be used for a neighbourhood grocery store.

P6-2 Explain in a brief essay why it is valuable for new small firm planners to make a statement of assets to be used, including land and building, even though they never plan to own the building.

P6-3 Make a list of some of the decisions which can be made to reduce the total investment in a new firm from the value of the assets listed on the statement of assets to be used.

P6-4 Ms. O'Brien has made a complete study of her expenses for the first year of operation. She finds that she will have cash expenses of $12,000 and noncash expenses of $3,000. The merchandise turnover of her business will be 6 times per year. How much cash should she plan to have on hand?

P6-5 Write a short essay explaining the importance of merchants providing investment capital to finance the open accounts receivable planned to be carried on the books. Include the rule as to how much they can expect this investment to be within one year.

CONTINUING PROBLEM:
THE SUCCESS HARDWARE STORE

Part 6. The Statement of Assets to Be Used

We know that a statement of assets to be used must represent a careful study of every asset of every kind which good operations of the firm will need. At this point we assume that we will buy the land and building which will be required. We must compute the cash balance to be needed and the amount of funds which will soon be invested in our accounts receivable. Cost of other assets is not our prime concern now. The most important thing is to include all assets. Hypothetical figures may be necessary for some asset values.

Assignment for Part 6

With a proper heading, prepare a statement of assets to be used for our new firm. Divide the assets into current and fixed assets, with subtotals for each.

REFERENCES FOR FURTHER READING

Broom, H.N., and J.G. Longenecker, *Small Business Management*, 2d ed., South-Western Publishing Co., Inc., Cincinnati, 1966, chap. 11.

Kelley, Pearce C., Kenneth Lawyer, and Clifford M. Baumback, *How to Organize a Small Business*, 5th ed., Prentice-Hall, Inc., Englewood Cliffs, N.J., 1973, chap. 10.

"Managing Your Fixed Assets," Pamphlet No. 7, Minding Your Own Business Series, Federal Business Development Bank.

"Planning and Budgeting . . . the Independent Business Way," Your Business Matters, No. 7, The Royal Bank of Canada, 1976.

CHAPTER 7

Developing an Opening Day Balance Sheet

An opening day balance sheet? I didn't know what a balance sheet was when I started this business. It scares me now to think that I ever started without it. Profits would have been better and come much sooner if I had known more about planning.

The Late Learner

We have seen from the previous chapter and our study of assets which will be needed to operate the planned business that a total of $100,500 would be required to finance all these assets if they were paid for outright by the proprietor. People with abundant personal capital might be satisfied just to go ahead and buy all these things and get started. Such people often decide not even to finance the land and building which we know to be necessary. A person with a modest amount of personal assets to invest would go to the opposite extreme and use every possible assistance in the form of credit. There are options between these extremes. Some of them are:

1 Invest $100,500 and buy all the assets outright. The business would then start without liabilities of any kind.

2 Finance construction of the building and purchase of the land and plan to make the mortgage payments out of profits or other capital to be obtained later.

3 Decide to rent a store space instead of investing $40,000 in order to own your own building.

4 Decide to sell on credit only to customers who have approved credit cards.

5 Purchase the inventory with a minimum down payment and pay the balance as the merchandise is sold.

6 Finance the acquisition of store fixtures, office furniture and fixtures, and the delivery truck on available 24-month contracts which are obtainable after 25 percent down payment has been made.

7 Decide to open the doors with less than the required cash on hand; give credit on open account, even though proper capital is not on hand; carry the receivables on the books in the hope that all will be collected on the first of each month; provide fewer than the desired store fixtures in the hope that the future profits will provide money to buy more later; leave the delivery service to a hit-or-miss arrangement with deliveries being made in the proprietor's personal car whenever a family member can be left in charge of the store.

Option 7 is included only because it demonstrates the errors made altogether too often by new firms. Adopting this plan defies all the planning we have been talking about and makes the firm immediately susceptible to the risk of failure. Such action is not even a calculated risk. It is foolhardy action which constitutes an invitation to failure.

Each of the other alternatives bears investigation. Final choices must be governed by such basic considerations as:

1 We anticipate $24,000 net profit before income taxes. (We originally planned on $15,000, but our market survey showed a sales volume which should produce $24,000 profit.)

2 Unless other investment capital is known to be available (including a possible loan from Grandma or Uncle John), we cannot let the payment of the liabilities incurred in the provision of the assets cut into out planned profits to the point that the proprietor's family expenses are impaired.

3 We cannot minimize the cash and inventory needs which have been carefully calculated in our planning.

4 It is good business to use any credit which is available without charge.

5 Excessive interest charges should be avoided whenever possible. The fact that interest expense is a deductible income tax item is little solace if profits disappear and there is nothing left on which to pay any tax.

PROCEDURE FOR DEVELOPING A BALANCE SHEET

The development of an opening day balance sheet necessitates making decisions on how each of the assets or services is to be provided. The decisions will vary with the individual owner. As hypothetical proprietors, we have the following facts or constraints to assist us in making these decisions:

1 We have about $20,000 to invest.

2 We will rent an excellent building located at the desirable site previously chosen. This will eliminate the large investment required to purchase the building. The landlord will now have funds invested in the building. Our planner will now show rent expense on the income statement, rather than a building on the balance sheet.

3 Uncle John has indicated a willingness to loan us up to $15,000 on a 5-year note with only the interest to be paid for the 5 years until the principal of the note becomes due. This is called a balloon note.

4 A wholesaler in our line has offered the usual terms in this type of business if they can sell us most of the inventory. These terms are 50 percent down and 50 percent in 30 days with no interest charge.

5 We have found a delivery truck, slightly used, which we can purchase for $2,000 with $800 down payment and monthly payments of $100 plus interest for 1 year.

6 We must have the new store equipment, but we find slightly used desks, files, and office machines which are available for $1,000 cash and which will meet the needs for office furniture and fixtures.

7 The store equipment (showcases, shelving, window displays, cash registers) can all be bought from one firm with 50 percent down and 50 percent due in 1 year.

8 We have decided to push credit-card sales and reduce the open accounts receivable we carry on our books. We expect this to reduce the amount we will need for our investment in these accounts. We will accordingly keep $6,250 in our savings account, where it will earn interest until it is needed to maintain current debt payment. We will list this on our opening day balance sheet as "other bank accounts." If this $6,250 were in the form of government bonds or other readily saleable securities, we could list it as "marketable securities."

Against this background of soundly gathered information, the proprietors are now in a position to make a first draft of an opening day balance sheet and test it for financial soundness. With explanatory comments, it would like Table 7-1.

TABLE 7-1
P.M. JONES COMPANY
OPENING DAY BALANCE SHEET
NOVEMBER 1, 1978

ASSETS			LIABILITIES		
Current assets:			Current liabilities:		
Cash on hand (as per calculation in statement of assets to be used)	$ 9,000		Accounts payable (due to wholesalers for balance of beginning inventory)	$16,250	
Other bank accounts	6,250*		Contract payable (one-year note on store equipment)	2,500	
Merchandise inventory	32,500		Notes payable (delivery truck)	1,200	
Prepaid expenses (supplies, insurance, etc.)	1,000				
Total current assets		$48,750	Total current liabilities		$19,950
Fixed assets:			Fixed liabilities:		
Store fixtures (half cash, half credit)	$5,000		Notes payable (five-year loan from Uncle John)	$15,000	
Office furniture and fixtures (paid for in cash)	1,000		Total fixed liabilities		15,000
Delivery truck ($800 cash, $1,200 credit)	2,000		Total liabilities		$34,950
Total fixed assets		$ 8,000	NET WORTH		
			P.M. Jones, proprietorship		21,800†
Total assets		$56,750	Total liabilities plus net worth		$56,750

* *Funds held until needed to finance accounts receivable.*
† *Assets, $56,750 – Liabilities, $34,950 = Net Worth, $21,800*

PUTTING THE OPENING DAY BALANCE SHEET TOGETHER

Remember that our opening day balance sheet must provide for each of the assets found to be necessary for proper planning, as reflected in our statement of assets to be used developed in the previous chapter. Our basic decisions, or constraints, listed in the preceding paragraph, tell us how each of those assets will be provided. The balance sheet lists all assets at full purchase price. Amounts owed on any of them are shown as liabilities.

We cannot compromise with proper cash on hand, so we can first insert $9,000 cash on hand as a current asset. Next we list the $6,250 as other bank accounts, which represents the funds we will hold to finance our accounts receivable. (Remember we reduced this amount from the $7,500 listed in the statement of assets to be used via a basic policy decision in our constraints in the preceding section.)

Next we list the full value of the inventory purchased, $32,500, as merchandise inventory. But we are not paying for the entire purchase now, so we list 50 percent of this amount as a current liability — accounts payable, $16,250. Then we can list as prepaid expenses the full value of these items (supplies and insurance — $1,000), which we pay for in full before opening day.

In the fixed asset section we can then list the full purchase price of the store fixtures ($5,000), the office furniture and fixtures ($1,000), and the delivery truck ($2,000). But we received some help in providing these by incurring some liabilities to cover the balance of their purchase prices. Therefore, we must list the $2,500 contract payable on the store fixtures as a current liability and the $1,200 still owed on the delivery truck as notes payable. We were also provided with $15,000 cash by Uncle John. This is not due, except for interest, for five years, so we list that note payable as a fixed liability.

If we now total our current and fixed assets, we find that we have total assets of $56,750. Our total current and fixed liabilities are $34,950. Following our basic accounting equation that assets minus liabilities equals proprietorship, we subtract the liabilities of $34,950 from the assets of $56,750 and find that Jones' needed proprietorship is $21,800. We then insert the proprietorship account in our balance sheet for this amount and we have a completed opening day balance sheet.

As our fledgling proprietors review this first draft of a proposed opening day balance sheet, the ratio analysis which we studied in Chapter 3 should be applied. We will find that we have proposed a current ratio in excess of 2 to 1 (current assets, $48,750, divided by current liabilities, $19,950), which is good. The quick ratio proposed is substantially less than the desired 1 to 1 (cash plus receivables, $15,250, divided by current liabilities, $19,950). The reason seems to be our decision about reducing the capital necessary to finance the receivables. The proprietorship ratio is less than 50 percent (proprietorship, $21,800, divided by total assets, $56,750). The 50 percent minimum would require an investment of $28,375 by Jones.

If we are to strictly apply the rules we have learned about financial soundness and ratio analysis, we would go back to the drawing board and make adjustments to bring the deficient ratios into line. Possibilities which appear are:

1 Do not buy the delivery truck, thus eliminating a $2,000 truck on the asset side and a $1,200 liability. This would add the $800 down payment to cash. It would also necessitate adding the cost of a hired delivery service to the operating expenses on the income statement.

2 Request that the contract on the store fixtures be lengthened to 2 years, thus making half the balance due a fixed liability (amounts due more than 1 year hence) rather than a current liability, all of which must be paid in 1 year.

3 Ask Uncle John to become a partner, silent or active as he desires. Offer him 5 percent of profits as an inducement. His note payable of $15,000 would thus be eliminated and we would have two proprietorship accounts in the net worth section of the balance sheet. Partners are co-owners, not creditors. This can be significant. You maintain control and your silent partner can be inactive and happy as you succeed. See Chapter 11 for more on this matter.

4 Incorporate the business and give Uncle John preference shares for his inducement (see Chapter 11).

If suggestions (1) and (2) plus either (3) or (4) were enacted into the financial plan, the proprietorship ratio would be well above the 50 percent minimum, the quick ratio would be improved, and the current ratio would be even better.

Proving again that principles should be adapted rather than always adopted, we can find some justification for the balance sheet suggested in the first rough draft. Its strengths and supporting facts include a good current ratio, a rich uncle who can be available in case of pressing financial needs, a variable policy which may be applied to the present program for giving credit, and the possibility for discounting receivables via a bank loan. The availability of other funds for investment by Mr. Jones without placing a second mortgage on his home would be another strength.

When an opening day plan is finally adopted, the reader may ask,

"Where is Mr. Jones's $21,800 now?" The organizing procedure begins with placing this amount and the $15,000 collected from Uncle John in a bank account in the company's name. Total deposit is $36,800. In our illustration, we have paid out $16,250 as the down payment on the merchandise inventory; we have paid out $800 as down payment on the delivery truck; we have paid out $2,500 on the store equipment and $1,000 for the office furniture; we have paid out $1,000 cash for prepaid expenses (supplies and insurance). The total of these checks written on the bank account is $21,550. This amount, plus the $9,000 on hand in cash and the $6,250 in the savings account, totals $36,800, the total cash invested by Jones ($21,800) and by Uncle John ($15,000).

While it would be desirable for Mr. Jones to make the suggested changes in the first draft balance sheet, if the potential strengths listed do actually exist it would appear that cautious management of funds should enable him to proceed accordingly. Each proprietor must decide what exceptions to the rule he or she will undertake. Most important is that each knows the rules of sound financing and knows when they are in violation.

Lest we forget, we should remind ourselves that we have now produced a plan or plans for soundly financing a business which will utilize more than $100,000 of the world's limited assets with an owner investment of $21,800. Remembering that accomplishment provides an understanding of how the business economy operates.

BALANCE SHEET VARIATIONS FOR PROPRIETORSHIPS, PARTNERSHIPS, AND CORPORATIONS

The opening day balance sheet which we developed for the P.M. Jones Company, Table 7-1, shows that there is only one owner, Mr. Jones. This is a proprietorship form of legal operation. We will pursue our study of different legal forms of organization in Chapter 11. It is valuable here, however, to see how our opening day balance sheet would look if we had adopted the alternative of making Uncle John a partner, or if we had incorporated and sold him preference shares.

Only the right side of the balance sheet shown in Table 7-1 would have been changed in either situation. Table 7-2 shows in the first column how the right side of the balance sheet would look under the partnership suggestion. Column 2 shows how it would look as a corporation.

TABLE 7-2

P.M. JONES COMPANY: LIABILITIES AND NET WORTH AS PARTNERSHIP AND AS CORPORATION

PARTNERSHIP			CORPORATION		
LIABILITIES			LIABILITIES		
Current liabilities			Current liabilities		
Accounts payable	$16,250		Accounts payable	$16,250	
Contract payable	2,500		Contract payable	2,500	
Note payable	1,200		Note payable	1,200	
Total current liabilities		$19,950	Total current liabilities		$19,950
Fixed liabilities		0	Fixed liabilities		0
Total liabilities		$19,950	Total liabilities		$19,950
NET WORTH			NET WORTH		
P.M. Jones, capital		$21,800	Preference shares outstanding		$15,000
Uncle John, capital		15,000	Common shares outstanding		21,800
Total net worth		$36,800	Total capital		$36,800
Total liabilities plus net worth		$56,750	Total liabilities plus net worth		$56,750

QUESTIONS FOR CLASS DISCUSSION

Q7-1 Why is it important to have a current ratio of 2 to 1 on the opening day balance sheet?

Q7-2 Why would a new business planner refuse all types of credit available?

Q7-3 What is the biggest danger in using too much credit?

Q7-4 "Payments on contracts to buy fixed assets come out of planned profits and are not operating expenses, which are deducted before profits are determined." Explain.

Q7-5 What is meant by the term, "trading on too thin an equity"?

Q7-6 What does a proprietorship ratio of 50 percent mean when measuring the soundness of the financial structure on the proposed balance sheet?

Q7-7 If the first rough draft of the proposed balance sheet fails to meet the standard ratio analysis, what should the planner do?

Q7-8 What is the error in ignoring high interest charges paid because "such charges are deductible for income tax purposes"?

Q7-9 Do you recall how we measure current assets? Current liabilities? Do you think these rules are too conservative?

Q7-10 In the example of the P.M. Jones Company in Chapter 7, Mr. Jones and Uncle John invested a total of $36,800. Where is that cash now? Who provided the balance of the $56,750 of total assets now invested? Explain.

PROBLEMS AND QUESTIONS FOR WRITTEN ASSIGNMENT

P7-1 Ms. Hill's balance sheet shows current assets of $40,000 and current liabilities of $20,000. She borrows $10,000 from the bank on a 90-day note. What effect will this new loan have on her current ratio?

P7-2 Mr. Stein's balance sheet shows current assets of $30,000 and current liabilities of $15,000. He then pays off a bank loan of $5,000. What effect will this debt retirement have on his current ratio?

P7-3 Explain why payments on a contract to purchase a delivery truck are not operating expenses but instead are a provision of investment capital. Can you illustrate the accounting entries?

P7-4 How can misunderstanding the statement in problem P7-3 get a business into trouble?

CONTINUING PROBLEM:
THE SUCCESS HARDWARE STORE

Part 7. The Opening Day Balance Sheet

Assignment for Part 7

After carefully studying your statement of assets to be used, *list the decisions* you will make on how the various assets are to be provided. Will you buy the land and building or rent a store building? Will you buy all new fixtures for the store and office? Will you carry your own receivables or sell on credit cards only? Will you operate your own delivery truck or use an available merchant's delivery service? What other decisions will you make? Assume that sales will be half for cash and half on 30-day credit. Divide credit sales between open accounts and credit-card sales as you desire.

Now transfer these decisions into a proposed opening day balance sheet for the store. Does it come out with proper current, quick, and proprietorship ratios? Perhaps a second or third draft will be necessary as you change some of your decisions to bring these ratios into balance. Perhaps your instructor will want to discuss the basic decisions on asset acquisition with you so that all students follow the same plan. Follow the procedure in the preceding chapter in making your balance sheet. Explain in parentheses the nature of each asset cost and liability incurred in providing it. Remember, assets minus liabilities equal net worth. In the net worth section of your balance sheet, you can list the net worth in one account, owner capital, for the present. We will detail that section in the next assignment.

REFERENCES FOR FURTHER READING

Kelley, Pearce C., Kenneth Lawyer, and Clifford M. Baumback, *How to Organize and Operate a Small Business*, 5th ed., Prentice-Hall, Inc., Englewood Cliffs, N.J., 1973, chap. 10.

Meigs *et al.*, *Accounting: The Basis for Business Decisions*, 2d Can. ed., McGraw-Hill Ryerson Ltd., Toronto, 1976, chap. 1.

Preshing, W.A., *Business Management in Canada*, Wiley Publishers of Canada Ltd., Toronto, 1974, chap. 34.

CHAPTER 8

Sources of Financing for New Small Firms

Getting friends to invest in my business was one of my toughest jobs. They now seem much more willing to purchase shares in my firm. And I always thought the corporation was just for very large firms.

The Late Learner

No firm should ever be started without a clear and positive understanding of where its total capital needs are coming from. As we have seen in previous chapters, a very important phase of the entire planning process is to determine what assets will be needed and how they are to be provided. When the amount of the net ownership capital needed has been determined, the proprietors turn to the problem of making sure that the entire amount is available. The total sum should preferably be deposited in the company's bank account before any commitments are made by the new owners.

When several sources of capital are available, the planners must still bear in mind that all sources may not be equally desirable. Borrowed capital is shown on the balance sheet as a liability. It must be paid back at specific periods. These repayments of principal amounts are not operating expenses which are deducted on the income statement before planned profits are produced. They are payments for the provision of investment capital and are to be paid out of the profits shown on the income statement. The author has found that failure to recognize this basic fact is the commonest cause of financial strain among small firms. It is important, therefore, to consider the repayment schedules in choosing among sources of financing.

The various types of financing available to business firms are usually classified as:

1 Short-term capital. This category is used to designate borrowed capital which is to be repaid within one year.

2 Intermediate capital. This title is applied to borrowed capital which is to be repaid in one to five years.

3 Long-term capital. This is capital whose repayment is arranged for more than five years in the future.

As new firm planners review the 12 sources of financial assistance which follow, they may find that some of these sources fall into different categories of the above listing. For example, a note payable to a commercial bank is generally considered short-term financing, but a three-year note payable to a finance company would be considered intermediate capital.

SOURCES OF FUNDS FOR SMALL FIRMS

1. Personal funds saved or inherited
2. Loans from relatives and friends
3. Trade credit
4. Loans or credit from equipment sellers
5. Mortgage loans
6. Commercial bank loans
7. Small Business Loans Act (SBLA) loans
8. Federal Business Development Bank loans
9. Federal and provincial development programs
10. Taking in partners
11. Selling capital shares
12. Other miscellaneous sources

Two things should be recognized when one is faced with the problem of obtaining outside capital assistance:

1 An established concern with a good record of operations usually has better access to available sources of capital than a new firm.

2 Some personal capital available for investment in the firm by the new owner is almost always essential to obtaining any type of outside assistance.

Against this background, we can investigate the possibilities of each of the 12 sources of funds listed.

Personal Funds Whenever potential creditors, partners, or stockholders are invited to invest in, or lend financial assistance to, a new firm, their first question is, "How much does the owner have invested?" Every business contains an element of risk, and outsiders who invest in a new firm wish to be sure that such risk is shared by the owner. We have seen that "trading on too thin an equity" means that the owner's investment is too small relative to the investment of outsiders. A financing plan which indicates that the firm is starting out on this basis does not usually invite confidence from creditors. As we saw in Chapter 7, this does not always mean that the new owners must have 50 percent of the total capital needs to invest, but it does mean that they should likely look to other ownership capital rather than only to creditor capital in their financial plan. In any event, it is important that the would-be owners have assets of their own to invest in the firm. The closer to 50 percent of the total capital needs that can be provided, the greater will be their independence and share of net profits.

Loans from Relatives and Friends Although this type of borrowing to provide original investment capital is generally frowned upon by experienced business operators, it remains one of the prominent devices used in small firm planning. Many new owners are encouraged in their enterprise by parents, relatives, or friends who offer to supply loans to the firm to get it started. Quite often, no other sources are available after normal trade credit and supplier contracts have been utilized.

It is unfortunate that many otherwise successful firms have been fraught with troubles because relatives or friends interfered with the operations. Mixing family or social relationships with business can be dangerous. Many such situations might have been averted if the terms of the loans had been more clearly specified, including the rights of the lenders to insist upon making operational policy. The best way to avoid subsequent problems is to make sure that loans are made on a businesslike basis. They should be viewed as business dealings. The right of the owner to make decisions should be respected by all parties involved. Arrangements for retiring such loans, including any options for early payment, and the procedure if loans become delinquent, should be clearly understood. The owner should be sure such loans are properly presented on the balance sheet — payments due in 1 year are current liabilities; the others are fixed liabilities.

Trade Credit Trade credit is the financial assistance available from other firms with whom the business has dealings. Most prominent are the suppliers of inventory which is constantly being replaced. We have previously noted that wholesalers who desire a retailer's business, for example, will offer generous terms for payment of invoices. Manufacturers will do the same for wholesalers whose business they desire. Financing the opening inventory usually represents onc of the larger investments in a typical small firm. If a $20,000 inventory can be purchased for $10,000 down payment and the balance in 30 days, the wholesaler has virtually provided $10,000 of required capital to open the business. The owner then has an opportunity to sell that inventory at a profit and thus to have the funds to pay off the original balance. As a record for successful operation is established, even more attractive terms may be offered on subsequent purchases. A grocer may have several such suppliers. Other firms may have only one or two major suppliers. The inducement of a sales discount for prompt payment of invoices should always tempt the owner to pay within the maximum discount period.

Loans or Credit from Equipment Sellers This type of financial aid is often considered another form of trade credit. It does, however, have distinct characteristics. The new firm may need counters, shelves, display cases, delivery trucks, and other equipment such as air conditioning, refrigeration units, food counters. These, too, are a large investment for the new small firm and are so recognized by the major suppliers of such items. The purchases, it is hoped, are not made on a regular basis but represent a large part of the capital needed to get started. The suppliers usually offer good credit terms with a modest down payment and a contract for the balance spread over 1, 2, or 3 years.

This type of credit, when financing charges are reasonable, can be most helpful to the planner. The caution is in its overuse — remembering, again, that the principal payments must be paid out of profits anticipated. Any principal repayments of this type, too, are for the provision of capital and are not operating expenses. Too much of this type of financing can distort the current and quick ratios and upset the firm's financial liquidity. Many cases are on record where the monthly payments on such fixed assets exceed the profits earned from sales in the month.

Mortgage Loans If the new firm planners own a commercial building, they can normally secure a mortgage on it with payments over as many as 20 years. It may be the building in which the new firm will operate. In that case, the planners will be making mortgage payments instead of rental payments to a landlord. They may wish to risk a mortgage on their homes. Even second mortgages are sometimes used, although not recommended. Mortgage loans are typically made by trust companies, credit unions and mortgage companies. When profits are uncertain, caution is advised in committing any assets to mortgage claims. As a clear profit pattern becomes more definitely established, the use of mortgage credit becomes less risky.

Commercial Bank Loans Historically, a line of credit at a chartered bank was designed to enable a merchant to purchase an inventory of merchandise. When the merchandise was sold at a profit, the bank was paid its loan. This situation is still followed by many banks. This use of bank credit is still the best way to establish credit with a commercial bank. Since the relaxation of bank restrictions in recent years, however, many other types of loans and financing are now available to qualified applicants. In fact, we have banks now which advertise, "If you are planning to go into business, come see us." The cold, hard facts of economic reality will be faced in such a visit, but the prospective firm owner with an otherwise sound financing plan, a reputation for integrity, and a business deemed likely to succeed may still establish some bank credit in the planning stage. Long-term loans are less generally available than short-term loans. Short-term loans are usually considered those for not more than 1 year. If adequate collateral is available, longer term loans may usually be obtained. Getting influential or wealthy friends to cosign notes also may be helpful.

The policies of several of the chartered banks should always be checked in the planning stage. Many small firm owners with experience have long described banks as "a place where you can borrow money when you prove that you don't need it." Some banks are earnestly trying to remove that image today. In keeping with our previously noted axiom that rewards must be commensurate with cost and risk, however, interest rates charged by banks to small firms are significantly higher than the rates charged to large firms.

Small Business Loans Act (SBLA) Loans The proprietor of a small business enterprise or one who is about to establish a new business may borrow funds under this program for the acquisition of fixed assets, modernization of premises (leasehold improvements) or the purchase of land or building necessary for the operation of the business. Working capital loans are not provided under the SBLA nor is it possible to refinance existing debt. It is hoped, however, that eventually the SBLA will be amended to include much needed working capital financing for small enterprises. A small business, be it a proprietorship, partnership, or a limited liability company, is eligible if its actual (or estimated) gross revenue does not exceed $1.5 million per year and is engaged in any one of the following activities: manufacturing, wholesale or retail trade, service, transportation, construction, and communication. The maximum which a business may have outstanding under the SBLA at any one time may not exceed

$75,000 and the loan must be secured by first charge on equipment, mortgage on the premises, and sometimes additional security may be required. The loans are provided and administered by the chartered banks and other designated lending institutions such as Credit Unions, Caisses Populaires, trust companies, loan companies, insurance companies, and Alberta Treasury Branches and are fully guaranteed by the federal government. The loans have fixed terms of repayments of the principal, typically 5 years, and since April 1978 the interest charged on these loans is fluctuating (floating) with the chartered bank's prime lending rate with an additional one percent above the prime rate.

The Federal Business Development Bank (FBDB) is a Crown Corporation which assists the growth and creation of business enterprises across Canada by providing them with financial and management services. It supplements such services available from others and it gives particular attention to the needs of smaller enterprises.

FBDB extends financial assistance to new or existing businesses of almost every type in Canada which do not have other sources of financing available to them on reasonable terms and conditions.

The qualifications for FBDB financing are that the principals of the business have sufficient investment in the business to ensure their continuing commitment and that the enterprise may reasonably be expected to be successful.

FBDB financing is available by means of loans, loan guarantees, equity financing, or leasing, or by any combination of these methods, in whatever manner best suits the particular needs of the business. Where loans are involved they are made at interest rates which are in line with those generally available to businesses. Security is usually a first charge on fixed assets. Where equity is involved, FBDB normally takes a minority interest and is prepared to have its investment repurchased on suitable terms.

Most of the customers of the bank use FBDB funds to acquire land, buildings, or equipment. Others use them to strengthen the working capital of a business, to establish a new business, and for other purposes.

FBDB financing ranges in size from a few thousand dollars upwards. Most loans are $100,000 or less. Close to half of them are for $25,000 or less and the average size of a loan is around $45,000. The amount that can be borrowed for a specific purpose depends upon the borrower's ability to satisfy the general requirements of the bank. Businesses may obtain FBDB assistance on more than one occasion if they meet its requirements.

In addition to its financial services the FBDB provides for small business management training through an extensive series of one-day management seminars at many centres across Canada, and it develops and distributes adult education courses on small business management topics. The Bank's Small Business Information Service is an enquiry and referral service available at its 90-odd offices across the country.

CASE (Counselling Assistance for Small Enterprise) is a management counselling service wherein retired business persons act as counsellors on behalf of the Bank. Its purpose is to assist owners and managers of business enterprises, particularly those of smaller size, to improve their methods of doing business. Also it provides an opportunity for retired business people to contribute to the development of the small business community by making available a vast store of knowledge and experience. To be eligible a business may already be established, or be about to engage in business in Canada.

Any proprietorship, partnership, or limited company conducting virtually any type of business enterprise in Canada can apply, provided that the enterprise does not have more than 75 full-time employees. There is a nominal charge ($20 per day at the present) for this service.

Federal and Provincial Development Programs The Enterprise Development Program (EDP) was launched by the Department of Industry, Trade and Commerce on April 1, 1977. Designed to increase the effectiveness of the Department's industrial support efforts, it has replaced a number of the department's previous programs. The EDP is intended to help smaller and medium-sized companies become more viable and internationally competitive. Its decentralized administration and decision-making makes the program more accessible to smaller and medium-sized businesses. EDP participates with eligible firms that undertake projects involving relatively high-risk innovation or modernization/expansion of production systems that can be expected to yield attractive rates of return on the total investment.

There are two primary methods by which the EDP participates in projects with a firm: (i) through sharing of project costs, or (ii) by providing insurance for a term loan which finances the project.

The Department of Regional Economic Expansion (DREE) objective is to stimulate increased manufacturing investment and employment in designated slow-growth regions. Cash grants and/or loans guarantees are used to encourage entrepreneurs to locate in regions designated for incentive assistance or, for industries already established in those regions, to expand or modernize.

At the present, these regions include all of the provinces of Newfoundland, Nova Scotia, New Brunswick, Prince Edward Island, Quebec (excluding Hull and its immediate environs), Manitoba, and

Saskatchewan, together with the northern area of Ontario, Alberta, and British Columbia, and all the Northwest Territories.

The Export Development Corporation is a federally owned commercial enterprise that provides financial facilities to assist Canada's export trade. It has assets well in excess of a billion dollars and lending, insurance, and guarantees capacities of nearly $9 billion. EDC operates to help Canadian exporters remain competitive in world markets. It does this by providing insurance, loans, guarantees, foreign investment guarantees, and other services. Any firm, large or small, is eligible for this type of assistance.

The provincial governments in every province of Canada have established Development Agencies or Crown Corporations. Their methods of operation and levels of activity vary from province to province, but all have similar objectives — mostly to stimulate economic growth in their areas and to provide financial assistance to firms unable to secure required financing.

Taking in Partners Despite all the cautions previously discussed, raising capital often necessitates taking one or more partners into the business. If more than one manager is not needed, the new partners may not be employed in the firm but may hold full partner status as a result of their investment in the firm. The partnership agreement (discussed in Chapter 11) is important here. Inducements can be offered to such a finance partner, but the duties, responsibilities, and authority of each partner must be clearly understood. At this point we are looking at the partnership only from the standpoint of providing a source of investment funds.

Selling Capital Shares Aside from the technical, legal, and operational advantages of the corporate form of legal organization, its advantages as a device for raising capital are extremely significant. Many small firm owners seem to believe that the corporate form was designed only for the very large business firms. This is false. It is true that this legal form has not been as widely used as it might be. This is believed to be due to lack of knowledge of its advantages. Chapter 11 explains details of the corporation.

Let us consider the new firm planner who needs $100,000 in ownership capital but has only $30,000 to invest. Would it not be desirable to go to a local investment dealer as a corporation and request the sale of $50,000 of 7 percent preference shares and $50,000 of common shares? The planner takes title to $30,000 of the voting common shares. The charter provides authorization to sell $100,000 of each type of shares. The planner can hold the unsold shares in the firm for possible future financing for expansion. The preference share is given a priority of dividends and may not have voting privilege. Usually only the common share has voting power. The planner still owns a majority of the common shares outstanding and has no problem of control. The investment dealer sells the shares to customers who are probably unknown. A detailed study of the plans of the firm is contained in a prospectus, which the investment dealers will prepare. The firm planner does not have to pursue relatives to plead with friends for financial "favours," does not have to take in undesired partners to raise capital, has assured a financial plan for expansion, and has all the protections of the corporate form of organization. The investment dealer will charge for this service. The charge will be higher if the dealer guarantees the sale of the full amount, and less if the stock is sold on a "best efforts" basis. The investment dealer's fee is chargeable to organization expense and can be amortized over the succeeding 5 to 10 years. This procedure is followed by the most informed new firm planners who desire growth. It should be investigated for appropriateness by many more. Details for forming a corporation are covered in Chapter 11.

The raising of funds described above is called "private placement" of limited share distribution. When stock market conditions are depressed, this financing route can be an important alternative to the public distribution of the company's shares — "going public."

Each province has a Securities Act, as well as several other laws affecting and controlling the raising of funds for business purposes from the general public. Securities Commissions in the provinces regulate public offerings of corporation securities, investigate and scrutinize the people involved in the companies' affairs, and the companies' books, and ascertain that the offering "prospectus" includes a full, true, and plain disclosure of all relevant facts — in general, to safeguard the public interest. In addition, certain rules are enforced by the various stock exchanges, by the Investment Dealers Association in Canada, and by the Broker-Dealer Association in Ontario, to ensure and to maintain an ethical standard of conduct by its members. It should be noted that the public distribution of shares is an expensive source of funds for the small- or medium-sized business. A share issue will cost from $50,000 to $100,000 in legal and accounting fees and commissions; offerings of less than $1 million are just not practical any more. With public ownership there are many statutory obligations for increased disclosure of company information, regulatory reporting, and the like.

Other Miscellaneous Sources of Funds Most of the other miscellaneous sources of funds are more available to going concerns than to persons who need financial aid for a newly planned business. If the new firm has equipment paid for through investment by the owner, if it has an inventory of merchandise which is free and clear, or if it has some accounts receivable from other sources which are being invested in the firm, loans against these can usually be obtained. *Commercial finance companies* are available in every town and most make loans against this type of collateral. Similar companies will make credit available in "floor planning" arrangements to make merchandise available. Others will purchase installment-loan contracts from the small firm owner. *Insurance companies* sometimes engage in long-term loans to substantial small business firms. These are usually secured by mortgages on real estate. *Personal finance companies* will make personal loans to small firm owners with precise repayment schedules. In the types of small firms where *factors* or *sales agents* are used to handle the bulk of the firm's business, working capital is often advanced to the firm by such factors or sales agents. The textile industry is the most prominent example of this type of business activity.

Leasing companies may be sources of funds for the acquisition of a wide variety of assets, including land and buildings, machinery and equipment, vehicles, fixtures, etc. Frequently, substantial cash may be generated by the sale and leaseback of a building owned by the business.

QUESTIONS FOR CLASS DISCUSSION

Q8-1 Why is it important for new firm planners to have some capital of their own to invest?

Q8-2 Do you think it is advisable to borrow from relatives and friends to raise capital to start a business?

Q8-3 How can loans from relatives and friends be made more businesslike?

Q8-4 What are the pros and cons of having partners in your business?

Q8-5 Are shareholders creditors or owners? Explain.

Q8-6 Are there possible dangers in borrowing too much, even if funds may be available? Explain.

Q8-7 What is the Federal Business Development Bank?

Q8-8 What is trade credit? Is it usually more expensive than bank loans?

Q8-9 Can trade credit be used in planning a new firm? How?

Q8-10 What other miscellaneous sources of funds may be used by small business firms?

Q8-11 Why do established firms have less trouble in getting outside financial assistance than newly planned firms?

Q8-12 How do equipment suppliers help provide financing for a new firm?

Q8-13 Does our government assist small firms in obtaining financing? How?

PROBLEMS AND QUESTIONS FOR WRITTEN ASSIGNMENT

P8-1 You are starting a new business. You have $15,000 available and the total assets required on your opening day balance sheet will cost $50,000. How would you suggest arranging the balance of the required capital?

P8-2 Under what circumstances could a small firm planner sell capital shares to the public?

P8-3 Under what circumstances can a commercial bank be reasonably expected to open a line of credit for a new small firm?

P8-4 What are the advantages of selling shares in a corporation as against borrowing on notes?

CONTINUING PROBLEM:
THE SUCCESS HARDWARE STORE

Part 8. Raising The Owner Capital

We must now decide how we will raise the amount of owner capital found to be necessary in our last assignment. Will we rely on additional long-term liability debt? Will this destroy our basic ratios of conservative financial structure? Will we take in partners to provide some of the needed investment capital? Should we incorporate and sell some shares? Preference or common? (See Chapter 11) How will we retain control?

Assignment for Part 8

Explain the alternatives you have in providing the needed owner investment and how you have decided to provide it. How much of your own money will you invest?

Prepare a refined net worth section on your opening day balance sheet, prepared in the preceding assignment, showing how your decisions will be shown in the finally adopted opening day balance sheet.

REFERENCES FOR FURTHER READING

Archer, M., *An Introduction to Canadian Business,* 3d ed., McGraw-Hill Ryerson Ltd., Toronto, 1978, chaps. 14,15.

Broom, H.N., and J.C. Longenecker, *Small Business Management,* 2d ed., South-Western Publishing Co., Inc., Cincinnati, 1966, chap 9.

"Equity for Small Business," Minding Your Own Business, Pamphlet No. 12, Federal Business Development Bank.

"Financing Canadian Industries," Department of Industry, Trade and Commerce, Ottawa, 1977.

"How to Finance Your Business," Your Business Matters, No. 1, The Royal Bank of Canada, 1975.

Kelley, Pearce C., Kenneth Lawyer, and Clifford M. Baumback, *How to Organize and Operate a Small Business,* 5th ed., Prentice-Hall, Inc., Englewood Cliffs, N.J., 1973, chap. 10.

"Management of Liabilities and Equities," Your Business Matters, No. 12, The Royal Bank of Canada, 1978.

Musselman, Vernon A., and Eugene H. Hughes, *Introduction to Modern Business,* 6th ed., Prentice-Hall, Inc., Englewood Cliffs, N.J., 1973, chap. 14.

"Presenting Your Case for a Term Loan," Minding Your Own Businss, Pamphlet No. 3, Federal Business Development Bank.

Preshing, W.A., *Business Management in Canada,* Wiley Publishers of Canada Ltd., Toronto, 1974, chap. 36.

Part 4

FORM AND STRUCTURE OF THE FIRM

CHAPTER 9

Location of the Firm

Location? Yes, we learned the hard way. We used to think that you just found an empty store for rent and went to work. We went broke once while wondering why customers didn't come to our store. Our new store is ideally located and we are now making good profits in the same town and serving the same people we tried to serve before.

The Late Learner

The subject of location is indeed a very large one. Many entire texts have been written on this one problem. At best, we can only point out some of the highlights here.

Small firm owners should distinguish between general location factors and site factors. In this sense, *location* means the region, the province, the county, or the city which represents the general market area for the planned firm. The *site* factors are the particular street, the corner, and the building within the location area. The advantages of a good location can be minimized by a poor site.

In the 1970s the three fastest-growing Metropolitan areas in Canada were Calgary, Kitchener/Waterloo and Edmonton. This means that expanded markets are developing in these areas. In isolation, these growing markets suggest that these areas would be good places in which to establish new firms. It would be foolhardy, however, to think that there are not many other areas of the country where location of a new firm would be desirable. Moreover, not all types of firms are needed in all growing areas. We must investigate even general location factors more closely.

Small business failures often reflect complete neglect of a consideration of specific location factors. Too many small firms are established in locations because a store space happened to be available for rent. Most students can probably recall a section of their home towns which became known as the cemetery for small firms. New ones come and go every year. Business firms which otherwise would have been quite successful suffer from the start when not properly located. Some new proprietors have as the prominent factor in their choice of location such things as a desire to live in their home town, to be close to friends or relatives, to locate in a climate they prefer, to be close to a particular religious group, to be near a particular ethnic group. Others attach a certain social atmosphere to their location. In themselves, these factors may not be bad for choosing a location, but it is important that within these considerations, the proper location and proper site be chosen. Never should a particular store space be selected merely because it is available, without subjecting it to some specific tests of suitability. Being well known in one's home town can be a great advantage if other considerations are in line. Knowing the population and its atmosphere, the mode of living and something of the business climate in the home town, and being known to your bankers can all be advantageous for a new proprietor if he chooses a location consistent with the considerations we will discuss below.

If the planner is not restricted by desire to locate in a particular town or region but is looking for a location anywhere in the country, he can apply all the following general considerations.

LOCATION FACTORS FOR RETAILING

1 Industry Study the industry of the area under consideration. Payrolls create buying power for your potential customers, and unless their permanence and growth seem probable, making a big investment is probably unwise.

The ideal is a community with substantial permanent industry, an upward trend in community payrolls, diversification of its industries, stability of its industries, and a minimum of seasonality in the total activity. Seasonal business firms can be very successful. The important thing is to know the facts about the seasonal variations.

2 Population Study the nature of the population in the area. Many students seems surprised to learn that there are many areas of our country where the population has actually decreased in recent years. Declining, stationary, or small populations do not suggest new firms for the area. Growing populations and wealthy populations desiring the goods or services you propose to offer in an expanding population area represent ideal situations. The mode of living of the community under consideration must be studied. The authors recall the proprietor of a small hardware store on the ground floor of a 20-story apartment building complaining about his lack of sales of garden hoses. When asked if apartment dwellers buy many garden hoses, he realized that the mode of living of most of his customers did not require many of such a product.

Study your potential market area in terms of the needs and desires of the people you want to serve. Are they home owners? Are they renters? Do they live in apartments? Are the rents high, low, or medium? Condominium owners may have a different mode of living than apartment renters. Another factor in the mode of living in a particular area is the general character of the population. Is it composed mostly of older people, a dominant religious group? Are the people native-born, mostly foreign-born, or a truly mixed group?

3 Competition Know your competition in advance. Our free enterprise system is based upon competition. Our business history has proved that customers are best served when healthy competition prevails. Competition should not be feared. It should be known and coped with.

The two time-honored justifications for opening a new firm in an existing line of business are (a) an expanded market, and (b) presence of inefficient firms. Expanded markets are almost always the result of expanding populations. The trend of our population to the cities in recent years has provided the basis for many new firms. Much of this population growth, of course, has been in the suburbs of the larger cities. The attendant growth of sales and new firms in the suburbs has been one of the outstanding characteristics of our recent business history.

As mentioned earlier, new planners can learn a great deal about a particular area relative to its population growth and existing competition. Chambers of commerce, trade development associations, county industrial planning boards, and similar organizations can provide details about many areas. Cities are divided into census tracts or other smaller areas for various purposes. The population of each is usually recorded annually and is available at least by census years.

When the population of an area is compared with the number of competing firms, a first conclusion can be made as to whether or not the area needs another firm in this field. For example, if it takes 700 people to maintain a modern grocery store and the area now has a grocery store for every 500 people, the conclusion, on this basis, must be that this is not a good place to establish another store. The total market has not expanded. If there is only one grocery store for 1,200 people, the evidence suggests this is a good location. Table 9-1 shows the size of population necessary to support various types of retail store.

TABLE 9-1
POPULATION REQUIREMENTS FOR VARIOUS TYPES OF RETAIL STORES*

Camera and photography supplies	40,000
Drugs	2,500
Dry goods	25,000
Florist shops	7,500
Grocery stores	700
Hardware stores	5,000
Hobby shops and toy stores	25,000
Household appliances	8,500
Jewelry stores	7,500
Men's and boys' clothing	7,500
Restaurants and lunch counters	1,000
Shoe stores	6,000
Sporting goods	12,000
Stationery stores	25,000
Women's clothing	5,000

**Source: Independent study made by a group of advanced business administration students at the University of Miami. Starting from established studies, their procedure was to use data from the United States census, census of business, trade reports, and local market surveys in order to update figures for this table. Their results do not vary widely from other established studies. They emphasized in their conclusions that varying localities and conditions need study before adopting these averages.*

In the former case, however, we can still consider the presence of inefficient firms. Customer reaction to existing stores, nature of stocks carried, services available, and the type of management reflected by competitors may present a situation in which a new, efficient firm would be successful despite the number of competitors now attempting to serve the same population.

Competitors should be studied in terms of their numbers, their management, how many of them are chain stores, the attractiveness of their stores, and the completeness and nature of their stocks of merchandise. If it is found that customers are dissatisfied with service, lines of merchandise, price ranges, attractiveness of stores, or other items, a basis may be found for successfully competing in that area.

4 Facilities Consider your city or town facilities. Is public transportation important to your plans, and if so, is it available with good service? Are there special problems in obtaining merchandise supplies through normal channels of distribution? Does the area have good banking facilities? Are civic associations, schools, churches, and professional services conducive to good community life and healthy business conditions? Is the local government attitude toward business encouraging or restrictive? If labour supply is important to your business, is an adequate supply available?

For manufacturers, the questions of nearness to raw materials or markets, the availability of cheap fuel, power and water, skilled labour of a special type, and financing facilities take precedence.

SITE FACTORS FOR RETAILING

Having decided upon a favourable city or even a part of a city in the preceding process, the planner can turn his attention to the specific site to be chosen within his generally desired location. Some of the site factors and their implications follow:

1 Parking Does the particular site provide easy parking and access and other comforts for customers? Grandpa never worried about this factor with his general store. Hitching posts provided a place to tie the horses and were usually provided by the local government. Fields surrounded many stores and were free parking areas. Likely the most significant change in downtown retailing management in recent years has been the expense and importance of

Even shopping centre parking lots can be inadequate.

providing parking space for customers. Parking and heavy traffic in urban areas have contributed greatly to the growth of suburban shopping centres. Today parking is a fundamental part of every "save the downtown" or "bring the customers back downtown" or "revitalize the main downtown" program. An hour's free or subsidized parking is now available in many department-store lots when a purchase is made. Small firms must rely upon availability of low-cost parking or follow the same policy.

2 Surrounding Firms What types of firms surround the site? It must be recognized that some types of business firms attract customers of one type and others attract other types. Good site choosing must consider this factor. What kinds of business firms surround the site you have under consideration? Sites close to department stores are generally considered good for most types of retail stores. The general appeal of the department store to all types of customers makes this so.

Market research has provided some conclusions in this regard. For example, studies have shown that men's stores should not be located next to gas stations, beauty shops, or women's apparel shops. Those who might disagree have not provided substantial evidence to support their views. Like electricity, it is more important that we know how to use research than to understand its foundation. Such neighbours just do not normally attract customers who are looking for men's clothing when visiting these shops. The innovation of clothing stores which sell both men's and women's apparel has not made sufficiently significant inroads on the principle to warrant its revocation.

3 Traffic Density What kind of traffic is there at this site, and is it adequate? Modern site analysis distinguishes between automobile and pedestrian traffic. If only automobile traffic were considered, most businesses would be located on expressways or main highways. Pedestrian traffic of potential customers is the key item here. Heavy automobile traffic adjacent to a suburban shopping centre can be very important, but the number of people who convert into pedestrian traffic is of even greater concern.

In urban sites, passing cars become less important. Getting these cars parked and bringing customers to the street and the store is the crucial consideration.

People traffic alone is not the most significant item in pedestrian traffic, however. Are they the type of people who are shopping for your type of merchandise? Why are they on this street at this time? Significantly, a large drug chain has staff people interview passerbys on a site it is considering. With clip boards and questions, they observe, interview, and study the traffic. They ask age bracket, record sex, ask about employment, income range, objective of the trip past this site, shopping habits, and interest in this type of store, etc. Their conclusion is that the site with the heaviest count of potential customers per half-hour between one and five o'clock in the afternoon and on Saturday evenings is the preferred site for the company's stores.

4 The "Going-Home" Side of the Street Marketing research has produced the principle that the going-home side of the street is usually to be preferred to the going-to-work side of the street. This may be only a reflection of people's buying habits, but it has proved true in cases studied by advanced students. Those interested in the psychology of human conduct can form their own reasons for this principle of site choosing.

5 The Sunny Side of the Street Market studies have also established that the sunny side of the street is less preferable for retail operations than the shady side. Our own research has found rents higher on the shady side in high-priced shopping areas. Perhaps in northern Alaska the reverse might be true because the sunshine is less frequent and may even be sought by shoppers. Merchants recognize the sunny-side-of-the-street principle by the installation of expensive awnings to combat the sun and make customers more comfortable.

Preferred Site

We must not leave this discussion with the implication that all types of retailers must be in prime, high-rent locations. Lower rents also have attractions, but they must be offset by higher advertising and promotion budgets to attract customers to the low-rent area. Some types of firms need such areas for best results. Firms that sell by mail or through travelling salesmen are obviously exempt from the considerations just discussed. Firms selling shopping merchandise should normally be close to their competitors, as we shall discuss in a later chapter. Firms concentrating on specialty goods emphasize comfort for their customers above all (see Table 9-2).

Site studies which have been made over many years, by both government agencies and private market research groups, have generally agreed that the preferred site can be associated with characteristics of the business in question. For instance, firms should generally seek low-rent locations if they have a high gross margin and low merchandise turnover, need much space of interior displays, sell merchandise which is low in value compared with bulk, sell what are considered shopping goods by most people in the area, have an established customer demand, resort to much advertising and promotion effort, or have high overhead expense. High-rent locations are more appropriate for firms which feature window displays, have a high rate of turnover, have low gross margins, appeal to transient trade, feature price appeal and convenience merchandise, sell merchandise of high value compared with bulk, have low overhead, and do little advertising.

TABLE 9-2
FIRM CHARACTERISTICS WHICH SUGGEST HIGH- OR LOW-RENT LOCATIONS AND FIRMS WHICH USUALLY ARE IN EACH CATEGORY

CHARACTERISTICS WHICH SUGGEST HIGH-RENT LOCATIONS	ILLUSTRATIVE FIRMS
Window displays featured	Department stores
High rate of turnover	Style clothing shops
Low gross margin	Urban drugstores, banks
Appeal to transient trade	Men's shops, drugstores
Feature price appeal and convenience merchandise	Discount stores
Sells merchandise of high value compared to bulk	Fine jewelry stores
Low overhead	Specialty tobacco and cigar stores
Does little advertising	Independent hardware stores
CHARACTERISTICS WHICH SUGGEST LOW-RENT LOCATIONS	**ILLUSTRATIVE FIRMS**
High gross margin	Furniture stores
Low merchandise turnover	Plumbing supplies
Need much space for interior displays	Automobile agency
Merchandise is low in value compared to bulk	Grain and feed stores
Merchandise is essentially shopping goods	Carpet stores, TV stores
Has an established clientele	Neighborhood drugstore
Does much advertising and promotion	Florist, grocery chains
Has a high overhead expense	Specialty food franchise, super service station

It is unlikely that the individual firm would meet all the characteristics suggesting either a high-rent or low-rent location. The decision is usually reached in the planning stage by determining which type of location is suggested by the preponderance of characteristics represented. If the firm's characteristics imply a low-rent location on a majority of the measures, prudence recommends that such a location be given serious consideration. The many exceptions to such rules only prove the rule. Local circumstances usually account for the exceptions. A study of such a list may aid policy making in merchandising.

Small factories can also be attractive.
Courtesy of Canadian Hanson Ltd.

LOCATION FACTORS FOR MANUFACTURING

Factory locations are usually restricted to specified industrial areas of any city. Recent trends show an increase in municipal regulations in this regard. As a first consideration, the new factory planner must check the zoning laws in his area. Some industrial zones allow some types of factories and not others.

Once the available industrial zones are determined, attention is turned to the adequacy of shipping facilities, adequacy of the types of buildings available for lease or rent, and distances from factory to market and attendant shipping costs.

The factory which can be located in the central part of its total market area usually has an ideal location. This holds true for most manufacturers of consumer and industrial goods. Nearness to market usually takes precedence over nearness to raw materials. Two notable exceptions are to be observed.

When the manufacturing process involves (1) much waste in the processing of the product, or (2) dealing with perishable raw materials, the factory should be located close to its raw materials. An obvious example of the first situation is a saw mill which makes finished lumber from giant logs. Shipping the logs to a mill near the final market would be wasteful and expensive. An example of the second situation is the processing of fresh fruit. Peach- and strawberry-canning factories must be near the lands where the fruit is harvested. Excessive spoilage and/or expense would result from long-distance hauling.

The speed of modern transportation systems has expanded many markets in ways not thought possible only a few short years ago. Planeloads of fresh tulips and other flowers are flown from Holland to many cities around the world. Fresh fruit from Mexico is available in Toronto as well as other markets without the benefit of freezing facilities. These instances, however, are the exception and not the rule. When considering utility versus uniqueness in consumer products, it is good to know that many people desire and can afford the products of uniqueness. The final test of any business economy, however, is the total goods and services which can be economically produced for its citizens. The average standard of living of any nation still depends on products of utility and their economical production. This truth is not intended to discourage innovations in manufacturing, distribution, and selling. It merely indicates that the greatest share of our total production is done with the objective of economical production a first consideration. The rules of experience still prevail.

LOCATION FACTORS FOR WHOLESALING

Wholesalers also are restricted by zoning laws in most cities. The objective is to be located as close to most customers as possible in a building which is suited to the type of operation planned. Good transportation facilities by rail or truck are essential for efficient reception of inventories. Local wholesalers make most deliveries by truck. When customers regularly visit the wholesaler, rather than phone in their orders, it is important that the customer area be attractive and efficient. This is not the normal situation. Most customers telephone their orders and desire speedy delivery. Emphasis should accordingly be placed on a location which makes this possible.

LOCATION FACTORS FOR SERVICE FIRMS

Locations for service firms are almost as varied as the types of firms involved. The beauty shop, the shoe repair shop, the TV repair shop, do not need high-rent locations. They have become largely residential-area types of businesses. Closeness to a shopping centre is usually considered ideal. Yet there are differences, even among these service shops. Beauty shops must be attractive. Shoe-repair shops have a character all their own, which is not necessarily attractiveness. Shopping-centre promoters do not encourage this type of shop, and they are usually found in an adjacent lower-rent area. The TV repair shop is seldom seen by the customers. The chief location problem is a suitable area for doing their work. By advertising, they compensate for avoiding the high-rent districts.

Travel agencies depend upon drop-in traffic and therefore require locations on busy streets. Firms selling theatre tickets may do all their business by phone or from an upstairs office.

The most important location factor for all service firms is to know the type of customer to whom they plan to appeal. With this knowledge, choose a location and site which best fit that customer group.

QUESTIONS FOR CLASS DISCUSSION

Q9-1 What is the difference between a good location and a good site?

Q9-2 In seeking a good general location, why should the nature of the industries in the community be studied?

Q9-3 What should be your attitude toward competition when seeking a good location for your business?

Q9-4 What are the two most important justifications for establishing a new firm in an exisiting line of business?

Q9-5 Where can information be found about a community's population growth, its industry, and its community facilities?

Q9-6 Why should the planner of a new small firm consider the nature of the other stores which surround the site being considered?

Q9-7 How should the traffic at a specific site be analyzed?

Q9-8 When should a factory be close to its source of raw materials rather than its markets?

Q9-9 Why is it important to know the buying habits of potential customers when choosing a site?

Q9-10 Should a dry-cleaning business be located in a high-rent district? Why?

PROBLEMS AND QUESTIONS FOR WRITTEN ASSIGNMENT

P9-1 On the basis of what you have learned about location, identify a suggested location in your neighbourhood for a dry-cleaning business, a grocery store, and a bank. Defend your suggestions.

P9-2 Can you point out a service station which is not located on any main road but is in a residential neighbourhood? Is this an exception to general location rules? Explain.

P9-3 From a location standpoint, where would you rent space for a suburban men's clothing store?

P9-4 Can you think of any firms which suffer from being on the wrong side of the street?

P9-5 Where would you locate a firm which converts copper ore into copper bars? Why?

CONTINUING PROBLEM: *THE SUCCESS HARDWARE STORE*

Part 9. Evaluating the Location

Assignment for Part 9

a List all the factors you have become familiar with which make for good locations. Include any regional, county, or city facts which have caused you to choose Edmonton, Alberta as the location for the firm. Answers can be real or hypothetical but should demonstrate your familiarity with what is important in this matter.

b List any site factors which appear important to you generally and which may apply to the site under consideration for this firm.

REFERENCES FOR FURTHER READING

Archer, Maurice, *An Introduction to Canadian Business,* 3d ed., McGraw-Hill Ryerson Ltd., Toronto, 1978, chap. 24.

Davidson, William R., and Alton F. Doody, *Retailing Management,* 3d ed., The Ronald Press Company, New York, 1966, chaps. 5, 6.

Gist, Ronald R., *Retailing,* John Wiley & Sons, Inc., New York, 1968, chap. 8.

Hastings, Paul G., *Introduction to Business,* McGraw-Hill Book Company, New York, 1968, chap. 7.

Markin, Rom J., Jr., *Retailing Management,* Macmillan Publishing Co., Inc., New York, 1971, chap. 8.

Preshing, W.A., *Business Management in Canada,* Wiley Publishers of Canada Ltd., Toronto, 1974, chap. 20.

CHAPTER 10

Layout

Those things you say about layout surely do seem to make a lot of sense. Funny we never thought of some of them before. Our sales have increased since we tried out some of those principles.

The Late Learner

Layout, or physical arrangement of a business, is another subject with which small firm planners and operators must concern themselves in order to achieve maximum results. Guiding principles of layout will vary with the type of business. These principles or guidelines are different for retailers and for wholesalers, for manufacturers and for service firms. In all types of firms, however, the objectives are maximum efficiency and hence maximum profits. Key considerations in good layout are best discussed in terms of the general type of firm involved.

LAYOUT FOR THE RETAIL FIRM

Layout for retailers has been defined as "a selling machine." This definition, the best one the authors have heard, encompasses much of what experienced business owners include in their applications of good layout. Good layout does a great deal to maximize sales and is a vital part of the selling objective. Its basic objective is to do just that—maximize sales. How is this accomplished? The answer lies in observing and applying generally accepted rules of layout. Some of them are outlined and discussed briefly below.

Guidelines to Good Layout for Retailers

1 Customer Buying Habits Know the buying habits of your customers. We have already noted the location of the dessert counter in a cafeteria and the prescription counter in a drugstore. These locations represent applications of knowing customers' buying

Ideal layout for most drugstores suggests the prescription counter should be at the back of the store with attractive displays of convenience and impulse merchandise along the path to that counter.
Courtesy of Boots Drug Stores (Canada) Ltd.

habits. The hungry patrons of a cafeteria are awed by attractive displays of desserts as they enter the food line. They happily pick one quickly before even knowing what their main course will be. If they had first chosen their vegetables, main dish, and salad, they would likely have been much more reluctant to pick up that luscious dessert. Studies have shown a large decrease in dessert sales when that counter is at the end of the line rather than at its beginning.

Customers who enter a drugstore with prescriptions from their doctors in hand are not concerned with convenience in finding the prescription counter as much as they are with getting the medicine. The purchase will not be lost because they do not find the druggist immediately. If they have been in this particular store before, they know that prescriptions are filled at the back of the store. As they pass along attractive counters of merchandise en route to the prescription counter, they see many other kinds of products and effective displays. That is the key to layout. In making that trip through the store, customers are likely to make many impulse purchases. Impulse purchases are those which the customers never anticipated when they entered the store. Each such purchase is a credit to the application of this layout principle.

Cafeteria sales are increased when the dessert section is at the front of the line.

2 Merchandise Display Display merchandise attractively. The day when all merchandise in a store was kept in closed drawers, locked showcases, or generally out of sight is long past. Customers want to find attractive displays of most items they desire to purchase. Ready comparisons are desired: comparisons of price ranges, styles, designs, or alternative products. This is all part of providing customer satisfaction. Open displays are important.

3 Customer Service Provide good services for customers. They can include pleasant surroundings and courteous personnel in charge of opening credit accounts, competent and agreeable sales people, clean rest rooms, and convenient passageways and stairs.

4 Physical Surroundings Make maximum use of light, ventilation, and heat. This layout guide serves the comfort of customers and employees as well. Customer comfort aids merchandise selection. The public image of a firm can be a reflection of how well this layout principle is observed.

5 Organization of Merchandise Display associated lines of merchandise close together. That is, products which most people tend to purchase at one time should be located in close proximity on shelves, in showcases, or on counters. Toothpaste and shaving cream are the classic examples. Shirts, blouses, and skirts are usually displayed adjacently. Customers' convenience is violated when they must travel around the store to find items they consider to be in the same group. There can be no final or all-inclusive answer on this matter because different customers associate different products in groups. Knowing your customers is a great help in this regard.

Occasional use of an "obstacle course" display situated between aisles can increase sales.

6 Visual Spaciousness Provide a maximum view of the entire store for customers, employees, and managers. Customers prefer seeing other departments when shopping in one. Spaciousness in image is encouraged. Managers can do a better job of handling such problems as relieving crowded departments by reassigning sales persons and detecting emergencies. Employees have better morale when they are in closer contact with, or in view of, other employees.

7 Separation of Activities Separate selling from nonselling activities. Generally, this means that such activities as the wrapping and accounting departments, credit offices, repair services, cashiers, public telephones, and customer-service counters should be located near the rear of the store. The front of any store is considered prime selling space.

8 Customer Image Store fixtures should reflect the desired customer image. If the appeal is mainly to men, the fixtures should reflect the he-man, male atmosphere. For women, a more refined image with a feminine touch is appropriate. Colours and decorations are important here. This feature of layout may be frequently observed in sports shops and hair salons. When customers are equally divided between men and women, general attractiveness is foremost.

9 Utilization of Space Know the value of your space and place merchandise accordingly. The average small retail store is 30 to 50 feet wide and from 50 to 100 feet deep. It has several departments or displays several lines of merchandise for its customers. How should those departments be arranged? Three governing principles apply:

a Most new shoppers turn to the right when entering a store.

b Space in the front of the store will have more customer traffic than rear sections. Front space is, accordingly, more valuable for sales.

c The type of merchandise offered must be considered. Convenience goods, shopping goods, and specialty goods demand different answers because buying habits vary with goods desired (see Chapter 14). It follows that allocation of space among departments should reflect these facts.

In terms of traffic and potential sales, the average floor space can be divided into specific areas. Dividing the total space into nine major sections, as in the floor plans shown in Figures 10-1 and 10-2, we can attach priorities of value for first, second, third, etc., choices.

It will be noted that of the nine areas two are tied for second choice, two for third choice, and two for sixth choice. Only areas (1), (4), and (5) seem to be clear choices.

Figure 10-1
Space Values in a Typical Retail Store

Sixth	Fifth	Sixth
Fourth	Third	Second
Third	Second	First
Windows	Door	Windows

Whether the individual planner adopts this valuation in total or not, the important thing is to realize the general relationship of the different areas. There is no definite rule for assigning specific departments or merchandise to these areas. Some guidelines are available. They include the following:

1 Impulse merchandise and other convenience goods should be located in the front areas.

2 Shopping merchandise (demand goods) should be located at the rear or upstairs in the multistoried store.

3 Nonselling departments and service departments should be in the rear.

4 It usually does not pay to move a successful department to a less valuable space in order to give a losing department a morc valuable space.

5 Wide aisles for customer comfort are recommended, but creation of an occasional "obstacle course" by placing sale merchandise or other special items in an aisle may be good merchandising.

6 Make good use of available window space by placing attractive displays in them as well as on the selling floor.

Figure 10-2
Possible Department Locations for a Small Department Store Showing Space Values and Types of Consumer Goods Sold

Office Credit Department Public Telephones	Beauty Salon Rugs Drapes	Rest Rooms Will-call Layaways
Yard Goods Knitting Supplies Major Appliances China Cutlery Fine Jewelry	Swim Wear Resort Wear Children's Wear Lingerie Shoes	Men's Shop Suits Shoes Shirts Sports Ties
Better Dresses Teen's Dresses Budget Dresses	Sweaters Hosiery Ladies' Bags	Toiletries Cosmetics Jewelry Watches
Windows	Door	Windows

LAYOUT, MERCHANDISE DISPLAYS, AND SHOPLIFTING

We have seen that a vital part of good layout is to have merchandise readily available for customers to view and compare. Many marketing tests have established that sales of particular items are much larger when the item is on an open table or open rack. At the same time, all merchants are confronted with the ever-increasing problem of shoplifting, which has attained tremendous proportions throughout the country in recent years.

There are two phases of the shoplifting problem: stealing by employees and stealing by visitors in the store. Many millions of dollars are lost by businesses every year in each category. The problem of employee stealing demands closer control of employee activities on the premises. It is unfortunate that the necessary measures are imposed on the honest as well as the dishonest employees. Common sense dictates, however, that these procedures should be viewed in the same light as the commonsense procedures against airplane hijacking. Application to all is a necessary evil to protect the innocent. If personal inconvenience for the innocent can eliminate or reduce the crime, the result must be to the benefit of all. Fidelity bonds may be purchased which insure the firm against employee thefts.

Stealing by outsiders in the store is a different matter. Even the laws of some provinces make it very difficult to arrest shoplifters on the premises. Public images sometimes suffer, even when obviously guilty persons are prosecuted. Large expenses are incurred in maintaining security staffs within stores. Yet the crime goes on in untold millions. Large and small firms suffer in the same manner.

Firms which acquire a reputation for prosecuting all shoplifting cases will find that the problem is reduced. Law enforcement officials recommend prosecuting as a strong deterrent to shoplifting.

Training sales people to be alert to the problem is also helpful. When people in a store are immediately welcomed with a "May I help you?" shoplifting is discouraged.

Various devices have been introduced to cope with this problem. One is the placing of metallic tags inside clothing items. These tags turn on alarm systems at all exits unless removed by the sales person when the item is paid for or the charge slip is signed at the cash register. Other alarm systems can be provided which buzz upon disconnection of attaching cords when items are removed from open counters. The cords allow ample space and distance for complete inspection of the merchandise, but only the sales person is to remove them, with the alarm system deactivated.

One significant conclusion has been forced upon retail firms. Limits must be placed upon the customer access to some types of merchandise. Items of small bulk and relatively large value must be kept in transparent showcases or glass-doored shelves, which may be necessarily protected by lock and key. Such items as wristwatches, expensive costume jewelry, diamonds, costly cutlery, and even expensive gowns may fall in this category. Some department stores protect expensive sweaters or dishwarc in this manner. It is important that the new firm owner be aware of this problem and be prepared to cope with it, at least to keep it to a minimum. It is a sad commentary on our society that we must accept the reality of this serious problem. It is only to be hoped that improved morality may soon eliminate the problem or reduce it to a minimum. It is the honest consumers who pay the final bill for this outrageous situation.

LAYOUT FOR THE WHOLESALER

Layout considerations for a wholesaling firm are dominated by the objective of filling orders with speed and economy. This goal also emphasizes the speed and economy with which inventories are stacked in the warehouse. Emphasis must be placed on the labour costs expended in the process of storing the inventories and in filling the orders received. More than 60 percent of total operating costs of the average wholesaler consists of labour costs, and the ability to compete depends on efficiency in controlling labour costs.

Methods which can be of assistance to wholesalers include:

1 Keeping most often demanded merchandise easily accessible.

2 Using conveyors, material-handling equipment, and overhead cranes wherever feasible.

3 Using the principle of gravity when possible. These devices help speed order filling and inventory stocking.

Wholesalers handle many different lines of merchandise. Hence, no one rule for inventory arrangement can be suggested. Common to all wholesalers, however, is the desirability of knowing the most frequently ordered items so that application of the suggested devices may be possible.

LAYOUT FOR THE FACTORY

Factories which produce only one product, or one product at a time, have the advantage of being able to use a *continuous-production layout*—usually called a *product layout*. All operations follow the same path through the manufacturing process. Materials are received where needed in the assembly or manufacturing process, all machines are placed at the point where needed without unnecessary moving of materials or products in process, and all product comes from the assembly line at one point.

The ideal product layout calls for having raw materials delivered at the factory door nearest to where the materials go into the assembly or manufacturing line, having a continuous conveyor belt move the product in process from one station to another nearby, having any required subassemblies delivered close to the point of need, and having all finished products arrive on the same conveyor belt, even packaged and ready for delivery.

The obvious goal of all factory layout is to minimize the unproductive movement of products and materials. Possibilities for doing this are much greater in continuous-production, or product, layouts.

Factories which produce different kinds of products, or even produce products to individual orders, cannot use this arrangement for their machines and operations because the routes through the manufacturing process are different for each product manufactured. They use a *process layout*—also known as *intermittent manufacturing layout.*

Foundries and job-order printing firms are examples of factories which produce many different products, each of which may require a special sequence of machines or other operations in the process of being completed. Each product usually follows a different path through the manufacturing process. The big problem in layout here is to minimize the movement of work in process which does not add value to the final product. Having people move half-finished products in wheelbarrows from one machine to another some distance away adds nothing to the value of the finished product. Yet, much movement is often necessary to complete the orders. Another problem is that some machines may be kept busy all the time, and others are in use only part of the time. Efficient layout therefore means having the most frequently used machines in proper quantity handy for all orders.

Because of the differences in product and process layouts, costs for process layout manufacturing are usually higher than for most product layout manufacturing.

With the guiding rule of keeping unproductive movement of materials and work in process to a minimum, new firm planners should first study their production lines to see how closely they can keep them to the ideal. Keeping the production-control and production-planning personnel in close proximity to the factory production line can contribute to this overall objective.

LAYOUT FOR THE SERVICE FIRM

Service firms are so varied that little can be said of common factors shared. A barber or beautician needs an attractive shop with enough chairs to handle customers in good time, space for all the equipment used for hair treatment, and an attractive space for waiting customers and a receptionist. Many of these shops also maintain a stock of products for sale. Repair shops for major appliances are seldom seen by their customers. Customers phone the TV repair shop or the washing-machine repair shop. The machinist visits the home, does the work, and is paid. The only need is for an efficient workshop at his or her headquarters. A travel agency, if catering to transient trade, needs a well-located office with adequate counters, phone service, and comfortable places for customers to wait or to be interviewed. A firm selling only theater tickets may operate from a home telephone or a hired desk in a business office. Others may maintain offices on a popular street if catering to drop-in traffic. A cleaning establishment needs to have its equipment arranged like a product-line factory and room to receive its customers and return finished dry cleaning. Laundries generally follow the product line in processing their services. Most of their customers may be served via delivery trucks, but counters are also usually provided to receive customers and make deliveries.

The one common factor shared by all service firms is the importance of keeping their facilities consistent with the volume and type of service they are rendering.

QUESTIONS FOR CLASS DISCUSSION

Q10-1 Why is the prescription counter in a drugstore usually found at the rear of the store?

Q10-2 Can you think of any practical reasons why grocery stores place the frozen goods close to the checkout stations?

Q10-3 How do displays of merchandise become important in layout?

Q10-4 Would you advocate open counter displays of wristwatches? If not, why not?

Q10-5 What do we mean by the relative value of space within a retail store?

Q10-6 Why shouldn't the nonselling activities be in the front of the store?

Q10-7 What are impulse goods? Where should they be located in a retail store?

Q10-8 Do you believe that window displays are an important part of total layout?

Q10-9 How would you combat the problem of shoplifting in your store?

Q10-10 What is the prime objective in layout for a wholesaler?

Q10-11 What is the difference between a product layout and a process layout?

Q10-12 "Factory layout seeks to minimize the unproductive movement of goods in process." What does this statement mean to you?

PROBLEMS AND QUESTIONS FOR WRITTEN ASSIGNMENT

P10-1 What are the motivations for impulse-item sales?

P10-2 Can layout encourage the sale of impulse items? How?

P10-3 Why are more and more firms selling cigarettes through machines rather than at the counter?

P10-4 In your buying habits, which of the following merchandise items are impulse purchases rather than shopping purchases: shirts, rugs, ice cream, aspirin, automobiles, sweaters, suits?

P10-5 Prepare a floor plan layout for a men's clothing store.

CONTINUING PROBLEM:
THE SUCCESS HARDWARE STORE

Part 10: Preparing a Layout

Assignment for Part 10

a List the various principles of layout which can contribute to greater efficiency of the firm.

b Prepare a simple floor-plan sketch of the store showing where major departments or activities will be located following the principles you have just listed.

REFERENCES FOR FURTHER READING

Archer, Maurice, *An Introduction to Canadian Business,* 3d ed., McGraw-Hill Ryerson Ltd., Toronto, 1978, chap. 20.

Davidson, William R., and Alton F. Doody, *Retailing Management,* 3d ed., The Ronald Press Company, New York, 1966, chap. 7.

Gist, Ronald R., *Retailing,* John Wiley & Sons, Inc., New York, 1968, chap. 9.

Preshing, W. A., *Business Management in Canada,* Wiley Publishers of Canada Ltd., Toronto, 1974, chap. 21.

CHAPTER 11

Choosing a Legal Form of Organization

I thought corporations were all huge firms. I couldn't tell by looking at a business whether it was a proprietorship, partnership, or corporation. I just assumed that if one person was running the place it was single proprietorship, and if two or more people were running it, the business was a partnership. Do you really mean my small store could be a corporation?

The Late Learner

New firm planners should do some serious thinking about the legal form chosen for the new firm. To the new student, this means determining what will be the status of the business in the eyes of the law. Very important consequences are at stake.

More than 99 percent of the more than 1 million businesses in Canada are organized legally as (1) single proprietorships, (2) partnerships, or (3) corporations. It is our intention here to evaluate the characteristics, advantages, and disadvantages of these three legal forms. Other legal forms, such as joint ventures or investment trusts, are rarely used and not considered pertinent to our purposes here.

When confronted with the choice of a single proprietorship, a partnership, or a corporation, too many students and small firm planners and operators mistakenly believe that the corporation is intended only for very large firms. All three of these legal forms are available to small firms. Different factors may affect the choice in a particular case. In all cases, all three forms should be looked at carefully. Some of the items which will affect the decision include plans for expansion, product or service being sold, needs for raising capital now and in subsequent years, liability characteristics of the planned firm, the proprietor's available investment funds, need for continued life of the firm, alternatives for bringing desired people into the firm, and legal requirements of the particular locality.

We can note that of the total number of business firms in Canada, approximately 60 percent are proprietorships which do about 30 percent of the total sales volume; approximately 12 percent are partnerships doing about 10 percent of the total sales volume; and approximately 30 percent are corporations doing more than 60 percent of the total sales volume in the country. It is this type of statistics which encourages the erroneous belief that the proprietorship is the almost exclusive choice of legal form for small firms. The data do not reveal to the casual observer the reasons why the larger firms have chosen the corporate form. Business prudence includes knowledge in this regard.

THE SINGLE PROPRIETORSHIP

By definition, a single proprietorship is a business owned and operated by one person. The owner and the business are synonymous in the eyes of the law. All assets in the firm are owned by the proprietor, subject only to the liabilities incurred in its establishment and operation. The proprietor is solely responsible for its debts, incurs any losses, assumes all its risks, provides all its capital, and provides its total management. The only requirement for its establishment is that the owner obtain any licenses required in the municipality and start operations.

This simplicity in establishment has probably accounted for the popularity of this legal form of operation. This choice may represent neglect of other factors which would indicate another legal form.

Advantages of the Single Proprietorship

The literature on business asserts that the proprietorship form has several advantages, such as:

1 Simplicity of organization
2 Owner's freedom to make all decisions
3 Owner's enjoyment of all profits
4 Minimum legal restrictions
5 Ease of discontinuance
6 Tax advantages

These alleged advantages should be carefully reviewed to distinguish between mere characteristics and true management advantages. Some thoughts in this regard are as follows:

1 Simplicity of Organization If the new firm owners choose a legal form of organization only because of its simplicity, they probably demonstrate that they lack overall business competence and a thorough knowledge of legal forms and that they are the type of owners who always look for the easiest way to make decisions. Simplicity of organization is truly a characteristic of the proprietorship, but no inherent management advantages are to be noted because of this simplicity.

2 and 3 Owner's Freedom to Make All Decisions and Enjoy All Profits To allege that one advantage of the proprietorship is that the owner is free to make all the decisions and to receive all the profits completely ignores the facts of a close corporation (explained later in this chapter). If these same business people have their businesses incorporated for 100 shares of common stock and they decide to give 1 share to their spouses, 1 share to a son or daughter, and retain 98 shares in their name. Who then makes all the decisions? Who then receives all the profits? Surely the owner has the same authority as if the firm were a proprietorship. So again, these alleged advantages become merely nonexclusive characteristics of a proprietorship.

4 Minimum Legal Restrictions This factor, in the sense of fewer reports to be filed with government agencies, no paid-up capital taxes to be paid, and no charter restrictions on operations, can be an advantage from the standpoint of time and expenses involved. Whether or not this advantage would dominate in the final selection remains to be seen after the total business scene has been reviewed.

5 Ease of Discontinuance This is truly a characteristic of the proprietorship. To discontinue a proprietorship means essentially closing the front door. When we recognize, however, that sound business firms are not organized with thought of discontinuing them, we must question whether this is truly an advantage of this particular form. Our concern is not the establishment of the Mom and Pop type of firms but solid business firms which may start small but have the potential for growth, good profits, and a good future for the owner. These objectives should be in mind as we choose our legal form of organization.

6 Tax Advantages Alleging tax advantages as a bonus of the proprietorship form of legal organization defies the fact that as taxable income increases, the rate on individual income is higher than on corporate taxable income or total taxes on the divided income of a partnership. Total federal and provincial income taxes are a prime consideration in the choice of any legal form. The government accepts business people to practise tax avoidance rather than tax evasion, and the choice of a legal form may be of assistance in this regard. Examples of various taxable income levels and the applicable income taxes for the different legal forms of organization are presented in a later section of this chapter.

Disadvantages of the Single Proprietorship
The literature also describes the various disadvantages of the proprietorship as follows:

1 Owner's possible lack of ability and experience
2 Limited opportunity for employees
3 Difficulty in raising capital
4 Limited life of the firm
5 Unlimited liability of proprietor

A brief evaluation of these items is the following:

1 The Owner's Lack of Ability and Experience The owner may truly lack these qualifications. It is to guard against this possibility that preownership experience is recommended for those planning to own their own firms. Sound college courses in management are available to college students. Participation in management development courses can be tremendously helpful. Those without formal study in management can learn much from working for other firms in the same line of business. Testing one's own competence through studies of good business texts should be a prelude to investing in and opening a new firm. Only when owners feel that they know a great deal about the particular firm they propose should they proceed. It should be pointed out, however, that this feature of the owner's capability is not inherent in the legal form of organization chosen. Lack of ability and experience can ruin a partnership or a corporation just as easily as it can a proprietorship.

2 Limited Opportunity for Employees This point has been overdone as a disadvantage of the proprietorship. Aggressive, capable employees may indeed desire more rewards faster than the firm can provide them. You can indeed promote some people only so far, and the best thing you can do for them is to promote them out the front door. But let us realize that if the same firm is a partnership or a small firm corporation, the employees' environment, potential rewards, and promotions are the same. Small firms generally face the problem of keeping good employees. All large firms face this problem. Also, probably a refreshing thought in this regard is that small firms have not fully utilized profit sharing, bonuses, or a share in the ownership of the firm in order to keep key people on the payroll. Possibilities of share ownership in a corporation add to these benefits. Good employees are a firm's most valuable asset. The problem of obtaining and keeping them is not solved merely through the choice of a legal form. Personnel policies are discussed in Chapter 20.

3 Difficulty in Raising Capital This can be a problem. On the average, two people have more capital than one. It follows that, on the average, two people would have more to invest in providing the capital needs of a new small business. Not all firms have this problem, however. If it does exist and the planner does not wish to share ownership of the firm, this would restrict the alternatives in raising adequate capital. When the planner has seriously faced the problem of building a sound financial structure for the firm, as we did in Chapters 6 and 7, its investment needs can be compared with available funds and a decision can be made. If the assets are adequate, the planner will have no disadvantage due merely to the difficulty in raising capital.

4 Limited Life of the Firm Discussions of this feature of legal forms are usually restricted to the partnership form of organization, but it also applies to proprietorships. What is involved is the matter of legal discontinuance of the firm. Untimely, unanticipated, or unplanned removal of the proprietor from operation of the business may have ramifications for creditors of the firm. Restrictions on credit granted may be founded in this matter of limited life. An owner's record for stability, honesty, and capability can largely overcome this practical problem. When these are unknown, as in the case of a new firm, it may have some application.

5 Unlimited Liability By far the greatest disadvantage of the proprietorship is its inescapable feature of *unlimited liability.* This disadvantage is one which applies directly to the owners. It means that, even though they believe that they have invested only part of their total capital in the business, they are liable to the full extent of their total assets for the liabilities of the firm. A damaging lawsuit lost, a judgment for injuries suffered by a customer on the premises, or a serious accident involving injuries to outside persons are some of the things which can create liabilities far beyond anything anticipated when the firm was planned. It is this feature of the proprietorship which causes many owners, when aware of unlimited liability, to put their homes in their spouses' names in order to keep the home from being available to pay such claims. The present divorce rate in our country hardly makes this a recommended procedure in all cases. The owner's savings accounts, investments, and any other assets are liable in these cases. As we noted earlier, in the proprietorship legal form, the owner and the business are synonymous, and all assets, not just those the owner thinks are invested in the firm, are liable to pay its debts. Insurance protection can be provided, of course, and this matter will be discussed in a later chapter.

THE PARTNERSHIP

A partnership is usually defined as an association of two or more persons to carry on as co-owners of a business for profit. Partnerships are based upon a partnership agreement. The partnership agreement should always be reduced to writing, even though this is not a legal requirement. It should cover all areas of possible disagreement among the partners. It should define the authority and the rights and duties of each partner, and the limits to such authority. It should include an agreement on how profits and losses are to be divided. Their treatment need not be the same. In the absence of an agreement to the contrary, profits and losses are divided equally among all partners. Partners may make special arrangements to pay members of the firm for services rendered, interest on capital investment, time spent, or advance drawings before the balance of profits is to be divided in an agreed ratio.

Many successful partnership firms have been dissolved because of serious disagreements between original partners which were not anticipated in the partnership agreement. Thoroughness in this matter cannot be overemphasized.

Advantages of the Partnership

The following advantages of the partnership form of organization are usually cited in business books:

1. Ease of organization
2. Combined talents, judgment, and skills
3. Larger capital available to the firm
4. Maximization of personal interest in the firm
5. Definite legal status of the firm
6. Tax advantages

With the benefit of our previous discussion of the proprietorship, we can quickly evaluate these alleged advantages. Ease of organization should not be a management consideration in starting a new firm. Greater financial potential is true only in average terms; personal interest of partners should be no greater than if each had shares in a corporate form of organization; and definite legal status can be important to creditors. In most income brackets, a group of partners would pay less total income taxes than the owner(s) would under either of the other chief legal forms.

Advantages of potential substance, then, as compared with the proprietorship, seem to be possibly greater capital available, generally less income tax on the same net profits, and a positive legal status. As compared with the corporation, only the tax consideration would remain as a potential advantage.

Disadvantages of the Partnership

The partnership has some very real disadvantages, which can be serious to well-meaning people who start their firms in good faith. Four disadvantages merit brief dicussion:

1 Unlimited liability
2 Limited life
3 Divided authority
4 Danger of disagreement

1 Unlimited Liability Just as this condition applied to the proprietorship, it is even more serious in the partnership. Not only is a partner liable for debts he or she contracts for the firm, but a partner is also responsible to the full extent of his or her resources for debts contracted by the other partners.

2 Limited Life Any change whatsoever in the list of general partners automatically ends the life of the existing partnership, and a new legal entity must be created by the remaining partners. Admission of a new partner, death of an existing partner, and withdrawal of any general partner are cases in point. Restatement of all assets and readmission of all liabilities and individual capital accounts are part of the process. This is also known as *mandatory dissolution.*

3 Divided Authority It is one thing for a good factory manager and a good sales person to combine their talents in a partnership. Each can have clearly defined areas of operation. Other areas, however, such as policy for the total firm, financing plans, personnel management, and ideas on expansion, can create divided authority and delay decisions for the firm. Some activities always seem to provide possibilities of conflicting authority.

4 Danger of Disagreement The ever-present possibility of a disagreement between the partners can be extremely serious. Even though a very thorough partnership agreement is written, clauses are subject to various interpretations, some partners may willfully exceed clearly defined authority, and discontent can develop between the partners. Only honest and capable people of great mutual respect should engage in partnerships.

Types of Partners

Partnerships are usually either *general partnerships or limited partnerships.* A general partnership is one in which each partner carries the unlimited liability for the firm's debts. A limited partnership is one in which some partners may have their liability limited to the extent of their investment. A firm must have at least one general partner (active partner) who carries the unlimited liability obligation. Withdrawal of a limited partner does not dissolve the partnership as withdrawal of a general partner will do. Limited partnership agreements must usually be filed with a government official. Without notice as to the acceptance of a limited partner, all partners are considered to be general.

There are many other special types of partners which new firm planners may wish to investigate. *Secret* partners are those who play an active role in the business but are not identified to the public as partners. *Silent* partners are those who are not active in operations but share in the profits. *Dormant* partners are those not active and not known to the public. An *ostensible* partner is one who lends his name and credit to the firm, but who has no financial interest in the business. Special circumstances may make it necessary to choose these types of partners, but their use is not normally recommended. It must be remembered that while these special classes of partners differ in their relationship to one another, they are all equally liable to the public for partnership debts and liabilities. The limited partnership, on the other hand, enables many new firm planners to obtain capital which might otherwise not have been available. In most such cases which we have reviewed, the corporate form of organization would have served everyone's purpose in a superior manner.

THE CORPORATION

Just as the problems of size and need for acquiring more capital motivated the creation of the partnership rather than the proprietorship, they also motivated the next step to the modern corporation as a legal form of organization. The second step was also made necessary by the problems of unlimited liability and limited life which characterized the partnership. The need of a developing industrial world was for a legal form of organization which would provide limited liability for owners and perpetual life for the business firm. Accordingly, in 1819 in the famous Dartmouth College case, Justice John Marshall gave the first legal recognition to a new type of business organization, which was to become known as the corporation. He defined it as "an artificial being, invisible, intangible, and existing only in contemplation of law." Its ownership would be divided into shares.

Though the corporate form of organization was originated in this background, it was never contemplated to be used only by giant firms. Its advantages and disadvantages have always been equally available to small firms as well.

HOW TO ORGANIZE A CORPORATION

In Canada, there are 11 general Companies Acts, one for incorporation under *federal* law and one each for incorporation under *provincial* law. A federal company incorporated under the Canada Business Corporations Act may carry on its business in all provinces as of right; no license is required for a federal company in Ontario, Quebec, and New Brunswick, although the other provinces impose a registration requirement. The Companies Acts of the provinces vary according to history and local requirements, however, in the main they are comparable to the general legislation under which federal companies are incorporated. If a provincially incorporated company wishes to conduct business in other provinces, as an "extra-provincial" company it will have to register (obtain a license) in those provinces. In the provinces of Ontario and Quebec, incorporation in either one allows the company to operate in the other. The decision regarding the jurisdiction (place) of incorporation will generally depend on factors such as the ease of incorporation, reporting requirements, fees payable, and the like. For small companies it is advisable to incorporate in the province where the company's business is conducted and where the principals normally reside.

The actual incorporation is done by filing *Articles of Incorporation* (Memorandum of Association) signed by the subscribers and paying the applicable fee. This sets out such information as the name of the company, the location of its head office, the objects for which the company is formed, provides details regarding directors, the authorized capital, and the shares which the subscribers to the

Memorandum agree to take. This will, then, become the charter of the company. Upon approval, the Registrar of Companies approves the application, issues a certificate of incorporation (in some provinces this may be called the granting of Letters Patent), and publishes a notice of incorporation in the provincial (or federal) "Gazette."

The selection and registration of a distinctive corporate name is an important step in the process of incorporation. The corporate name must convey the information that the firm has the protection of limited liability for its members. It is required that the words "Limited," Incorporated," or "Corporation," or the abbreviations "Ltd.," "Inc.," or "Corp." be the last word of the company's name. Names liable to conflict with another existing business organization, whether incorporated or not, are not acceptable.

It is permissible for a company to have a bilingual name, i.e., a name in an English and a French form. The practice is to separate the English and French forms with a hyphen, as for example "XYZ OF CANADA LIMITED - XYZ DU CANADA LIMITÉE."

Total incorporation costs vary from $500 to $800 depending on location and the complexity of the situation. Although the use and counsel of a lawyer is generally advisable, a small businessman can actually do the incorporation himself and save several hundreds of dollars in legal fees. There are publications available in most bookstores providing step-by-step instructions and guidance regarding the procedures involved.

TYPES OF CORPORATIONS' SHARES

The authorized capital of a corporation is divided into shares with par value or without par value or both, and may consist of shares of more than one class (type).

Most small firms have only one class of shares called *common shares.* If the corporation is federally incorporated, these must be without nominal or par value. There are other classes of shares which have special preferences, rights, conditions, and restrictions attached thereto. *Preference shares* have a priority over other classes of shares as to the payment of dividends. Stated preference share dividends — such as 8 percent preference — must receive its dividends before any dividends may be declared on the common shares. *Cumulative preference* means that the preference share must receive its dividends for any years in which no dividends were paid before the common may receive dividends. *Participating preference* means that the preference shares must share in any further dividends after the common has received a specified maximum dividend. *Redeemable* means that the corporation may purchase or redeem the shares upon the demand of the corporation, or that the corporation is required to purchase or redeem such shares at a specified time or upon the demand of a shareholder. Holders of *convertible shares* have the privilege of converting their shares, under specified conditions, into another class of shares.

ADVANTAGES OF THE CORPORATION

After discussing the operation of the other forms of organization, we can find little to argue with in the claimed advantages of the corporation. These are:

1 Limited liability to shareholders
2 Perpetual life
3 Ease of transferring ownership
4 Ease of expansion
5 Applicability to all sizes of firms

1 Limited Liability to Shareholders Rather than risk their entire assets to the debts of the business, the new firm owners or investors buy shares at a given price, and this investment is the total liability to which they can be subjected. Only those assets which a small firm planner turns over to the firm in exchange for shares become corporate property. Total corporate liability is the assets listed on its balance sheet. No longer need the owners of a small corporation fear the unexpected judgment against them as a threat to their other assets.

2 Perpetual Life If all the shareholders of a given corporation died on the same day, the business would go on as a legal entity. Shares would pass to the heirs of the original owners and they would inherit a going concern.

3 Ease of Transferring Ownership Any shareholders can sell their shares when they want to. Formal transfer of share certificate titles is normally handled by a fiduciary agent, usually a trust company, that will issue a new certificate in the name of the new owner of the shares. Operations of the company are not affected by this transfer.

4 Ease of Expansion of the Company Although additional share sale is not the only way to raise capital for expansion, it is usually easier to sell additional shares when expansion is contemplated. Many corporations, large and small, will receive permission from the appropriate authorities to sell more shares than originally planned for sale. The balance is held as "authorized but not issued" shares. It should appear on the balance sheet in the net worth section for informational purposes. If all authorized shares have been sold, a corporation may request permission to sell additional shares when an expansion is contemplated.

5 Applicability to Both Large and Small Firms Truly an advantage of the corporate legal form is its versatility. Regulations and charter requirements are the same for small or large corporations.

Other advantages often claimed for the corporation, such as that it permits employee profit sharing and encourages efficiency in management, must be termed as possible but not exclusive characteristics. Profit sharing is possible other than through shares in any legal form of organization. Efficiency in management is not guaranteed to any firm because of its legal form. This is the responsibility of management in all cases.

DISADVANTAGES OF THE CORPORATION

The chief disadvantages are:

1 Government regulation
2 Expense of organization
3 Capital tax

1 Government Regulation All good things demand some sacrifice. In the case of the corporation, the chief sacrifice is the necessary acceptance of government regulation. This begins with the necessity of obtaining a charter from the federal government or from the home province of the corporation. For small firms operating in only one province, it is recommended that the charter be obtained in that province.

2 Expense of Organization There is an expense in organizing a corporation. The use of an attorney is to be recommended when applying for a charter. Total expenses for this process range from $600 to $1,000 in most cases. Requirements for the charter include specifying the business activity in which the firm will engage, types of shares it desires to issue, and quantities of each to be authorized.

3 Capital Tax The province in which the firm is incorporated may levy an annual capital share tax on paid-up capital. The activities of the corporation will be restricted to those specified in the charter. For instance, a small firm authorized to engage in the men's clothing business cannot open a grocery store unless the terms of the charter are broad enough and/or so specify. The sometimes cited disadvantage of impersonal management of a corporation need not apply to small firms using the advantages of the corporate form of legal organization.

How, then, will the new planners decide upon their legal form of organization? As previously mentioned, they will consider the importance of unlimited liability, the protections available through public liability insurance, the expansion plans, the nature of the product, dangers inherent in the service or product, and the relative incidence of risks in normal operations which might provoke lawsuits and judgments against them. Through the potential of preference shares, a corporation can attract investors who prefer dividends to increased market price. Preference shares do not normally carry voting power, and the planner is able to keep control of the company by retaining 51 percent of the voting common shares. It is the authors' view that far too many small firms have neglected the use of the corporate form. Its protections and potentials should be carefully considered by any new firms which plan to grow large and profitable.

INCOME TAXES AND LEGAL FORMS OF ORGANIZATION

Students have often heard that tax considerations play an important part in most business decisions. The choice of a legal form of organization can be one of those decisions with significant tax consequences. It is never too early for college students to get an idea of the taxes to which they will be subjected as business owners or as salary earners.

There are three levels of taxation in Canada — federal, provincial, and municipal. The federal government levies both direct and indirect taxes, the most important of which are the corporate and personal income taxes and manufacturers' sales tax (currently at 9%). The provincial governments levy direct taxes, such as income tax, retail sales tax, special taxes on specific primary industries (mining, logging), and in some provinces, paid-up capital taxes. Municipalities function under the guidance of provincial legislation and impose direct taxes on real estate, water consumption, and places of business. Income taxes imposed by the provinces are collected by the federal government except in the cases of corporate taxes imposed by the provinces of Quebec and Ontario and personal income tax imposed by Quebec.

Because provincial and local taxes vary, we can concentrate here only on federal income taxes currently in effect.

Generally speaking, all companies resident in Canada are liable to federal income tax. The tax is applied upon income received or receivable during the taxation year from all sources inside or outside of Canada, less certain deductions permitted by the Income Tax Act.

There is no one form of legal organization which claims the best advantage in all instances. The applicable federal income tax is affected by the amount, the distribution, and the source of net taxable income involved in any business. Income tax rates for proprietorships and partnerships are progressive — the higher the income bracket, the higher the tax rate. These rates vary for the individual owners from 0 percent at $2,000 of net taxable income to 34 percent at $100,000 of such income. Of course, provincial taxes are additional (see Tables 11-1, 11-2, and 11-3). For corporations the Federal Income Tax Act contains a number of special income tax rate adjustments which apply to special types of income. The two most significant ones are the Small Business Incentive and Manufacturing and Processing Deduction.

Canadian controlled private corporations enjoy a 21 percentage point tax rate reduction from the top basic rate of 46 percent on active business income of up to $150,000 annually to a cumulative total of $750,000. This latter is defined as the total amount of the corporation's Canadian before tax business earnings accumulated after 1971, less four-thirds of any taxable dividends paid out since 1971. Any income in excess of the small business limits is taxed at the top corporate rate (46%). When planning the amount and timing of salaries, bonuses, hirings of additional staff, and other reasonable expenses which may be used, within reasonable limits, to reduce business income, particular attention should be given to eligibility for the Small Business Incentive. Similar to the federal incentive, some provinces also have a special, lower, small business tax rate applicable to small business income.

All corporations resident in Canada are entitled to a reduced rate of tax on their profits derived from manufacturing and processing. This reduction amounts to 5 percent for income eligible for the Small Business Incentive rate and 6 percent for other corporate income. There are complex rules and calculations required to determine the amount of the manufacturing and processing profits, as compared to profits arising from other corporate activities such as selling and distribution.

Let us clearly understand that we are talking about tax rates on net taxable income and what that term means. Net taxable income is the remaining income after all legitimate deductions have been taken. Charitable, educational, and dependent deductions, for example, are subtracted from gross income earned to arrive at net taxable income.

There is one very important difference between legal forms of organization in computing the taxable income of the firm. In proprietorships and partnerships, any withdrawals of cash by the owners during the year are considered as withdrawals of capital for tax purposes, even though the owners may consider them as regular salaries for themselves. In closing the books at the end of the year, such amounts are charged to their capital account balances and may not be recorded as operating expenses of the business. Proprietors and partners pay income taxes on the total profit shown on the income statement irrespective of any withdrawals made during the year. It will be recognized from our definition of proprietorships and partnerships that they are not taxable units at law but are part of the owners' personal identities as taxpayers. It is the individual in a proprietorship and the partners in a partnerhip who pay the taxes—not the firm.

TABLE 11-1
NET TAXABLE INCOME LEVELS NECESSARY TO REACH CERTAIN TAX RATE BRACKETS FOR FEDERAL AND ONTARIO INCOME TAXES*

FOR SINGLE PROPRIETORS FILING INDIVIDUAL RETURNS			PARTNERSHIPS	CORPORATIONS
	FEDERAL	COMBINED FED. & PROV.		
1,000	0%	0%	The income levels remain the same, but each partner pays income tax only on his/her share of the firm's profits as determined by the profit-and-loss sharing ratio.	Income eligible for the small business incentive and the manufacturing and processing deduction: 20%
2,000	0%	0%		
4,000	7%	14%		
6,000	11%	18%		
8,000	13%	21%		
10,000	15%	23%		Income eligible for the small business incentive only: 25%
16,000	18%	27%		
20,000	20%	29%		
26,000	23%	34%		Income not eligible for the small business incentive but eligible for the manufacturing and processing deduction: 43%
32,000	24%	35%		
40,000	26%	38%		
50,000	29%	41%		
70,000	31%	45%		
100,000	34%	49%		Income not eligible for the small business incentive nor for the manufacturing and processing deduction: 49%

*Source: *Official 1978 Tax Guide*

This is quite different from the corporation. By definition, the corporation is an artificial being (person) at law. It is, therefore, recognized as a separate unit for tax purposes. Small firm owners who operate as corporations can charge reasonable salaries to the

TABLE 11-2
SAMPLES OF TOTAL INCOME TAXES CURRENTLY (1978) PAID ON INCOME BY DIFFERENT LEGAL FORMS OF ORGANIZATION IN ONTARIO

NET TAXABLE INCOME	SINGLE PROPRIETOR	TWO-PERSON PARTNERSHIP	CORPORATIONS (1)	(2)	(3)
$16,000	$ 4,298	$ 3,316	$ 3,200	$ 4,000	$ 7,840
32,000	11,135	8,596	6,400	8,000	15,680
50,000	19,741	15,820	10,000	12,500	24,500

(1) Income eligible for the small business incentive and for the manufacturing and processing deduction.

(2) Income not eligible for the manufacturing and processing deduction but eligible for the small business incentive.

(3) Income not eligible for the small business incentive and not eligible for the manufacturing and processing deduction.

business, and these become operating expenses of the firm. Such salaries are accordingly deducted before arriving at net taxable income for the corporation. It is the remaining income which is taxed at the various corporate rates, as explained earlier. The owner of the small corporation then files a separate individual tax return and pays individual rates on the salary withdrawn and charged to the corporation.

It is this situation which gives rise to the much quoted and often misunderstood "double taxation" which is attributed to corporations. The owners pay personal income taxes on their salaries, which is a deductible operating expense to the corporation. They also pay individual income tax rates on any dividends declared on the stock of the corporation, which they own. Dividends paid by a corporation are not a deductible expense to the corporation, but are considered a distribution of remaining profits.

A sole proprietor is not permitted to deduct salaries paid to a spouse and where the spouse of one of the partners in a partnership is paid a

TABLE 11-3
SAMPLES OF TOTAL INCOME TAXES CURRENTLY (1978) PAID ON INCOME OF $32,000 BY CORPORATIONS ELIGIBLE FOR SMALL BUSINESS INCENTIVE IN DIFFERENT PROVINCES

PROVINCE	TAXES PAID	
	(1)	(2)
Alberta	$6,720	$8,320
British Columbia	7,040	8,640
Manitoba	6,720	8,320
Newfoundland	7,040	8,640
New Brunswick	6,080	7,680
Nova Scotia	7,040	8,640
Prince Edward Island	6,400	8,000
Saskatchewan	6,720	8,320
Ontario	6,400	8,000
Quebec	7,040	8,640
Northwest Territories	6,400	8,000

(1) Income eligible for reduced rate of tax on manufacturing and processing profits.

(2) Regular rate of tax on profits.

salary, that partner is not allowed to claim the salary expense of the spouse which relates to his or her proportionate share of the partnership expenses, therefore a legitimate business expense may be lost. On the other hand, a spouse may be employed by the corporation and paid a reasonable salary. This provides income splitting as well as making the spouse eligible for benefits under the Canada Pension Plan and any corporate benefit plans which may be instituted.

A close study of Tables 11-1, 11-2, and 11-3 will reveal valuable information for decision making by new small firm owners. For example, they may minimize total income taxes by drawing salaries close to the amount where individual income tax rates equal the corporate rate. They may find it desirable to qualify members of their families as salaried employees (which means they must render service to the company) or as bona fide partners, and share the profits equitably in a profit-and-loss sharing ratio. Thus, they will reduce total taxes on the firm. This is not a suggestion to risk fraudulent practices but merely to practice legal tax avoidance, which the government allows all citizens to do. Students are often amazed to discover the rates of federal income taxes paid by business firms. Therefore, it is good to realize the extent to which business firms do contribute to maintaining government and social services. New respect for parents' business ability can also result.

It should be noted that following the November 16, 1978, budget, in December 1978 draft income tax regulations were issued for planned changes in the small business tax incentive. The draft regulations scheduled for introduction in Parliament in 1979 deal primarily with problem areas related to the small business deduction: the incorporated professional, the incorporated employee, the related service corporation, and the investment corporation. The professional income of doctors, dentists, lawyers, and accountants will not qualify for the small business incentive. Also excluded are businesses whose principal purpose is the provision of managerial, administrative, and financial services. Concerning incorporated employees, the small business deduction will not be available to individuals who, in corporate form, provide essentially the same services as employees. Accordingly, the lower tax rate will only be afforded if less than two-thirds of the gross revenue is derived from one client. Investment companies holding bonds, shares, mortgages, and real property for purposes of earning income will qualify for the small business tax rate only if the corporation has more than five full-time employees who are not themselves or related to "specified shareholders" in the corporation, i.e., persons who hold 10 per cent or more of the voting shares.

QUESTIONS FOR CLASS DISCUSSION

Q11-1 Why would a small business proprietor ever consent to being a general partner and allow a partner to be a limited partner?

Q11-2 Evaluate "ease of discontinuance" as an advantage of the proprietorship form of legal organization.

Q11-3 Is the owner of a small corporation as "free to make all the decisions" as a single proprietor? Explain.

Q11-4 What are the legal requirements for starting a business as a proprietorship?

Q11-5 Is "limited opportunity for employees" an exclusive problem for small firms? How does this problem affect large firms?

Q11-6 What does "limited liability" really mean to holders of shares of corporation?

Q11-7 Can lack of ability and experience in small firm owners be corrected solely by their adopting another legal form of organization for the business?

Q11-8 What is a partnership agreement? What should it include?

Q11-9 At what level of net taxable income does a Canadian citizen reach the 30 percent combined income tax level? 35 percent? 40 percent?

Q11-10 What are the federal and provincial income tax rates on corporations eligible for small business deduction?
Q11-11 What factors in a business would suggest to you that limited liability should be in effect?
Q11-12 How could expansion plans affect the choice of a legal form of organization?

PROBLEMS AND QUESTIONS FOR WRITTEN ASSIGNMENT

P11-1 Your law or business library has samples of corporation charters and of partnership agreements. See if you can find one of each, and then list the important features of each.
P11-2 Write a short essay explaining why you agree or disagree with the fact that charters limit the business activities of a corporation.
P11-3 Explain in one paragraph the difference between tax avoidance and tax evasion.
P11-4 Write a brief essay on the practical implications of having a legal form of organization defined as an artificial being, invisible, intangible, and existing only in contemplation of law.

CONTINUING PROBLEM: *THE SUCCESS HARDWARE STORE*

Part 11. The Legal Form Chosen and Why

Assignment for Part 11

Prepare a written report explaining which legal form you have chosen for the firm. Which advantages or characteristics governed your choice? Or was it the disadvantages of another legal form which determined your selection?

REFERENCES FOR FURTHER READING

Archer, M., *An Introduction to Canadian Business*, 3rd ed., McGraw-Hill Ryerson Limited, Toronto, 1978, chaps. 2, 3.
Canada Corporations Law Reporter, CCH Canadian Limited, Toronto.

A loose leaf system of Statute Law, explanations and forms with respect to Federal and Provincial laws related to companies.

Hume, Frederick, R., *Anger's Digest of Canadian Law,* 20th ed., Canada Law Book Company Limited, Toronto. (In preparation, expected: 1979)

Iacobucci, F., M. L. Pilkington, and J.R.S. Prichard, *Canadian Business Corporations,* Canada Law Book Company Limited, Toronto, 1977.

Part 5

MERCHANDISING AND SALES

CHAPTER 12

Developing Sales Volume: Advertising and Promotion

I like that discussion about established *versus* created *demand. But I was always afraid of advertising. I tried once, and the increased sales didn't pay the cost of advertising. Maybe I used the wrong type.*

The Late Learner

THE NATURE OF DEMAND

The total demand for the goods or services offered by any small firm can be divided into (1) established demand and (2) promoted, or created, demand.

Established demand is that volume of sales which comes without conscious outside promotion by the firm. It assumes that the firm is established with some degree of attractiveness and relies basically on that fact to bring customers to the firm to buy products or services. Reliance is also placed on the fact that people see the store and think of it, perhaps, when products or services are considered. It is recognized that pedestrian traffic is already in the area and that some of the people will stop en route to other places. Distance from competitors will usually assist in bringing in established demand for most types of merchandise.

Promoted demand, by contrast, is the volume of sales which results from the firm's engaging in all types of activities to draw people to the firm. Promoted-demand customers, if pleased, can become established customers.

It is not true that small firms cannot operate profitably when they rely solely on established demand. However, those firms which supplement this established demand with promoted demand show much better sales volume and profits. Too many small firms restrict their operations by ignoring the possibilities of creating more sales. Case studies often show that the reasons are a lack of working capital to pay expenses of promotion, a belief that their market is inelastic, or a lack of knowledge of how to design a sales promotion program.

All the activities that go into the development of sales can be grouped under the title *sales promotion.* Sales promotion can use either *direct* or *indirect* methods. There are no guarantees that any one method will show a precise dollar return in sales, but the effectiveness of each can usually be measured with some degree of accuracy. Every small firm owner should think about using some of the following types of sales promotion:

Direct Promotion Methods

1 Advertising
2 Publicity
3 Displays
4 Special event sales
5 Manufacturers' aids
6 Personal selling

Indirect Promotion Methods

1 Public relations
2 Customer relations
3 Customer services
4 Product styling and packaging

Each of these promotion methods may be important in the individual case, and surely all of them are valuable ways of trying to expand business sales, in either the short run or the long run.

DIRECT SALES PROMOTION

Advertising

Running a business without advertising is like winking at a pretty girl in the dark — you know what you're doing but she doesn't.[1]

[1]Copyright, General Features Corporation. Reprinted with permission.

Attractive store fronts lure shoppers. Unattractive store fronts may drive potential customers away.

The president of one of the largest advertising companies in New York concluded a formal address on the billions of dollars spent on advertising each year in the United States by saying,

> *We know that half of these billions were wasted. The only trouble is we don't know which half.*

These two statements point out the importance of advertising and the size of the advertising bill in this country every year, and caution all business people to make their advertising effective. This caution is even more true for small firms which normally cannot absorb wasteful expenditures as well as larger firms.

At the same time it must be recognized that advertising is essential to almost every business. Large-scale advertising has made possible the benefits of mass production by creating a demand for the increased flow of products and services which mass production has made possible. Unit costs have been reduced in most cases because the economies of large-scale production have more than offset the cost of advertising.

Advertising can be defined as commercial messages to the public, designed to inform potential and established customers and to encourage sales for the advertiser. Advertising can be either *institutional* (designed to sell the firm name) or *direct action* (designed to sell the firm's product or services). An advertisement saying, "Our employees subscribed to the United Way 100 percent" is an example of institutional advertising. "Raincoats are on sale today at $66.95!" is an example of direct-action advertising. Most small firm advertising is of the direct-action type. Service firms may stress the services available from the firm, but this is still direct action to sell that service.

Types of Advertising Media Among the media generally used in advertising are:

1 Television
2 Radio
3 Newspapers
4 Magazines
5 Outdoor billboards
6 Specialty advertising (distribution of such items as matchpads, pencils, calendars, blotters, gummed labels, telephone pads, shopping bags)
7 Public transportation
8 Yellow pages
9 Direct mail
10 Other media (catalogs, samples, handout leaflets, etc.)

Small firms have a special problem in choosing the medium or type of advertising which is best for them. Big city *television* is not appropriate for most. Large city *newspapers* are too expensive for a firm which services only a small part of the city (although local newspapers can be used, as we will discuss later). It is worthy of note that some large newspapers have attempted to cope with this problem by having special small firm advertising sections where a dozen or more individual small firm ads can be displayed on a single page. More attractive advertising rates have made such advertising possible for more small firms. Effectiveness of such ads has been demonstrated in many cases. *Magazines* usually cover too much territory for a small local firm. Metropolitan *radio* advertising has adjusted somewhat to the problems of the small firm through multi-sponsored programs. In smaller cities and towns, the local radio station and newspaper may cover the market of the small firm well.

Billboards are most effective when used near the actual site of the small firms. Political campaign use of billboards has demonstrated their effectiveness, although their appeal in elections is usually to a much wider audience than that of the market of a particular small firm. Commercial billboards are quite expensive for individual firms, but they are often custom-made for sites which are available on less expensive terms to the particular firm, such as on another of the owner's buildings, or a friend's vacant lot.

Effectiveness of *specialty advertising* has been proved by many small firms. Its appropriateness will vary with the type of business.

It can take almost limitless forms. Pencils for children when school begins, calendars distributed in attractive shopping bags to neighbourhood homes, matchpads, telephone pads for firms taking telephone orders, blotters, ball-point pens with company name inscribed, and even gummed labels for various uses have all been effective in particular cases. All should prominently show the firm name, address, and phone number. Experience will demonstrate the effectiveness of any particular devices used.

Advertising in *public transportation* vehicles has become big business and can be effective for small firms if it is possible to coordinate the particular vehicles used and the firm's market. Local streetcars, buses, subways, and taxis are most popular.

Yellow-page advertising is recommended only when the firm is dealing in shopping goods or has a market where customers may be looking for a firm which is first contacted by telephone.

Despite its abuse over the years, *direct-mail advertising* remains the most effective advertising media for the great majority of small firms. It has the advantages of being selective in its coverage, less expensive, more flexible, adjustable to any size firm, and subject to measurement of its effectiveness. Because of past abuse, however, it must be done well to avoid being tossed into the nearest wastebasket.

Measuring Advertising Effectiveness Whenever possible, every advertising program undertaken should be checked for its effectiveness. Some of the ways the small firm can do this are:

1 Advertise one item in one ad only. Have no references to the item on the sales floor. Then count the calls and requests which result.

2 Place separate identifying marks in an ad which appears in two places. The reader is asked to bring the ad to the firm to obtain a special price or prize. See how many ads come in from each source.

3 Omit a regular advertising project for the intermittent periods and watch any change in sales.

4 Check sales results when a new advertisement is placed.

While the results of these and similiar advertising programs cannot be measured precisely, they can give some indication of effectiveness. Timing, products advertised, weather, and attractions offered, such as valuable coupons, will affect results. If no results are observable, it can be said that the program is not effective as direct action advertising. Even then it may have notified some people of the existence of the firm, and they may include it on future shopping journeys. It will thus have served an institutional purpose.

Are your judgments based on what you know or what you hear?

The Man Who Sold Hot Dogs

There was a man who lived by the side of the road and sold hot dogs.
He was hard of hearing so he had no radio.
He had trouble with his eyes so he read no newspapers.
But he sold good hot dogs.
He put up signs on the highway telling how good they were.
He stood on the side of the road and cried: "Buy a hot dog, Mister?"
And people bought and profits were good.
He increased his meat and bun orders.
He bought a bigger stove to take care of his trade.
He finally got his son home from college to help him out.
But then something happened.
His son said, "Father, haven't you been listening to the radio?
Haven't you been reading the newspapers?
There's a big depression.
The European situation is terrible.
The domestic situation is worse."
Whereupon the father thought, "Well, my son's been to college, he reads the papers and listens to the radio, and he ought to know."
So the father cut down on his meat and bun orders, took down his advertising signs, and no longer bothered to stand out on the highway to sell his hot dogs.
And his hot dog sales fell almost overnight.
"You're right, son," the father said to the boy.
"We certainly are in the middle of a great depression."

It should be obvious that the most important thing in designing an advertising program for any small firm is knowing your market — knowing where the present and potential customers you seek are located. The more owners know about their customers, the better they can devise ways to get their advertising messages to them. If many live in a condominium, for example, an ad in the local house paper may be most effective. If many live in private homes in a small town and take the local newspaper, newspaper advertising is recommended. These are only obvious examples. Time spent in studying the potential customer market will pay good dividends. Much of the wasted expenditures for advertising can be traced to careless preparation of the advertising, not knowing the market and hence misdirecting the advertising, and using the wrong media.

Once an advertising program has been decided upon, it must be consistent and continuous throughout the year. Special features or special events are appropriate for extra expenditures at certain times, but the basic program must be continuous, with both a long-run and a short-run objective in view at all times.

Publicity

Publicity has often been described as advertising which is not paid for. It includes such things as public news about the owner of the firm which tend to brighten the firm's image or make friends for the business. Notices of support given to community activities, awards won by employees for excellence in their industry, public citations for service rendered, election to office in community organizations, sponsorship of a team in the Pee Wee Hockey League, notices of new services or techniques available are examples. Such activities give the firm a reputation for being interested in and related to the community interests, for striving to give the latest and best services, for having competent people to serve its customers, or for just being a desirable place to do business. Their effect may often be more indirect than direct promotion, but, in any event, the potential of publicity should be exploited wherever possible.

Displays

Displays are an on-site method of sales promotion. Products which are not normally considered impulse items to most people are often sold through an effective display in the windows or on the sales floor. Displays enable the merchant to add changes, interest, and brightness to the standard layout, and when done well, can do much to increase sales. Even the occasional use of a display as an "obstacle course" item can be effective if not overdone. Windows can be used for sophisticated displays, such as in men's clothing stores, or for giving information about special sales or events, for example in grocery stores. The use of home-made window signs to advertise prices on Saturday or week-end specials has become a vital activity in many consumer goods firms.

Special Events

Using special events as direct sales promotion has become a well-established feature of most consumer goods businesses. They are also used by industrial goods firms, but less often. The firm's anniversary, Victoria Day, the firm president's birthday, the addition of a new service for customers, the start of the spring and fall seasons, etc., can all be used as occasions to promote sales. Making the most of such events may entail use of other direct promotion methods, such as advertising, but special events justify classification as a separate direct promotion method.

Manufacturer's Aids

Manufacturer's aids are any form of assistance provided by the manufacturer to small wholesalers and retailers for promoting sales. These aids may take the form of national advertising of the products involved, assignment of sales representatives to be in the particular store, provision of attractive window and floor displays, or actual contributions to an advertising program. Such products as home appliances, automobiles, television sets, and men's suits and shirts are often accompanied by such assistance from the manufacturer. Firms having franchises and/or distributorships are frequently aided by the parent firm in many of these matters.

Personal Selling

Personal selling means all those activities and characteristics of the individual sales person which make for successful sales. If it is recognized that all people are not good sales persons, we can appreciate that there are certain things which make good ones. Some of these are being able to discover potential customers, knowing methods of acquainting potential customers with available merchandise, and ability to close a sale. The type of skills required will vary with different types of firms and products.

Fundamental to all good personal selling is a thorough knowledge of the merchandise by the sales person. The advantages, various uses, and special qualities of the merchandise must be thoroughly known. Discerning customers look to the sales person for such knowledge. They know quickly if the sales person is competent or incompetent in this regard. If a sales person is only an order taker, this fact is soon obvious to such customers. If equipment or machinery is involved, the sales person must be able to demonstrate the product efficiently. In retailing, such characteristics as pleasant personality, good appearance, knowledge of prices, and interest in finding a product to fill an expressed need become more important. Confidence in firms is developed through successful personal selling. A positive training program for all sales people should be a must for all small firms, just as it is in large firms. Advertising may produce a first inquiry from potential customers or bring them into a retail establishment. Unless the personal selling which follows is satisfactory, not only the first sale but all potential repeat business is in jeopardy.

The four basic steps in making any sale have often been summarized as follows:

1 Gaining the prospective customer's attention
2 Arousing interest

3 Creating desire for the product — overcoming objections
4 Closing the sale

The detailed sales plan in applying these four steps varies with the type of product and type of business. The drugstore sales person will need to give less attention to these steps because the customers come in with an interest in a particular product. The person who is selling an electric saw to a prospective customer will need to pay attention to every detail of the sales plan.

INDIRECT SALES PROMOTION

We have observed earlier in this chapter that indirect sales-promotional methods are usually classified as public relations, good customer relations, customer services, product styling, and packaging of products. These may all be applied to the established demand customers we have previously discussed, but they can also be applied to the developement of new customers.

Public Relations

A firm's public relations determine its image, or popular reputation, in the general community. The nature of its public relations, good or bad, is reflected in the community's attitude toward the firm. Every business has public relations, either consciously or unconsciously, and a good image cannot normally be purchased. It is the responsibility of every person associated with the firm. Every act of the firm's representatives contributes to the overall image of the firm. Good public relations are a cumulative net result, which is more easily destroyed than built. Good public relations develop goodwill and sales. Every owner should be aware of the importance of good public relations and should be sure that each employee knows their importance and how they are built. Building good relations in the community is a never-ending project. Every proposed business policy should first be analyzed in terms of its effect upon the company image. Every crisis decision must always consider the possible effect upon the firm's image.

Customer Relations

Good customer relations build sales independently and also contribute to the total image of the firm. Satisfied, happy customers are the best form of advertising. Word-of-mouth advertising results from happy customers. Good customer relations are basically the result of past transactions with the firm. Such items as speedy handling of complaints, assistance in emergencies, favours in obtaining items, and abiding by announced policies all assist in developing good customer relations. Courteous, competent, and pleasant treatment of customers is most important.

Customer Services

Customer services can be a part of both public relations and good customer relations. Many customers want special services and seek out firms which supply them. Examples are air-conditioned stores, night hours for shopping, credit accounts, delivery service, and lines of merchandise not generally available. Pricing policy may be adjusted to a particular customer group. Trading stamps may provide an attraction as a customer service. Effective administration of any services offered is essential to making them valuable as sale developers. Firms selling industrial products have found recently that the most valued customer services are on-time deliveries, conformity to specifications of products sold, and efficient accounting procedures.

Product Styling and Packaging

Product styling and product packaging are obvious aids in developing sales volume. Customers who desire to be first with the latest seek out the merchants with the latest styles. When similar products are offered in various styles, they seek choices. Packaging can be an equal attraction. The cosmetic field is an excellent example of products which have been presented in all types of beautiful bottles and packages. Even the choices in packaging of bread have recently been of concern to some customers, some preferring the type of package which either has a detachable tie (device to reclose the package after opening) or the inner wrapper supplied by some bakers. Such customer preferences probably reflect a desire for uniqueness as against the utility of the product which we previously discussed.

All the indirect sales promotion methods also reflect a conviction that the customer is still the most important part of any successful business. There can be no profit in the absence of sales. Efforts to keep present customers happy and to develop new ones constantly are essential to continued profits and growth.

QUESTIONS FOR CLASS DISCUSSION

Q12-1 How would you describe established demand as contrasted with promoted demand?

Q12-2 How would you define advertising?

Q12-3 Is advertising as important to small firms as to large ones?

Q12-4 How is the problem of choosing the advertising media different for small firms and for large ones?

Q12-5 What is specialty advertising? Give some examples.

Q12-6 Would you recommend advertising on "Canada A.M." show for a small-town department store? Why?

Q12-7 How do you recommend that direct-mail advertising be made effective?

Q12-8 What do we mean by "checking the effectiveness of advertising"? What are some of the methods by which this can be done?

Q12-9 What is meant by saying that creating an "obstacle course" with a display can increase sales of an item of merchandise?

Q12-10 What are the four basic steps in successful selling?

Q12-11 Do you agree that good public relations can normally not be purchased? Why?

Q12-12 What is meant by saying that product styling can be an indirect sales promotion device?

PROBLEMS AND QUESTIONS FOR WRITTEN ASSIGNMENT

P12-1 The owners of a small department store plan to spend $3,000 on advertising during the coming year. The store is located in a typical Canadian town of 35,000 people. They ask you to prepare an advertising budget showing how the $3,000 would be spent. What would you recommend? Would you spend the same amount each month?

P12-2 If you were asked to design a training program for sales people in a ladies' clothing store, what items would you emphasize to assure that good personal selling was achieved?

P12-3 Can you think of other ways than those cited in the chapter to check the effectiveness of advertising? List them.

P12-4 List any special events which could be used as the basis for a special sale by a men's clothing store. How would you promote each event?

P12-5 Name three types of business firms for which you would recommend specialty advertising as being particularly effective. What form would the advertising take for each type of business?

CONTINUING PROBLEM:
THE SUCCESS HARDWARE STORE

Part 12. Developing Sales for the Store

Assignment for Part 12

Prepare a report showing your recommendations for a program of sales promotion for the new firm. Will you rely on established demand or actively pursue created demand? Which promotion methods will you use? What advertising media do you suggest? How will you measure effectiveness of your advertising? What other points might you cover?

REFERENCES FOR FURTHER READING

"Advertising and Sales Promotion," Your Business Matters, No. 15, The Royal Bank of Canada, 1979.

Archer, Maurice, *An Introduction to Canadian Business,* 3d ed., McGraw-Hill Ryerson Ltd., Toronto, 1978, chap. 11.

Gist, Ronald R., *Retailing*, John Wiley & Sons, Inc., New York, 1968, chap. 13.

Hastings, Paul G., *Introduction to Business,* McGraw-Hill Book Company, New York, 1968, chap. 19.

Kelley, Pearce C., Kenneth Lawyer, and Clifford M. Baumback, *How to Organize and Operate a Small Business,* 5th ed., Prentice-Hall, Inc., Englewood Cliffs, N.J., 1973, chap. 18.

Markin, Rom. J., Jr., *Retailing Management*, Macmillan Publishing Co., Inc., New York, 1971, chaps. 19, 20.

Preshing, W.A., *Business Management in Canada,* Wiley Publishers of Canada Ltd., Toronto, 1974, chap. 18.

CHAPTER 13

Pricing Policies

When I started this business, I just put the price I wanted to charge on each item. I always wondered why some products sold better than others. Funny how many things can affect your prices when you really are informed.

The Late Learner

FACTORS AFFECTING INDIVIDUAL PRICES

The prices which any firm can charge for its merchandise are subject to many influences. Some or all of the following considerations may apply in a particular case:

1. Combines Investigation Act (fair trade law)
2. Nationally advertised prices
3. Desired customer clientele
4. Competitor price policies
5. Market strategy
6. Manufacturer's suggested prices
7. Type of merchandise handled
8. Policy on loss leaders
9. Seasonal nature of sales

10 Demand factor for certain products
11 Price lining
12 Target return pricing

A word about each of these factors will introduce us to the total scene of setting prices. In addition to the Combines Investigations Act, a federal statute, three provinces have laws governing unfair trade practices: Ontario has the Business Practices Act, Alberta has the Unfair Trade Practices Act, and British Columbia has the Trade Practices Act. *Nationally advertised prices* must be recognized by small firms as at least an upper limit to the prices they place on items so advertised. *Competitor prices* on similar lines or merchandise with similar quality must be recognized when active competition exists between firms. *Market strategy* is a policy of setting prices and quality in a range not served by competitors.

Where a *special clientele* is served, its buying can be reflected in price policy. For example, if affluent people want special services and special merchandise, they are willing to pay for such service. In other cases, the desired clientele may be price-conscious people and price policy will be directed to serve them.

Manufacturers' suggested prices are designed by the manufacturers to protect the quality image of their products and protect profit margins for the individual retailer. Price policy is significantly affected by the *type of merchandise handled* by the firm, whether convenience, shopping, or specialty merchandise. This subject is pursued in detail in a later chapter. Novelties or special-interest items normally carry higher markups.

Price maintenance by a supplier is illegal, that is, a manufacturer cannot maintain fixed prices at the resale level. The rule is that a manufacturer may suggest a maximum price but may not set a minimum. An exception is when the manufacturer has evidence that the products supplied are being repeatedly used as "loss-leaders," i.e., there is a *practice* of using the products as promotional (advertising) means. *Seasonal nature of sales* can affect pricing policy by making it possible to alter prices with the high and low seasons of sales volume. The *nature of overall demand* is likewise a consideration in setting individual prices. Elastic demand suggests lower prices. Specialty goods, such as luxury items and style merchandise, carry higher prices. *Price lining* is a policy of keeping merchandise in fairly well defined price ranges. Dresses at $19.95, $24.95, and $29.95 would be an example.

Target return pricing is a relatively recent development in the theory of pricing. It involves adding a desired percentage return on investment or a specific dollar amount return to total fixed costs in setting retail prices. This higher fixed cost total is then added to variable costs in setting prices. This method assumes a given volume in terms of units of product against which the procedure is applied. For example, a factory plans to sell 10,000 units of its product in the coming year. Fixed expenses are $150,000, variable expenses are $300,000 and it is desired to earn a profit of 10 percent on its investment of $500,000 (or $50,000). Using the target return pricing principle, the owner would add the $150,000, the $300,000 and the $50,000 for a total of $500,000. This total is the amount which must be received in sales of the 10,000 units of product in order to produce the desired return on investment. This means that the unit price would be $50 (10,000 times $50 equals $500,000). We can only hope that the many other circumstances which affect pricing, including the competitor's prices, would not change this price calculation.

From this maze of influences on individual prices, some always present and some justifying irregular application, there are basic considerations which take overall precedence in the determination of the price policy for the individual firm.

AVERAGE MARKUP AND INDIVIDUAL PRICES

Up to now, we have used average markup figures for our type of business in setting up the projected income statement. We have found that if a firm has sales of $100,000 and gross margin of $40,000, it has an average markup on total sales of 40 percent. This does not mean that every item in the store was marked up 40 percent of sales. (The principle of markup on sales, not on costs, will be explained later.) Some had more than this average markup and others undoubtedly had less than 40 percent markup. The total year's sales probably included some loss leaders, or items which were sold below actual invoice cost. Pricing policy in total must recognize these facts — while always bearing in mind that the overall average markup must be maintained to arrive at the planned profit.

Pricing policy can be expressed diagrammatically, as in Figure 13-1.

The days when many businesses operated on a basis of a standard markup on every item in the store are long past. Almost every firm today has sales in each of the four areas shown in Figure 13-1. Dynamic pricing policy demands that owners be aware of the aggregate sales volume in each area so that overall total sales will average out to the markup necessary to provide desirable overall profits. Individual prices will reflect the many points discussed above. If loss leaders are a desirable part or necessary condition of the total merchandising plan, they must be offset by extra profit margins on other items. Loss leaders are still illegal or regulated in some states.

Any merchandise sales in the less-than-average markup area must also be offset by sales in the above-average markup area.

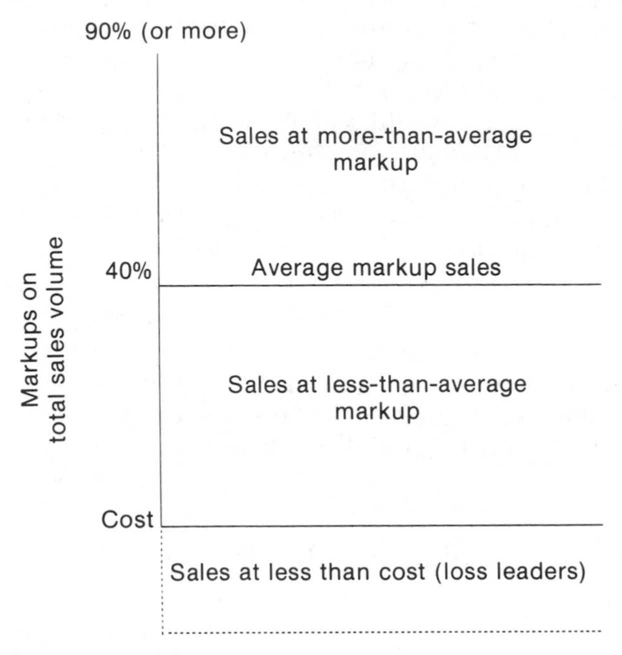

Figure 13-1 Pricing policy

Understanding this pricing policy will explain why the price of Cream of Wheat may be 49 cents (its normal markup price) one day in a grocery, 37 cents on another day, and 57 cents on still another. Saturday specials, other sales prices, and special attractions will alter the prices of the same product from time to time. These variations are intended to attract customers who are price-conscious, yet compensate for the deficiencies in gross margin on other occasions. We can see this policy well applied in the Saturday specials of grocery stores. It should be especially noted that the prices of many of these specials are subject to a "minimum order of $7 excluding cigarettes." The idea of attracting sales by using less-than-average markup items is practised by retailers in almost every line of consumer goods. They may be used with equal effectiveness by sellers of many industrial goods.

THE NATURE AND COMPUTATION OF MARKUP

Markup represents the difference between what is paid for merchandise and the price at which it is sold to the customer. That markup, or gross margin, is the merchant's reward for rendering a social service in bringing the merchandise to the customer. The merchant has given the merchandise place utility. The basic justification of any profit is a reward for rendering this service.

The markup should always be computed as a percentage of the retail price, not as a percentage of the cost of merchandise. The most competent proprietor will compare sales records from period to period in terms of the percentage of sales and average markup represented for each department or type of merchandise. The total of all operating expenses, cost of goods sold, and profits must equal 100 percent of sales. Statement analysis is always facilitated when all items on the income statement are stated as a percentage of the sales figure.

We must recall here the proprietor who insisted that the accountant was wrong in stating that there was an operating loss for the period rather than a profit. The proprietor contended that there was a profit because "markup was 25 percent, while operating expenses were 23 percent, including my salary, and therefore I must have a net return on investment of 2 percent of sales." Of course, the accountant was correct; the owner's markup was based on cost and not on sales. A markup of 25 percent of cost is equivalent to 20 percent of sales. The firm had actually incurred a net loss from operations of 3 percent of sales. (See Table 13-1).

To illustrate this situation, consider merchandise costing $100. Marked up at 25 percent of cost, the sale price would be $125 (.25 times $100, added to $100). But operating expenses are 23 percent of sales. This amounts to $28.75 (23 percent times $125). Net result is a loss of $3.75 on each $125 of sales or $100 of cost of merchandise. (Markup of $25 is $3.75 less than operating expenses of $28.75.) No firm can long endure under such a condition. Obviously, this owner had to increase the markup or reduce operating expenses to get back into a profit position.

Initial prices on merchandise must cover all these items:

1 Markdowns
2 Shortages
3 Damaged merchandise
4 Employee discounts
5 Operating expenses
6 Cost of goods sold
7 Profits

The new firm may not know how to estimate the volume of some of these items. Data gathered for comparable firms in the planning stage can assist in making realistic estimates. None can be neglected. It is much safer to use a generous estimate than to be short in the calculations. Operating expenses and desired profits are clearly set forth on the budgeted income statement. The other items will be reflected in a lessened net sales figure and will not normally appear in the expense accounts. It is always hoped that markdowns, shortages (like shoplifting losses), and damaged merchandise will be kept to a minimum. Employee discounts are usually desirable as a basic part of personnel policy. A popular figure used in retailing to represent the first four items listed above is 3 percent of net sales. This will vary, of course, with different firms and different policies.

TABLE 13-1
MARKUP EQUIVALENTS

DESIRED PERCENTAGE OF SALES	EQUIVALENT PERCENTAGE OF COST
10	11.1
13	15
15	17.7
20	25
25	33.3
30	42.9
33 1/3	50
35	53.9
40	66.7
50	100

INITIAL PRICE: MARK-ON VERSUS AVERAGE MARKUP

It is because of the implications of the preceding paragraphs that marketing experts draw a distinction between *mark-on* and the *average markup*, as the latter term is computed from the year-end income statement. The distinction is based on the fact that many of the items just discussed (markdowns, shortages, damaged merchandise, and employee discounts) are normally not shown on the income statement as such. In most cases it would be impossible to put a dollar amount on these items. Markdowns are recorded at lower sales prices; shortages like shoplifting are not sales at all, but the merchandise lost is still included in the cost of goods sold; damaged merchandise sold at a discount is merely a lessened sales item; and employee discounts are usually recorded as sales at lessened prices. Importantly, however, all of these items must be covered in the initial price set upon the merchandise. Hence the term mark-on denotes the total amount added to the cost of merchandise in setting the *initial price*.

In contrast to this, when we refer to average markup shown on an income statement (gross margin divided by sales), we are using the net sales which resulted after all of the above items have had their effect on the sales figure, or have been included in the cost of goods sold when they were shortages instead of sales. The average markup reflected on the income statement may be 38 percent, but if the items of markdowns, damaged merchandise, shortages, and employee discounts amounted to 4 percent of net sales, a mark-on of 42 percent would be necessary in setting the initial price.

The fundamental lesson to be learned by small firm operators is that if you wish to maintain an average markup on net sales of a given percentage, you must use a somewhat higher percentage of sales in setting the initial price.

PRICE CALCULATIONS

If 25 percent of net sales is required to cover operating expenses, if 3 percent is required to cover markdowns, shortages, damaged merchandise, and employee discounts, and if 12 percent is the desired profit, then an average total markup of 40 percent of sales must be applied to maintain the planned profit. This leaves 60 percent of sales price for the cost of merchandise.

Looked at another way, the initial price of any merchandise offered for sale can be computed as follows:

Initial price in dollars must equal cost of merchandise, plus operating expenses, plus markdowns, plus shortages, plus damaged goods, plus employee discounts, plus profits.

How is the retail price of a particular item computed when the markup as a percentage of sales is known? Let us take a case which illustrates our figures above. Markup is now 40 percent of sales. An item — a dress, say — costing $25 would retail for $41.67. Computation is as follows:

If markup is 40 percent of sales price, the cost of goods must be 60 percent of sales price. We know the cost is $25. Divide $25 by 60 to find 1 percent of sales. Multiply by 100 to find 100 percent of sales price.

```
          .4167 × 100 = $41.67
60 )  25.00
      240
       100
        60
        400
        360
         400
         420
```

If the item involved in this calculation were to be sold in various price ranges, it would be placed in the next price range above $41.67. Dresses, for example, might be sold at $35, $45, and $55. The $25 dress would likely be put on the $45 rack.

We should stress here what the retail price would have been if the markup had been computed on cost rather than sales price. We would merely take markup percentage, 40 percent, of $25 ($10), and add it to cost ($25) to establish a retail price of $35. It is this ease of calculation which has made this method more popularly understood and also has contributed to the errors in statement analysis previously mentioned.

To ease the problem of retail pricing and still assure that markups are based on sales prices, tables have been prepared to show what percentage of cost is necessary to provide the desired percentage of sales price in the markup. A segment of such a table is shown in Table 13-1.

It can be seen from Table 13-1 that 20 percent of sales, for example, is equivalent to 25 percent of cost. If a 20 percent markup on sales is desired and if it is easier for persons pricing merchandise, they can just take 25 percent of the cost and add it to the cost to arrive at sales price. The important thing is to quote the markup as 20 percent of sales price and use this figure in statement analysis.

QUESTIONS FOR CLASS DISCUSSION

Q13-1 What does market strategy mean as a price policy?

Q13-2 What does price lining mean as a price policy?

Q13-3 What is a loss leader? Would you ever recommend its use?

Q13-4 Does average markup mean that every item in a store has the same markup?

Q13-5 What items must be covered by markup other than normal operating expenses and planned profits?

Q13-6 How would you compute the sale price for an item which costs $8 and is to be marked up 20 percent of sales price?

Q13-7 Do you believe employee discounts are justified for most types of business firms?

Q13-8 How does a store owner achieve an average planned markup on total sales for the year?

Q13-9 If an item sells for $10 and has been marked up one-third of selling price, what did it cost the firm?

Q13-10 Do inventory losses usually show up as a specific operating expense on the income statement? If not, how is this expense accounted for?

Q13-11 How does target pricing work?

PROBLEMS AND QUESTIONS FOR WRITTEN ASSIGNMENT

P13-1 You are in charge of setting prices on merchandise for your school's bookstore. Give an example of when you would mark up a particular item at 90 percent or more of sales price. When would you use average markup, when less-than-average markup, and when would you recommend an item as a loss leader?

P13-2 If you planned to use a table of markup equivalents and wanted a markup of one-third of sales, what cost equivalent would you use? Give details for merchandise costing $30.

P13-3 Explain why a desired gross margin of 40 percent on the income statement may necessitate a markup of 45 percent on individual items in any store.

P13-4 Losses from shoplifting do not appear on the income statement. How are they accounted for in that statement? How about employee discounts? Damaged merchandise?

CONTINUING PROBLEM:
THE SUCCESS HARDWARE STORE

Part 13. Setting Price Policies

Assignment for Part 13

Prepare a report on your planned pricing policy for this business. Will you strive to have an image of a bargain-price store? Will your image be one of quality merchandise? Will outside influences affect particular prices in your store? Which merchandise will carry above-average markup, which average markup, which less-than-average markup? Will you have occasion to use loss leaders? How will you assure maintenance of an average markup for total sales during the year? Will special sales affect your pricing policy? What other pricing decisions should be considered?

REFERENCES FOR FURTHER READING

Broom, H.N., and J.G. Longenecker, *Small Business Management*, 2d ed., South-Western Publishing Company, Inc., Cincinnati, 1966, chap. 18.

"Control Over Direct Costs and Pricing," Your Business Matters,

No. 6, The Royal Bank of Canada, 1976.
Hastings, Paul G., *Introduction to Business*, McGraw-Hill Book Company, New York, 1968, chap. 17.
Kelley, Pearce C., Kenneth Lawyer, and Clifford M. Baumback, *How to Organize and Operate a Small Business*, 5th ed., Prentice-Hall, Inc., Englewood Cliffs, N.J., 1973, chap. 17.
Markin, Rom. J., Jr., *Retailing Management*, Macmillan Publishing Co., Inc., New York, 1971, chaps. 13, 18.
Preshing, W.A., *Business Management in Canada*, Wiley Publishers of Canada Ltd., Toronto, 1974, chap. 16.

CHAPTER 14

Types of Merchandise Sold and Merchandising Implications of Each

---

I never did understand that stuff about convenience, shopping, and specialty products. If the same product can be a convenience good to one customer, a shopping good to a second customer, and a specialty good to a third, why the heck should we bother to study details about each?

The Late Learner

The particular type or types of merchandise sold by the individual firm should be reflected in the total nature of the operations.

All products can be classified into two major groups: (1) consumer goods and (2) industrial goods. Within these broad classifications, many further characteristics should be noted. We will first examine consumer goods and then turn our attention to industrial goods.

CLASSIFICATION OF CONSUMER GOODS

Consumer goods are those products purchased at retail by customers for their own use. They may be generally separated into three groups:

1 Convenience goods

2 Shopping goods
3 Specialty goods

1 Convenience Goods Convenience goods are products which the customers desire to buy with a minimum of effort. The more convenient their purchase, the better they like it. Price is not a major factor when they seek such a product in a hurry. Customers do not search around or shop in different stores for convenience goods. Most convenience goods are purchased when the customer makes a special trip to obtain them. Other convenience goods may be purchased on impulse, perhaps in response to an attractive display. Most convenience goods are staple items of low value.

Examples of convenience goods, to most people, are tobacco, drugs, gasoline, soft drinks, newspapers, and ice cream. These are obviously items which, when wanted by customers, are wanted as quickly as possible.

2 Shopping Goods Shopping goods are those items which most customers buy after comparing prices, fashion, quality, and service of several different sellers. Buyers do shop around before making a final decision on the particular item to be purchased. Most shopping goods are relatively high in value and are not bought frequently. This is why comparisons are so important to most people. Husband and wife usually consult the family budget first when considering the purchase of shopping goods. Individual buyers may place different relative values on price, fashion, quality, and service. Only when they are satisfied that they have found the best value for their situation do they make the final decision to buy.

Examples of shopping goods, for most people, are furniture, rugs, suits, shoes, jewelry, chinaware, automobiles, and television sets. Each can represent a substantial item in the family budget and demands close comparison before purchase.

3 Specialty Goods Specialty goods are items which the individual buyer believes have special qualities that make him prefer them. They are usually items of high value. Price is not of major concern to most specialty goods customers. Their preference is usually expresseed for a particular brand. They insist on this brand to the exclusion of all others.

Examples of specialty goods, for many people, are stereo sets, expensive shirts, television consoles, tires, period antiques, or even brand-name chocolates. People who believe that they should have only an RCA or Zenith television console, or Goodyear or Firestone tires, for example, will not be concerned that these goods are not available conveniently in their neighbourhoods. They will go out of their way to find a merchant in their town who carries their desired brand.

It should be observed that not all people fall into these general categories of buying habits. Cigarettes may be a shopping item for some families. People without shopping time may buy shopping goods without adequate comparison. What some customers consider specialty goods — expensive shirts, for example — may be shopping goods or even convenience goods to others. The important thing for the small firm owner is to know as much as possible about the customers' buying habits. Knowing your market is crucial in so many ways in successful business operation.

The classification of consumer goods and the examples within each classification represent what is considered the majority view of most consumers. If the firm owner finds, from study of the market, that it is in accord with these classifications, attention can be turned to the management implications for each type of consumer merchandise. Any notable exceptions found in the market can be adjusted for in merchandising policies.

MERCHANDISING IMPLICATIONS FOR DIFFERENT TYPES OF CONSUMER GOODS

The three types of consumer goods generally influence merchandising in the following ways:

1 Convenience goods
- **a** Less capable sales persons are needed.
- **b** Nearness to competitors is undesirable.
- **c** Store hours can usually be longer and still be profitable.
- **d** Variety of products in one line is not of prime importance.
- **e** Displays of impulse items are important.
- **f** Location in store is important.

2 Shopping goods
- **a** Location should normally be near competitors so that customers can compare goods.
- **b** High-rent areas are not essential.
- **c** More capable and higher-paid sales people are necessary.
- **d** Ability to explain advantages of merchandise over competing products is essential.
- **e** Assistance to customers in value determination is important.

3 Specialty goods
- **a** Attractive, comfortable selling space for customers is important.
- **b** Advertising can cover wider areas of the city productively.

c Efficiency in installations is important.
d Customer services are a premium item.
e Special sales may be less important.
f Publicity emphasis is on location and brands more than on price.

INDUSTRIAL GOODS

Industrial goods are those products which are sold to other business firms, either for their own consumption or for use in their own manufacture of other products. These goods, too, are extremely varied. They may be classified as follows:

1 Raw materials: oil, grain, logs, unprocessed tobacco, wool, fresh fruits, etc.

2 Semimanufactured goods: sheet aluminum or steel, leather, ores, pig iron, etc.

3 Parts: blades for cutting machines, automobile wheels, bearings, ax handles, etc.

4 Supplies: cleaning compounds, plastic bags, wrapping paper, fuel, office stationery, etc.

5 Machinery and equipment: all machines and equipment items used in the factory, office, or store.

Note that the same product can be both a customer good and industrial good. The customer's purpose in buying the good will decide into which classification the particular item falls. For example, coal purchased for a factory is an industrial good, whereas coal purchased for the home is a consumer good.

Small firms do engage very much in the manufacture of many industrial goods. Individual firms may both sell their product to industrial firms and distribute them through wholesalers to retailers to consumers. The selling process in these two areas has distinct differences.

Special Features of Industrial Goods Selling

Any small firm selling to industrial users should recognize these special characteristics of industrial sales:

1 Industrial goods buyers are better informed about the products they buy. They buy products on the basis of performance and not because of advertising or emotion.

2 Many industrial goods are sold directly by the factory to the user without the use of any intermediaries.

3 There are fewer customers for individual goods, but the average sale is usually much higher.

4 Factories will often request products made to their own specifications.

5 Many industrial goods are sold with the seller providing installation and repair service.

6 Industrial goods prices are more sensitive to changing business conditions.

The implications of these characteristics for small firm manufacturers are that they must have sales people capable of demonstrating the performance of the product; they must be prepared to call on business customers rather than await buyers at the business; they must know where the potential users of the product are located (which relates to their own locations) and be prepared to offer installation and repair service either by their own staffs or through competent agents. And they must recognize the sensitive nature of industrial prices by keeping aware of business conditions.

All these factors will not apply in every case. The normal procedure in the particular line of products must be understood, however, and then the organization and services which apply must be arranged.

COST OF DISTRIBUTION

It is never too early in business education for students, small firm owners, and informed citizens to address themselves to the often-heard complaints about "the excessive costs of distribution." It is generally contended that efficiency in distribution has not kept pace with the economies of mass production. The facts bear investigation. Our best marketing studies show that up to 50 percent of the consumer dollar goes for distribution costs and about 50 percent for manufacturing costs. Marketing costs have increased over recent years but only as a percentage of the retail price. In true dollar cost, marketing costs have also declined. There are definite reasons why they have not declined as much as manufacturing costs. An example of the retail cost of a popular consumer good today will illustrate the facts.

Let us consider the price of a popular line of radios or coffee makers.

It will be seen that manufacturing cost has been reduced from $20 to $12—a reduction of 40 percent. Distribution cost has been reduced from $16 to $12—a reduction of 25 percent. Retail price has been reduced from $36 to $24—a reduction of 33 1/3 percent.

Former price and its breakdown	Today's price and its breakdown
$20 for manufacturing cost	$12 for manufacturing cost
$16 for distribution cost	$12 for distribution cost
$36 former retail price	$24 present retail price

If these percentages are seen in isolation, it would appear that distribution efficiency has not kept pace with manufacturing economies. It is this first impression that has caused most of the complaints that are heard.

Some of the ignored facts are the following:

1 Distribution costs have actually been reduced. In this example they are cut 25 percent. New ideas in distribution are constantly being tried. Distribution markets are open to all in a free economy, and anyone who can save money can corner a large percentage of the market. Some of the new ideas which have been applied include piggy-back trucks, carload rates, area distribution centres, large-size order requirements, and attractive discounts for large orders.

2 Mass-production economies necessitate wider markets in which to distribute the increased production. The wider the market served, the greater are expenses of distribution. Thus, mass production itself has added expense factors to distribution costs.

3 Consumers today have established a demand for products with high costs of distribution. As a society becomes more affluent, its increased purchasing power is reflected in a demand for more expensive consumer goods. Frozen foods entail greater distribution costs than fresh local vegetables. Imported products, which customers are demanding in rising quantities, carry extra distribution costs. Heineken is more expensive than Molson's, largely because of the distribution costs. We did not have frozen bakery goods until relatively recently. They demand refrigeration and expensive handling throughout the distribution process.

4 Some consumers, in fact an increasing percentage of them, have demanded costly marketing services. They are willing to pay for them and want them in expensive shopping centres. These services include delivery, free parking, evening shopping hours, air-conditioned stores, and sales on account. Such services are expensive and add to the total costs of distribution.

When these items have are considered, it is obvious that without great ingenuity in distribution activities, little or no reduction in distribution costs could have been achieved.

QUESTIONS FOR CLASS DISCUSSION

Q14-1 When you buy a shirt or blouse, do you consider it a convenience, shopping, or specialty item? How do you distinguish these three types of consumer goods?

Q14-2 Why should shopping goods firms generally be located in the same area of town?

Q14-3 Why can a firm selling convenience goods usually have less capable sales persons than one selling shopping goods?

Q14-4 Do you agree that factories should be located close to their markets?

Q14-5 When should a factory be located close to its source of raw materials?

Q14-6 How could the same product be both an industrial good and a consumer good?

Q14-7 "Industrial goods are bought on a basis of performance and not on emotion." What does this mean to you? Give examples.

Q14-8 Are there more or fewer customers for industrial goods than for consumer goods? Explain.

Q14-9 How has an affluent society increased distribution costs?

Q14-10 Have distribution costs per unit of product really increased with the increase in mass production?

PROBLEMS AND QUESTIONS FOR WRITTEN ASSIGNMENT

P14-1 In your home, is a new rug a convenience item, a shopping item, or a specialty item? Explain why.

P14-2 Explain how a new tire for the car can be a convenience item for one person, a shopping item for another person, and a specialty item for a third person.

P14-3 Name five different kinds of industrial goods which would be purchased by a maker of custom-built cars.

P14-4 Using the case of a popular consumer item, such as watches or shoes, explain why distribution costs have been unable to keep pace with manufacturing costs. Does this mean distribution is inefficient?

P14-5 Do you agree that more capable people are needed to sell specialty or shopping goods than convenience goods? Explain.

CONTINUING PROBLEM:
THE SUCCESS HARDWARE STORE

Part 14. Merchandising Implications for Goods Sold

Assignment for Part 14

Write a report explaining how you would classify the various items in your inventory between convenience, shopping, and specialty goods. Is one classification dominant for the customers you are seeking? If so, have you applied the implications for that category in your merchandising policy? How? How would you arrange your products in your store layout?

REFERENCES FOR FURTHER READING

Archer, Maurice, *An Introduction to Canadian Business,* 3d. ed., McGraw-Hill Ryerson Ltd., Toronto, 1978, chap. 9.

Davidson, William R., and Alton F. Doody, *Retailing Management,* 3d. ed., The Ronald Press Co., New York, 1966, chaps. 10, 13.

Gist, Ronald R., *Retailing,* John Wiley & Sons, Inc., New York, 1968, chap. 10.

Kriz, Joseph A., and Curtis J. Duggan, *Your Dynamic World of Business,* McGraw-Hill Book Co., New York, 1973, chap. 2.

Markin, Rom J., Jr., *Retailing Management,* Macmillan Publishing Co., Inc., New York, 1971, chap. 14.

CHAPTER 15

Seasonal Variations in Sales and Their Effect on Management Decisions

---

If you can't show a profit in March and October, why not just close the store during those months? And if you don't have enough customers on Tuesday and Wednesday each week, why not keep the store closed on those days?

The Late Learner

Almost every business, large or small, has a very definite seasonal variation in its monthly income during the year. Stable firms such as grocery stores, for example, generally report that sales are heaviest in September, November, and December. Summer months, when schools are closed, when people are off on vacation or moving to other cities, show a decline in sales. In resort towns, firms do their biggest business in the months which are vacation time for other people.

For example, at Miami Beach until about 15 years ago, the seasonal variation in business was so great that most hotels closed up completely from April until December. Today, because of huge expenditures by tourist development boards and airlines to encourage year-round vacations, most of the hotels stay open. But even here the seasonal factor has another aspect. In the summer, a different income group is served and policies are different. In the peak season of

January, February, and March, room rates are very high and many additional services are available for the "carriage trade." In the summer months, hotel managements frankly seek to produce enough income to cover fixed expenses and possibly to pay for renovations necessary for the following peak season. Room rates are lower, services are more limited, and the extras available in winter, such as golf privileges, are greatly reduced. Thus we see a different application of management decisions to cope with the seasonal factor in income. Some hotels in Miami Beach still close in the summer months because their operators own or operate other hotels in the Catskills or other northern summer-resort areas where the season is just the opposite of that in South Florida.

Most retailers and manufacturers do not have such a clear choice in adjusting to their seasonal variations in total income throughout the year. It is still important, however, that they know the extent of the variations. There are other things they can do in the best interests of their business firms.

CHARTING SEASONAL SALES VARIATIONS: A CASE STUDY

In an actual case reviewed recently by one of the authors, a small department store made a study of seasonal variations in sales income. The approximate monthly sales figures were as follows:

January	$ 60,000
February	50,000
March	40,000
April	40,000
May	45,000
June	45,000
July	30,000
August	30,000
September	40,000
October	40,000
November	60,000
December	120,000
Total sales for year	$600,000

These monthly variations were plotted on graph paper. The results are shown in Figure 15-1.

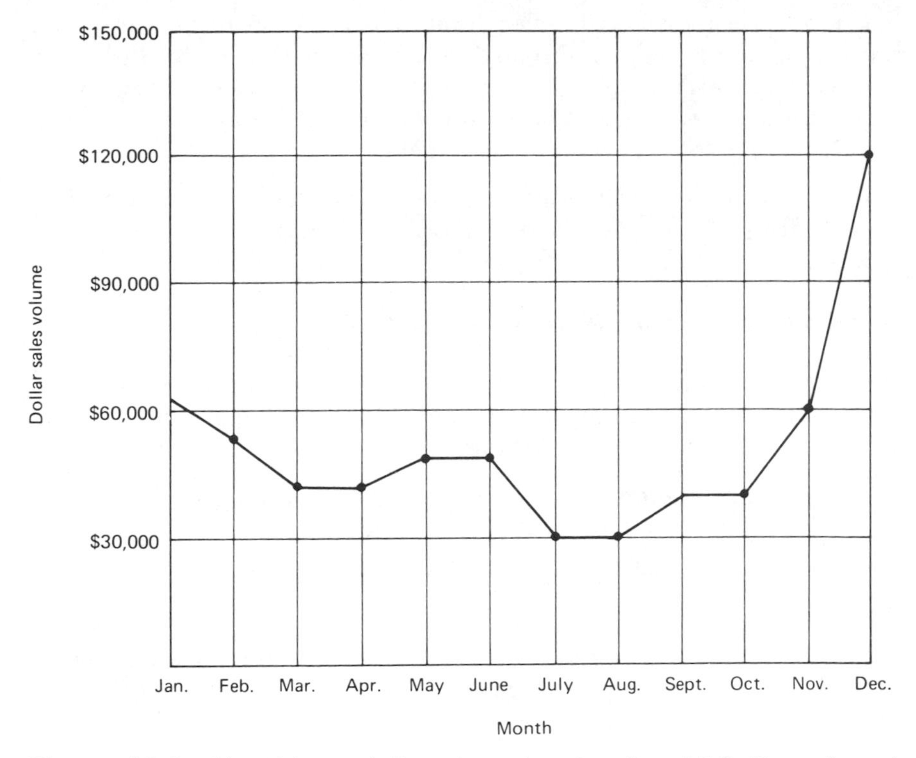

Figure 15-1 *Monthly variation in sales for the ABC Department Store.*

Analysis of a Seasonal Sales Chart

When the results of the analysis of seasonal variations were discussed with the owner of the store, several very interesting facts came to light. Some of them were:

1 The owner had been using only an annual break-even chart based upon annual sales of $600,000. This suggested that an average monthly sales volume of $50,000 was needed. A monthly break-even chart which would reflect the actual differences in sales volume in the summer months was never made.

2 Although sales dropped badly in the slack season, no special action to adjust expenses accordingly was taken.

3 The fact that 40 percent of annual sales were made in the three months of November, December, and January was not noted. The three slack summer months provided only 17 percent of annual sales.

4 Inventories had been kept at normal levels during the year, but some extra orders were made for the holiday trade.

5 Employees each had several years' service with the store, and their loyalty was well established. As a reward, they were allowed to take their vacations any time during the year. Because of this, part-time employees were hired in the spring and fall months, as well as in the December rush, to handle customers.

6 The owner was reluctant to make policy changes because "after all, we did show a profit for the year."

Decision Making from Seasonal Sales Analysis

The consulting report sent to the owner listed the errors in some of the situations cited. It recommended several positive steps to improve the firm's profitability. These included:

1 Part-time employees should be hired only during November, December, and January.

2 All employee vacations should be granted only in July and August.

3 Inventory policy should reflect the lower sales in the summer months by reducing purchases of year-round merchandise in the spring and early fall.

4 A positive program of sales promotion for the slack periods should be studied. Perhaps special sales, attractive prices, or other ideas could increase sales in the slack months.

5 Monthly break-even charts and income statements should be made.

When it was pointed out to the owner that several thousand dollars was the estimated saving from applying the first three suggestions, the reaction was most enthusiastic about them and possibly other decisions that could be made. At last report, consideration was being given to closing the store entirely during July and August and reopening when school began in September, when a community-covering, dynamic advertising program would be launched.

This case is recited in detail mainly because its implications are appropriate for so many small firms. Even in the planning stage of a new small firm, seasonal variations for the type of business at hand can be determined within reasonable limits. Decisions like those recommended in the case just described can be enacted from the beginning. Existing firms should study their situation for possible policy changes.

Many students have probably heard of the two small airlines which accidently compared their monthly revenues and found the peak season for one was the slack season for the other. The result was an agreement between them to lease planes to each other during their respective peak seasons rather than have planes idle for one season. Each obtained leasing revenue without buying additional equipment, and maintenance costs were reduced for both lines. Their seasonal variations are shown in Figure 15-2.

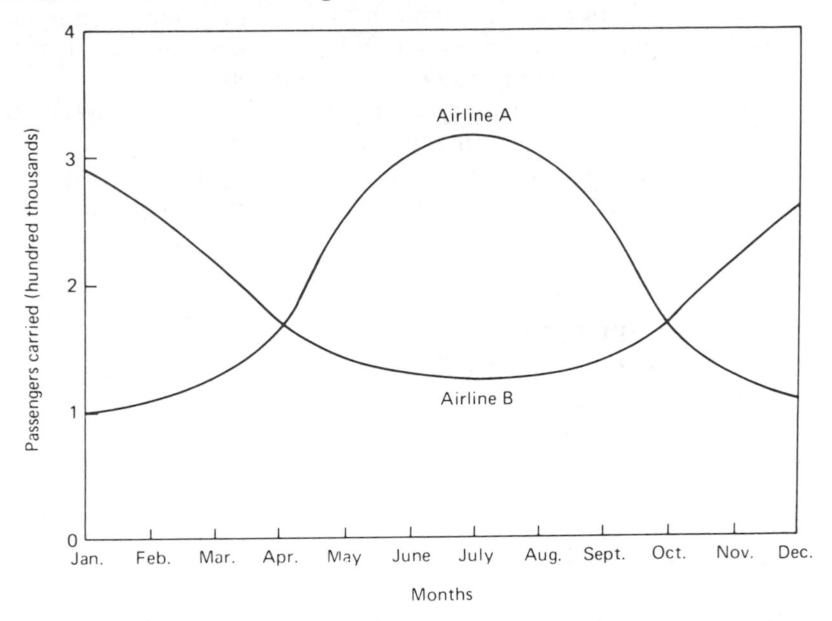

Figure 15-2 *Comparison of seasonal variations for two airlines.*

In summary, all small firm owners should know their seasonal variations. When significant variations are apparent, every attempt should be made to adjust operating expenses accordingly. We have noted some of the ways this may be done.

QUESTIONS FOR CLASS DISCUSSION

Q15-1 What could cause seasonal variations in the sales volume of a neighbourhood grocery store?

Q15-2 Are there any variations in the monthly sales of most small department stores? What could cause them?

Q15-3 How drastic do you think the seasonal variations are for a resort restaurant in a far-north village?

Q15-4 Is the fact that "we made a profit last year" a good reason to neglect study of seasonal variations? Explain.

Q15-5 What are some of the things an owner can do to aid profits when significant variations in seasonal business are normal?

PROBLEMS AND QUESTIONS FOR WRITTEN ASSIGNMENT

P15-1 Prepare a chart showing seasonal variations in sales for a small firm which did 8 percent of its business in each of the months of February, April, May, October, and November; 5 percent of its annual business in January, March, June, and July; 15 percent in September and December; and 10 percent in August. Total annual sales were $360,000.

P15-2 Does your chart show any clearly defined variations which can be of value in making management decisions?

P15-3 Explain the personnel problems which might be confronted by the owner of a business which operates only 6 months of the year.

CONTINUING PROBLEM:
THE SUCCESS HARDWARE STORE

Part 15. Seasonal Variations Anticipated

Assignment for Part 15

a Break down the total yearly sales into monthly totals. If actual data are not obtainable, divide the total on the basis of your best ideas as to how sales will vary from month to month in this type of business.

b Prepare a line chart similar to the one in Chapter 15, showing graphically how the seasonal variations would appear.

c Assuming that rather wide variations are to be observed on your chart, what decisions will you consider to make income and expense coincide more closely in the lighter months?

REFERENCES FOR FURTHER READING

Davidson, William R., and Alton F. Doody, *Retailing Management*, 3d ed., The Ronald Press Co., New York, 1966, chap. 17.

Gist, Ronald R., *Retailing*, John Wiley & Sons, Inc., New York, 1968, chap. 11.

"Managing the Future Sales," Your Business Matters, No. 16, The Royal Bank of Canada, 1979.

Markin, Rom J., Jr., *Retailing Management*, Macmillan Publishing Co., Inc., New York, 1971, chap. 15.

CHAPTER 16

Purchasing and Inventory Control

I only have one policy on purchasing and inventory control. Keep the warehouse full, and you never lose a sale. I know it costs money to carry inventory, but it also costs profits to lose sales. If you always keep the warehouse full, your inventory will take care of itself.

The Late Learner

The term "merchandising" is used very broadly in business. It usually covers all facets of the business which have to do with merchandise: acquiring it, handling and displaying it, seeking out potential customers for it, selling it, and rendering services to customers who have bought it. These activities can be divided into at least the following subjects:

1. Purchase of inventories
2. Inventory control
3. Sales promotion and advertising
4. Publicity
5. Displays of merchandise
6. Selling activities
7. Pricing policies
8. Customer services

Each of these subjects is a large one and many books have been written on the theory and practice of each. For the student or new firm planner, we can attempt here only to summarize some of the key considerations in each area. Such a summary can also be used to check the actual performance of an existing firm. This chapter will cover purchasing and inventory control.

PURCHASING MERCHANDISE

The key questions which the small firm owner must ask himself or herself are: Am I buying through the established channels of distribution for this type of business? Is there another source which would give me the same dependability and service? Am I getting the best prices available for comparable quality? In what quantities should I be buying merchandise?

Most small retailers have wholesale houses available in their own locality which are eager and willing to serve them. Most consumer goods are normally distributed from manufacturer to wholesaler to retailer. In addition, there are sales people from out-of-town suppliers who will call on the merchant to present their products. Job-lot dealers may operate in the area and have special quantities of merchandise for sale. A basic decision the new owner must make is whether to buy only from established wholesalers who serve the area or to buy wherever needed types of merchandise are available. If the firm has a distributorship for a particular line of merchandise, the source of supply is assured as part of the distributorship arrangement. Most small firm retailers carry similar merchandise in different price lines. Each price line may be served by a different wholesaler or distributor. Experience will soon tell the owner which are the most popular lines with their customers, and they will buy accordingly.

The inventory investment is usually the largest investment in the new small firm. Because of this, the owner must constantly be concerned with making this investment as profitable as possible. Assistance is available in the following ways:

1 Determining how much to buy on each order
2 Taking advantage of all purchase discounts offered
3 Combating the constant problem of slow-moving merchandise

The object is to have the proper merchandise turnover.

DIFFERENT TYPES OF WHOLESALERS

New retailers are often confused as to the various types of wholesale establishments which may be available to serve their procurement needs. New wholesalers are often not sure of how their planned firms fit into the generally accepted organization of the wholesale function. The following comments should clarify the situation for both groups.

Wholesalers are generally classified as:

Full-service wholesalers (also called merchant wholesalers)
Limited-function wholesalers
Agent middlemen (also called intermediaries)

Full-service wholesalers are the most numerous in most lines of consumer goods. They usually buy their inventories directly from the manufacturers and thus take title to the merchandise. They store the merchandise in their own warehouses, deliver and/or assemble the products involved, and maintain a location where customers may inspect the products and place orders. They do not work on commission, but rely upon their ability to sell their products at a profit to make their own operations successful. They are called *full-service wholesalers* because of the extra services they extend to their customers—such as granting credit on sales, providing delivery service, and supplying current market information.

Limited-function wholesalers render fewer marketing functions for their customers. *Jobbers,* who specialize in odd-lot sales only, are often placed in this category. Wholesalers who merely sell merchandise that is delivered by the manufacturer to the customer are another example. They are often called *drop shippers.* Wholesalers who do not grant credit to their customers but make cash sales only are similarly classified.

Agent middlemen are wholesalers who actually provide a procurement function for their customers. Most do not take title to the merchandise they buy or sell for their customers. They merely arrange for such sales through their customers and contacts. They usually work on commission only. Any extra services extended to their customers are the exception, not the rule. Examples of this group are *brokers* who arrange sales for their clients without ever taking title or possession of the merchandise products involved; *selling agents* who often contract to take the entire output of a small factory and sell it wherever the market may be; and *manufacturers' agents* who usually represent their manufacturer in only a certain specified territory and make sales of their product for delivery by the manufacturer.

Commission merchants are also usually classified as agent middlemen, but they operate somewhat differently. They do not take title but usually assume physical possession of the merchandise they are employed to sell. They often provide temporary storage until they have completed their sales. They usually provide delivery service of the merchandise when sold. Sometimes they grant credit to the firms to which they sell, but this is not uniform practice. They are paid for their services by a commission on the selling prices they develop. Special arrangements with the principal they represent may add other compensation.

HOW MUCH TO ORDER AND WHEN

How much of each item should be purchased on each order? The most important consideration here is to avoid stockouts while keeping the investment under control and the working capital active and available. Most retailers determine a minimum size in the inventory of any item as the reordering point. This minimum stock must take into consideration the time necessary to get a new order placed and delivered. Some allowance for contingencies in this regard is usually advisable. For example, if canned milk is sold at the rate of a case per week and it takes one week to get a new order placed and delivered, such an order could be placed when the stock is down to one case. Prudence suggests ordering a bit sooner.

But how many cases should be ordered? If local wholesalers are easily available with speedy delivery or pick-up service, if there is no price advantage in ordering more, and if storage space is limited, grocers cannot be accused of hand-to-mouth buying if they keep a reserve of one case and just have one case delivered each week. Such a situation does not usually exist. Even the problem of bookkeeping and totaling several invoices during the month would probably suggest that the grocers buy one month's supply each time. More likely, they have opportunities for purchase discounts for prompt payments of invoices, and lower prices for larger-quantity purchases. These factors would cause them to increase their ordering quantities. Larger orders would be encouraged by their wholesalers. Keeping track of every item in a large inventory is a big job, and some system should be established for keeping information available. Some small firms use tags taken from each item to post against inventory on hand. Others determine monthly usage and order just that amount each month until a physical inventory is taken.

FOR FACTORIES—THE SQUARE ROOT FORMULA FOR INDUSTRIAL BUYING

Industrial buyers have a basic formula which applies more effectively to their type of buying. It is popularly known as the square root formula for determining economic ordering quantities. The individual order considers the dollar amount used in the previous year; the cost of issuing a purchase order; and the cost of storing, insuring, protecting, and maintaining inventory on hand. When these factors are known, the formula is as follows:

$$\text{Economic ordering quantity} = \sqrt{\frac{2AB}{i}}$$

Where A = annual usage in dollars
B = cost of issuing a purchase order, in dollars
i = cost of carrying inventory,
expressed as a percentage of the inventory value

To illustrate the use of this formula, let us consider a firm which used $10,000 of product P last year; it costs $1 to issue a purchase order; and it costs 5 percent of the inventory value to store, insure, and protect it (0.05 percent). When we insert these figures into the formula, it becomes:

$$\text{Economic ordering quantity} = \sqrt{\frac{2(\$10{,}000)\,1}{.05}} = \sqrt{\frac{\$20{,}000}{.05}}$$

$$= \quad \$400{,}000$$

The square root of $400,000 is $633, as follows:

```
           6  3  3
        ___________
       / 400,000
      √  36
         ---
          40 0
          36 9
          ----
           3 100
123
   -
1263
    -
Proof       633
            633
            ---
           1899
          1899
         3798
       --------
       $400,689
```

The most economic ordering quantity is, therefore, $633 each time an order is placed.

This formula uses a square root, but the time spent calculating it is worthwhile. It takes the guesswork out of the buying process. (Tables of square roots are available.) Different product groupings with similar usage patterns can be placed together so that calculations are minimized. The ordering quantity is recorded on each inventory sheet for future use. The formula does have some limitations, such as schedule changes, price changes, commercial practices, packaging limits, and the perishable nature of products, which will prevent strict adoption in some cases. These can all be handled as adjustments, however, in the initial calculation.

Beginning inventories for a new factory must be based upon close scrutiny of available industry statistics and planned production schedules. As experience is gained in operations, the techniques of the square root formula can be applied.

As factories grow larger, management will usually find it desirable to utilize even more refined economics-purchase order formulas, which can be operated on computers. Many of these formulas have as many as 15 variables to be considered in arriving at precise ordering quantities.

In small factories the responsibility for initiating new purchase orders for material and supplies must be the responsibility of the person in charge of inventories. A minimum inventory is established which allows for the normal lead time in getting stocks replenished (the time necessary to get purchase orders issued and new materials received). When that minimum point is reached, immediate action is necessary. Notice that the minimum inventory which has been reached can be given in different ways. One is to have the minimum stock in separate bins or shelves. Another is to post to a current inventory record all material issued to production. This record adds all incoming shipments, deducts material issued, and thus has a perpetual inventory of balances on hand. The size of that minimum inventory may be adjusted because of new business developments such as transportation strikes, supplier problems, etc. It may also be affected by attractive prices available or changes in the production demands due to new products or extra usage of particular items in the total inventory.

Regardless of which system is used to keep control of inventory, the most important thing is to work the system. Practising the old idea of always having more than enough on hand to avoid stockouts or machinery shut-downs without regard to the adequacy of the inventory or the investment involved is prime evidence of inefficient management. Special circumstances may create exceptions. Too much inventory is wasteful. It ties up working capital unnecessarily, increases storage costs, and increases the risks of obsolescence and deterioration of the products.

INVENTORY CONTROL CONSIDERATIONS FOR RETAILERS

What is the ideal amount of inventory? For retailers, it is that inventory which does not lose profitable sales and can still justify the investment in each part of its total.

For manufacturing firms, it is that inventory which maintains production schedules with a minimum investment in inventory.

Let us quickly admit that the ideal inventory is easier to describe than to determine in particular cases. Some examples will serve to illustrate the rule. If a drugstore has repeated requests for an aerosol spray product but does not have this item on its shelves, it is losing profitable sales by not stocking that item. If the owner's reason for not carrying the item is that it is only bought seasonally, the reasoning is not good; such a policy is driving potential customers to competitors. If it is seasonal, the owner should arrange the stock so that little or no investment is tied up in the item during the off season.

Carrying too many brands or sizes in a particular item can easily produce a situation where the total investment is not justified. Stocking many brands of toasters in one drugstore would be an example. People who want to buy a toaster in a drugstore are not usually concerned with a particular brand. Brand-conscious customers in this case would likely go to the brand distributor. Other consumer items which can easily fall into this category for various types of retailers are dishware, shirts, hammers, men's suits, and dresses. A choice may be desirable but excessive brands are not usually necessary. The type of store and type of customer must, of course, always be considered, but the underlying principle of inventory control remains continually important. Knowing the customers you have or are seeking is the best information to have in this regard.

Some items which are not generally popular may still have to be carried in minimum quantities for other reasons. For example, few drugstores still carry bar shaving soap. In one case, the druggist admitted that his shelves always had one dozen bars in stock because of two customers who regularly made substantial purchases in the store and who demanded this product from time to time. Giving up the small investment in bar shaving soap would have driven those customers to another store, together with their profitable purchases. A slow-moving item was justified here, even though its own sales probably could not justify even the small investment.

Retail Inventory Control Techniques

The problems of inventory control are really more difficult for most retailers than for factories. The factory was a specific production schedule, and the inventory of raw materials is adjusted to that positively planned usage. Retailers, however, may have the demands on their inventories change with the whims of their customers, with style changes which are often unpredictable, or with the changing character of their market. They may drop or add new products or new lines of products at any time. Yet the importance of efficiently managing this largest investment for most retailers remains. Even if the ideal inventory has been approached, it is often subject to change on short notice. And the problems of different retailers vary in many ways. Some of the techniques which can be used to assist inventory control are:

1 Keep a constant vigil of sales results and inventories. There is no substitute for this. All other techniques only assist actual experience.

2 Set minimum reordering point and maximum inventory on all basic stock items. Such basic stock is not liable to most frivolous demand changes.

3 Obtain data from modern cash registers to identify key items for sales. These will reflect increased or decreased sales of such items.

4 Have a detachable portion of sales slips which will record sales of particular items. A two-part price tab, half of which can be detached at time of sale, will accomplish the same purpose. Summaries of this data will provide sales information to govern purchases.

5 Rely on suppliers who regularly visit the store to maintain proper inventories without wasteful expenditure. (The bread truck driver knows how many loaves of each kind of bread to leave each morning.)

6 Use wholesaler or manufacturer recommendations if products represent a distributorship for certain brands or products.

PURCHASE DISCOUNTS

Good management demands that all purchase discounts should be taken. The excuse that cash is not available is not valid. A purchase discount is a reduction in the price on any invoice offered in return for prompt payment of the invoice. The most common discount offered by suppliers is 2/10, n/30. This means that if the invoice is paid within 10 days, 2 percent of the gross amount can be deducted, but in any event the entire amount is due in 30 days. An invoice for $1,000 of merchandise can thus be settled in full for $980 if paid within 10 days, instead of $1,000, which would be due on the thirtieth day. Net saving is \$20. A saving of 2 percent for paying bills 20 days sooner is saving at the rate of 36 percent per year. (It is earned in 20 days and there are 18 periods of 20 days each in the year.) The often observed tendency to avoid paying such bills within the discount period represents neglect of good financial management. The typical drugstore must sell many units of shaving cream, cigarettes, or magazines to clear \$20 in profit. One of the differences between efficient large firms and inefficient small firms lies in the attention given to this matter.

A study some years ago of over 1,000 small firms showed that most were lax in taking advantage of purchase discounts. It also showed that 2 percent of purchases was more than the majority paid in federal income taxes.

If adequate cash is not available, the competent proprietor with a good credit standing can borrow the necessary amount from his bank for the 20 days involved in the case above. At 6 percent interest, the \$980 would cost \$3.27 in interest. Even deducting this interest from the \$20 saved, the proprietor is still \$16.73 ahead by paying the invoice within the discount period. Such clear gains cannot be ignored.

While advocating taking advantage of all purchase discounts for prompt payment, and all quantity discounts where the quantities involved are justified by the company's inventory policy, we should also caution about ordering too large quantities in order to receive quantity discounts. One year's supply should be the maximum order placed, regardless of attractive prices on larger quantities. In many cases, an order of this size cannot be justified.

THE PROBLEM OF SLOW-MOVING MERCHANDISE

One of the hardest lessons for new retailers to learn or to accept is the desirability of selling slow-moving merchandise at less than normal markup or, in some cases, at less than cost. Every firm faces this problem to some degree. Stores selling style merchandise are particularly vulnerable to the risk of being stuck with an inventory of slow-moving products which will lose value as the style fades. Bathing suits and fashion shoes are examples of products that should be marked down as seasons or styles pass. Merchants sell Christmas cards at half-price the day after Christmas to combat this problem. They don't want working capital tied up in the cards for a whole year. Other products are subject to deterioration, fading, or other defects when kept in stock too long. Wise merchants who find such items in their inventory act to sell them as best they can as soon as they can.

Special sales, markdowns, and advertising are some of the devices employed.

The Federal Business Development Bank and the Royal Bank have prepared several aids for small firm owners. They include ideas on how to move such products and generally reduce the problem. All proprietors should take advantage of these services. Suggestions for liquidating slow-moving inventory would include:

1 Make traffic obstacles of large displays of the items.
2 Offer special discounts for quantity purchases.
3 Put specially coloured lights on displays.
4 Offer 1-cent sales.
5 Place slow-moving goods next to best sellers.
6 Have grab-bag sales.
7 Use specially coloured price tags.
8 Offer "Special of the Day" items.

MERCHANDISE INVENTORY TURNOVER

Some attention was paid to inventory turnover in Chapter 2, where we needed to know the average turnover for our type of firm. We can now return to that concept with more experience.

We have found that the ideal merchandise inventory is the one which does not lose productive sales and can still justify each part of its investment. We have investigated many of the ramifications of achieving that happy state. We know that the turnover is computed by dividing cost of goods sold by the average inventory. It is also clear now that too much inventory can lessen the turnover and result in inefficiency in total operations.

A time-honoured measure of efficiency in management has been this turnover figure. When comparing two firms, the one with the higher inventory turnover is usually assumed to be the more profitable. An erroneous conclusion has resulted in many cases. We are regularly reminded in these instances that a profit is made every time the inventory is turned. It is assumed, therefore, that the higher the turnover, the higher the profits. This is not always true. It does not measure profitable sales lost because no merchandise was available. To illustrate with an extreme case: Consider the hardware store with an inventory consisting of one hammer. No other merchandise is on the shelves. The owner sells a hammer each day. After the sale, the owner goes to the nearby supply house and buys another hammer. At the end of the month, there is a merchandise inventory turnover of 30 times per month, or 360 times per year. But has it been efficient? Many productive sales were lost through lack of inventory. A proper inventory with a turnover of 5 times per year would have produced much better results.

Experience has demonstrated that too much inventory is usually less harmful than inadequate inventory and stockouts. The ideal inventory as described earlier may never be exactly achieved. Nevertheless, it has great value as a principle and should always be pursued.

QUESTIONS FOR CLASS DISCUSSION

Q16-1 What are the advantages, if any, of buying regularly from the same wholesalers?

Q16-2 How can it be dangerous to buy very large quantities of a particular item in order to receive an extra discount?

Q16-3 How do distributorships assure steady supply of merchandise?

Q15-4 Do you agree that the merchandise inventory is usually the largest investment of small firms?

Q16-5 What is the ideal inventory for a retailer?

Q16-6 What is the ideal inventory of raw materials for a factory?

Q16-7 What is hand-to-mouth buying?

Q16-8 If a factory used $20,000 of one raw material last year, should it order this amount on January 1 next year? Explain.

Q16-9 What are the possible advantages of placing large orders if so doing is consistent with inventory needs?

Q16-10 How can carrying too many competing items adversely affect the inventory investment and consequent profits?

Q16-11 Why can an efficient merchant not afford to neglect purchase discounts?

Q16-12 A saving of 2 percent in 20 days represents an annual rate of 36 percent. Explain how this is true.

Q16-13 Can the merchandise turnover ever be too high? Explain.

PROBLEMS AND QUESTIONS FOR WRITTEN ASSIGNMENT

P16-1 Explain in a brief essay the problems of having too much or too little inventory.

P16-2 Do you agree that it is usually considered better to have too much than too little inventory? Explain why.

P16-3 Using the square root method, how much of product A should a factory buy on each order if it used $20,000 worth last year, if it costs $2 to issue a purchase order, if it costs 5 percent of the cost of inventory to maintain it, and prices are expected to be the same next year?

P16-4 Explain some of the things which should be considered when determining the size of the minimum inventory to be used as a reordering point in a factory.

P16-5 What method would you suggest to control inventories for a neighbourhood drugstore? Be specific.

CONTINUING PROBLEM:
THE SUCCESS HARDWARE STORE

Part 16. Inventory Control and Purchasing Policy

Assignment for Part 16

Prepare a short report explaining your plan for inventory control. Will you adopt one of the control plans recited in the chapter? How will your plan work? What protection will you have against stockouts? Will you avoid excessive inventory? Will your minimum inventory for various items of merchandise be different? What other things should be included in your plan?

REFERENCES FOR FURTHER READING

Archer, Maurice, *An Introduction to Canadian Business,* 3d ed., McGraw-Hill Ryerson Ltd., Toronto, 1978, chaps. 21 and 22.

Broom, H. N., and J. G. Longenecker, *Small Business Management,* 2d ed., South-Western Publishing Co., Inc., Cincinnati, 1966, chap. 25.

"Control Over Inventory Investment," Your Business Matters, No. 8, The Royal Bank of Canada, 1976.

Davidson, William R., and Alton F. Doody, *Retailing Management,* 3d ed., The Ronald Press Co., New York, 1966, chap. 18.

Glos, Raymond E., and Harold A. Baker, *Business: Its Nature and Environment,* 7th ed., South-Western Publishing Co., Inc., Cincinnati, 1972, chap. 16.

Kriz, Joseph A., and Curtis J. Duggan, *Your Dynamic World of Business,* McGraw-Hill Book Co., New York, 1973, chap. 4. "Pointers on Raw Materials Inventory Control (2)," *Small Business Administration* Publication 1.10/2:12, Annual No. 12, No. 155.

Preshing, W. A., *Business Management in Canada,* Wiley Publishers of Canada Ltd., Toronto, 1974, chap. 22.

Part 6

FINANCIAL MANAGEMENT AND CONTROL

CHAPTER 17

Fixed and Variable Expense Analysis: The Break-Even Chart

I don't see the value in studying expenses to see if they are fixed or variable. They are all expenses, and they all have to be paid. No small business owner likes expenses, and he always tries to keep them down as much as possible.

The Late Learner

A business which has only variable expenses, all varying directly and proportionately with sales, cannot possibly operate at a loss. Such a business would be very unusual. Yet the idea is more than merely an academic or theoretical concept. Such firms are known to the authors.

The foregoing statements are offered here in the hope they will stimulate the student's interest in a study of the nature and consequences of fixed and variable expense relationships in any business firm.

Basic to such a study should be recognition of the fundamental law of business that the greater the risk, the greater must be the potential profits. It follows that when the risk of loss is removed or even lessened, the potential profits must be less. Some sacrifices must be made in exchange for the protection against loss. In the case of the firm which has only variable expenses which vary directly and proportionately with sales, the sacrifice is that the profit margin on the first dollar of sales is the same as the profit margin on the last dollar of sales. Such a firm which has total expenses of 85 percent of sales will have a profit of 15 cents on the first dollar of sales and a 15-cent profit on the one hundred-thousandth dollar of sales. Many small firm owners of long experience would likely welcome such an arrangement in exchange for this protection against loss if, indeed, it was possible to attain such an expense position. Although such a position is extremely rare, in fact impossible in almost all cases, the facts involved can be useful in making decisions for any business.

WHAT ARE FIXED EXPENSES?

By definition, fixed expenses are those which do not change with the sales volume. No matter what the sales are, the expense stays the same. A good example is the set monthly rent paid for the store or factory premises. The rent may be $400 per month. This is known as a flat rental. Such a rental has no relation to the volume of sales made by the business during the month. It must be paid every month whether sales are good or bad. This is a true fixed expense. Other fixed expenses in a typical small firm are depreciation expenses on fixed assets, skeleton-staff salaries, property taxes, amortization of organization expense, and most insurance premiums. In all these cases, too, the expense goes on at the same amount without reference to sales made.

WHAT ARE VARIABLE EXPENSES?

By definition, variable expenses are those which change with the sales volume of business. One type varies directly and proportionately with sales, the best example being commission expense. If all sales persons, for example, receive commissions only and no sales are made, there is no commission expense. As sales grow larger and larger, the commissions grow accordingly. If all sales persons receive commissions of 10 percent of sales, the commission expense account grows directly and proportionately to total sales. Such expenses are the exception.

Most variable expenses do *not* vary directly and proportionately with sales. In fact, there are all degrees of variability. As a result, most variable expenses are really *semivariable*. Let us examine some of the typical variable expenses to determine how closely they vary with sales.

1 Cost of Goods Sold Normally, the expense of cost of goods sold will bear a close relationship to sales made. But it may vary somewhat if there are increases in the price paid for merchandise which cannot be offset by increases in sales prices, or if special bargain purchases are made which increase profit margins. These situations seldom make a large percentage change in the relationship between cost of goods sold and sales. Strong competitive pricing situations may force owners to adjust their prices unwillingly in order to maintain average margins. Cost of goods sold can, therefore, be considered in most cases as bearing a direct and almost proportionate relationship to sales.

2 Utilities Expenses Utilities expenses cover the cost of such items as telephone, electricity, water, and gas. If these expenses are billed on a flat per-month charge, they are truly fixed expenses. If they are charged on a usage basis and the use varies from period to period during the fiscal year, a distinct variable factor is involved. Telephone and telegram expenses usually have a tendency to rise with increased sales volume. Heating in the winter by electricity or gas, or cooling in summer may bring variability into these utility charges. Many firms have a policy of charging the basic telephone bill as a fixed expense and the extra charges for long-distance calls and telegrams as variable expenses. Where the variations are small from month to month in total utilities expense, most firms consider the total as a fixed expense.

3 Advertising and Promotion Expense If a specified amount is set aside for these items in the yearly budget and if it is spent on a regular program or at specified periods, the total can be considered a fixed expense. If the policy of the firm is to increase or decrease its expenditures for advertising and promotion on a basis of monthly decisions, for example, it becomes a variable expense. Many firms have a policy of planning a specific advertising budget but remain open to extra advertising for special occasions. In these cases, the planned budget could be considered a fixed expense and the extra expenditures would be considered variable when analyzing the total operation for a specific period.

4 Salaries for Sales Staff A common mistake is failure to analyze the expense of salaries for sales staff and to assume that it is 100 percent variable expense. So doing neglects the concept of a skeleton staff. By skeleton sales staff we mean the minimum number of sales persons who must be on hand to keep the doors open for business.

Salaries for these people are a fixed expense. The variable portion of sales salaries is all salaries which will be expanded or contracted with changes in the sales volume. Competent managements study the need for adding sales people as sales grow. Often they find the need for part-time people in certain seasons or on certain days of the week, or even during certain hours of the day. Sales salaries still do not vary directly and proportionately with sales volume. As sales increase, new sales persons are added to the payroll so that four people are doing the work in a leisurely way that three persons were doing last week under considerable pressure. Thus sales and sales salaries do move in the same direction but not proportionately at any given time. Figure 17-1 illustrates the relationship of sales and most semivariable expenses. Points *A, C, E,* and *G* might represent the addition of a new sales person, a new bookkeeper, or a second delivery boy. At these points there is a vertical increase in the dollar total of the variable expenses. Between points *B* and *C, D* and *E, F* and *G,* and *H* and *J,* the variable expenses stay the same. As sales increase, each semivariable expense tends to increase also.

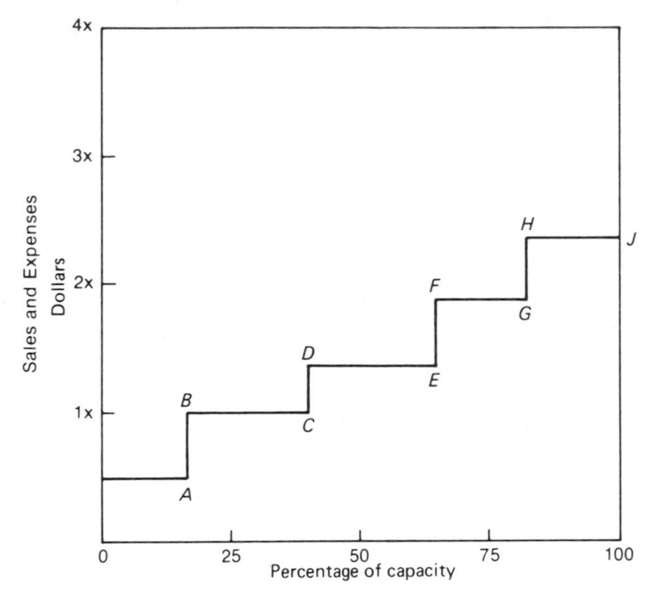

Figure 17-1 *Relationship of sales and semi-variable expenses.*

5 Rent Expense and Percentage Lease Rentals Landlords have long demonstrated that they are more competent in knowing the value of store or factory space than most small firm owners. In most big cities especially, the percentage lease rental arrangement is replacing the flat rental previously mentioned. A percentage lease provides a minimum flat fee plus an additional charge made on sales above certain amounts. For example, the total rental charge may call for a minimum of $400 per month plus 1 percent of sales over $100,000 annually and 2 percent of sales over $200,000. In such a case, the $400 flat charge is a fixed expense and the additional charge is a variable expense. Small firm planners must be prepared to evaluate the type of lease they are offered. Under the flat rental plan, the proprietor has a chance to retain more profits when business is very good. Under the percentage lease, the proprietor shares the profit of extra sales with the landlord. It would be most unusual for the landlord to give the firm a completely variable rental contract. Some instances are known. Requests for such rental arrangements may be appropriate.

6 Delivery Expenses Are they fixed or variable? Would the delivery boy be discharged if sales were down 50 percent? Not if the same routes were to be covered but with fewer deliveries. Perhaps the deliveries would be less frequent each day. Perhaps the bookkeeper would operate the truck half the time. Gas, oil, and maintenance expenses should reflect some variation with a wide variation in sales volume. The policy of the owner on these matters in any given situation will determine whether the total is considered fixed, variable, or divided into parts of each.

THE BREAK-EVEN CHART

Knowing what the total expenses are and how to make a break-even chart are essential to good management. A correct break-even chart is valuable as a supplement to budget making, pricing policies, decisions on sales policies, and expense control and expansion plans, among other things. The completely competent business person should know what sales volume is necessary to break even (the point where there is no profit and no loss). The break-even chart can indicate the profits to be achieved at different levels of expanded sales. It can tell the results of changes in price policies and the benefits of expense reductions which might be available.

A break-even chart shows the relationship of fixed, variable, and total expenses to sales at all volumes of sales. It measures all expenses and income from sales on the vertical axis and the units sold or percentage of capacity on the horizontal axis. Profits at any level of capacity or at any volume of sales are measured by the vertical distance between the total expense line and the sales income line.

An accurately drawn break-even chart tells firm owners what sales volumes are necessary to reach the break-even point and the percentage of their capacity this sales volume represents. It tells them the profits to be derived from any planned expansion of sales. These relationships are measured against a presently existing set of facilities and expense analysis. Any change of store space, for example, would call for the creation of a new chart made for the expanded facilities and expenses.

An example of a complete break-even chart is shown in Figure 17-2. It has been prepared for the Jones Department Store, which had sales for the year of $300,000, fixed expenses of $50,000, variable expenses of $150,000, and total expenses of $200,000. The firm operated at 60 percent of capacity during the year. Students should study this chart to see how each line is plotted, where the two connecting points for each line are, and the reasons for each. Be sure you can tell how to measure the profit for the year on this chart.

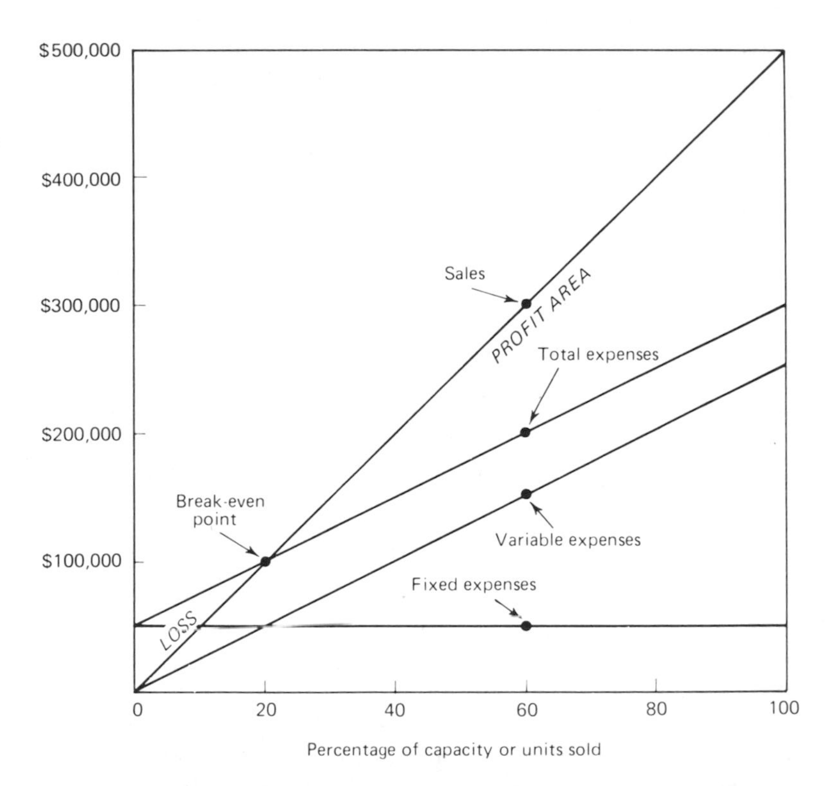

Figure 17-2 *Break-even chart for the Jones Department Store.*

Making Your Own Break-Even Chart

Most students and most owners of small firms will recognize the preceding example of a break-even chart and appreciate its usefulness. The actual construction of such a chart for a specific firm is not so widely understood. All small firm owners should know how to construct such a chart and how to use it for purposes of analyzing their operations.

The following is a step-by-step explanation of how to construct a break-even chart for any business when the percentage of capacity is known. Each step is illustrated on the break-even chart shown in Figure 17-3.

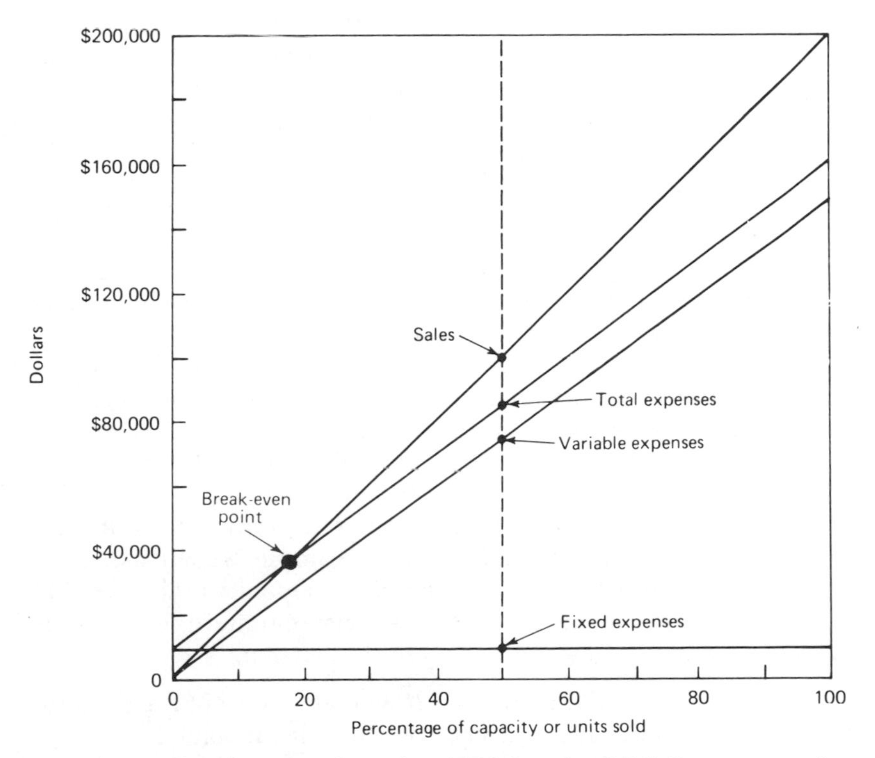

Figure 17-3 *Break-even chart for 1978 for the ABC Company when the percentage of capacity is known.*

Step 1 Analyze each operating expense on the income statement (or planned income statement) to determine whether it is fixed, variable, or divided between these two according to the policies of the owner. List the fixed expenses in one column and the variable expenses in another column. Total the columns and add the cost of goods sold to the variable expense column. For this illustration we will use the ABC Company, which had sales of $100,000 for the year, costs of goods sold of $50,000, and operating expenses of $35,000, broken down into fixed and variable expenses as follows:

Fixed expenses		Variable expenses	
Flat rental paid	$6,400	Sales salaries	$15,000
Taxes	1,200	Office salaries	8,000
Depreciation	400	Percentage lease, extra payment	500
Delivery expense	1,400	Telephone & telegrams	500
Utilities expense	600	Advertising & promotion	1,000
		Subtotal	$25,000
		Cost of goods sold	50,000
Total fixed expense	$10,000	Total variable expense	$75,000

Step 2 On a blank sheet of paper (or graph paper), draw the vertical and horizontal axes for your chart. The chart should be about 5 inches square. Label the vertical axis "Dollars (sales and expenses)" and the horizontal axis "Percentage of Capacity" or "Units Sold." Divide each axis into equal parts and mark each division with a dot. Place dollar amounts on each dot on the vertical axis, beginning with zero at the lower left corner and increasing in equal amounts to the top of the vertical axis. The dollar amount at the top of the vertical axis should represent sales at 100 percent of capacity if known. This amount is broken up into 10 equal amounts. In our example, we will assume that operations for the year were at 50 percent of capacity and use $200,000 as the top figure on the vertical axis, with cumulative divisions of $20,000 each as the scale starts from the bottom.

Step 3 Draw a solid line from the lower left corner of the chart to the upper right corner. This will become the sales income line.

Step 4 Find the point of 50 percent capacity on the horizontal axis. Draw a vertical dotted line from the bottom of the chart to the top of this at 50 percent capacity point.

Step 5 On the vertical dotted line, mark the points representing $10,000, $75,000, $85,000, and $100,000, all measured against the left axis. These points mark the total of fixed, variable, and total expenses and the sales volume at 50 percent of capacity.

Step 6 On the left axis, mark the point for $10,000. This is the total fixed expenses and total expenses at zero sales, or zero percentage of capacity.

Step 7 Every complete break-even chart should have four lines. We drew the sales line in step 3, which bisects the square chart. Now draw the other three lines. Fixed expenses, by definition, are the same regardless of sales volume. Therefore, connect the $10,000 mark on the left axis and the $10,000 mark on the vertical dotted line, and extend the straight line on across the chart. Variable expenses, by definition, are zero at zero sales and $75,000 at 50 percent of capacity. Therefore, connect the point zero on the left axis with the $75,000 mark on the vertical dotted line, and extend the straight line on across the chart. Total expenses are the combination of both fixed and variable expenses. That total is $10,000 at zero sales and $85,000 at 50 percent of capacity. Therefore, connect the $10,000 point on the left axis and the $85,000 mark on the vertical dotted line, and extend the straight line on across the chart.

We now have a break-even chart for the ABC Company. It tells us many things about the operations. Among these things are the following:

1 The break-even point for the firm is a sales volume of $40,000. This is the point in sales volume where neither profit nor loss will result. On the chart it is found at the point where the sales line and the total expense line cross. Any sales less than $40,000 would put operations in the loss area of the chart. As sales expand into the profit area, profits become larger and larger.

2 Only 20 percent of possible capacity is necessary to reach the break-even point. This is found by comparing the break-even point with the horizontal scale. It follows that $40,000 of sales represents 20 percent of capacity.

3 Profit on the $100,000 of sales for the year was $15,000—measured by the vertical distance between the total expense line and the sales line, read against the vertical dollar axis.

4 As sales volume expands, the profits on each succeeding dollar of income is greater than on the preceding dollar. A sales increase from 50 to 60 percent of capacity will not yield as much profit as an increase from 70 to 80 percent of capacity. The reason is that after we pass the break-even point, all fixed expenses are covered and only the variable expenses must be borne by subsequent sales.

5 We can measure the profit results of a 10 percent increase in prices, for example, by superimposing another sales line from the lower left corner across the chart connecting through the vertical dotted line at the point of $110,000 ($100,00 plus 10 percent). We can also observe the results of a 10 percent reduction in total expenses by superimposing a line from $9,000 ($10,000 less 10 percent) through the point $76,500 ($85,000 less 10 percent) on the vertical dotted line. This type of analysis may be necessary if the firm is faced with the necessity of increasing income or reducing expenses. In any event, it provides good information for decision making and study of the operation.

6 If sales could be expanded to 100 percent of capacity, profits would rise to $40,000—again the vertical distance between sales and total expenses on the right axes. As a practical matter, we can observe that if this point is even approached, most small firms have already made plans to expand their facilities.

Finding the break-even point by formula:
If the only objective is to ascertain the dollar volume necessary to break even when sales, fixed expenses, and variable expenses are known, the following formula will give a ready answer:

$$\text{B.E.P.} = \frac{\text{fixed expenses}}{1 - \text{variable expenses over sales}}$$

Applying this formula to our problem above will show the same 40,000 break-even point in dollars:

$$\frac{\$10{,}000}{1 - \$75{,}000/\$100{,}000} = \frac{\$10{,}000}{1 - 0.75} = \underline{\underline{\$40{,}000}}$$

Finding the break-even quantity by formula:
If you would like to calculate the volume of output to break even (i.e., total revenue is exactly equal to total costs) at a given selling price, use the following formula:

$$\text{B.E.Q.} = \frac{\text{fixed expenses}}{\text{price per unit sold} - \text{variable expenses per unit}}$$

In our example, if the variable expenses are $1.00 per unit and the selling price is $1.33, then:

$$\text{B.E.Q.} = \frac{\$10{,}000}{\$1.33 - \$1.00} = \frac{\$10{,}000}{\$.33} = \underline{\underline{30{,}000 \text{ units}}}$$

The Problem of Measuring Capacity

The problem of determining at what percentage of capacity the firm operated has prevented many small firm owners from making maximum use of a break-even chart. This problem can be easily removed.

A factory operation which has machines which can produce 100 units of its products a day can easily determine 100 percent of its capacity. It merely multiplies working days times 100 units to find what production will be if full production is maintained during the month or year. By then comparing actual production with this capacity, the percentage is determined. For example, if the plant operates 250 days per year and 100 units is capacity per day, maximum production at 100 percent capacity would be 25,000 units. If actual production is 15,000 units, the percentage of capacity for operation during the year is 60 percent (15,000 divided by 25,000).

For retail and wholesale operations, the measurement of utilized capacity is not easily determined. Some retailers use a flat amount of sales per sales person (for example $300 per day) to represent 100 percent of capacity. This method must include the number of sales persons who can conveniently operate in the available sales space. Others attempt to combine average sale, time required per sale, sales people's time on the sales floor, and number of sales people who can conveniently operate in the sales space, to arrive at a figure which would represent 100 percent capacity sales for a given period. Store hours must be considered in any such calculation.

How to Make a Break-Even Chart When Percentage of Capacity Is Not Known

It is not necessary to resort to these types of calculations to have the benefit of a break-even chart. The chart in Figure 17-4 has been constructed without reference to the percentage of capacity at which the firm operated. Its construction is explained in detail following the chart.

Figure 17-4 shows the break-even chart when the percentage of capacity or number of units is not known. The same ABC Company data is used.

Step 1 Find any convenient point on the vertical scale to insert the $100,000 sales volume. Any point about midway up the scale is normally used unless it is felt that close-to-maximum capacity has been achieved. In that case, choose a higher point on the vertical scale.

Step 2 Bisect the angle on the grid at the lower left corner. Extend this line far enough across the grid so that it allows for the maximum length of the horizontal and vertical lines. This is the sales line on any break-even chart.

Step 3 Scale the vertical axis in even units from the point where you inserted the $100,000 amount for sales.

Step 4 Draw a horizontal dotted line from the $100,000 sales point completely across the grid. Where the horizontal dotted line crosses the sales line, draw a vertical dotted line from bottom to top of the grid.

Step 5 On the vertical dotted line, plot the points for fixed, variable, and total expense against the vertical axis scale.

Step 6 Draw the lines for fixed, variable, and total expenses from the left axis to the plotting points on the vertical dotted line. Remember sales and variable expenses connect at the point zero on the vertical axis, and fixed expenses and total expenses connect at the point of fixed expenses ($10,000) on the vertical axis.

When we compare this chart with Figure 17-3, it will be seen that the

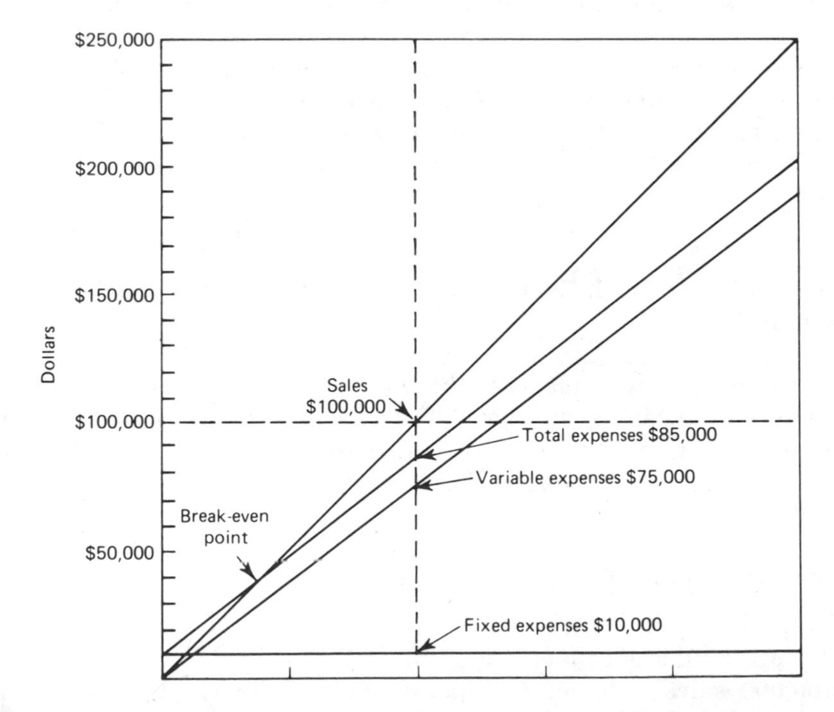

Figure 17-4 *Break-even chart for 1978 for the ABC Company when the percentage of capacity is unknown.*

scale is different, but all readings are identical. The break-even point calls for the same volume of sales, and profits are the same at all sales volumes. The only thing unknown is the percentage of capacity represented at each measuring point. The profit effects of an increase in sales can still be measured in the same manner.

QUESTIONS FOR CLASS DISCUSSION

Q17-1 Is it possible for any business to be immune to loss? How?

Q17-2 What sacrifices must a business make to reduce risk?

Q17-3 What types of expenses increase directly and proportionately with sales?

Q17-4 What expenses increase directly but not proportionately with sales?

Q17-5 If the rent is $400 per month plus 1 percent of sales over $50,000, how would you classify the total rent expense?

Q17-6 What do we mean by the "skeleton staff expenses"?

Q17-7 What are the three most important things you believe a break-even chart tells you?

Q17-8 Does an annual break-even chart reflect seasonal variations in sales volume?

Q17-9 Why is the cost of goods sold added to the variable operating expenses when making a break-even chart?

Q17-10 Is it true that the greater the fixed expenses, the further to the right is the break-even point? Why?

Q17-11 What other uses can an owner make of an accurate break-even chart?

Q17-12 Do you consider delivery expenses a fixed or a variable expense? Explain.

PROBLEMS AND QUESTIONS FOR WRITTEN ASSIGNMENT

P17-1 On a 5-inch grid, draw a break-even chart for a firm which operated at 60 percent of capacity with sales of $450,000, variable expenses of $300,000 including cost of goods sold, and fixed expenses of $100,000.

P17-2 From your break-even chart, determine the amount of profit earned for the year. What was its break-even point both in dollars of sales and in percentage of capacity? What would its profits be if it operated at 90 percent of capacity?

P17-3 Construct your own break-even chart with your own figures for two different kinds of firms. Make the fixed expenses much higher for one firm than for the other. When you compare the two charts, which firm needs a higher capacity of sales to reach the break-even point? Can you explain why?

CONTINUING PROBLEM:
THE SUCCESS HARDWARE STORE

Part 17. Expense Control and a Break-Even Chart

Assignment for Part 17

a Using your budgeted income statement as the basis, prepare a list of the fixed expenses in one column and the variable expenses in a second column. Add the cost of goods sold to the variable expense total. Some expenses may be divided between fixed and variable.

b Using the column totals, prepare a break-even chart for the hardware store on a 5-inch grid. Assume that the store operated at 60 percent of capacity during the first year. Below the chart indicate the sales volume in dollars and the percentage of capacity required at the break-even point.

REFERENCES FOR FURTHER READING

Broom, H.N., and J.G. Longenecker, *Small Business Management,* 2d ed., South-Western Publishing Co., Inc., Cincinnati, 1966, chap. 10.

Gist, Ronald R., *Retailing,* John Wiley & Sons Inc., New York, 1968, chap. 18.

Hart, Donald J., *Introduction to Business in a Dynamic Society,* 2d ed., Macmillan Publishing Co., Inc., New York, 1970, chap. 11.

Meigs *et al., Accounting: The Basics for Business Decisions,* 2nd Can. ed., McGraw-Hill Ryerson Ltd., Toronto, 1976, chap. 27.

Preshing, W.A., *Business Management in Canada,* Wiley Publishers of Canada Ltd., Toronto, 1974, chap. 35.

CHAPTER 18

Selling on Credit: Administering a Credit Program

When I started my business, I knew that people had to have credit to buy things when they wanted them rather than waiting for payday. But I thought they would always pay me the next payday. Was I wrong! I had to borrow money to pay my own current bills while waiting for customers to pay their accounts. And some of them never paid me. Thank goodness for credit cards.

The Late Learner

CREDIT SELLING WILL INCREASE SALES

There are very few axioms in the world of business. But one of them is "if you sell on credit you will increase sales, even to the same customers to whom you previously sold for cash only." This alluring proposition has great appeal to small business firms. Sales are the foundation of profits, and anything which will help to increase sales commands the attention of competent business owners.

But there is more to credit selling than meets the eye. Every retail business must first decide whether it will offer credit arrangements to its customers. If credit is to be available, a decision must be made about the kind of credit to be extended. Will the firm sell to its customers on open account and carry these accounts receivable on its own books until they are paid? Or will it sell to credit card holders who have been approved for credit by one or more of the many credit-card companies now so active throughout Canada? In this chapter we will review the details of both of these types of consumer credit.

TRADE CREDIT VERSUS CONSUMER CREDIT

Trade credit is credit extended from one business firm to another. *Consumer credit* is credit given by retailers to their customers, who are the final users of the products or services sold. Sales by manufacturers and wholesalers are almost always made on a credit basis. Retail sales on credit are now about half of the total retail sales in the country. Only the growing popularity of chain grocery stores and others which sell for cash only has kept retail sales on credit from growing larger.

Trade credit almost always carries a sales discount for prompt payment. We have seen in Chapter 16 that "terms of sale 2/10, n/30," for example, means that 2 percent of the total amount may be deducted if the invoice is paid within 10 days, but the entire amount is due in 30 days. Such discounts are extremely rare in consumer credit. The trend is quite the opposite. Most retail sales on credit carry a charge to customers for the privilege of postponing their payment to a later date. Large firms have adopted this practice more than small firms. Various types of consumer credit accounts will be discussed later in this chapter.

THE BUSINESS WORLD OPERATES ON CREDIT—OF NECESSITY

Our business world could not operate without credit. There is not enough currency and coin in the country to finance the business transactions carried on every day. Total bank deposits exceed the actual money in the country several times over. The key is credit extended throughout the economy. Without credit from banks, credit from other business firms, and the sale of securities, large and small manufacturers could not operate. Without credit from manufacturers, banks, and other sources, wholesalers could not operate. Retailers depend on credit from banks and wholesalers. Without credit terms available, the average family could not buy a home, an automobile, major appliances, or finance expensive vacations. The importance of the credit standing of the business firm and of individuals is obvious. Unless a reputation for prompt payment of obligations is developed, credit sources will not be available. A good credit standing is essential to business success. Business owners must look for the same good credit standing of firms or individuals to whom they grant credit.

OPEN ACCOUNT CREDIT

Open account credit means that the merchant allows customers to say "charge it" when they make purchases. A copy of the sales slips for each purchase is recorded on the firm's books. The total charges for each customer are added and shown on a statement, which is sent to the customer, usually on the first of the following month. Such unpaid balances appear on the firm's balance sheet as accounts receivable. Open account credit operates quite differently from credit-card credit, which we will investigate later in this chapter.

Great care in granting such open account credit is most important. We have seen in Chapter 6 that, even when such credit is carefully granted, the firm will soon have a total investment in accounts receivable of 45 to 60 days' credit sales when they are selling on a 30-day credit basis. Careless credit granting will greatly increase this amount. Accounts receivable tie up the working capital of the firm. We have stressed in Chapter 6 the importance of the firm having sufficient cash in the business to be able to invest in such accounts receivable.

THE COSTS OF OPEN ACCOUNT CREDIT

Whenever a business firm, large or small, makes open account credit available to its customers, it automatically assumes additional costs. These should be seriously considered before a business owner embarks upon a general credit policy. Too many new small firms fail to recognize some of these costs. They include:

Bookkeeping costs to record customer purchases and payments received

Printing of sales slips, statement forms, letterheads, envelopes, and credit memos

Postage costs for mailing statements

Interest on working capital invested in accounts receivable

Collection costs for delinquent customers

The inevitable bad debts which are never collected

Full recognition of these costs has caused more and more small firms to turn to credit-card sales rather than carrying customer accounts on their own books.

The seriousness of the credit problem is emphasized by the aggregate losses on bad debts incurred every year by Canadian business firms. The most conservative estimates run into the millions. The most efficient firms are satisfied to keep their bad-debt losses below 2 percent of their credit sales. Studies show that small firms which exercise inadequate control over their credit extensions have often had losses on bad debts which exceed 5 percent of their credit sales. Profitability can be seriously affected in such cases. Such data point up the need for care in credit extension.

The longer a credit sale is carried on the books, the greater is the likelihood of its not being collected in full. This fact shows the necessity of close follow-up on accounts which become past due. Small firms too often have been lax in enforcing good collection procedures.

With the benefit of the foregoing facts about the world of credit, new firm planners can make choices for their firms. If they decide to sell on open account, either exclusively or in connection with credit-card sales, they must turn their attention to the question of which customers should be granted credit and on what basis.

ADMINISTERING A CREDIT PROGRAM

It has been seen that credit sales may increase total sales and profits. This is only true, however, if the increased sales do not cost more in administration expenses and bad-debt losses than the profits on the credit sales. Every firm should therefore have a procedure for granting credit. Any customer who asks for credit desires the use of the firm's capital. In exchange, the customer should be willing to comply with reasonable rules for granting of that credit. No exceptions should be made.

The credit manager always wants to be sure that the account will be paid. The manager must find out the applicant's record for payment, capacity to pay, and how much credit the applicant can properly handle. Everyone is worth some credit; the question is how much. No business does its customers favours by granting them more credit than they can handle. Such a credit policy only invites ill will from the customers in the long run and might even force them to consider bankruptcy. Giving credit is a serious responsibility.

Well-managed companies take the following steps in granting credit:

1 Have the applicant for consumer credit fill out a credit application blank which calls for such basic information as name, address, age, present and past employment, length of employment, salary, home ownership details, past credit extended, payments now being made on other accounts, bank accounts, family status including dependents, and other asset information. An example of a credit application blank is shown in Figure 18-1. Applicants for trade credit should submit their companies' official financial statements.

PLEASE PRINT IN BLOCK LETTERS

LAST NAME	FIRST NAME	INITIALS	TELEPHONE NO.	SOCIAL INSURANCE NO.	NO. OF CARDS REQUIRED 1 ☐ 2 ☐
NO. AND STREET NAME (SPECIFY ST., AVE., RD., ETC.)		APT. NO.	☐ SINGLE ☐ SEPARATED ☐ MARRIED ☐ DIVORCED ☐ WIDOW(ER)	DATE OF BIRTH MONTH DAY YEAR	SPOUSE (FIRST NAME)
CITY	PROVINCE	POSTAL CODE	AT PRESENT ADDRESS ☐ OWN ☐ RENT $ PER MONTH ☐ WITH PARENTS	NO. OF DEPENDENTS (EXCLUDING SPOUSE)	DRIVER'S LICENSE NO.

PREVIOUS ADDRESS (IF AT PRESENT ADDRESS LESS THAN 2 YEARS)				HOW LONG?
EMPLOYER—NAME AND ADDRESS	TELEPHONE	OCCUPATION	HOW LONG?	GROSS MONTHLY INCOME $
PREVIOUS EMPLOYER (IF WITH ABOVE LESS THAN 2 YEARS)	TELEPHONE	OCCUPATION	HOW LONG?	GROSS MONTHLY INCOME $
SPOUSE NOW EMPLOYED BY—NAME AND ADDRESS	TELEPHONE	OCCUPATION	HOW LONG?	GROSS MONTHLY INCOME $
NAME AND ADDRESS OF NEAREST RELATIVE NOT LIVING WITH ME				RELATIONSHIP

REFERENCES					
BANK	BRANCH	☐ LOAN $ ☐ SAVINGS ACCT. NO.		☐ PCA NO. ☐ C/A NO.
HOME: FINANCED BY		$	$	$
		ESTIMATED VALUE	AMOUNT OWING	MONTHLY PAYMENT
AUTO: YEAR AND MAKE	FINANCED BY	$	$	$

OTHER LOANS (CREDIT CARDS, DEPT. STORES, FINANCE CO'S, ETC.)			
NAME	ADDRESS	$	$
		AMOUNT OWING	MONTHLY PAYMENT
NAME	ADDRESS	$	$
NAME	ADDRESS	$	$
		AMOUNT OWING	MONTHLY PAYMENT
NAME	ADDRESS	$	$

I, the undersigned, hereby certify the above information to be true and, if this application is accepted, request card(s) be issued to me, and renewals or replacements thereof from time to time. In connection with such issuance, renewal or replacement, the undersigned authorizes and consents to the receipt and exchange of credit information and agrees to abide by the terms of the issuing Cardholder's Agreement. Use of such card shall evidence receipt of such Cardholder's Agreement.

DATE ________ APPLICANT'S SIGNATURE X ________

Figure 18-1 *Typical application for credit used by large firms. Small firms should be equally careful in extending credit.*

2 Check the applicant's credit record with local credit bureaus and other credit agencies. Find out what limits were placed on the applicant's credit by other firms. Remember you are always looking for evidence of the applicant's possession of the "four C's of credit." These are character, capital, capacity, and conditions. Trade-credit applicants are checked by credit bureaus and/or by Dun & Bradstreet, a general trade-credit agency. (See Figures 18-2 and 18-3.)

3 On the basis of knowledge gathered from an independent investigation plus confirmation of information on the application, determine the limit of credit you feel can safely be granted. If the investigation proves that an applicant is a high risk, the decision must be to deny any credit at all. Assuming that investigation proves an applicant worthy of credit, compare the desired merchandise purchase with the limit you have set. This will determine whether the applicant should be granted credit on an installment-loan basis, a revolving-account basis, a budget-account basis, or an open charge account. (These accounts are explained below.)

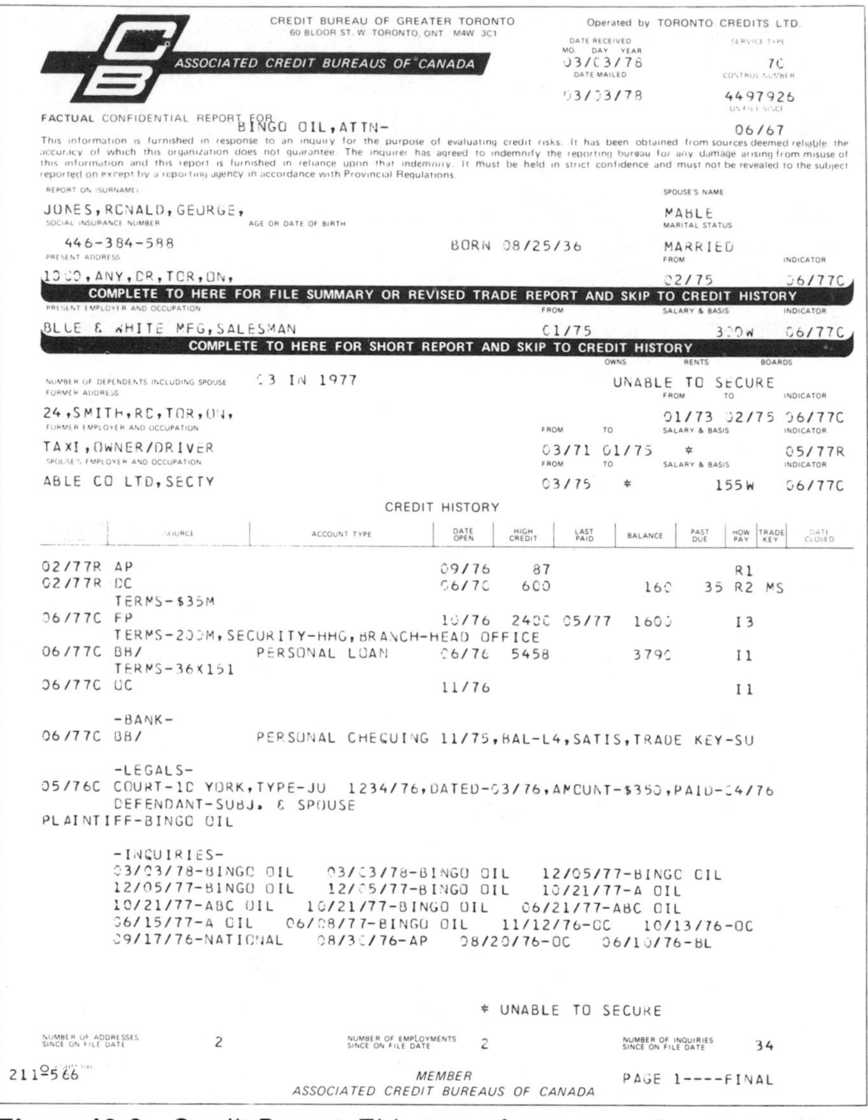

CREDIT BUREAU OF GREATER TORONTO
60 BLOOR ST. W. TORONTO, ONT. M4W 3C1

Operated by TORONTO CREDITS LTD.

ACB ASSOCIATED CREDIT BUREAUS OF CANADA

DATE RECEIVED MO. DAY YEAR: 03/03/78
SERVICE TYPE: 7C
DATE MAILED: 03/03/78
CONTROL NUMBER: 4497926
ON FILE SINCE: 06/67

FACTUAL CONFIDENTIAL REPORT FOR BINGO OIL,ATTN-

This information is furnished in response to an inquiry for the purpose of evaluating credit risks. It has been obtained from sources deemed reliable, the accuracy of which this organization does not guarantee. The inquirer has agreed to indemnify the reporting bureau for any damage arising from misuse of this information and this report is furnished in reliance upon that indemnity. It must be held in strict confidence and must not be revealed to the subject reported on except by a reporting agency in accordance with Provincial Regulations.

REPORT ON (SURNAME): JONES,RONALD,GEORGE,
SPOUSE'S NAME: MABLE
SOCIAL INSURANCE NUMBER: 446-384-588
AGE OR DATE OF BIRTH: BORN 08/25/36
MARITAL STATUS: MARRIED
PRESENT ADDRESS: 1000,ANY,DR,TOR,ON,
FROM: 02/75 INDICATOR: 06/77C

COMPLETE TO HERE FOR FILE SUMMARY OR REVISED TRADE REPORT AND SKIP TO CREDIT HISTORY

PRESENT EMPLOYER AND OCCUPATION: BLUE & WHITE MFG,SALESMAN
FROM: 01/75 SALARY & BASIS: 300W INDICATOR: 06/77C

COMPLETE TO HERE FOR SHORT REPORT AND SKIP TO CREDIT HISTORY

NUMBER OF DEPENDENTS INCLUDING SPOUSE: 03 IN 1977
OWNS / RENTS / BOARDS: UNABLE TO SECURE
FORMER ADDRESS: 24,SMITH,RC,TOR,ON,
FROM: 01/73 TO: 02/75 INDICATOR: 06/77C
FORMER EMPLOYER AND OCCUPATION: TAXI,OWNER/DRIVER
FROM: 03/71 TO: 01/75 SALARY & BASIS: * INDICATOR: 05/77R
SPOUSE'S EMPLOYER AND OCCUPATION: ABLE CO LTD,SECTY
FROM: 03/75 TO: * SALARY & BASIS: 155W INDICATOR: 06/77C

CREDIT HISTORY

	SOURCE	ACCOUNT TYPE	DATE OPEN	HIGH CREDIT	LAST PAID	BALANCE	PAST DUE	HOW PAY	TRADE KEY	DATE CLOSED
02/77R	AP		09/76	87				R1		
02/77R	DC		06/70	600		160	35	R2	MS	
	TERMS-$35M									
06/77C	FP		10/76	2400	05/77	1600		I3		
	TERMS-200M,SECURITY-HHG,BRANCH-HEAD OFFICE									
06/77C	BB/	PERSONAL LOAN	06/76	5458		3790		I1		
	TERMS-36X151									
06/77C	OC		11/76					I1		

-BANK-
06/77C BB/ PERSONAL CHEQUING 11/75,BAL-L4,SATIS,TRADE KEY-SU

-LEGALS-
05/76C COURT-1D YORK,TYPE-JU 1234/76,DATED-03/76,AMOUNT-$350,PAID-04/76
DEFENDANT-SUBJ. & SPOUSE
PLAINTIFF-BINGO OIL

-INQUIRIES-
03/03/78-BINGO OIL 03/03/78-BINGO OIL 12/05/77-BINGO OIL
12/05/77-BINGO OIL 12/05/77-BINGO OIL 10/21/77-A OIL
10/21/77-ABC OIL 10/21/77-BINGO OIL 06/21/77-ABC OIL
06/15/77-A OIL 06/08/77-BINGO OIL 11/12/76-OC 10/13/76-OC
09/17/76-NATIONAL 08/30/76-AP 08/20/76-OC 06/10/76-BL

* UNABLE TO SECURE

NUMBER OF ADDRESSES SINCE ON FILE DATE: 2
NUMBER OF EMPLOYMENTS SINCE ON FILE DATE: 2
NUMBER OF INQUIRIES SINCE ON FILE DATE: 34

211-5 66

MEMBER
ASSOCIATED CREDIT BUREAUS OF CANADA

PAGE 1----FINAL

Figure 18-2 *Credit Report. This type of report may be obtained from local credit bureaus when a business owner is checking on the eligibility of credit applicants. Courtesy Credit Bureau of Greater Toronto*

4 Discuss your decision with all applicants. Explain the reasons for the decision if asked. Support your decision by explaining that applicants' payments must be in line with their available income and that you are protecting them from getting too far into debt.

5 Follow up on new credit accounts regularly. This can be done

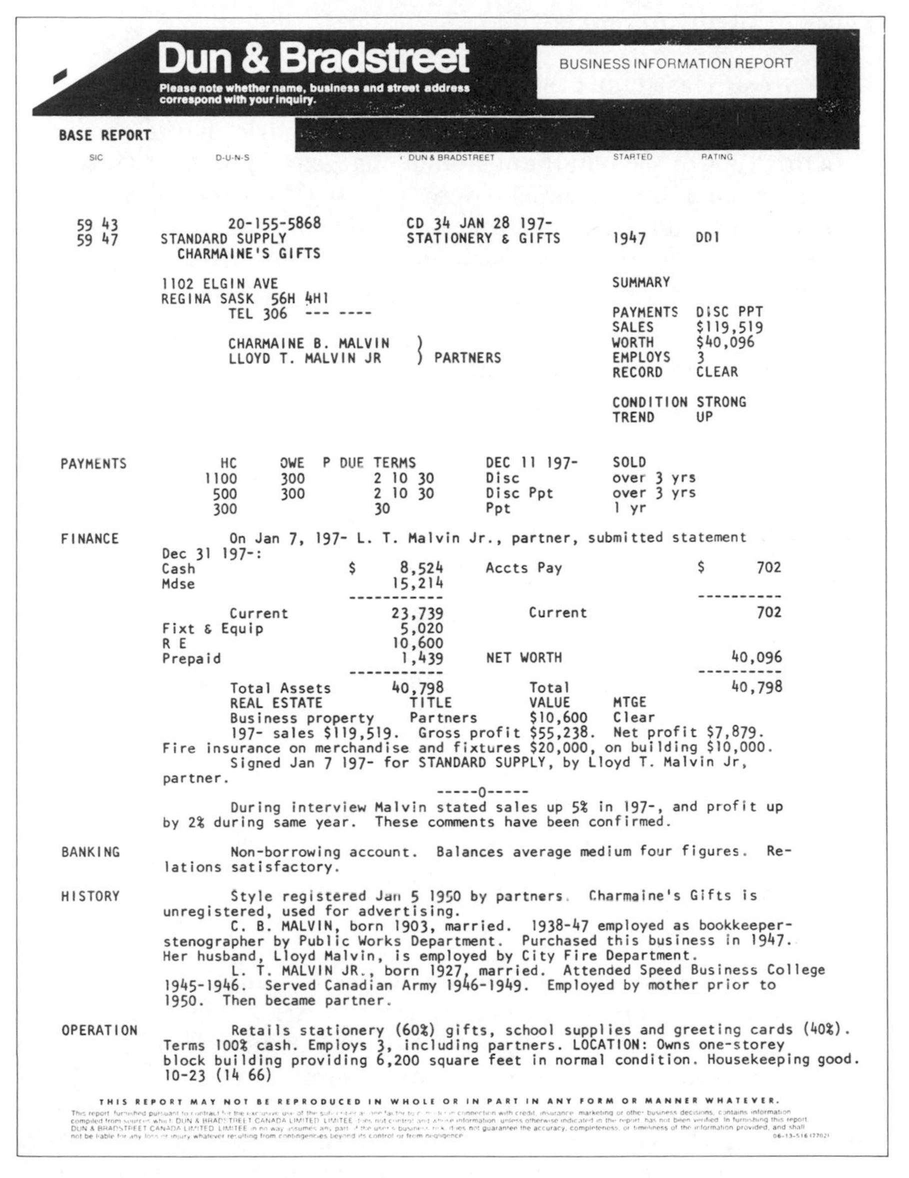

Dun & Bradstreet

Please note whether name, business and street address correspond with your inquiry.

BUSINESS INFORMATION REPORT

BASE REPORT

SIC	D-U-N-S	© DUN & BRADSTREET	STARTED	RATING
59 43	20-155-5868	CD 34 JAN 28 197-		
59 47	STANDARD SUPPLY CHARMAINE'S GIFTS	STATIONERY & GIFTS	1947	DD1

1102 ELGIN AVE
REGINA SASK 56H 4H1
TEL 306 --- ----

CHARMAINE B. MALVIN
LLOYD T. MALVIN JR } PARTNERS

SUMMARY

PAYMENTS	DISC PPT
SALES	$119,519
WORTH	$40,096
EMPLOYS	3
RECORD	CLEAR
CONDITION	STRONG
TREND	UP

PAYMENTS

HC	OWE	P DUE	TERMS	DEC 11 197-	SOLD
1100	300		2 10 30	Disc	over 3 yrs
500	300		2 10 30	Disc Ppt	over 3 yrs
300			30	Ppt	1 yr

FINANCE

On Jan 7, 197- L. T. Malvin Jr., partner, submitted statement Dec 31 197-:

Cash	$ 8,524	Accts Pay	$ 702
Mdse	15,214		
Current	23,739	Current	702
Fixt & Equip	5,020		
R E	10,600		
Prepaid	1,439	NET WORTH	40,096
Total Assets	40,798	Total	40,798

REAL ESTATE	TITLE	VALUE	MTGE
Business property	Partners	$10,600	Clear

197- sales $119,519. Gross profit $55,238. Net profit $7,879. Fire insurance on merchandise and fixtures $20,000, on building $10,000.

Signed Jan 7 197- for STANDARD SUPPLY, by Lloyd T. Malvin Jr, partner.

-----0-----

During interview Malvin stated sales up 5% in 197-, and profit up by 2% during same year. These comments have been confirmed.

BANKING

Non-borrowing account. Balances average medium four figures. Relations satisfactory.

HISTORY

Style registered Jan 5 1950 by partners. Charmaine's Gifts is unregistered, used for advertising.

C. B. MALVIN, born 1903, married. 1938-47 employed as bookkeeper-stenographer by Public Works Department. Purchased this business in 1947. Her husband, Lloyd Malvin, is employed by City Fire Department.

L. T. MALVIN JR., born 1927, married. Attended Speed Business College 1945-1946. Served Canadian Army 1946-1949. Employed by mother prior to 1950. Then became partner.

OPERATION

Retails stationery (60%) gifts, school supplies and greeting cards (40%). Terms 100% cash. Employs 3, including partners. LOCATION: Owns one-storey block building providing 6,200 square feet in normal condition. Housekeeping good.
10-23 (14 66)

THIS REPORT MAY NOT BE REPRODUCED IN WHOLE OR IN PART IN ANY FORM OR MANNER WHATEVER.

This report furnished pursuant to contract for the exclusive use of the subscriber as one factor to [illegible] in connection with credit, insurance, marketing or other business decisions, contains information compiled from sources which DUN & BRADSTREET CANADA LIMITED LIMITEE does not control and whose information, unless otherwise indicated in the report, has not been verified. In furnishing this report DUN & BRADSTREET CANADA LIMITED LIMITEE in no way assumes any part of the user's business risk, does not guarantee the accuracy, completeness, or timeliness of the information provided, and shall not be liable for any loss or injury whatever resulting from contingencies beyond its control or from negligence. 06-13-516 (7702)

Figure 18-3 *A typical business information report by Dun & Bradstreet Limited/Limitée.*

even before an aging of accounts receivable (to be explained later in this chapter) is made. When payments are delinquent and notices and other steps taken have been ignored, it may be necessary to exercise right of repossession if it is available. If all has worked out well, it would be desirable to inform the customer that better credit terms can be arranged in the future.

Types of Credit Accounts

There are at least four basic types of consumer credit accounts.

1 Open Accounts Open accounts are ordinary charge accounts. With this type of account the customer charges all purchases throughout the month and is expected to pay the total charges when a statement is sent by the firm. Most firms send out statements monthly, but full payment each month is not insisted upon. No interest charges are normally made against such accounts.

2 Revolving Accounts It would appear the revolving accounts were designed for customers who live with eternal indebtedness. The firm sets an upper limit to the amount that may be charged, and any purchases below that limit are automatically approved for credit sale. The customer must then pay a certain amount or a specified percentage of the total charges at the end of each month. Interest is charged on the unpaid balance each month, and credit purchases can continue to be made against the account up to its limit.

3 Installment Accounts Installment accounts were specifically designed to make possible the sale on credit of larger purchases. The customer makes a down payment, preferably at least 20 percent of the total purchase price, and the balance is spread over a monthly payment plan. Good business practice limits such payments to not more than 3 years. Many installment accounts are for a shorter period. Carrying charges are added to the amount due, usually about 1½ percent per month. Most such sales are protected by a chattel mortgage on the item being sold or a conditional sales contract, so that the merchant may repossess the item if payments are not made. The customer obtains title only when the payments have been completed.

4 Budget Accounts Budget accounts are designed to handle payments which ordinarily fall between short-term open accounts and longer term installment accounts. No down payment is required and customers are normally given 3 months to remit the total price in equal payments. Customers are expected to make payments without reminders in the form of statements from the seller. Service charges are made only when the original plan of payment is not maintained.

Each of these four types of accounts necessitates special forms and clear identification to the buyer. Payment plans for each must be explained and understood.

ACCOUNTS RECEIVABLE TURNOVER

The accounts receivable turnover is the relationship of the credit sales made during the year and the average amount of accounts receivable carried on the books. It is computed by dividing the total credit sales for the year by the average accounts receivable.

$$\frac{\text{Credit sales for the year}}{\text{Average accounts receivable}} = \text{accounts receivable turnover}$$

When seasonal variations in credit sales are normal during the year, it is especially important to average the accounts receivable to obtain a more accurate measure of their turnover. Firms selling to one another on a basis of trade notes receivable should include the balance of any such notes receivable in their receivables in computing the turnover.

Every good management keeps a close check on the turnover figure and makes decisions based on the trend of this turnover. This figure also serves as a check on the paying habits of the firm's credit customers and on the credit-extension policies of the credit department. Increasing turnover indicates that customers are paying their accounts more quickly. If the turnover is decreasing, customers are paying more slowly, and/or the credit department is granting unjustified credit.

An example will illustrate computation of the accounts receivable turnover and its significance in evaluating performance.

The AAA Company is a small department store which sells to many customers on a 30-day credit basis. In 1978 its credit sales were $300,000. The average accounts receivable on the first of each month was $50,000. Its accounts receivable turnover, therefore, was six times per year. In other words, it took one-sixth of a year (60 days) to collect the average amount of receivables carried on the books. But the firm was selling on 30-day credit. If all customers paid their account balances on the first of the month, the turnover would have been 12 times per year. Management considerations in such a situation involve answers to questions such as the following:

1 Can the company carry these receivables without impairing its cash position?

2 Has credit been granted unwisely to customers who average 60 days to pay 30-day accounts?

3 Is this account-paying schedule normal for this type of business?

4 Has the loss on bad debts been increased because customers take 60 days on the average to pay current charges?

5 If bad-debt losses are not out of line, would it be desirable to arrange financing to enable the firm to carry its accounts receivable for this longer period?

6 Can anything be done to encourage more prompt payment of credit accounts by customers?

7 Would an interest charge on past due accounts stimulate more prompt payment?

Circumstances will vary from firm to firm as answers to these questions are sought. The important thing is to know the facts in regard to the accounts receivable turnover and to make policies accordingly. New restrictions may have to be placed on credit granting. Or perhaps credit will be granted only through credit cards. On the brighter side, a turnover of 12 times per year for the AAA Company may suggest that profits could be expanded by further granting of credit. Such a turnover rate indicates that customers are paying their bills on schedule and that losses on bad accounts are at a minimum.

AGING OF ACCOUNTS RECEIVABLE

To combat the problem of delinquent accounts, an *aging of accounts receivable* should be regularly made by the small firm owner. An example of such a statement is presented in Table 18-1. The first two columns show the customer's name and current balance. In the other columns, that balance is broken down into what portion of it was

TABLE 18-1
ABC COMPANY, AGING OF ACCOUNTS RECEIVABLE
OCTOBER 1, 1978

CUSTOMER NAME	CURRENT BALANCE	NUMBER OF DAYS ON BOOKS				
		0-30	31-60	61-90	91-120	OVER 120
M. Jones	$375	$ 75	$300			
H. Harris	160	60	50	$50		
G. Salzman	50	50				
P. Miller	500	300	100	100		
G. Geipel	50	—	—	—	$50	
B. Thompson	75		75			
H. Strauss	35	10	—	25		
J. Hegner	125	100	—	—	—	$25
T. Nathan	400	100	100	100	100	
A. Cohen	425	25	200	200		
G. Young	75					75
J. Osborg	200				100	100
Totals	$37,000	$22,000	$8,000	$5,000	$1,000	$1,000

charged in the last 30 days, what portion has been on the books 30 to 60 days, what portion 60 to 90 days, and what portion over 90 days. As we observe our axiom that the longer an account is on the books the more likely is its failure to be paid in full, we can see that prompt action should be taken via an established collection procedure whenever a balance gets past due. The exact point and exact steps will be decided by firm policy. Alternatives are presented later.

In this case, $37,000 represents the balance of the accounts receivable account for the firm. The total of all other columns is also $37,000. This statement shows the proprietor that $22,000 is current month charges, $8,000 is less than 60 days old, $5,000 is less than 90 days old, but $1,000 is more than 90 days old and $1,000 is over 120 days old. When the proprietor estimates the bad-debts expense for the year, serious consideration should be given to charging off the last $2,000. Its collection is definitely in doubt when it has been on the books so long. Accounts once charged off as a loss can always be reported as income if their unlikely collection should occur.

Number of Days' Sales in Receivables

An even more precise measure of customer paying habits is the number of days' sales represented in the accounts receivable on a given date. This figure is found by dividing the total accounts receivable at the end of the year by the average daily credit sales. The latter figure is found by dividing the credit sales for the year by 365. If the firm has $50,000 of accounts receivable on December 31 and the average daily credit sales are $1,000, the receivables represent 50 days of credit sales. This calculation can also be made in terms of business days rather than calendar days by dividing the credit sales for the year by the number of business days the firm is open for operation rather than by 365, as shown above.

We should note that the example of the AAA Company's selling on 30 days' credit and having 50 days of credit sales on its books is not a farfetched one. You will recall that in the planning of an opening day balance sheet (Chapter 7), it was recommended that we be prepared to finance 1½ to 2 times the credit sales in the maximum credit period. Most new firms which carry their own receivables will reach such a position within the first or second year of operation.

HANDLING DELINQUENT ACCOUNTS

Credit customers who do not pay on schedule cause the firm several problems. Their credit is cut off so that they are lost as future customers even if their finances improve, the old balances restrict liquidity of the working capital, and the net result is usually an uncollectible account which becomes bad-debts expense. Partial collection by attorneys or collection firms involves much expense. No merchant likes to make credit sales in good faith and then have the sales cause these problems. The best course of action when accounts become overdue is to minimize the eventual losses by taking the following steps:

1 Send a second statement in 60 days from purchase. This could include a note to the effect that "Perhaps our first statement was not received or was mislaid. We know you would not want your credit status impaired. Please advise us if there is any complaint about our products or service."

2 Telephone the customer or send a telegram in 70 days, asking the reasons for nonpayment.

3 Send a third statement in 75 days. Include a note to the effect that "Your credit status is at stake. We are forced to turn over accounts 75 days old to our collection agency or attorney."

4 Send a registered letter in 80 days, including a certified copy of the statement, saying that the account is being referred to the collection agency.

5 Turn the account over to the agency or the firm's attorney for legal action in 90 days.

Small firm owners usually have an advantage over large firm owners in this situation, since they know their customers better. If this is so, they can usually accomplish more through personal contact with the customer than by resorting to the steps just described. If they find that a genuine customer complaint exists, they may open the door to making a fair adjustment and keeping the customer. But the possible delinquent situation should always be anticipated by picking the right credit customers in the first contact.

PERSONAL AND COMPANY CHECK CASHING IS ANOTHER FORM OF CREDIT

Credit extension is normally thought of as allowing customers to charge their purchases to the firm at the time of purchase, with the balances due to be paid at least once a month. Cashing checks for customers and companies, however, is another form of credit extension. Few merchants will not confess to having cashed checks for customers which came back from the bank marked "NSF" (not sufficient funds) or "no account here." One major airline reported to the authors some time ago that it had accepted more than $2 million in bad checks in one year. It now encourages the use of credit cards whenever possible. These facts point up the necessity of a policy on check cashing. The natural result has been an increasing reluctance to accept such checks.

Devices are now available to aid in this problem. "Debit cards" have been introduced. These are plastic cards, held by customers, which may be inserted into an electronic box by the merchant to confirm that check-writers have funds in their accounts to cover their checks. Check guarantee companies, which will guarantee personal checks to the merchant, now exist. Many banks have machines available 24 hours a day to enable their card holders to get cash from the machines by inserting their cards. These machines not only make it easier for customers to get cash; they also reduce the use of personal checks. Merchants must be cautious in cashing checks for people they do not know. We will see more and more evidence in this chapter that the small firm should restrict its credit sales to credit cards and not attempt to carry many open account receivables on its own books. Neither should it accept personal checks without substantiation of the customer's identification and/or assurance that the check is good.

CREDIT-CARD CREDIT

The huge increase in the use of credit cards in Canada in the past ten years has truly been one of the major merchandising and financial developments. In 1978 it was estimated that there were more than 9 million individual credit cards outstanding. Many families have as many as ten cards in effect. Outstanding dollar balances exceed $2 billion, or almost $400 for every family in the country.

Credit cards are being used today for ever-increasing types of purchases. They originally were designed to assist travelers with the problem of cashing personal checks when they were away from home. They were used most often for purchasing airline tickets and paying hotel bills, auto rentals, and gasoline purchases. *Today retail purchases of consumer products and services represent their widest use.* In California credit cards can be used to pay property taxes, buy auto tags, and even to pay state income taxes. Other newer uses could include payments to doctors and dentists, political parties, churches, etc. Most credit cards are issued free of charge for approved applicants. This includes the most popular: Master Charge and Chargex (VISA). Each card specifies the maximum credit the holder may charge.

A recent development has been the charging of an annual fee to holders of some credit cards, for example, American Express and Diners Club. These charges range from $10 to $20 per year.

The cards named above are all issued by general credit-card companies. Many can be used around the world. But we should also observe that many individual service and product companies still issue their own credit cards. These are called *single-firm credit cards*. Oil companies, department stores, hotels, and chain restaurants are most prominent examples. The objective is to stimulate sales of the firm's own products or services while avoiding the costs of the general credit-card companies. Some oil companies even honour the credit cards of other oil companies. Oil companies charge no fee to service stations, garages, or other firms using their cards. Most of these individual company cards carry no service charge to customers who pay their monthly balances promptly. When such cards are issued by smaller firms, the effect is usually comparable to open account selling. They may still have good advertising and sales development value.

How Credit Cards Operate for the Customer

When a cardholder wishes to make a purchase against a credit card, he or she must first ascertain whether the firm honours that card. Most small firms which accept credit cards have signs displayed in their front window or door indicating the types of cards accepted. To make a purchase, the customer merely shows the merchant the credit card. The merchant, who may phone the credit card company or a credit bureau to confirm the customer's credit limit, processes a multiple-copy bill called a *charge notice*. The customer signs the notice and keeps one copy. The merchant files the other copies and returns the credit card to the customer.

At the end of the month the credit-card company sends the cardholder a statement of the total charges and the minimum payment required on the total. A due date for the payment, in full or in part, is indicated on the statement. If the cardholder decides to make the minimum payment only, he or she is charged interest at the rate of 1½ percent per month, or 18 percent per year, on the unpaid balance.

Credit-card companies prefer customers who do not pay in full each month—but who do pay in full, with interest, some time in the future. In 1976 one large credit-card company in the New York area established a flat service charge to customers who paid their bills in full each month. This charge was subsequently declared illegal and it obviously was not popular with credit card holders.

How Credit Cards Operate for the Merchant

When sales are made on credit cards, the business is assured of full collection of those sales, less the credit-card company charge, each

Small firms offering credit card sales find it profitable to tell customers the specific cards they honour by listing them on the front door.

month. The owner merely tallies the total credit-card sales slips and takes them to the credit-card company. The settlement date is usually the fifth of each month. With some credit cards, sales slips may be deposited in a commercial bank in the same manner as currency or checks. Credit card charges to large and small business firms vary from 1 percent to 6 percent. The rates are lower now than when credit cards were first introduced.

The charge to the specific firm will vary with two basic factors: (1) the total volume of credit-card sales and (2) the average dollar sale. Thus, an airline which discounts $2 million per week with a credit-card company and has an average sale of $100 may receive a charge of 1 percent. The average charge for a small volume of credit sales and a much lower average sale is 5 or 6 percent. For an additional 1 percent discount, merchants may cash in their slips sooner. Most small firm owners do not know that the rate they are charged is negotiable. Competition between credit-card companies is keen, and small firm owners should always take advantage of this fact in requesting a lower rate from their credit-card companies.

Are Credit Card Companies' Charges Too High?

Credit-card companies are not philanthropic organizations. We would not wish them to be. They render positive services to business firms, small and large, and are organized to make a profit. They have large administrative costs. One credit-card company executive reports that the average cost of each computerized entry is 28 cents.

The companies suffer losses from misuse of stolen cards and when accounts for which they have advanced funds to the individual merchants are not paid. Credit-card companies "buy" accounts without recourse to the merchant. This means that unpaid accounts are losses to the credit card company. They cannot collect losses from the merchants to whom they advanced money.

The companies' only sources of income are the discounts charged to merchants when accounts are bought and the interest charged to cardholders who do not pay in full each month. In addition, the major general credit-card companies face stiff competition. Their reported profits have not been out of line with the services rendered, and many companies report that any profits were long in coming.

Should Small Firms Encourage Credit-Card Credit?

The predominant answer to this question that we have gathered from successful small business owners is yes. There may be communities where customers still demand open account credit. In such circumstances the individual small firm must satisfy the customers and meet the competition. However, the general trend throughout the country is obviously toward wider and wider consumer use of credit cards. Manufacturers and wholesalers who supply small firms must abide by the prevailing trade credit terms. As we have noted, little if any business between firms is done on a credit-card basis.

The small retailing firm which is adequately financed to carry its own open accounts receivable must measure its costs of open account credit against the cost of credit-card credit. Experienced firms can do this most effectively. If the total costs of bookkeeping, printing, postage, interest, collection costs, and bad debts are less than the discount paid to the credit-card company, it pays to have open accounts available. If the individual firm is inadequately financed to carry its own receivables, if the owner does not want the bother of the bookkeeping and other aspects of administering a credit program, and if no community demand exists for open account credit, a program of credit-card credit seems preferable. The cost differences between the two plans of credit are often slight. Many small firms still offer both open account and credit-card credit, but the trend is definitely toward more credit-card selling.

Laws Governing Consumer Credit Practices

The great current interest in consumerism in our country has been accompanied by new legislations designed to protect consumers. Chief among these are:

— Provincial Consumer Protection Acts
— Provincial Credit Reporting Acts
— Amendments to the federal Bills of Exchange Act

It is most important for all business firms which extend credit on their own books to become familiar with these Acts and related Regulations. Space prohibits even a condensed summary here; we can only note the main provisions:

All disclosure Acts in Canada now require disclosure of both the dollar costs and the effective annual rate of interest to enable credit consumers to discover the terms of their borrowing before actually purchasing a good on credit. If the full cost of credit is not disclosed, the borrower is only required to pay the amount disclosed. Non-disclosure is also a criminal offence, punishable in Ontario, for example, by imprisonment for up to one year, a $2,000 fine, or both.

In recent years, legislation has been passed in several provinces to control the activities of credit reporting agencies: a Personal Investigations Act was passed in Manitoba in 1971; a Credit Reporting Agencies Act was passed by Saskatchewan in 1972; the Ontario Consumer Reporting Act was passed in 1973; and similar Acts were passed by Nova Scotia and British Columbia in 1973. The main purpose of these Acts is to ensure: the consumer's right to expect responsible conduct from businesses engaged in gathering, storing, assembling, or using credit and personal information; the right to

CREDIT BUREAU POLICY

Members of the Associated Credit Bureaus of Canada pledge themselves to the improvement of the consumer credit industry, both locally and nationally. In its efforts to achieve the highest possible excellence for the credit industry, the Association co-operates fully with all levels of government, business and educational organizations interested in consumer credit.

The Association does not grant credit, but strives constantly to protect those who use credit by maintaining strict control over the dissemination of credit information. Only credit-granting customers who have a contract with a member bureau of the Association can obtain information concerning a consumer's credit record.

Members of the Association are committed to provide courteous and understanding interviews to any person who comes to their office to discuss his credit record. They provide supervisory personnel to conduct interviews in privacy without charge. Members are required to investigate and correct file information if it is necessary and update files by re-investigation on request and record new credit references when furnished.

The Association carries on a continuing and effective educational program, which stresses the importance of sound credit, its proper use, and the joint responsibility of credit granters and consumers to make the use of credit of real value to both the economy and the consumer.

The Association takes every step necessary to insure that all inquiries and all information processed by its members are treated in the strictest confidence. At no time is credit information made available to any inquirer whose operations are of an illegal nature or reveal a tendency to be adverse to the public good.

Each member undertakes to provide information that is factual and has not been altered, amended, colored or qualified in any way possible. For example, members of the Association never use private investigators or interview neighbours to gain information.

Members of the Association commit themselves to the provision of a worthwhile service by fulfilling all their responsibilities in an honest, accurate, unbiased and efficient manner. They must operate under a strict set of rules, regulations and standards, which insures that bureau operations are conducted in a most exemplary manner.

Figure 18-4 *Credit Bureau Policy*

know what is being reported and to whom it is reported; and the right to correct false information. Figure 18-4 shows the Code of Ethics prepared by members of the Associated Credit Bureaus of Canada.

In order to give greater protection to the consumer, the federal *Bills of Exchange Act* was amended in 1970 to require that a promissory note signed in connection with a sales agreement, such as a conditional sales contract, must be marked "consumer purchase." This has the legal effect that the creditor cannot sue the consumer on the basis of the promissory note if the seller has not met his obligations under the sales contract — for example, sold defective goods.

Another federal legislation to be noted is the *Small Loans Act*, enacted in 1939, which provides for uniform, all-inclusive credit charge ceilings for all loans of $1,500 or less.

In 1977 the federal government proposed a *Borrowers and*

Depositors Protection Bill. After much debate this Bill has "died," and new legislation, tentatively called "Fair Credit and Savings Act," is now being drafted by the Consumer and Corporate Affairs Canada.

All of this new legislation has contributed to the increasing use of credit cards by customers and the increasing encouragement of credit-card sales by small business firms. Only large firms and credit-card companies can normally stand the expense of staff experts to administer credit programs and to make sure the firm complies with the abundant rules and regulations. Key details and forms may be obtained through trade associations or bankers or other friends of small firms.

Credit-card sales now give the customer more protection than ever. As one credit-card company executive reports, "The consumer who doesn't use credit cards today is short-changing himself." It seems a fair prediction for the decade of the 1980s that more and more credit programs will be under the jurisdiction of credit-card companies who have the expertise to make their programs comply with the abundant legislation which now governs credit granting. That same expertise may also help to protect people from using excessive and unwarranted credit.

It May Still Be Worthwhile for Customers to Pay Cash Another feature of the current wave of consumer legislation makes it legal under the Amended Combines Investigation Act to give a discount of up to 5 percent to retail customers who pay cash. This law was deemed necessary to avoid charges of price discrimination.

SUMMARY

The business world operates on credit. From the grower of raw materials to manufacturers, distributors, transportation companies, or retailers, business operations necessitate credit. Consumer credit to buyers of all products is a vital part of the entire credit system in this country. Trade credit is that offered by one business firm to another. Consumer credit is that offered by retailers to buyers of consumer goods. Without credit most families would be unable to purchase their homes, their cars, their major appliances, and many other items.

Granting of credit must always be based upon the applicant's ability to repay debts incurred within a specified schedule. For the small firm, this necessitates careful granting of credit in the first place and careful administration of a credit program once it is established. The costs of a credit program are significant. They include bookkeeping costs, postage, supplies, interest on investment in receivables, costs of collection, and eventually bad debts expense for those accounts which are never collected. Some loss on bad debts should be anticipated whenever a general program of credit is undertaken.

Small firms usually have a choice of carrying their own receivables on open accounts or restricting their credit sales to credit cards. More and more small firms are finding it desirable to accept credit cards, even though the average charge is still about 5 percent of all credit-card sales discounted with the credit-card companies. It is a genuine service to small firms to be able to collect their credit sales in full by the fifth of the following month, less the credit card company charge, and avoid the expenses and losses of their own program. New credit legislation suggests that businesses of the future will have more credit based on credit cards and administered by experts in the field.

QUESTIONS FOR CLASS DISCUSSION

Q18-1 Would you sell on credit and carry the accounts on your own books if you owned a dress shop? Why?

Q18-2 What are the advantages to small firm owners of selling on customers' credit cards? The disadvantages?

Q18-3 What is an "aging of accounts receivable"? How often would you recommend that one be made for small firms?

Q18-4 What is the difference between trade credit and consumer credit?

Q18-5 How would you explain the statement, "The world operates on credit"?

Q18-6 Do you believe the statement that "a firm will sell more merchandise, even to its present customers, if credit accounts are made available?" How do you explain this?

Q18-7 How does a revolving account work?

Q18-8 Is an installment account different from a revolving account? How?

Q18-9 When would you recommend use of a budget account?

Q18-10 How is the credit reputation of an applicant checked?

Q18-11 Do you agree that you do not do a person a favour by granting credit which he or she cannot likely afford? Explain.

Q18-12 What kind of a policy would you establish to handle delinquent accounts?

PROBLEMS AND QUESTIONS FOR WRITTEN ASSIGNMENT

P18-1 As the new credit manager for a small department store, you are asked how you decide which of your four types of consumer-credit accounts you offer to a particular customer. What would you answer?

P18-2 Explain with a concrete example how a small firm owner may have real advantages in collecting delinquent accounts that the large firm may not have.

P18-3 If you agree that giving credit is not a favour to applicants, how would you explain this to them?

CONTINUING PROBLEM:
THE SUCCESS HARDWARE STORE

Part 18. Policy for Credit Sales

Assignment for Part 18

Prepare a report on your suggestions for handling credit sales. Cover the following points:

1. Advantages of selling on credit
2. Dangers of selling on credit
3. Types of credit accounts which may be used
4. Pros and cons of selling on credit cards
5. Program you recommend

REFERENCES FOR FURTHER READING

Archer, Maurice, *An Introduction to Canadian Business*, 3d. ed., McGraw-Hill Ryerson Ltd., Toronto, 1978, chap. 14.

Broom, H.N., and J.G. Longenecker, *Small Business Management*, 2d ed., South-Western Publishing Company, Inc., Cincinnati, 1966, chap. 20.

"Credit Management and Collection," Your Business Matters, No. 10, The Royal Bank of Canada, 1977.

Davidson, William R., and Alton F. Doody, *Retailing Management*, 3d ed., The Ronald Press Company, New York, 1966, chap. 19.

Gist, Ronald R., *Retailing*, John Wiley & Sons, Inc., New York, 1968. chap. 15.

"Giving Credit to Your Customers," Minding Your Own Business, Pamphlet No. 2, Federal Business Development Bank.

Kelley, Pearce C., Kenneth Lawyer, and Clifford M. Baumback, *How to Organize and Operate a Small Business*, 5th ed., Prentice-Hall, Inc., Englewood Cliffs, N.J., 1973, chap. 19.

Musselman, Vernon A., and Eugene H. Hughes, *Introduction to Modern Business*, 6th ed., Prentice-Hall, Inc., Englewood Cliffs, N.J., 1973, chap. 14.

CHAPTER 19

Risks and How to Deal with Them

All those risks the experts talk about could scare a person out of starting a new business. And then you realize that most of these risks apply to all of us every day in our personal lives. Then you get smart and figure out how to protect yourself in the best manner.

The Late Learner

Every business firm operates daily with risks. The small firm is no exception. A risk can be defined as the chance of damage, injury, or loss. The total dollar costs incurred from risks may be much greater for large firms, but they are relatively more important for small firms. The small firm is characteristically less able to absorb losses from risks. These facts make it very important that every small firm understand the risks to which it is subject. Once these are known, a policy can be established on how best to handle the risks so as to keep losses to a minimum.

Risk is a vital part of everyday life. Each of us takes chances in driving to work, crossing the street, owning a house, travelling on public transportation, buying food, attending the movies, and eating in restaurants. Accidents happen in the best-regulated routines, and they may result in injury, damage, or loss to the person affected.

Individuals, like businesses, take steps to protect themselves from many of these risks. People install burglar alarms and window guards in their homes as protection against risk of loss from robbery. Generally, they tend to guard themselves and their families by shifting the chance of loss to an insurance company. They purchase life insurance policies to protect their families in case of death; they buy title insurance on their homes to be sure that they are protected against any defects in the title which may be discovered later. Most automobile owners buy insurance to protect them in case of collision damage, bodily damage, and property damage to others. Almost any type of risk can be insured against, but the question is, how much can one pay in insurance premiums? If every possible risk in an individual's life were insured against, the cost of insurance would be prohibitive for most people.

The small business owner has all the previously mentioned risks and many more. For small firm owners, competence demands that they give serious attention to what risks they assume when they start operations. They face the same losses, damages, and injuries that are faced by individuals, and the losses, damages, or injuries to the business may be even more serious to the success of the business. Most common risks are generally recognized, but a serious investigation may reveal some that are not usually noted.

RISKS FACED BY THE SMALL FIRM

1 Damage to Property The property of most small firms is represented by its inventory and its building if it is owned by the firm. The building and the inventory are constantly subject to the risks of damage and loss from fire, theft, floods, hurricanes, and riots. Cars and trucks owned by the firm are also open to loss through theft or damage.

Property damage to business firms in Canada is estimated to be as high as $350 million yearly, placing it at the top of the list of possible risks for most firms.

2 Liability to Employees All employers are responsible for the health and safety of employees while they are performing their duties for the firm. Legislation giving employers such responsibility has been one of the greatest developments in social responsibility in recent years. The employer's liability is no longer left to individual court action but is assured by the requirement that workers' compensation insurance be carried by employers to provide this protection to employees.

3 Liability to the Public This type of risk is often illustrated by the proverbial slip on a banana peel by a customer in the store. Store owners are liable for injuries received by persons on their premises. This liability applies to apartment houses, factories, and wholesale establishments, as well as to popular retail establishments. This risk includes not only physical injuries, but also damage to the property of others. It further covers liability for defects in merchandise which the firm has sold. Readers may recall cases in which cosmetic firms have been sued for alleged harmful results from using cosmetic products of a particular firm, or canned food companies being sued because people were made ill by spoiled contents, restaurants being sued for illness from eating on the premises, airlines and railroads and bus companies being sued for injuries incurred when travelling, or theatres being sued for injuries sustained in a theatre fire or accident. All these risks are examples of possible liability to the public.

4 Death of Key Employees Valuable employees are a firm's best asset. Real losses could be sustained if they should die suddenly. Fortunately, this is a possible loss which can be insured today.

5 Excessive Loss from Bad Debts We have noted in other chapters the importance of extending credit carefully and on the basis of a well-established procedure. Losses due to inability to collect accounts receivable can be severe. Protection against such losses can be expensive, as we shall see later in this chapter.

6 Faulty Title to Real Estate Students may not recognize the importance of being sure that real estate purchased does, indeed, have a clear title that cannot be challenged at law. Typically, in Canada, the purchaser will rely on a solicitor's "certificate of good title," however, there are a few insurance companies providing real estate title insurance policies.

7 Shoplifting This serious management problem seems to be growing in our society. It cannot be dismissed, because no firm seems free from the attendant losses. Legal action is expensive and difficult to administer. We will consider management ideas on the problem later in this chapter.

8 Loss Through Dishonest Employees No business people like to admit that they have dishonest employees. Countless cases of employee theft are reported every year. This is another real risk that must be recognized and coped with.

9 Financial Hardship Financial hardship has probably caused more small firms to go out of business than any other single risk. It is especially sad to see a firm with otherwise excellent prospects suffer because illiquidity has been allowed to dominate its financial condition.

10 Marketing Risks Marketing risks cover such things as having an inventory of merchandise suddenly fall in value because the market price has dropped. The risk of having a location lose its value is a marketing risk. In style merchandise, situations occur where the style has fallen out of favour, and the remaining merchandise on the owner's shelves has lost most of its value. The small miller may have bought a large supply of wheat, for which he paid the market price 2 months ago. His finished product, flour, will bring a price which reflects the price of wheat when he sells the flour. All merchants face some of these types of marketing situations and should be cognizant of their existence. When all prices are rising, as in a period of inflation, the risk will not be present. In a period of declining prices, the risk becomes greater.

These risks are only 10 of the more prominent types faced by many small firm owners. Individual cases may produce other risks which should be recognized.

WHAT TO DO ABOUT RISKS

When the existing risks are known, business owners may turn their attention to the matter of what to do about them. They will realize that some risks are easier to control than others. In all cases, good management will do some of the following:

1 Eliminate risks
2 Minimize risks
3 Shift risks
4 Absorb risks

The action taken will vary with the desired policy, services, and circumstances of the individual firm, and the business owner has several choices.

DEVICES AVAILABLE TO COPE WITH RISKS

1 Remove the Cause If losses are being incurred from injuries to workmen handling dangerous equipment, install safety guards on the machinery. Replace equipment that has proved it is defective. Faulty wiring should not be tolerated. Employ an outside delivery service if necessary to remove the risk of keeping your own delivery equipment.

2 Create Self-insurance Under a self-insurance plan, a specified amount is set aside in a reserve fund each year to be available to cover any losses incurred. Rather than the owner paying premiums to an insurance company, the cash is held in this reserve fund. Unfortunately, this plan has been used with bad results by many one-store small firms. This self-insurance plan can be recommended only when the business has several geographically separated units. School systems and small chains of hamburger shops or grocery stores are ideal candidates for self-insurance. A small loss on one will usually be covered by the reserve fund. A significant loss for a one-store firm usually results in a net loss for the firm because the reserve fund has not yet become large enough to cover losses. Unless the reserve fund is well built up, the risk remains and protection is inadequate.

3 Purchase Outside Insurance An insurance policy shifts the risk to the insurance company. Insurance can be purchased from established insurance firms to cover many of the risks listed here. These are considered normal business risks. In addition, Lloyd's of London will insure any nonbusiness risks—for a price.

As we review the 10 risks listed earlier and consider the case of a typical small firm retailer, it would appear that there is no alternative to buying insurance to protect the inventory and building against various possible losses such as fire, theft, floods, or hurricanes. Owners are required by law to carry workers' compensation insurance to cover their employees. They surely should carry public liability insurance to cover risk of liability to people on their premises. If key personnel are sufficiently valuable to the business, owners may buy life insurance on their lives, payable to the company.

For loss from excessive bad debts, only the loss in excess of what is normal for the particular line of business can be insured. Credit insurance is not available to cover what are considered normal losses. The cost of such insurance is very high, and it is not recommended for small businesses. Proper administration of a credit program, as outlined in Chapter 18, is preferable.

Fidelity bonds may be purchased to protect any firm from losses incurred by employee thefts. Only established losses are reimbursed, and such establishment is often difficult. In business practice these bonds have been used much more to cover cash losses than merchandise losses. Too many firms buy such protection only for those employees who operate cash registers or handle money in other operations. It is common knowledge today that the losses incurred by business firms from merchandise stolen by employees far exceed losses in the form of cash. This situation suggests that fidelity bonds should be used more widely to cover losses of both cash and merchandise.

Surety bonds, which will protect the firm for losses incurred as a result of the failure of others to perform on schedule, may be purchased. Failure of a contractor to complete an important addition to the store in time for the Christmas trade under the terms of a contract would be an example. In such a case the insurance company would pay the firm for the established loss incurred.

Title insurance is available on all real estate purchases for a small sum, and it should always be requested.

Insurance is either not economically available or not usually recommended to cover the other risks on our list.

4 Hedging Any small firm that buys quantities of products quoted on well-established commodity exchanges should know about hedging and should practice it to protect normal profits. Hedging is often misunderstood as a device to make additional profits, but it is only to protect normal profits.

A few of the commodities regularly traded on the commodity exchanges are sugar, wheat, corn, citrus fruits, soybeans, soybean oil, cocoa, wool, oats, rye, silver, and copper. Whenever merchants buy large quantities of a product listed on the exchanges for use in manufacturing and sell it later as a part of their final product, they can protect themselves against losses in the price of the commodity by *hedging*. On the day they purchase the material, they also sell a futures contract on the exchange. The difference between the price paid for products delivered today (spot price) and the price in the futures market is roughly the cost of insuring and storing the same commodity for the period of time from today to the date of the futures contract. When the merchants sell their manfactured products, they will neutralize any loss in the price of the raw material commodity by buying a futures contract. The profit or loss on the commodity (spot) sales will be offset by the profit of loss on the purchase and sale of the futures contracts.

5 Good Management Good planning and good management are probably the best protection against most of the other risks we have considered. Price fluctuations of any normal retail inventory may be upward or downward. Good management will keep itself informed of price trends. Study of population trends and business activity will warn merchants early if their location is losing its value. Good accounting records and study of operations against a budget will warn of any developing adverse trends. To handle the risks of shoplifting and dishonest employees, good management will provide devices for detecting shoplifters, such as internal security guards and signal systems. These are often expensive but necessary. Personnel policies will provide means of checking employees whose honesty is questioned. Inspection of employees at checkout time is being used by manufacturing firms. It is recommended for wholesalers and retailers when losses in this area are deemed a high risk. As we have seen, fidelity bonds may be purchased to protect the firm from losses by dishonest employees.

The risk of financial hardship can best be coped with by proper financial planning and financial management. This popular risk has caused the downfall of many firms which otherwise had a most profitable future. Good planning along the lines we have reviewed in this text, watching the key financial ratios in the financial statements, the cash adequacy rule, the investment in receivables, and having a cash flow statement are devices to protect against this risk. Having a good performance record for honesty and fair dealing will help the business person secure financial help when it is needed.

Chapter 25 is devoted to managing the daily operations of the firm. It will demonstrate how danger signals may appear which may affect financial standing of the firm. Thus warned, the owner can quickly apply corrective action.

COINSURANCE FOR BUSINESS FIRMS

Small firm owners should know how coinsurance works. It is a subject often misunderstood. For example, a building owner who has a $20,000 building insured against fire loss of $10,000 would not collect in full for an $8,000 fire loss.

Insurance companies are not in business for charity, nor should they be. As business organizations, their function is to pool the risks of many and pay those who incur losses. Their premiums must provide them with adequate income to cover these losses, their operating expenses, and a profit.

They know from experience that fire damage to business buildings, for example, rarely results in complete loss of the building. To protect themselves and the client against having to pay insurance on the total cost of a building only partially destroyed, for example, they offer a coinsurance clause in their policies. Coinsurance means that owners of a building can literally share the potential loss with the insurance company if they are willing also to share the premium cost.

Business buildings, like residential buildings, may be protected against losses in varying degrees under such coinsurance clauses. This means that potential losses may be shared by the owner and the company while major protection is still given to the owner.

For example, a building owner may wish to insure his building at 50 percent of its market value. His savings in annual insurance premium costs may be considered as an offset to any potential losses incurred. This does not mean, however, that any losses incurred up to 50 percent of the building value will be paid in full by the insurance company. He becomes subject to the coinsurance clause in his policy.

The most common percentage of market value of buildings used in coinsurance is 80 percent. If the building is insured at 50 percent of its value and 80 percent is the coinsurance percentage, the owner will recover fifty-eightieths of losses incurred. If he has an $8,000 loss, he will recover $5,000. Coinsurance truly means a shared risk.

Let us review a more detailed illustration of how coinsurance works.

ABC Manufacturing Company has a small factory building valued at $40,000. It is insured under a coinsurance policy at 80 percent of market value, or $32,000. This amount is the face value of the owner's policy ($32,000). The insurance company will be liable for the full amount of any losses up to $32,000. A complete loss on the building, or $40,000, would result in the owner's bearing an $8,000 loss and the insurance company's paying him $32,000.

The formula for computing insurance company liability in such cases is as follows:

$$\text{Insurance company liability} = \frac{\text{face value of policy}}{80\% \text{ of property value}} \times \text{amount of loss incurred}$$

As we apply this formula, we can see that if the ABC Company had insured its building for only $16,000 (less than 80 percent of market value) and then incurred a $16,000 loss, it could collect only $8,000 (16/32, or ½, times $16,000). This is true even though the face value of the policy was $16,000.

If a building is insured for more than 80 percent of its market value, the insurance company pays any losses in full up to that of the face value of the policy. Insurance never pays more than the face value of the policy.

OTHER FACTS ABOUT CASUALTY INSURANCE FOR SMALL BUSINESSES

The small firm owner should be aware of the following facts.

1 A regular (standard) fire insurance policy pays the policyholder only for losses that are directly due to fire. Other indirect losses, known as consequential losses, may be even more important to the small firm's welfare. Some of these consequential losses are:

- **a** Loss of use of the building.
- **b** Continuing expenses after a fire, such as salaries, rents paid, and interest obligations.
- **c** Loss of rental income on buildings owned and rented out.
- **d** Extra expenses of obtaining temporary quarters.

Most fire insurance policies have available a consequential loss clause to cover such losses. An extra premium is charged for such a clause, of course.

2 Fire losses caused by windstorms, tornadoes, or hurricanes are not covered by a standard fire policy. A windstorm policy is essential to have protection in such cases.

3 Flood insurance is designed to protect buildings and inventories against such risks as overflowing rivers and tidal waves. Water damage insurance, as distinct from flood insurance, covers such risks as roof leaks, bursting water tanks, and leaking pipes.

4 Marine insurance covers merchandise while it is in transit. There are two types:

- **a** Ocean marine insurance, covering transportation of merchandise and products on water.
- **b** Inland marine insurance, which covers both land and water transportation.

5 Automobile collision insurance is considered a must by prudent business people. Business cars and trucks, as well as personal cars, should be insured. This insurance can be purchased under both a full-coverage policy (which pays all losses from collision damage in full) or a deductible policy, which carries a lower premium but provides that the owner is responsible for the first $50 or $100 in damage from each accident.

6 Comprehensive policies are available to cover fire and theft losses on automobiles. They can protect the owner against many risks of damage or loss, including flood, windstorm, riot, glass breakage, robbery in the car, theft of the car, fire damage, or even hail damage. Collision damage is not included in these policies. Rates on policy premiums vary from state to state in accordance with the loss record for the particular area.

7 The *relative incidence of loss* means the likelihood of the risk's causing a loss to the firm. The relative chance of an automobile collision, for example, is greater for most people than the risk of losing a limb. Thus, collisions are said to have a higher incidence of risk. It follows that the higher the incidence of loss, the more important it is to have insurance protection.

8 An *insurable interest* means that the person buying insurance is subject to a loss if the property or person insured should be damaged or deceased. Such an insurable interest is a prerequisite to the purchase of any insurance policy. Key-man or key-woman insurance, the right of a company to insure the life of valuable employees, is a relatively recent large development in the business field. A business firm, large or small, has an insurable interest in the lives of its key employees when the business would suffer should those persons be removed by death. Under certain conditions, group insurance policies on the lives of employees may be charged as expenses to the firm.

BASIC FACTS ABOUT LIFE INSURANCE FOR BUSINESS AND FOR BUILDING PERSONAL ESTATES

We have seen the importance of having adequate protection against casualty risks in business management. Whenever the incidence of such risks as fire, theft, and other damage is high, most business owners shift the risks to insurance companies. But the matter of life insurance is of growing interest and value to small firms as well. Small firms, like large ones, can carry key-man (or woman) life insurance on the lives of valuable employees to protect them against the loss of such employees. The fact that a company can carry a group life insurance policy on all of its employees up to $50,000 each and charge the premiums as business expense can be a major part of a personnel policy and help retain good employees.

Because life insurance can be used to serve business purposes or in the building of personal estates, it should be important to all informed citizens to know the basic facts about different kinds of life insurance policies. But first we should be sure we understand the basic terms used in connection with such policies. Some of these follow.

Terminology of Life Insurance

Face amount of the policy	The amount paid by the insurance company in the event of the death of the insured, for example, $1,000.
Premium	The amount paid annually to maintain the face of the policy in force, for example, $20 per year.
Beneficiary	The person designed to receive the face amount of the policy in the event of the death of the insured.
Insured	The person whose life is covered in the policy.
Cash Value of policy (Cash Surrender Value)	The amount the insurance company will pay if the policy is cancelled.

Loan value of policy	The amount the insurance company will loan to the insured if he or she wishes to borrow against its cash value.
Paid-up policy	A policy on which no further premiums are required, or a new policy for less than the face value, given to an insured person who desires to cancel the original policy, take a policy for less than the original face, and pay no more premiums.

TYPES OF LIFE INSURANCE POLICIES

There are four basic types of life insurance policies. Some special policies may include features of more than one of these types. If we understand the basic types, we can evaluate special policies which may be under consideration at any time. These four basic types, their characteristics, and their uses, plus a word of explanation of each, are as follows:

1 Term Life Insurance Policies This is the least expensive type of life insurance (see Table 19-1). It can be written for short periods, such as one year, or for longer periods of years. It is seldom written for more than 20 years. It provides full payment of the face of the policy to the designated beneficiary if the insured dies during the life of the policy. Term insurance is unique in that no payment of face value is ever made if death occurs after the stated expiration date of the policy. This very feature, plus the inexpensive premiums, have made the policy extremely valuable in the business world.

Such term policies are increasingly used to provide collateral security for firm or personal obligations. Bank loans or mortgage debts on plant and equipment can have a provision that the borrower take out a term policy on his or her life payable to the creditor, which will assure full payment of the obligation in the event of his or her death. It is often called *credit life insurance* when used in this manner. Only a small addition to regular payments on such obligations is needed in most cases to pay for the insurance. Creditors thus are not forced to interfere with the business firm's operations to collect the debt.

Financial advisors recommend to all young married couples with a mortgaged home or condominium that they take out a term life policy on the life of the breadwinner of the family to assure that the mortgage will be paid in full in the event of the insured's death. The home is thus fully paid for and the remaining spouse is no longer faced with this debt. Many mortgage companies and other financial institutions are encouraging, if not requiring, such insurance protection for both the borrower and the lender. Family protection and estate building usually suggest that the amount of any life insurance carried should be proportionate to the current debts and present versus future earning powers of the family.

Term life insurance is unique in other ways. Historically it has no cash value, no loan value, and no paid-up policy is available. These features are also part of the price paid for the inexpensive premiums required.

2 Straight Life Insurance Policies This is the type of life insurance on which the great American insurance industry was built. Premiums are based on actuarial figures of life expectancy, as in all insurance. When a policy is once taken out on the life of an individual, that person normally pays the annual premium until death. The face amount of the policy is then paid to the designated beneficiary. In recent years many insurance companies have introduced provisions that no further premiums are to be paid after some ripe old age, such as 90 or 99, is reached, if the policy has been in effect a minimum number of years. The policies are considered paid up for the full face value at that time. Face value plus any accumulated dividends or interest are paid to the beneficiary at the death of the insured.

Most straight life policies may be cancelled after a minimum existence and the insured given a paid-up policy for a lesser face value than the original policy. The insured may also borrow against active policies up to the amount of the cash value or cancel the policy if desired and receive the cash value. Straight life insurance is more expensive than term insurance but less expensive than the following types.

3 Limited Pay Plan Life Insurance The very fact of longevity and the continued payment of premiums on straight life policies motivated the development of limited pay plans. The most popular pay period is 20 years, but other periods of time may be used. Premiums are higher than straight life policies. Many people are willing to pay a higher premium in exchange for limiting the number of years the premiums are to be paid. The insurance becomes a fully paid-up policy at the end of the designated years. This insurance is similar in all other ways to straight life insurance.

Limited pay policies have the features of cash value, loan value, and a paid-up policy of lesser value if cancelled prior to payment of the premiums for the specified years.

4 Endowment Life Insurance Policies Endowment policies have the unique feature that when the premiums have been paid for the specified number of years, the insured may collect the face value. Endowment policies are sold on a basis of premiums being paid only for the number of years specified in the policy. In exchange for the right to collect face value in full at maturity, premiums are the highest for any form of life insurance. Full protection on the insured's life for the entire life of the policy is assured. A beneficiary must be named who will collect the face value if the insured's death occurs before maturity. This type of insurance has been dubbed by some "the insurance for people who want to take it with them."

Endowment policies have all the characteristics of loan value, cash value, and an available paid-up policy.

LOAN VALUE OF LIFE INSURANCE POLICIES AS A SOURCE OF TEMPORARY WORKING CAPITAL

When any life insurance policies, except term, have been in force a few years, they build up a loan value, as we have noted. This loan value may be used to assist business owners in times of cash shortages or special needs. The interest rate charged on such loans against life policies is not as high as that charged by most financial institutions. Such loan value can be counted on to be available without risking a refusal on a loan application elsewhere. The full face value of life insurance policies remains in effect during the period of such loans, subject to the outstanding loan.

TABLE 19-1
APPROXIMATE ANNUAL PREMIUM COSTS OF LIFE INSURANCE AT AGE 22*

TYPE OF INSURANCE	ANNUAL PREMIUM PER $1,000 FACE VALUE
Term	$ 3
Straight life	9
Limited pay plan (20 payments)	15
Endowment	22

**These rates assume no dividends are paid on the policies.*

From this brief review of the fundamentals of casualty and life insurance it should be clear to students and the experienced small firm owner that *every business needs a good insurance agent.* Competent business owners today *buy* insurance to fit their needs and do not have to be *sold* insurance protection. They analyze the relative incidence of each risk to which they are subject and plan their casualty insurance accordingly. They then decide how they can use life insurance for business purposes or personal estate building and choose appropriate policies. A thoroughly competent and conscientious insurance agent who specializes in the problems of small firms can be an invaluable asset to any small firm owner.

QUESTIONS FOR CLASS DISCUSSION

Q19-1 What is meant by saying we all live with risks every day of our lives? What are some of these risks?

Q19-2 What risks are incurred by ownership of a building?

Q19-3 If you rent a building for your store, should you still insure the inventory of merchandise? Why?

Q19-4 What is workmen's compensation insurance? How does it work?

Q19-5 What kinds of risks does the owner of a department store incur as far as the general public is concerned?

Q19-6 What is title insurance? Do you think it is important?

Q19-7 How would you cope with the risk that your location may lose its value?

Q19-8 What is the best way to protect a business against the risk of financial hardship?

Q19-9 What do we mean by "shifting the risk" as a means of coping with possible loss?

Q19-10 When is self-insurance a practical idea?

Q19-11 Should you protect against all risks by buying insurance?

Q19-12 If your answer to question 11 is no, give an example of risks you would not insure against. How would you handle them?

PROBLEMS AND QUESTIONS FOR WRITTEN ASSIGNMENT

P19-1 Prepare a list of risks which can be eliminated. Explain the method you would use to eliminate them.

P19-2 Prepare a list of risks which you would be willing to absorb in your business.

P19-3 Prepare a list of risks which should never be absorbed and tell what you would do about each.

P19-4 Can you identify some small firm employees who would be valuable enough to the firm that the owner could justify taking out key-man or key-woman life insurance on them? Would you recommend this practice?

P19-5 From your studies in this course so far, name several ways in which good planning can serve to minimize risks.

P19-6 Name some ways in which term life insurance is used in business.

CONTINUING PROBLEM: *THE SUCCESS HARDWARE STORE*

Part 19. Risks Taken and How We Will Face Them

Assignment for Part 19

Prepare a list of all the important risks you understand the business will face. Which have the highest incidence of loss? What is the difference between eliminating, reducing, shifting, and absorbing risks? What will you do about each of the risks on your list? Will you have occasion to use coinsurance?

REFERENCES FOR FURTHER READING

Archer, Maurice, *An Introduction to Canadian Business,* 3d ed., McGraw-Hill Ryerson Ltd., Toronto, 1978, chap. 18.

Kriz, Joseph A., and Curtis J. Duggan, *Your Dynamic World of Business,* McGraw-Hill Book Co., New York, 1973, chap. 2.

Musselman, Vernon A., and Eugene H. Hughes, *Introduction to Modern Business,* 6th ed., Prentice-Hall, Inc., Englewood Cliffs, N.J., 1973, chap. 15.

CHAPTER 20

Personnel and Organization for the Small Firm

In the depression years we had no trouble keeping good employees because they were thankful to have jobs. It isn't that way today. When our labour turnover increased, we decided we had better find out why. The things you talk about have helped us keep our good employees today.

The Late Learner

College students today usually have positive ideas about the personnel policies of business organizations. Their opinions and attitudes have been largely influenced by the decade of the sixties, when employers sought employees in what was a seller's market. The demand for workers usually exceeded the supply of able people. In the late 1970s, when unemployment in many areas became high, employers became unwilling to hire people without proper training and ability. Jobs are not so easily obtained in such periods, and applications are scrutinized more closely.

Successful business firms, however, have always recognized the difference between finding and retaining good employees. In big business we have seen great programs of employee on-the-job training, sensitivity training, opportunities to try different positions, merit raises to provide regularly increased income for productive workers, and supervisory and executive programs of various types. All are designed to improve employee productivity, encourage creativity, and generally make workers happy and convinced they have an attractive future with the firm.

At the same time, the past decade has seen an increasing percentage of trained people going into business for themselves in preference to working for large corporations. One large midwestern university reports that regular studies of its graduates show that those who went into business for themselves have the highest average income. This is healthy for small business, but it also means that small business owners must fully understand the problems of obtaining and retaining good employees.

It is a refreshing experience for students to consider these problems from the employer's viewpoint. They now sit on the other side of the desk. They must devise a personnel program for their contemplated firms, and it must be a good one if the business is to be really successful.

Everyone recognizes that good employees are a firm's most valuable asset. Many customers are "turned off" and do not come back to a business whose employees have been discourteous or incompetent or have given other bad impressions. It is often said that a retailer can lose established customers much more easily than he can gain new ones. Customers are the lifeblood of any business. Their continued patronage is essential to its profit objectives. Good employees can do much to assure this objective. Even those not in contact with actual sales contribute much to keeping the entire organization efficient and able to render proper service to customers.

Against this background, small firm owners can start their personnel programs with a review of those things which are important to employees. Their desires may not be in the order presented here, but all of them are influential.

THE FRAMEWORK FOR PERSONNEL PROGRAMS

Before taking a look at suggestions about what employees want from their jobs and suggestions for achieving the goal of an efficient, happy, and productive staff of employees for any business, we should recognize the legal framework in which all personnel policies operate. Personnel programs are not left to the sole discretion of business owners in the modern business world. Even well-meaning policies which have proved successful in the past may run into conflict with a barrage of legal regulations which all employers must abide by today.

Chief among the governmental regulations for employers today are minimum wage laws, fair employment regulations, the right of employees to collective bargaining and to form their own unions, requirements for withholding income taxes and other items from employee paychecks for the federal government (Unemployment Insurance, Canada Pension Plan), and public policy relative to being an equal opportunity employer. It is not our purpose here to evaluate such regulations but only to indicate to new firm planners that it is important to check the current status on all such regulations at the time they are starting new firms.

Fringe benefits, health and safety programs, profit-sharing plans, pensions, and vacation policies are all part of a complete personnel program. Surely all successful business owners must recognize today that fair wages which are competitive, fringe benefits which are attractive, desirable working conditions, and a sense of concern for employees are important parts of building a staff of dedicated and efficient employees.

WHAT DO EMPLOYEES WANT FROM THEIR JOBS?

1 Fair Wages Wages must be more than enough to buy the essentials of life. Employees want sufficient money to have adequate insurance, to be able to educate their children, and to provide for their old age. They want real wages to increase from year to year so that they can enjoy an improving status. They want to feel that their wages bear a relation to their contribution to the firm.

2 Continuous Employment Even when wages are quite satisfactory in all respects, employees still want to know that their employment is assured into the future. They will often take other positions at less pay, only because the outlook for permanent employment is better. Yearly earnings are more important than weekly earnings for most employees.

3 Reasonable Hours of Work Even good employees who truly want to work for a living still want the hours of work to be reasonable. When the 8-hour day was established, it was hailed as a great achievement for all wage earners. Today we are on the threshold of a further reduction in the workday and/or workweek, and small firms must abide by the rules of society. They can often adjust their working hours more easily than the large firms because their employees usually live close to their work and because of the close rapport possible among staff and employers. Some employees are more willing to work split shifts, for example.

4 Pleasant and Safe Working Conditions Factory workers want a minimum of risk of industrial accidents, occupational diseases, fatigue-creating elements such as noise, disturbances, and vibration. Factory, wholesale, service, and retail employees all want healthy working conditions in a pleasant environment.

5 Sense of Improving Status Employees desire assurance that they can feel a sense of status improvement with years of experience with the firm. This may take the form of opportunities to use talents other than those which got them their first job, a chance to participate in decision making for the firm, or a chance to demonstrate improved status through a title which their friends will respect.

6 Feeling of Contribution Despite any contrary impressions which appear in the newspapers during labour strife, most employees really do want to feel that they are making a contribution to the firm. Nothing is more frustrating to good employees than not knowing where their jobs fit into the total operation, not knowing the value of the work they do, and, even more, not having anyone display interest in what they are doing. Here again, the small firm has advantages over the larger firm because of the relative size of the business.

7 Respect for Management Employees are much happier and better workers when they respect the management of their firm and think that it is competent, fair, and alert to employees' contributions.

Small business has often been accused of being unable to provide all these conditions for employees. Competent owners refuse to accept such an accusation. The numerous small firms whose employees have many years of service with them demonstrate that small business can successfully compete for and keep good employees.

ADVANTAGES OF SMALL FIRM EMPLOYMENT

Among the advantages of employment in a small firm are the following:

1 The small firm can provide employment for people who want to work in the area where they live.

2 Employees are often neighbours and enjoy social life and sporting events together, with or without the owner, thereby creating spirit and harmony among the group members.

3 The firm is small enough so that employees can be close to the employer at all times. Therefore, complaints and irritations can be solved at once, rather than be sent to a committee.

4 Small firms can readily observe and compliment any exceptional achievements of employees.

5 Employees have greater opportunities to try different jobs in small firms because employers can pay close attention to their talents and desires.

6 Employees can more easily take part in decision making and be made to feel they are a part of that process because of their highly regarded and sought-after opinions.

7 Wages can be comparable to the wages paid by large firms while the wage earner maintains the advantages of working for a small firm.

8 Group benefits, such as life insurance and company-supported activities, are equally available in small firms.

9 Profit-sharing plans which aid firm growth and profitability can easily be set up.

10 Employees can easily become shareholders if the legal form of organization is a corporation.

These advantages do not exist automatically. They must be the result of a deliberate personnel policy. Some suggestions to be included in such a policy follow.

PERSONNEL POLICY SUGGESTIONS

The small firm owner can take certain steps to assure a good personnel policy.

1 Create an image that the firm is good to work for. Word of mouth from employees can do much to aid this objective.

2 Don't limit employee applications to people who happen to stop in and ask for a job. Go out and recruit employees. This can be done at schools and universities which maintain job placement bureaus for their students, at established government and private employment agencies, and through referrals from friends and other business firms. Advertising in newspapers or other media can also be very effective.

3 Establish applicants' capabilities before hiring them. Physical examinations are a must, including tests of vision, movement, strength, stamina, and hearing as appropriate to the job. Mental tests are also recommended. Hiring the handicapped is a fine thing, but don't do handicapped persons wrong by expecting them to fill positions they cannot handle.

4 Have all applicants fill out a detailed application blank and give references. See the sample form in Figure 20-1. Check references carefully, including credit references and other personal data. Check further than references whenever possible.

5 Always have an extended interview with the applicant—in pleasant surroundings—and have his or her application blank in front of you. The interview should enable you to rate the applicant. The interviewer should direct discussion into various channels to find out as much as possible about the applicant: background, previous

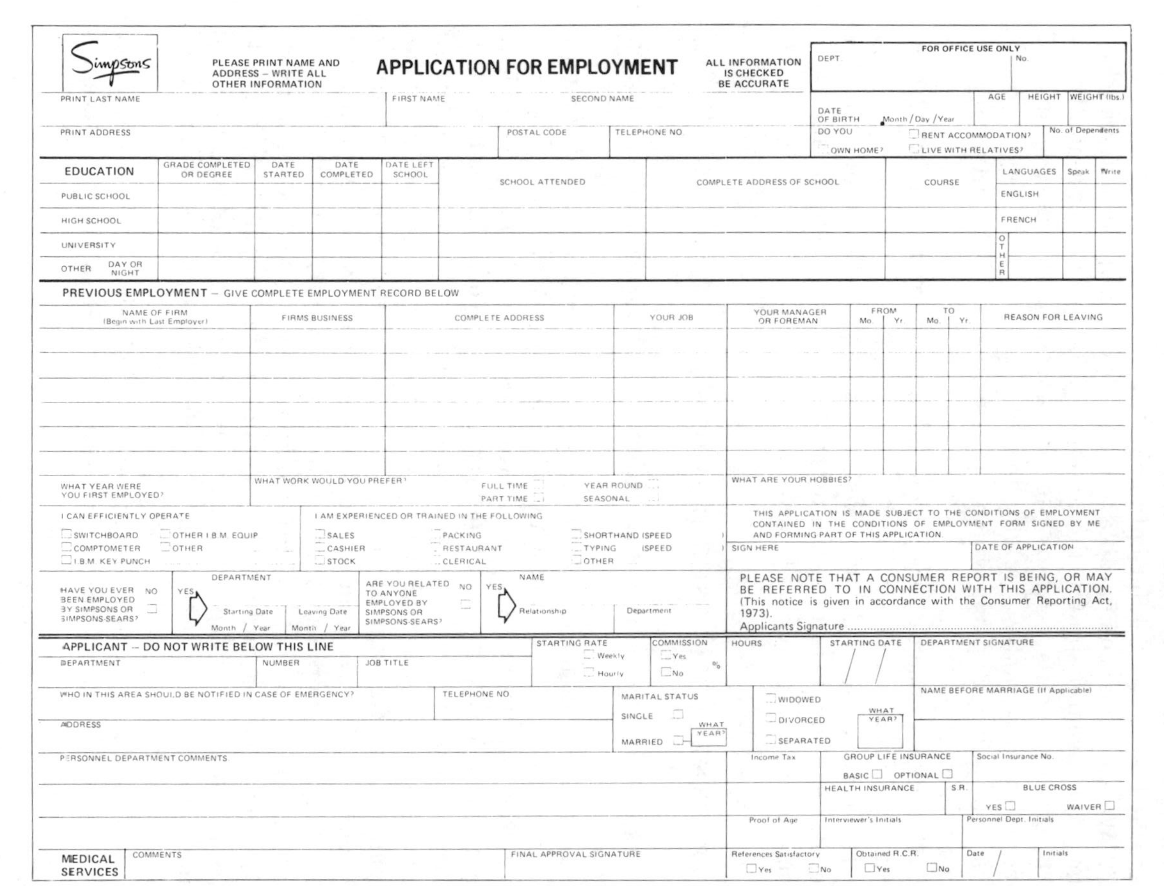

Simpsons

PLEASE PRINT NAME AND ADDRESS – WRITE ALL OTHER INFORMATION

APPLICATION FOR EMPLOYMENT

ALL INFORMATION IS CHECKED BE ACCURATE

FOR OFFICE USE ONLY
DEPT | No.

PRINT LAST NAME | FIRST NAME | SECOND NAME

DATE OF BIRTH Month / Day / Year | AGE | HEIGHT | WEIGHT (lbs.)

PRINT ADDRESS | POSTAL CODE | TELEPHONE NO

DO YOU ☐ OWN HOME? ☐ RENT ACCOMMODATION? ☐ LIVE WITH RELATIVES? | No. of Dependents

EDUCATION	GRADE COMPLETED OR DEGREE	DATE STARTED	DATE COMPLETED	DATE LEFT SCHOOL	SCHOOL ATTENDED	COMPLETE ADDRESS OF SCHOOL	COURSE	LANGUAGES	Speak	Write
PUBLIC SCHOOL								ENGLISH		
HIGH SCHOOL								FRENCH		
UNIVERSITY								OTHER		
OTHER DAY OR NIGHT										

PREVIOUS EMPLOYMENT – GIVE COMPLETE EMPLOYMENT RECORD BELOW

NAME OF FIRM (Begin with Last Employer)	FIRMS BUSINESS	COMPLETE ADDRESS	YOUR JOB	YOUR MANAGER OR FOREMAN	FROM Mo.	FROM Yr.	TO Mo.	TO Yr.	REASON FOR LEAVING

WHAT YEAR WERE YOU FIRST EMPLOYED?

WHAT WORK WOULD YOU PREFER? FULL TIME ☐ PART TIME ☐ YEAR ROUND ☐ SEASONAL ☐

WHAT ARE YOUR HOBBIES?

I CAN EFFICIENTLY OPERATE
☐ SWITCHBOARD ☐ OTHER I.B.M. EQUIP
☐ COMPTOMETER ☐ OTHER
☐ I.B.M. KEY PUNCH

I AM EXPERIENCED OR TRAINED IN THE FOLLOWING
☐ SALES ☐ PACKING ☐ SHORTHAND (SPEED)
☐ CASHIER ☐ RESTAURANT ☐ TYPING (SPEED)
☐ STOCK ☐ CLERICAL ☐ OTHER

THIS APPLICATION IS MADE SUBJECT TO THE CONDITIONS OF EMPLOYMENT CONTAINED IN THE CONDITIONS OF EMPLOYMENT FORM SIGNED BY ME AND FORMING PART OF THIS APPLICATION

SIGN HERE | DATE OF APPLICATION

HAVE YOU EVER BEEN EMPLOYED BY SIMPSONS OR SIMPSONS-SEARS? NO ☐ YES → DEPARTMENT Starting Date Month / Year Leaving Date Month / Year

ARE YOU RELATED TO ANYONE EMPLOYED BY SIMPSONS OR SIMPSONS-SEARS? NO ☐ YES → NAME Relationship Department

PLEASE NOTE THAT A CONSUMER REPORT IS BEING, OR MAY BE REFERRED TO IN CONNECTION WITH THIS APPLICATION. (This notice is given in accordance with the Consumer Reporting Act, 1973).
Applicants Signature ....

APPLICANT – DO NOT WRITE BELOW THIS LINE

DEPARTMENT | NUMBER | JOB TITLE | STARTING RATE ☐ Weekly ☐ Hourly | COMMISSION ☐ Yes ☐ No % | HOURS | STARTING DATE / / | DEPARTMENT SIGNATURE

WHO IN THIS AREA SHOULD BE NOTIFIED IN CASE OF EMERGENCY? | TELEPHONE NO | MARITAL STATUS SINGLE ☐ MARRIED ☐ WHAT YEAR? | ☐ WIDOWED ☐ DIVORCED ☐ SEPARATED WHAT YEAR? | NAME BEFORE MARRIAGE (If Applicable)

ADDRESS

PERSONNEL DEPARTMENT COMMENTS

Income Tax | GROUP LIFE INSURANCE BASIC ☐ OPTIONAL ☐ | Social Insurance No.

HEALTH INSURANCE | S.R. | BLUE CROSS YES ☐ WAIVER ☐

Proof of Age | Interviewer's Initials | Personnel Dept. Initials

MEDICAL SERVICES | COMMENTS | FINAL APPROVAL SIGNATURE | References Satisfactory ☐ Yes ☐ No | Obtained R.C.R. ☐ Yes ☐ No | Date / | Initials

Figure 20-1 *Application for employment.*

employment experience, ambition, sincerity, likes and dislikes, hobbies, sporting interests, living habits, family associations, responsibilities, etc. The applicant's self-evaluation is important also. Discuss past salaries and expected future salaries.

6 Even small firms should have job descriptions[1] available to discuss with applicants. These should be carefully explained, including salaries. The normal sequence of advancement in the firm should be described, including opportunities for such advancement, salary ranges, and average time at each level. If the firm has an organization chart, it should be shown and explained to the applicant.

7 A positive program of orientation of new employees should be established, preferably in writing. When new employees first come to work, a supervisor should be assigned to introduce them to fellow employees, the company layout, the facilities of the firm, and their own positions. Any printed material for employees should be given to them.

8 Have regular meetings with employees to discuss matters of mutual interest. Invite opinions, even contrary ones.

9 If training programs are desirable or necessary, establish them for regular presentation. No exceptions should be made for employees deemed able to benefit. Most small firms will do actual job training on the job.

10 Have a specified trial period for each new employee. Be sure that he or she knows about it. Do not hesitate to terminate a new employee whose work is unsatisfactory during this period. Weak employees hurt the morale of all who carry their share.

11 Provide at least an annual review of each employee's progress and productivity. Such reviews should be discussed with employees so that they know how they stand with the firm.

12 Keep salaries in line with the competition, or better than elsewhere—if this can be justified. Have a merit system of pay raises within a rank to be put into effect if they are earned. Be sure all new, and older, employees know the salary ranges available to them if they are promoted.

[1] *Personnel managers have three techniques to assist them in getting people into appropriate jobs:*

Job analysis—A detailed study of jobs, including identification and examination of the elements and characteristics of each job and the requirements of the person assigned to the job.

Job description—Description of the objectives of the job, the work to be performed, responsibilities involved, skills needed, working conditions, and relationship to other jobs.

Job specification—Description of the special qualifications required to fill a particular job including experience, education, special skills, and any physical requirements.

These are parts of a total job-evaluation program.

ORGANIZATION WITHIN THE SMALL FIRM

Most small firms do not make a formal chart of their organization, but this may become necessary if the firm grows and additional delegation of authority and responsibility becomes appropriate. A typical organization chart for a drugstore is shown in Figure 20-2. The owner may perform one or more of the functions shown. The size of the firm will determine when more people are assigned to other functions, that is, how many functions are carried out by the owner and how many are delegated.

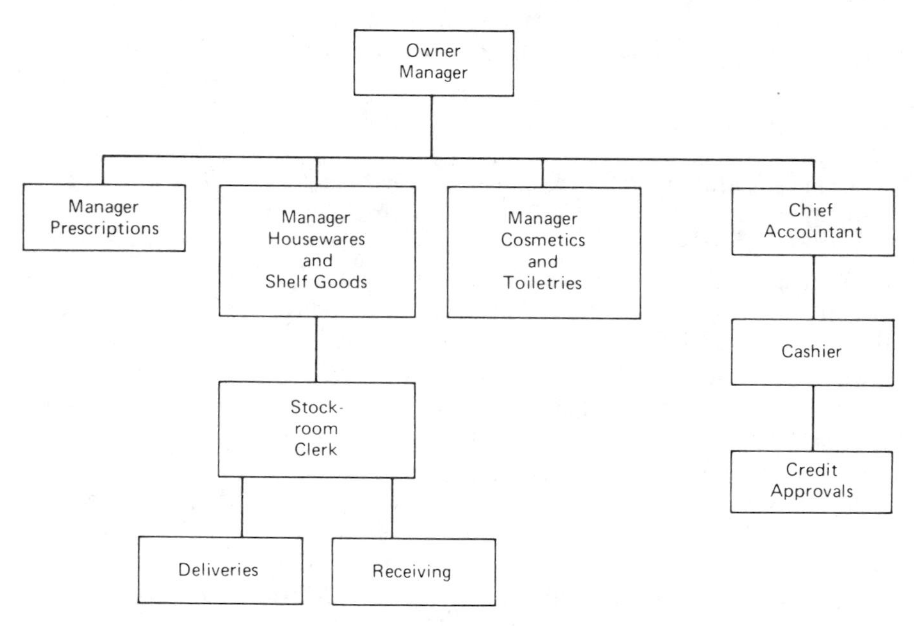

Figure 20-2 *Organization chart for a drugstore.*

In any small firm, even one without a formal organization chart, it is important that each employee knows precisely his or her responsibility and authority. If the owner works with the business each day, the owner is the top authority. If he or she is confident of the abilities of the employees, certain authority will be delegated to them to facilitate getting things done and to expedite the many routine decisions which must be made every day. For example, the company may have a policy on customer exchanges of merchandise sold. All competent sales persons should normally be able to handle most steps in this procedure. Approval of credit applications is a different matter. This authority can be specifically delegated, but it carries a responsibility which requires special analytical ability. One person should be assigned final authority in this regard.

All employees, from the stockroom workers to the sales manager, should know what is expected of them and their authority in performing their assigned tasks. It is an old principle of organization that authority must be commensurate with responsibility. This is another way of saying that if you give a person a job to do, give the authority necessary to do it. When policies are established for the firm, all employees should know what the policies are and who is responsible for their administration.

QUESTIONS FOR CLASS DISCUSSION

Q20-1 If "good employees are a firm's greatest asset," how would you assure good employees for your business?

Q20-2 How can employees do harm to a business?

Q20-3 Do you agree that it is easier to lose customers than to develop them?

Q20-4 What do you think employees really want from their jobs?

Q20-5 Would a 50 percent increase in all salaries solve the personnel problems of all business firms?

Q20-6 Do you agree that most employees really want to feel they are contributing in their jobs? How can this be achieved?

Q20-7 What are some of the advantages which small firms have in assuring that they have happy and productive employees?

Q20-8 Would you recommend a profit-sharing plan for your own small firm? How would you devise such a plan?

Q20-9 What features would you build into your personnel policy?

Q20-10 What is a formal organization chart? Do you think such a chart is appropriate for small firms?

Q20-11 What do we mean by "making authority commensurate with responsibility"?

Q20-12 What should be the relationship of the warehouse manager and the floor manager in a modest-sized department store? Can this relationship be shown on the typical organization chart?

PROBLEMS AND QUESTIONS FOR WRITTEN ASSIGNMENT

P20-1 Draw an organization chart for a small foundry business in which the owner is active and makes final management decisions. The owner has three separate departments for welding, die making, and production. One person is in charge of all production activities and reports to the owner. One person works as bookkeeper and secretary in the office. Another employee is in charge of the warehouse and materials. A shipping department sends out orders as they are completed and sends copies of shipping orders to the bookkeeper, as well as copies of invoices, which are checked against the shipments. The firm has 22 employees. Payrolls are produced each week by the bookkeeper.

P20-2 What is meant by the statement "personnel programs are not left to the sole discretion of employers"?

CONTINUING PROBLEM:
THE SUCCESS HARDWARE STORE

Part 20: Keeping Good Employees

Assignment for Part 20

You are now the owner of your own business and you know the importance of having good employees. Write a report on your personnel program. Include the following points:

1 Your understanding of employee desires
2 Policies you would establish for personnel
3 Salary plans and fringe benefits
4 Training policies if any are planned
5 Why you think this business is a good place to work
6 How you would handle employee problems
7 Whether you recommend job classification and job descriptions
8 Whether an organization chart is recommended

REFERENCES FOR FURTHER READING

Archer, Maurice, *An Introduction to Canadian Business,* 3d ed., McGraw-Hill Ryerson Ltd., Toronto, 1978, chaps. 25 and 26.

Broom, H. N., and J. C. Longenecker, *Small Business Management,* 2d ed., South-Western Publishing Co., Inc., Cincinnati, 1966, chap. 12.

Davidson, William R., and Alton F. Doody, *Retailing Management,* 3d ed., The Ronald Press Co., New York, 1966, chap. 9.

Kelley, Pearce C., Kenneth Lawyer, and Clifford M. Baumback, *How to Organize and Operate a Small Business,* 5th ed., Prentice-Hall, Inc., Englewood Cliffs, N.J., 1973, chap. 15.

Preshing, W. A., *Business Management in Canada,* Wiley Publishers of Canada Ltd., Toronto, 1974, chaps. 25, 26, 27, and 28.

CHAPTER 21

Buying an Existing Firm versus Starting a New One

I bought this business and later found out that I had paid too much for it. I guess it is all right to buy one, but I wish I had started a new one instead. I had no way of telling a fair price for the firm I bought. Thank goodness we have knowledge available now to measure fair prices.

The Late Learner

For persons who want to own and operate a small firm, there are several ways to achieve their wish. They may follow all the steps we have covered in the process of planning and establishing a new firm, or they may purchase an existing one in their desired line of business. Many students of management may even inherit a business from their parents or relatives. Our interest here is in choosing between the first two possibilities.

The case for buying an existing firm as against setting up a new one is not clear-cut either way. Each case must be decided on its merits. There are advantages and disadvantages to each. The hard world of reality in business suggests caution and competence when considering either route to ownership.

ADVANTAGES OF BUYING AN EXISTING BUSINESS

If an existing business can be purchased at the proper price (a matter we will discuss later in this chapter), it usually has the following advantages:

1 A going concern with a good history increases the likelihood of successful operation for the new owner.
2 It has a proved location for successful operation.
3 The time, cost, and energy required to do a thorough planning job for a new firm are eliminated. Profits can be earned sooner.
4 It already has an established clientele.
5 Its inventory is already on the shelves, and suppliers are established.
6 Its equipment is already available, and its resources and capabilities are known in advance.
7 Financing is restricted to a single purchase transaction.

While these advantages appear at first reading to be very significant, each must be studied very carefully in the individual case.

DISADVANTAGES OF BUYING AN EXISTING BUSINESS

Against the preceding list of advantages, even if they all stand the test of careful study, there are some important disadvantages:

1 The buyer inherits any ill will of the existing firm.
2 Lines of merchandise are already established and may not conform to the buyer's best judgment.
3 Certain employees may be inherited who are not assets to the firm.
4 The inherited clientele may not be the most desirable, and changing the firm's image is usually difficult.
5 Precedents set by the former owner are well established and may be difficult to change if the new owner doesn't like them.
6 The building itself and the layout inside the firm may not conform to modern standards and may entail substantial expense in modernization.
7 The landlord's attitude and practices may not be conducive to a pleasant and profitable relationship.
8 The purchase price may not be justified and may therefore create a burden on future profits.

Buying an existing firm does not always have disadvantages, but potential ones must be investigated thoroughly in every firm whose purchase is being considered.

EVALUATING AN OPPORTUNITY TO BUY

The problem for the prospective buyer is, how do I confirm the advantages and the disadvantages so that I can make a sound evaluation?

Any evaluation should proceed by the potential buyer's asking very specific questions and finding very specific answers. The list of questions and suggestions for finding the answers is as follows:

1 What has been the trend of profits for the firm? By trend of profits we mean more than merely the past year. At least 5 years should be reviewed. To find the answer we *(a)* ask for copies of financial statements, *(b)* review the firm's books, *(c)* study copies of bank deposits for the period, and *(d)* study copies of income tax returns for the past 5 years. If the seller (or business broker who has the firm listed for sale in his office) is not willing to provide these items, the buyer should be suspicious of the claimed profitability.

2 Is the business growing, declining, or relatively stable? The prime measure here is sales volume. Authenticity of sales claims should be verified. Audit reports are most valuable. Sales records, both cash and credit, are essential.

3 Are profits consistent with sales volume? We know now about comparative statistics which are available for almost every line of business. Any significant variation, up or down, from standard profits for this type of firm should be investigated.

4 Why does the present owner wish to sell? There may be entirely legitimate reasons for the decision, such as health, age, or a desire to move to Florida. The potential buyer must be sure that the current owner is not merely looking for a chance to sell at an inflated price or because of serious problems in the firm's operation.

5 Does the balance sheet for the firm reflect a sound current financial condition? By applying our basic current ratio, quick ratio, and proprietorship ratio rules (Chapter 3), we have a first approximation of financial soundness. From this point we must confirm the soundness of the assets. Are the accounts receivable current or a collection of long past due accounts? Is the inventory composed of fresh, modern merchandise, or does it include much obsolete merchandise which will be hard to sell? Only investigation of the accounts receivable ledger and inspection of the inventory will find the answers here.

6 Are the fixed assets properly valued, considering their cost and depreciation charges? Are they modern? Are they in good condition? The answers are to be found in purchase invoices, amounts of depreciation charges for past years, recognition of modern versus old equipment, and thorough checking of its condition by inspection and operation.

7 Are expenses in line with average statistics for this type of firm? The answer here is to refer again to comparative statistics while recognizing that there may be reasons for variations in the particular case.

8 If the store is rented, what is the nature of the lease? Can it be renewed? For what periods of time? Is it a percentage lease? What are those percentages? (See Chapter 17.) What is the landlord's attitude toward the business? If one of the chief advantages in buying the firm is the location involved, the lease and an option to renew become of great importance. Options should be in writing.

9 What is the competition in the area? By buying instead of organizing a new firm, one competitor has been eliminated. The nature of remaining competition is still important. It should be known. Chances for successful competition with other firms should be reviewed as carefully as if a new firm were planned.

10 What are the present owner's plans after the sale? Too often new buyers find that the seller is in competition with them soon after the sale. The best assurance against this is a clause in the sales agreement stating that "the seller agrees to not engage in the same business within 10 miles for five years." Such a clause is widely used today.

11 Will I need any of the present employees? Are they satisfactory? Honest sellers will usually give a prospective buyer an honest evaluation of their personnel. They may even assist in choosing only superior employees if they are going out of business for good. Interviews with employees and observations of their activities on the job can assist the potential buyer in making any necessary decisions.

12 What are the prospects for increasing profits? Even though the business has been profitable in the past, the competent buyer will analyze the floor space, the layout, the lines of goods carried, the market area, and the services now rendered in terms of whether or not a greater volume of sales and profits would be possible. Chain stores which purchase one-unit firms have a remarkable record of increasing sales after purchase. Individual buyers of such firms can do the same thing.

13 What is the customer and neighbourhood attitude toward the firm? Interviews with customers within or outside the store and door-to-door neighbourhood surveys are the vital devices to find answers to this question. Some ill will may be discovered, but ways to overcome it may be devised. The important thing is to know what customer and neighbours think of the firm.

14 What is the reputation of the firm among business people in the area? Visits to surrounding firms, the chamber of commerce, or service clubs will provide answers. The seller may be known as a "poor payer" in the trade, a dealer in shoddy merchandise, a "sharpie," or one who is lacking in community support or renders too few services. Again, if any of these opinions are discovered, they do not in themselves cancel the idea of purchasing the firm, but ways should be devised to change its reputation if possible. Information is important.

15 Are there any nationality, religious, or political factors in the area which would discourage purchase? Despite advances made in promoting goodwill among all peoples, it remains true that if a community is predominantly of one religious group, one nationality group, or even one political group, business people who are not members of that group have a tougher time in developing successful business firms. Check the facts.

16 Do suppliers regard the seller favourably? Although any critical attitude discovered may be overcome, relations with suppliers are a measure of business competence. If the firm owns valuable distributorships, it is important that their maintenance is assured. The same is true for franchises.

17 Is the community to be served growing? Population growth means new potential customers. It also means new competitors in most cases. Being established gives existing firms the first chance to maintain preeminence.

18 Are all liabilities correctly stated on the balance sheet? Individual contracts and other obligations may be checked in detail. The best protection for the new buyer is a clause in the sales agreement providing that any other claims or liabilities are those of the seller. Purchase of the specific assets and stated claims by a separate legal entity may be appropriate.

19 Would the investment make as high a return as could be made by starting a new firm? The answer usually is found in the purchase price, to which we will now turn our attention. We know that profits can be realized sooner, but we must also consider the future situation.

HOW MUCH IS A BUSINESS WORTH?

When the desirability of buying an existing firm has been confirmed, the important question becomes, "What is the price?" Business brokers, even more than the seller, will bandy about such terms as goodwill value, capitalized earnings basis, and replacement cost of assets. The majority of sales of small firms are made on a basis of asset value less liabilities, with possibly some adjustment for profits in excess of a good salary for the owner plus a satisfactory return on his investment.

Goodwill as a Basis of Value

Goodwill may be described as the asset value of established patronage and an established name or image which is publicly recognized. It is usually assumed to give a firm profits above the average. The product names "Jello" and "Beechnut" have great asset, or goodwill, value. "Smitty's Drugstore" has very little in comparison. Most small firms have little or no goodwill as an asset of sale. Their goodwill is usually the owner's personality, which is not part of the sale. They may have special assets, such as a long-term lease on a prime location or a coveted distributorship which can command high prices.

Capitalized Earnings as a Basis of Value

Capitalized earnings as a basis of value are sometimes used alone for determining the value of a business. For example, if a firm regularly earns an annual net profit of $20,000 after the owner's salary and interest on the investment have been deducted, and the rate of capitalization is 20 percent, the value of the business is said to be $100,000. (The computation involves finding the amount, 20 percent of which is $20,000. In this case, $20,000 divided by 20 equals 1 percent which, when multiplied by 100, equals the firm's value on this basis.)

The rate of capitalization varies with the riskiness of the particular type of business. If risks are believed to be normal, the rate of 20 percent is popularly used. Firms considered to have less risk, such as a local water company, may use a lower capitalization rate with a consequent higher value. For example, a water company earning net profits of $20,000 capitalization at 10 percent would be valued at $200,000. (The $20,000 is 10 percent of $200,000, computed as just shown.)

When the risk is considered to be very high, the rate of capitalization is higher. Many neighbourhood beauty shops, service stations, or dry-cleaning firms facing rough competition may be capitalized at a rate as high as 100 percent. This would mean that the value is equal to 1 year's profits.

When only capitalized earnings are used as a basis of value, the net value of assets is ignored in finding value. It is recognized that adequate assets exist to produce the earnings. Liabilities are, of course, confirmed, as is the value of the assets and other items which have been reviewed in analyzing the firm to be purchased, but these do not enter into the determination of sales price.

It should be emphasized again that only the profits in excess of what the buyer expects as salary for the time and effort involved operating the firm and a desired rate of return on invested capital are the basis for using the capitalized earnings method of determining value.

Replacement Cost as a Basis of Value

Replacement cost of assets is a poor basis on which to determine their value for purposes of sale of the firm. Only in very rare circumstances, such as an extremely scarce supply situation, would assets ever have nearly the value of new assets to replace them. Book value (the original cost less reasonable depreciation) is usually a sound basis for sale value. This is the value used for most small firm sales. Straight line depreciation is assumed here. Chapter 22 will discuss alternative methods of depreciation.

Even the new student will recognize from these comments that goodwill value, capitalized earnings, and replacement values usually leave something to be desired in arriving at a precise price for a particular business. It will also be seen why it was said that most small firm purchase prices represent an agreed net asset value (assets minus liabilities assumed), with possibly some adjustment for profits in excess of the desired profit for the buyer plus a satisfactory rate of return on the investment.

A Practical Way of Finding Value

Let us see, using a realistic example, how the value of a small firm can be determined. A business has $60,000 net assets, with reasonably expected profits of $30,000 per year. The potential buyer values her time and energy at $20,000 and desires 10 percent on her investment. She would be willing to pay a premium for the profits in excess of the amount sufficient to cover her salary and interest. If a purchase price of $80,000 is offered, she would need $28,000 to cover salary ($20,000) and interest ($8,000, or 10 percent of $80,000) if she invested the entire amount on the date of sale. This would be an attractive price because she can still contemplate $2,000 of extra profits. If the price is still being negotiated, she would be prepared to capitalize this extra $2,000 at 20 percent, or $10,000, if risks are only normal, and have a maximum price of $90,000 in mind during the negotiating sessions.

QUESTIONS FOR CLASS DISCUSSION

Q21-1 If you are considering the purchase of an existing firm, why would you be interested in seeing its tax returns for the past 5 years?

Q21-2 What are some reasons for saying, "Buying an existing business increases the certainty of successful operation for the new owner"? Is this necessarily always true?

Q21-3 Can time be saved by purchasing an existing firm, rather than by doing a thorough job of planning and establishing a new firm?

Q21-4 Can the ill will of an existing firm be overcome if you purchase the firm? How?

Q21-5 What are the advantages of audited financial statements, in comparison with an owner-produced report, when evaluating a firm for purchase?

Q21-6 How can bank-deposit records be useful in firm evaluation?

Q21-7 What ratios would you look for on the books of a firm you planned to purchase?

Q21-8 Would you be interested in the cost and depreciation charged off on fixed assets by a firm you wished to buy? Why?

Q21-9 Would you want to know the details of the lease if you were buying an existing firm? Why?

Q21-10 Do you believe in protecting yourself when buying a firm by having the seller agree in writing not to be in competition within 10 miles for 5 years? Is this a violation of the seller's civil rights?

PROBLEMS AND QUESTIONS FOR WRITTEN ASSIGNMENT

P21-1 A small firm is for sale in your home community, where you wish to live. It has net assets of $15,000 and a 10-year lease on its store building at a flat rental of $200 per month. It has shown an average profit of $15,000 for the first 3 years of its operation. It is a normal-risk type of business and the owner is required to move because of his wife's health. How much would you be willing to pay for this firm?

P21-2 A desirable small firm is for sale. Your investigation reveals that the present owner has alienated the community with some of his policies and his personality. The price is attractive. Would the owner's reputation cause you to decline the purchase? If not, how would you overcome the reputation which he has established?

P21-3 After analyzing the books of a business you plan to buy, you find that the firm has an excellent current ratio and a good quick ratio but is short of cash and has not been paying its current bills on time. How could this be possible?

P21-4 A college graduate is endeavouring to make a decision. She has been offered a job with a large company at $12,000 a year. Her father wants her to be an independent business person and has investigated a small firm which is for sale and should conservatively earn $15,000 per year. What advice are you able to give her?

REFERENCES FOR FURTHER READING

Broom, H.N., and J.G. Longenecker, *Small Business Management,* 2d ed., South-Western Publishing Co., Inc., Cincinnati, 1966, chap. 7.

"Changes of Ownership," Minding Your Own Business, Pamphlet No. 10. Federal Business Development Bank.

Kelley, Pearce C., Kenneth Lawyer, and Clifford M. Baumback, *How to Organize and Operate a Small Business,* 5th ed., Prentice-Hall, Inc., Englewood Cliffs, N.J., 1973, chap. 5.

CHAPTER 22

Inventory Valuation Methods and Depreciation Methods

It still strikes me as rather funny to think that the same inventory can be valued at four or five different figures. Different possible depreciation charges on the same asset give me the same reaction. Are you sure there isn't something crooked about this?

The Late Learner

The student who has had a 1-year course in accounting, business owners who have become familiar with the accounting for their own businesses, and students who have understood the preceding chapters should now be ready for a more detailed look at the problems associated with valuation methods which may be applied to inventories, and depreciation rates which may be applied to fixed assets.

The subjects of valuation and depreciation are particularly appropriate for new firms because the owners have a completely free choice of methods available for both. Final decisions can be postponed until the end of the first year. Operations for the first year can easily affect the choices made. New firm owners can make better decisions if they know the various methods.

Historically, inventories were always valued at the *lower of cost or market.* This method is still popular, and it has advantages in many cases. Its chief disadvantage for the small firm is that if the market value is lower than cost, the firm actually takes inventory losses before they have been incurred through sale of the merchandise. This will be explained fully in the following examples and discussion.

METHODS OF VALUING INVENTORIES

Today the small business firm has a choice of at least five major methods of valuing its inventories. Expediency, tax considerations, operation results, and the outlook for the future are some of the considerations which will affect the choice made in the particular case. These five methods are:

1 Lower of cost or market
2 First in, first out (FIFO)
3 Last in, first out (LIFO)
4 Weighted average cost
5 Retail price method

To illustrate the application of each of these methods to a specific inventory, let us consider the small firm which sells a relatively high-priced product. This could be a piano store or a firm selling block-making machines. Full data to value its inventory, using the first four methods, follow. A separate example is given showing the retail price method.

Company X sells product A. Its purchases of this product during 1978 were as follows:

January—10 units at $6,000 each
March—5 units at $6,500 each
June—15 units at $7,000 each
September—10 units at $8,000 each
December—10 units at $8,500 each

On December 31, the market price from the supplier was $9,000 per unit. Inflation had continued. On December 31, company X had 22 units of its product on hand as the year-end inventory. Of these 22 units, 8 were purchased in December, 8 in September, 4 in June, and 2 in January.

The company is interested in knowing how these 22 units could be valued under each of the five cited methods of valuation.

Detailed computation of the value of the inventory using each of the methods follows.

Lower-of-Cost-or-Market Method

This method necessitates computing two values, cost and market, and then using the lower of these two figures. The market value is easy. Market value on December 31 was $9,000 per unit. Therefore, market value is 22 times $9,000, or $198,000. Computing cost value of the 22 units in the inventory necessitates finding the invoices for each unit, subtracting the value of those particular units in the inventory, and totaling the result. In our problem, that is done as follows:

8 units purchased in December × $8,500	= $ 68,000
8 units purchased in September × $8,000	= $ 64,000
4 units purchased in June × $7,000	= $ 28,000
2 units purchased in January × $6,000	= $ 12,000
Total cost of the 22 units	= $172,000

When we compare market value of $198,000 and actual cost value of $172,000, under the lower-of-cost-or-market method the value of the inventory would be $172,000.

First In, First Out (Fifo) Method

This method is the most commonly used method in Canada and it coincides with the normal movement of merchandise in most inventories. At least, almost every small firm owner hopes that inventory will move smoothly through the process of acquisition to sale. Exceptions are, of course, to be recognized in some special types of firms.

FIFO means that the first inventory received is the first sold and, therefore, the remaining inventory is assumed to be the last merchandise purchased. In our problem, the 22 units in the inventory would be the 10 purchased in December, the 10 purchased in September, and 2 of the units purchased in June. The student will immediately recognize that this statement probably does not conform to the facts of the firm. No doubt some of the units purchased in September and December have been sold. Nevertheless, FIFO is an approved method of evaluation, and its calculation would be as follows:

10 units purchased in December × $8,500	= $ 85,000
10 units purchased in September × $8,000	= $ 80,000
2 units purchased in June × $7,000	= $ 14,000
Total FIFO value of the 22-unit inventory	= $179,000

The student will see that already we have some variation in value. Lower of cost or market gave us a value of $172,000, while FIFO indicates a value of $179,000. The importance of the valuation method should begin to unveil itself. But other values are available under the remaining methods. Let us continue.

Last In, First Out (Lifo) Method

As the name of this method indicates, the method assumes that the last units purchased were the first ones sold. Normal retailing activities would not suggest this movement of the inventory in most cases. Yet, in such lines as style merchandise, this may be true more often than suspected. Nevertheless, even though this is an often used method of inventory valuation, the Department of National Revenue does *not* accept the LIFO method for purposes of income tax returns.

Under LIFO, the 22 units in the inventory would be the earliest units purchased—the 10 units purchased in January, the 5 units purchased in March, and 7 of the units purchased in June. Calculation of a LIFO value would, therefore, be as follows:

10 units purchased in January × $6,000	= $ 60,000
5 units purchased in March × $6,500	= $ 32,500
7 units purchased in June × $7,000	= $ 49,000
Total LIFO value of the 22 units in inventory	= $141,500

This LIFO value, arrived at under the circumstances of rapidly increasing purchase prices, is substantially less than either of the preceding two value computations. The significance of its potential use will be seen later in this chapter.

Weighted Average Cost Method

This method is more than merely an average cost. It demands that the average cost be weighted to reflect the number of units purchased at different prices. This necessitates that we compute the total cost of units at each price and divide that total by the number of units bought during the year to find the weighted average cost of one unit. This figure is then multiplied by 22 to arrive at the inventory value. That calculation is done as follows:

10 units in January at $6,000	=	$ 60,000
5 units in March at $6,500	=	$ 32,500
15 units in June at $7,000	=	$105,000
10 units in September at $8,000	=	$ 80,000
10 units in December at $8,500	=	$ 85,000
Total cost of 50 units	=	$362,500

First, $362,500 divided by 50 (units purchased) equals $7,250, the weighted average cost of one unit. Then, 22 times $7,250 equals $159,500, the weighted average cost of the 22 units in the December 31 inventory. Inventory value under this method is, accordingly, $159,500.

Retail Price Method

This method of inventory valuation is particularly appropriate for retail firms which carry hundreds of items in their inventories. Its application involves gathering all costs and expected retail prices on the beginning inventory and the purchases during the year. Freight-inward charges are then added to the cost total and additional markups are added to the original expected retail price total. Markdowns would be deducted from total expected sales price.

The dollar difference between these totals (markup) is then computed in dollars and as a percentage of the sales total. Actual sales are then deducted from this sales value of all merchandise handled during the year to give a retail value of the inventory remaining. By deducting the average markup from this figure, we arrive at the inventory value.

For example, if total invoice costs of beginning inventory, purchases, and freight-inward charges during the year total $60,000, and normal retail prices plus additional markups or less any markdowns total $90,000, the planned markup is $30,000, or 33 1/3 percent of retail. Then, if actual sales at retail are $45,000, the remaining inventory has a retail value of $45,000. By deducting the markup percentage (33 1/3 percent) from $45,000, we arrive at a cost value of the inventory of $30,000.

Adjustments can be made in this method for employee discounts, inventory shortages, etc., in computing the cost percentages. An advantage of this plan for retailers is that employees need only list retail prices when taking inventory counts from the shelves. All cost data and summary work can be quickly completed in the office.

To apply the retail price method strictly to our same problem with company X and the data used in the previous valuation methods, we must set a retail price on the 50 units purchased during the year and record actual sales of the 28 units sold (50 purchased less the 22 in the ending inventory), as shown in Table 22-1.

TABLE 22-1
COMPUTATION OF INVENTORY VALUE USING RETAIL PRICE METHOD

	COST	RETAIL
Beginning inventory	0	0
This was a new firm; all units were purchased during the year.		
Purchases during year (50 units)	$362,500	$517,850
The difference between this cost and retail is $155,350, which is the gross margin or markup percentage of 30% of retail. Cost is, therefore, 70% of retail.		
Actual sales for the year (28 units)		$289,350
Inventory value at retail (22 units)		$228,500
70% of retail value is the cost of the inventory (30% is markup)		.70
Inventory value under retail price method		$159,950

WHICH VALUATION METHOD TO USE

In our various methods, we have seen that the value of the 22 units in company X's inventory ranged from $141,500 to $179,000. How is the new small firm owner to make a choice? Several factors may be important in the decision.

First, profits and inventory value vary directly. The higher the inventory, the higher the resulting profit; i.e., if closing inventory is overvalued as compared with opening inventory, costs will be understated and profits will accordingly be overstated. Taxes may therefore be important in the choice made. The firm owner should also consider the outlook for sales in the immediate oncoming years. Will they be as good as this year? Were there windfall profits or other unexpected profits this year, so that profits exceeded expectation? Can such profits continue? Are there some antagonistic shareholders scrutinizing operations to be sure that the firm earned sufficient profit to pay their preference share dividend? Will the firm show a profit regardless of which valuation method is used?

When all these factors are considered, the firm owner will choose the method which will be best for all concerned.

It should be pointed out that in the purposely inflationary market example we used in this chapter, LIFO showed the lowest inventory value and FIFO the highest. In a declining wholesale market, the opposite would be true. The other methods illustrated show a greater tendency to reduce wide variations in resulting values.

The uninitiated are often shocked to learn that a specific inventory of products or merchandise can have different values. Critics often think of this as an inherently evil situation. But who is to say what is the true value of merchandise which is yet unsold or has been on the shelves for a long period? Just as we recognize that there can be no profit in the absence of sale, so it would seem unfair to take an inventory loss in the absence of its sale. Consistency in method used will usually even out the value variations over time. Merchants or manufacturers cannot choose the method which favours their own purposes each year.

It is generally recognized commercial and accounting practice that inventories must be valued in the same manner from year to year and that the method of valuation cannot be changed unless there is good reason for the change and the new method is likely to remain in effect for a considerable time. The Income Tax Act provides that the inventory at the commencement of any taxation year is to be valued at the same amount as at the end of the immediately preceeding taxation year.

Inventory allowance In computing his business income for a fiscal period commencing after 1976, a taxpayer is allowed to deduct an amount equal to 3% of the cost amount of the opening inventory of tangible property of a business. The deduction must be prorated if the taxation year of the business is less than twelve months to reflect the proportion that the number of days in the fiscal year bears to 365.

The method of valuation of inventory for the purposes of computing income from a business was discussed above. These rules are applicable in determining the cost amount of the inventory for the purpose of computing the inventory allowance. Inventory eligible for the inventory allowance must be held in the taxpayer's inventory in respect of a business and held for sale or for the purpose of being processed, fabricated, manufactured, incorporated into, attached to, or otherwise converted into, or used in packaging of, property for the sale in the ordinary course of the taxpayer's business.

Examples of tangible property which would be eligible for the inventory allowance include: (i) finished goods inventory held for resale; (ii) tangible work in process; (iii) raw materials which will enter into the production process; (iv) materials used for packaging finished goods, such as wrapping, boxes, and returnable containers; (v) inventory separated from real property, such as stockpile of ore that has been mined; and (vi) livestock or crops held by a farming business.

Examples of property not eligible for the inventory allowance would include: (i) real estate or an interest therein; (ii) spare parts for machinery and equipment or vehicles (unless held for sale); (iii) office or other supplies to be consumed in the course of business but not directly in the manufacturing process; and (iv) stocks and bonds of a stockbroker or investment company.

The 3% per annum deduction does *not* reduce the cost of the inventory as carried in the books and its main purpose is to compensate for significant inflation and is, in fact, in lieu of allowing LIFO method of valuation for tax purposes.

METHODS OF DEPRECIATING FIXED ASSETS

The investment which any business has in its fixed assets must be recouped. Fixed assets wear out, or become obsolete, out of style, or technologically inadequate. As they render their services to the firm, their costs are just as truly business expense as the gasoline for the delivery truck. To provide the firm with capital to replace them, their costs must be charged to operations by way of depreciation expense. At the end of each fiscal period, a charge should be made to a depreciation expense account (debit) and a credit made to a minus asset account entitled allowance for depreciation. Each fixed asset should have such accounts in the records. These depreciation expenses are noncash expenses. No checks are written for them. But the depreciation expense accounts appear on the income statement as expenses, and the allowance for depreciation accounts are shown on the balance sheet as deductions from the cost value of the appropriate fixed asset accounts. These depreciation charges do not result in the creation of a cash fund to replace the assets, but they do provide a cross section of assets from which demands may be made for necessary capital to replace the assets.

The question for good management is how to charge off the assets as depreciation expense. How much should be charged each year? How long will the asset last before it must be or should be replaced? Small firm owners must make decisions on these matters. When they decide on answers to these questions, they can turn to a method of depreciation.

There are several methods of computing depreciation charges. Each has merit in particular cases. Small firm owners should be familiar with the details of each. The most common are known as:

1 Straight line
2 Use or production
3 Declining balance
4 Sum of the years digits (In the USA only!)

It may surprise the new student to know that the depreciation charges on a particular asset can also vary, just as an inventory can have different values. We will illustrate this variation in charges by computing the annual depreciation charge on a specific machinery and equipment fixed asset. The data necessary to illustrate all four methods are as follows:

A small factory has machinery and equipment which cost $150,000. Their estimated life is 10 years. It is estimated that their salvage value at the end of 10 years will be $20,000. Best estimates indicate that they will turn out 100,000 units of the company's product. During the firm's first year of operation, it produced 15,000 units of its product.

What is the depreciation charge for the first year under each of the four methods listed above?

Straight Line Method

This method provides for an equal charge in each year of the life of the fixed asset. It necessitates knowing the *depreciable value.* Depreciable value is *cost less salvage value.* In our problem, the cost of $150,000 and the estimated salvage value of $20,000 result in a depreciable value of $130,000. Straight line depreciation then spreads this $130,000 out evenly over the 10 years of estimated life of the asset. This means an annual depreciation charge of $13,000.

Straight line depreciation is expressed as a formula as follows:

$$\frac{\text{Depreciable value}}{\text{Estimated life}} = \frac{\$130{,}000}{10 \text{ years}} = \$13{,}000 \text{ annual charge}$$

Under this method the adjusting entry at the end of each fiscal period would be a debit to depreciation expense, machinery, $13,000, and a credit to allowance for depreciation, machinery, $13,000. Profits will accordingly be reduced this amount for the year, and the asset account value will be modified to this extent by the allowance account, which will be deducted from the cost value on the balance sheet.

Use or Production Method

This method seeks to ascertain what proportion of the total estimated production was achieved in the subject year. This percentage of the total is applied against the same depreciable value used above. In our illustration, the machinery produced 15,000 of the estimated 100,000 units in the first year, or 15 percent of the total. Accordingly, this method would charge off as depreciation expense in the first year 15 percent of $130,000, or $19,500.

Expressed as a formula:

$$\frac{\text{Annual production}}{\text{Total estimated prod.}} = \frac{15{,}000}{100{,}000} \times \text{depreciable value (\$130,000)} = \$19{,}500$$

Under this use or production method, the depreciation charge will vary from year to year. If only 10,000 units are produced in the second year, for example, the charge would be 10 percent times depreciable value, or $13,000. If 20,000 units are produced in one year, the depreciation charge would be $26,000.

Declining Balance Method

This method of computing depreciation has the distinction of being the only one which ignores salvage value. It is particularly suited to firms or assets which merit speedier depreciation of the total cost. It uses an accelerated rate and applies it to the cost of the asset. The most commonly used rate is twice the straight line rate which would normally apply. In our problem, this would be 20 percent. Applying 20 percent times cost, $150,000, this method produces a first-year depreciation charge of $30,000.

Expressed as a formula:

$$2 \times \text{straight line rate (20\%)} \times \text{cost (\$150,000)} = \$30{,}000 = \text{first year charge}$$

It is called the declining balance method because in subsequent years the annual charge is always computed against the new book value of the asset. In our example, the book value of the asset after the first year is $120,000 ($150,000 less $30,000). In the second year, the charge for depreciation would be 20 percent times $120,000, or $24,000. The book value is then reduced to $96,000, which is the basis for the depreciation charge in the third year. The book value of any asset is its cost less its accumulated depreciation.

Sum of the Years Digits Method

This method, much used in the USA (but not in Canada), also recognizes that assets normally give more service in their first years of operation than when they grow older and require more maintenance or repairs. It possesses arithmetical nicety in that its total charges reduce each year, but the total charge neatly fits the exact amount of the depreciable value at the end of the asset's estimated life.

By "digits" is meant the years of the estimated life. In our example, the years are 1, 2, 3, 4, 5, 6, 7, 8, 9, 10 . . . one digit for each year of estimated life of the asset. The sum of the digits is the total of these years numbers, 55. This total, 55, becomes the denominator of a fraction, which is applied to the depreciable value. The numerator changes each year. The numerator is the number of years of estimated life remaining at the beginning of the year in which the charge is being computed.

In our example, there are 10 years remaining at the beginning of the first year, so the numerator is 10 over the denominator, which always remains at 55. In the first year, ten fifty-fifths ($22,636.36) of the depreciable value ($130,000) is charged off. In the second year, nine fifty-fifths would be charged off, in the third year eight fifty-fifths, etc. In the tenth year, only one fifty-fifth of the depreciable value remains in the asset account and it is then charged off, reducing the asset account to its estimated salvage value.

As a formula, this method appears as follows:

$$\frac{\text{Years remaining at beginning of year}}{\text{Sum of the years digits}} \times \text{depreciable value} = \text{annual charge}$$

or

$$\frac{10}{55} \times \$130{,}000 = \$23{,}636.36$$

WHICH DEPRECIATION METHOD TO USE

The best authorities in the field will usually admit that depreciation methods are only intelligent guesses at best. No asset is going to fall apart on New Year's Eve because that date marks the end of 10 years of service. Most business people agree that new assets render more service at less expense when brand new. Even a new delivery truck carries a better image in its first years of service. Yet who is to decide the exact schedule for recouping the investment in any of a firm's fixed assets?

All the methods illustrated are open to a new small firm in its first year of operation, as noted earlier. Government officials insist that the same method be used for taxing purposes unless permission is granted in writing to change it.

It is to be observed that using one method approved by Revenue Canada for income tax purposes and another method for the firm's bank, its creditors, or its shareholders is not illegal or immoral. Full disclosure as to methods used via footnote on the balance sheet is recommended for both depreciation methods and inventory valuation methods.

The tendency of many small firms to ignore depreciation charges altogether in an attempt to maintain apparent profitability is to be seriously frowned upon. Any "window dressing" of financial statements usually results in the owner's being more misled than the creditors.

The decision as to which method to use will rest on the same factors cited earlier in this chapter relative to choice of an inventory valuation method. A gloomy picture for the next 2 or 3 years suggests a faster method of depreciation. Heavy taxes and/or technological obsolescence both suggest faster rates of depreciation. Straight line depreciation is still the most popular among small firms, but it may not always be the best for the particular case. Knowing the preceding details about the major alternatives should help the new firm owner to make the decision best suited to the situation.

Just as uninformed critics of business sometimes mistrust different valuations of the same inventory, they usually respond to knowing that different amounts may be charged as depreciation on a specific asset with a frown and a suspicion that something crooked must be going on. Let us clarify that situation. *In any of the methods illustrated, no firm can ever charge off more depreciation than the cost of the asset.* Whether that cost is charged off faster or more slowly, the total depreciation is limited to the firm's investment. In this modern age, no one has yet found the exact answer which will serve the economics involved. It would indeed be a rarity if a fixed asset were sold or salvaged for exactly the amount of its estimated salvage value. Business people know that fixed assets do depreciate. They use the best methods known to measure when that asset value is used up. They never recover more than they have invested.

Another constraint of note is that of the Income Tax Act which specifies the maximum allowable rates for various kinds (classes) of assets. The rates vary, for example, from 4% per annum for asphalt surface, storage yard (class 1); through 35% per annum for outdoor advertising signs (class 11); to 100% for patterns and moulds (class 12). The taxpayer can claim *less* than the allowable maximum in any given year, but never more.

QUESTIONS FOR CLASS DISCUSSION

Q22-1 How would you describe the lower-of-cost-or-market method of evaluating an inventory at the end of the year?

Q22-2 What do the letters LIFO stand for in accounting methods? Do you believe there is any logic in this method of valuing an inventory? Does it apply to any business firms you know?

Q22-3 What is weighted average? Can you think of any uses for a weighted average other than inventory valuation?

Q22-4 Do most firms you know move their inventory in the exact order in which it is purchased? Name such firms.

Q22-5 If market price is lower than its cost and you are using the lower-of-cost-or-market method for inventories, do you feel the firm should take an inventory loss before sale of the goods?

Q22-6 Where would the loss in the preceding question show up in the income statement?

Q22-7 Should a physical inventory be taken regularly by all business firms? Why?

PROBLEMS AND QUESTIONS FOR WRITTEN ASSIGNMENT

P22-1 Jones Grocery purchased a new delivery truck for $3,500. It was estimated that it would render good service for 75,000 miles, have a trade-in value of $600 in 4 years, and have an estimated life of 4 years. The first year the truck was driven 20,000 miles. What would be the first-year depreciation on this truck under each of the four major methods of depreciation?

P22-2 If a piano store purchased five pianos at $600 each, eight pianos at $500 each, and three pianos at $900 each, what is the weighted average cost of all its purchases?

P22-3 Which inventory valuation method would you recommend for your neighbourhood independent grocery store? Why?

P22-4 Do you believe that new showcases render better value to a store in their first year than in their tenth? Why?

P22-5 Explain why the rate of depreciation does not affect the depreciation that may be charged as expense.

REFERENCES FOR FURTHER READING

Archer, Maurice, *An Introduction to Canadian Business,* 3d ed., McGraw-Hill Ryerson Ltd., Toronto, 1978, chap. 21.

Broom, H. N., and J. G. Longenecker, *Small Business Management,* 2d ed., South-Western Publishing Co., Inc., Cincinnati, 1966, chap. 15.

"Control Over Inventory Investment," Your Business Matters, No. 8, The Royal Bank of Canada, 1976.

Kelley, Pearce C., Kenneth Lawyer, and Clifford M. Baumback, *How to Organize and Operate a Small Business,* 5th ed., Prentice-Hall, Inc., Englewood Cliffs, N.J., 1973, chap. 23.

Meigs *et al., Accounting: The Basis for Business Decisions,* 2d Can. ed., revised, McGraw-Hill Ryerson Ltd., Toronto, 1976, chaps. 10 and 11.

Preshing, W. A., *Business Management in Canada,* Wiley Publishers of Canada Ltd., Toronto, 1974, chap. 24.

CHAPTER 23

Essential Accounting Records and a Simplified Accounting System

---

I never took a course in accounting and believed that I would always be dependent on my accountant for every bit of information from the records. I know now that I can operate a simplified accounting system for my business and keep myself better informed between accounting periods.

The Late Learner

Telling owners or planners of small firms that they must keep good accounting records seems to cause a reaction of bewilderment, and they have visions of countless hours spent on ledgers, journals, and posting. A good double-entry bookkeeping system is too often thought of as something requiring at least one full-time employee who makes decisions under divine guidance. Nothing is further from the truth.

At the same time, in too many small firms the owners do not understand accounting and fail to keep proper records. It is amazing that many proprietors do not know whether their business operated at a profit or a loss until many weeks after the close of their fiscal year because they are waiting for an outside accountant to come in and summarize their operations for the year. Audit reports are valuable, but timely knowledge on operating results is even more important to successful business management.

Yet, the objectives of small firm owners should be to find ways to get essential accounting information economically, quickly, and with a minimum of desk effort. Unless the owners are completely unable to record figures, they can easily obtain the basic information using the methods outlined in this chapter. We studied the basic accounting statements in Chapter 3. Now we must devise ways to obtain the underlying information for those statements.

By now it should be obvious to the student that if the firm would keep records of at least its daily cash and credit sales, its cash receipts and payments, its invoices for purchases of merchandise, and all expenses paid or owed, the basic information for making an income statement could be obtained. Likewise, if purchases, sales, and exchanges of fixed assets are recorded at least in memorandum form, a balance sheet could be produced. Accountants employed to prepare these statements often have little else to work with.

It is nevertheless surprising how many firms do not keep even this basic information readily available in their files. Substantial guesswork is often necessary to produce the barest details for annual statements. Even when this basic information is available, however, the owner does not have the benefit of an analysis of operations from month to month or week to week. It is this type of owner who doesn't know the firm's profit position until long after the fiscal period has ended. Such neglect of good accounting information is a prime measure of management incompetence.

Day-to-day decisions in any business must depend upon the financial condition of the firm. Adverse income/expense relationships cannot be corrected, or even detected, without good accounting information. The sooner financial problems or undesirable trends are detected, the more quickly corrective action can be taken.

The simplified record keeping and the basic accounting system outlined in this chapter are designed particularly for retailers and wholesalers, but they can easily be adjusted for manufacturing. The discussion is divided into three parts:

1 Minimum information needs
2 How to gather the required information
3 Operation of a combined journal-ledger and a summary work sheet

MINIMUM INFORMATION NEEDED FROM ACCOUNTING RECORDS

1 Sales The owner should know not only the total sales by day, week, month, quarter, and year but should be able to easily break these sales down into departments, products, or types of merchandise as may be appropriate to the particular business. A grocery store usually divides its sales into meats, produce, dairy and staple groceries. A separate division may be needed for a delicatessen if one is part of the store. Drugstores may divide sales into prescriptions, housewares, shelf medicines, tobacco, and magazines, and even have a separate category for gift cards.

These divisions of sales are necessary for the owner to be able to decide on the profitability of each department or line and make decisions about it.

2 Operating Expenses Information is needed for total expenses, departmental expenses, product expenses, and any other appropriate divisions. Retailers' expenses may be classified into selling expenses and general expenses. Owners of factories will want to divide total expenses ino manufacturing, selling, and administrative expenses.

3 Accounts Receivable Records of total sales for cash and total sales on account must be available. A current record of balances owed by credit customers is fundamental. Sales to be charged to credit-card companies must be easily accessible so that statements may be submitted to those companies for payment.

4 Status of Accounts Payable Every debt incurred must be recorded and the total debts outstanding at any time must be easily accessible. The records must provide a way to pay invoices within discount periods. Other due dates must be known and observed.

5 Inventory The accounting records must provide ways to give the owner regular information on the total inventory and its major divisions. We discussed inventory control in Chapter 16.

6 Payroll Record Payrolls involve much more than issuance of weekly, bimonthly, or monthly cheques to employees. The requirements of withholding taxes, payments towards Unemployment Insurance, Canada Pension Plan, Health Insurance Plans, and other payroll deductions must be noted in detail for each payday.

7 Taxes Municipal, provincial, and federal taxes are an unavoidable part of managing any business. Details will vary from one location to another, except for federal income taxes. Requirements must be determined, and then provision for getting the proper information can be arranged.

HOW TO GATHER INFORMATION

1 Cash Register use a modern cash register. This essential piece of business equipment can be invaluable in assuring accuracy in recording transactions. But it can do much more. Modern cash registers can provide classification of sales and expenses paid in cash into almost any groups desired. Sales can be divided into departments, products, or lines of merchandise. The register will then provide daily subtotals for each classification, as well as total sales for the day. It will also provide subtotals for cash sales and credit sales. The representatives of companies selling these machines will show the individual firm how best to use their potentials.

2 Accounts Receivable and Accounts Payable Set up records for accounts receivable and accounts payable. If sales are made on credit and the company is carrying its own receivables, a record for each customer is essential. Such a record need not be elaborate. Many small firms use a 5- by 8-inch card for each customer on which each credit sale and each payment on account is recorded. A simple book of lined paper with a separate sheet for each customer will also suffice. Copies of sales slips are necessary to post each sale. This book is known as an accounts receivable ledger.

When sales are made on credit cards, it is only necessary to keep all such sales slips together by credit company to form a basis for sending statements to the company for collection.

PAYROLL JOURNAL

DEPT OR PLACE　　PAYROLL PERIOD ENDING　　SHEET NO　OF　SHEETS

NAME	EMPL. NO.	PERIOD ENDING	TIME WORKED: REGULAR	TIME WORKED: O.TIME	RATE	EARNINGS: REGULAR	EARNINGS: OVERTIME	EARNINGS: TOTAL EARNINGS *	U.I.C. INS. EARNINGS	DEDUCTIONS: HEALTH INS.	DEDUCTIONS: CANADA PENSION PLAN	DEDUCTIONS: INCOME TAX	DEDUCTIONS: HOSP. INS.	DEDUCTIONS: UNEMP. INS.	DEDUCTIONS: CAN. SAV. BOND	DEDUCTIONS: MISC. CODE	DEDUCTIONS: MISC. AMOUNT	DEDUCTIONS: TOTAL DEDUCTIONS	NET PAY	CHEQUE NUMBER	
H. Jones	07	Nov. 15	40	-	4.85	194.00	=	194.00	194.00	4.75	3.15	27.55		2.91	6.00	VW	2.00	46.36	147.64	618	1
P. Sibley	12	Nov 15	40	8	4.85	194.00	38.80	232.80	232.80	4.75	3.85	39.05		3.49	3.00	VW	2.50	56.63	176.17	619	2
J. Barlow	13	Nov 15	40	4	6.25	250.00	25.00	275.00	240.00	9.50	4.57	31.95		3.60		VW	2.50	52.12	222.88	620	3
J. Rejto	14	Nov 15	40	-	6.50	260.00	=	260.00	240.00	9.50	4.30	25.15		3.60	3.00	VW	3.00	48.55	211.45	621	4
																					5
																					6
Ms. D. Smith	29	Nov 15	30	-	4.75	142.50	=	142.50	142.50	4.75	2.22	13.60		2.14		VW	2.00	24.71	117.79	636	7
F. Carvaille	30	Nov 15	40	-	5.05	202.00	=	202.00	202.00	9.50	3.29	11.85		3.03	3.00			30.67	171.33	637	8
J. Miller	31	Nov 15	40	10	5.95	238.00	59.50	297.50	240.00	9.50	5.02	32.45		3.60	9.00			59.57	237.93	638	9
																					10

* A separate record of cumulative totals for each employee must be kept throughout the year for tax purposes, etc.

Figure 23-1 *Sample payroll sheet.*

A record of accounts payable operates similarly to the accounts receivable record above. In both cases, it is important to be able to tell immediately the current amount owed by a customer or the amount owed to a creditor. The record of amounts due to others is known as an accounts payable ledger.

3 Payroll Sheet Devise an adequate payroll sheet. Before each payday a complete payroll sheet must be completed. This sheet must have columns for employee identification, pay rate, overtime worked, taxes withheld, UI and CPP contributions, and other authorized deductions, such as United Way, Canada Savings Bond, etc. Once the form has been devised, it can be completed easily for each succeeding payday. Standard payroll sheets are available in stationery stores (Figure 23-1). Employers must also contribute to the Unemployment Insurance (UI) Fund and to the Canada Pension Plan (CPP). The employer's premium rate is 1.4 times the employee's premium for UI, and to CPP every employer is required to make a contribution of an amount equal to the contributions deducted from the employees.

4 Inventory Control Establish an inventory control procedure. The procedure will vary with the type of firm. Many retailers keep inventory records by accumulating price tags from merchandise sold. Accumulated tags show when reordering is appropriate. Other firms set minimum inventories and regularly check shelves and warehouse to see that stocks are above that minimum. Alert cashiers can report when sales of particular items suggest an inventory check. Analysis of sales records shows which items are getting more or less popular and whether inventory size needs checking. Physical inventories should be taken regularly, never less often than once a year. A perpetual inventory may be appropriate for some kinds of firms—which means checking each item sold as a deduction and each item received in stock as an addition in the inventory. Owners should devise their own plans for keeping themselves informed on adequacy of inventories.

5 Office Supplies Provide the firm with a businesslike set of supplies. Any firm's image, its public relations, and its accuracy in record keeping are all served by using attractive and businesslike supplies. These include sales books, statements to be sent to customers, invoice forms, receipt forms, letterheads and envelopes, and wrapping and packaging supplies.

6 Business Papers Carefully preserve all underlying business papers. All purchase invoices, receiving reports, copies of sales slips, invoices sent to business firm customers, all cancelled cheques, all receipts for cash paid out, and all cash register tapes must be meticulously retained. They are not only essential to maintaining good records but may be important if legal involvement is ever incurred on any of these items.

7 Accounting Records Install a basic set of accounting books in a combination journal-ledger system. Such a system is illustrated in the remainder of this chapter. This is the heart of the accounting records. This basic record, plus a worksheet to summarize operations at the end of the month or fiscal period, will enable the owner to make formal balance sheets and income statements regularly. Any student who has had a high school course in bookkeeping should easily handle both. Others can teach themselves by reviewing Chapter 3 and studying this chapter.

TIME REQUIRED TO MAINTAIN GOOD RECORDS

If the foregoing system still sounds as if it requires much time and expert knowledge to maintain, the following statements may help to dispel such thoughts. A men's clothing store which installed a similar system reports that less than 30 minutes a day of uninterrupted time was all that was needed to maintain daily recordings. A small department store with annual sales in excess of $700,000, with an average of 18 credit sales per day and 20 purchase invoices per month, reported that less than 1 hour per day was sufficient. The owner handled this work himself as the system was established. He then trained one of his sales people to do the work, and she did it during her slack periods on the sales floor or before the store opened each morning. Monthly summaries involving completing a worksheet, preparing formal statements, and preparing and mailing customer statements do require additional time. Many small firms engage a student as a part-time employee to handle the accounting details. Owners should not be occupied in these details when their time can be spent more valuably on other things.

THE JOURNAL-LEDGER ACCOUNTING SYSTEM

Figure 23-2 is an example of a segment of one page of a journal-ledger. It illustrates most of the possible types of entries which a small firm will have during the course of a month. The entries and their explanation are on the pages following. The column headings can be arranged to fit any desires of the owner. For example, we have combined operating expenses with a column of brief explanation to facilitate finding subtotals for each type of expense.

EXPLANATION OF JOURNAL-LEDGER ENTRIES

October 1 H. Jones opened a retail store, investing $2,000 in cash, store fixtures valued at $1,500, and an inventory of merchandise valued at $2,000. All assets were paid for in full, so no liabilities existed on opening day.
Debit cash (for increases) $2,000, debit Fixed Assets (for

H. JONES COMPANY
Journal-Ledger
October, 1978

Date		Description or Explanation	Cash and Bank Debit	Cash and Bank Credit	Accounts Receivable Debit	Accounts Receivable Credit	Sales Credit
1978 Oct.	1	Jones opened Business with $2,000 Cash; $1,500 Store Fixtures, and $2000 Merchandise - Total $5,500	2000 –				
	2	Paid Oct. Rent - Cheque #1		200 –			
	3	Cash Sales	300 –				300 –
	4	Credit Sales			350 –		350 –
	5	Merchandise purchased from Fincher Co. on account					
	6	Store Supplies - Rex Co. - Chq #2		200 –			
	8	Cash and Credit Sales	600 –		200 –		800 –
	9	Purchased Insurance on Inventory from Acky Ins. Co. - Chq #3		75 –			
	10	Collections on Acct. (Hernandez)	100 –			100 –	
	11	Jones withdrew cash		100 –			
	12	Paid Fincher Invoice 206 - Chq #4		600 –			
	13	Merchandise received from ABC Co.					
	15	Sales Return (from Cook)				25 –	DR. 25 –
	16	Payroll - Chqs 5–8		480 –			
	23	Paid ABC Co. Invoice of 10/13 - less disc.		980 –			
		Omitted Transactions					
	31	Sent gov't. checks for withholding taxes - UI - C.P.P. Chqs 10, 11, 12		440 –			
	31	Purchased showcases - XYZ Co. - Chq 13		100 –			
			9300 –	6500 –	4100 –	3000 –	11 600 –

Figure 23-2 *A segment of one page of a journal-ledger.*

increases) $1,500, debit Merchandise Inventory $2,000, and credit H. Jones, Capital (for increases) $5,500. The assets invested are explained in the description column so that any transaction can be traced later.

October 2 Paid rent on the store building for October, $200, by cheque. Debit Operating Expenses (for increases) $200, credit Cash (for decreases) $200. The description column notes that the expense was for October rent so that all the items in the Operating Expenses column can be subtotalled at the end of the month.

October 3 Cash sales for the day, $300.
Debit Cash (for increases) $300, credit Sales (for increases) $300.

October 4 Sales on account for the day, $350, as follows: Consuelo Hernandez, $100; Alan Cook, $150; Marie Smith, $100. Debit Accounts Receivable (for increases) $350, credit

Merchandise Purchases	Purchase Discounts	Accounts Payable		Supplies	Operating Expenses	
Debit	Credit	Debit	Credit	Debit	Debit	
2 000 –						
					200 –	
600 –			600 –			
				200 –		
					75 –	
		600 –				
1 000 –			1 000 –			
					700 –	
	20 –	1 000 –				
Omitted Transactions						
			300 –			
10 620 –	20 –	1 900 –	4 125 –	550 –	1 975 –	

Sales, $350. It is then necessary to go to the accounts receivable ledger and post debits to Ms. Hernandez's Mr. Cook's, and Mrs. Smith's individual accounts. This ledger is a supplemental record and does not require equal debits and credits.

October 5 Purchased merchandise for the inventory, $600, on account, from the Fincher Wholesale Company.
Debit Merchandise Inventory $600, credit Accounts Payable $600.
It is then necessary to record the liability owed in the accounts payable ledger by opening a sheet for Fincher Wholesale Company and crediting it for $600. This record is also a supplemental record and does not require equal debits and credits.

October 6 Purchased supplies for the store, $200. Gave cheque in full payment.

H. JONES COMPANY
Journal-Ledger
October, 1978

Date		Description or Explanation	Due to Government Agencies Debit	Due to Government Agencies Credit	Fixed Assets Debit	H. Jones Withdrawals Debit	H. Jones Capital Credit
1978 Oct.	1	Jones opened business with $2,000 Cash; $1,500 Store Fixtures, and $2,000 Merchandise - Total $5,500			1500 –		5500 –
	2	Paid Oct. Rent - Cheque # 1					
	3	Cash Sales					
	4	Credit Sales					
	5	Merchandise purchased from Fincher Co. on account					
	6	Store Supplies - Rex Co - Chq # 2					
	8	Cash and Credit Sales					
	9	Purchased Insurance on Inventory from Acky Ins Co. - Chq #3					
	10	Collections on Acct. (Hernandez)					
	11	Jones withdrew cash				100 –	
	12	Paid Fincher Invoice 206 - Chq # 4					
	13	Merchandise received from ABC Co.					
	15	Sales Return (from Cook)					
	16	Payroll - Chqs 5-8		220 –			
	23	Paid ABC Co. Invoice of 10/13 - less disc.					
		Omitted Transactions					
	31	Sent gov't checks for withholding taxes - UI, CPP. Chqs 10, 11, 12	440 –				
	31	Purchased showcases - XYZ Co. Chq #13			400 –		
			440 –	440 –	1900 –	400 –	5500 –

Figure 23-2 *A segment of one page of a journal-ledger (cont.).*

Debit Supplies $200, credit Cash $200. The description column will indicate what was bought and from whom to enable the owner to analyze details at the end of the month.

October 8 Sales for the day, $800, of which $600 was for cash and $200 on account.
Debit Cash $600, debit Accounts Receivable $200, credit Sales $800.
Then debit the individual customers in the accounts receivable ledger for their purchases from the copies of the sales slips.

October 9 Purchased insurance policy covering the inventory and fixtures in the store. Premium, $75, paid by cheque.
Debit Operating Expenses $75, credit Cash $75.
If insurance coverage extends beyond the period when the books are normally closed, the premiums may be charged to a Prepaid Expense account, which is an asset.

Then, at the end of each period, the amount used up may be taken from this account and placed in the Expense account.

October 10 Received cheque for $100 from Consuelo Hernandez to pay for her credit purchase on October 4.
Debit Cash $100, credit Accounts Receivable $100.
Then go to the accounts receivable ledger and credit Ms. Hernandez's account for $100.

October 11 Mr. Jones withdrew $100 from the business for personal expenses.
Debit Mr. Jones, Withdrawals $100, credit Cash $100.

October 12 Sent cheque for $600 to Fincher Wholesale Company to pay for invoice covering merchandise purchased on October 5.
Debit Accounts Payable $600, credit Cash $600.
Then go to accounts payable ledger and debit (for decreases) the account for Fincher $600.

October 13 Purchased and received merchandise from ABC Company.
The terms of sale are 2/10, n/30. Invoice for $1,000.
Debit Merchandise Purchases $1,000, credit Accounts Payable $1,000.

October 15 Alan Cook returned merchandise, $25, which was part of his credit purchase on October 4. Merchandise was defective. We gave him full credit on his account.
Debit Sales Returns $25, credit Accounts Receivable $25.
Then credit Mr. Cook's account in the accounts receivable ledger for $25.
If such transactions are infrequent, it is not necessary to open a special column for sales returns. Such entries can be placed in the Sales Credit column and circled to indicate that they are debits. The circled items can be totalled at the end of the month to find sales returns for the income statement.

October 16 Issued paycheques to employees covering the bimonthly payroll. Gross pay was $700, but withdrawals were made as follows: Withholding taxes, $175; UI, CPP, and Health Insurance $30; United Way, $15. Take-home cheques, therefore, totaled $480.
Debit Operating Expenses $700, credit Cash $480, credit Due to Government Agencies $220.
All this information will come from the payroll sheet (see Figure 23-1). The amounts due various governmental agencies will be kept current from the payroll sheets and sent on due dates to those agencies.

October 23 Sent cheque to ABC Company for $980, covering invoice for $1,000, dated October 13, less 2 percent discount for payment within 10 days.
Debit Accounts Payable $1,000, credit Cash $980, credit Purchase Discounts $20.

October 31 Sent cheques to government agencies for withholding taxes collected for the government out of employees' paycheques, $350, UI, CPP, and Health Insurance payments of $60, United Way payments, $30.
Debit Due to Government Agencies $440, credit Cash $440. The amounts due will be taken from the payroll sheets since the last payment to the agencies.

October 31 Purchase new showcases for the store, $400. Paid $100 cash and signed contract for $300 to be paid in 3 months.
Debit Fixed Assets $400, credit Cash $100, credit Accounts Payable $300.
Again the description column will identify what was bought and from whom, so that analysis of the Fixed Assets column can be made whenever desired.

QUESTIONS FOR CLASS DISCUSSION

Q23-1 After studying this chapter, does bookkeeping still seem a great mystery to you?

Q23-2 Can you think of situations where small firm owners could make wrong decisions because they lacked good accounting information?

Q23-3 Why should the owner of a drugstore want to have sales broken down by departments?

Q23-4 Have you ever closely observed a modern cash register? What things can it do for firm owners to help them have good accounting information available?

Q23-5 What is an accounts receivable ledger? How does it work?

Q23-6 What is an accounts payable ledger? How does it work?

Q23-7 What type of inventory control system would you recommend for a business firm you would like to own and operate?

Q23-8 Are withholding taxes taken from employee salaries an expense to the business or a part of its total salary expense? Explain.

Q23-9 Why are attractive supplies important to any business firm?

Q23-10 Why can underlying business papers, such as invoices, become important in case of legal involvement?

Q23-11 Could you post 18 credit sales and 1 purchase invoice to a system such as outlined in this chapter in 1 hour?

Q23-12 If you had not taken a course in bookkeeping, do you think you could learn to operate a journal-ledger system as outlined here? How much study would it take?

REFERENCES FOR FURTHER READING

"Financial Reporting and Analysis," Your Business Matters No. 5, The Royal Bank of Canada, 1976.

Meigs *et al.*, *Accounting: The Basis for Business Decisions,* 2d Can. ed., revised, McGraw-Hill Ryerson Ltd., Toronto, 1976, chaps. 2 and 14.

CHAPTER 24

Worksheet, Formal Statements, and Cash Flow Statements

Accounting can be fun after you get the worksheet completed. I was so proud of myself when I first achieved that goal. It didn't take long to teach myself, either.

The Late Learner

Experienced bookkeepers can prepare a balance sheet and an income statement directly from the totals of the columns in the journal-ledger. They will make the necessary adjustments in the process. A worksheet as a permanent record is recommended.

The worksheet has been described as the best friend a bookkeeper ever had. On this one multicolumn sheet there is a complete summary of operations for the period, from a trial balance through the adjustments to the formal statements.

All accounts in the journal-ledger are listed in the left column. In the first set of dollar columns, the totals of each account are inserted. These are the totals at the bottom of the journal-ledger. If an account has a column for both debits and credits, the difference between these amounts is inserted. This is the account balance.

In the second set of columns, adjustments are made to bring the accounts up to date. This usually involves recording the new merchandise inventory, the supplies used, and any depreciation expenses which are to be charged. Other adjustments may be necessary. Actual debits and credits are made to the specific accounts involved.

When the adjustments have been completed, the first and second sets of columns are combined to make an adjusted trial balance. All additions and subtractions are made as we read across the page to the third set of columns.

Completing the worksheet from the adjusted trial balance involves transferring the income statement accounts to the income statement column and the balance sheet accounts to the balance sheet column.

On the completed worksheet shown in Figure 24-1, adjustments were necessary for the following items:

1	New merchandise inventory	$3,000
2	Depreciation expense on store fixtures	$25
3	New inventory of store supplies	$400

Each step in completing the worksheet and the method of preparing statements from it are explained in the following pages.

COMPLETING THE WORKSHEET

Trial Balance Columns

All accounts in the journal-ledger are listed horizontally in that record. Their names are listed vertically on the worksheet. Opposite each account name, insert the totals from the bottom line of the journal-ledger in the trial balance columns. Four of our accounts (cash, accounts receivable, accounts payable, and due to government agencies) had both a debit and a credit column. In these cases, insert the difference between the debits and credits (the account balance) in the trial balance column. Be sure to list the balance on the appropriate side of the trial balance. When all accounts are inserted, add the debits and credits to be sure that the books are in balance.

Where a summary account title has been used, such as Operating Expenses, the trial balance can break the total down into any classification desired. By inspecting the individual items in our Operating Expense column, we have broken the total of $1,975 into Rent, $200; Employee Salaries, $1,400; Advertising, $200; Delivery Charges, $50; Insurance, $75; and Miscellaneous Expense, $50. The Fixed Assets total of $1,900 has been similarly divided into Store Fixtures, $1,500 and Showcases, $400. If this detail is not desired, only the totals can be used.

H. JONES COMPANY Worksheet Oct. 31, 1978	Trial Balance		Adjustments		Adjusted Trial Balance		Income Statement		Balance Sheet	
	Debit	Credit	Debit	Credit	Debit	Credit	Debit	Credit	Debit	Credit
Cash	2,800				2,800				2,800	
Accounts Receivable	1,100				1,100				1,100	
Sales		11,600				11,600		11,600		
Merchandise Purchases	10,620			(1) 7,620	3,000				3,000	
Purchase Discounts		20				20		20		
Accounts Payable		2,225				2,225				2,225
Supplies on Hand	550			(3) 150	400				400	
Operating Expenses ($1,975)										
Rent	200				200		200			
Employee Salaries	1,400				1,400		1,400			
Advertising	200				200		200			
Delivery Charges	50				50		50			
Insurance	75				75		75			
Miscellaneous Exp.	50				50		50			
Due to Gov't. Agencies	0	0			0	0				
Fixed Assets ($1,900)										
Store Fixtures	1,500				1,500				1,500	
Show Cases	400				400				400	
H. Jones, Withdrawals	400			(4) 400	0	0				
H. Jones, Capital		5,500	(4) 400			5,100				5,100
	19,345	19,345								
Cost of Goods Sold			(1) 7,620		7,620		7,620			
Deprec. Exp.-Store Fix.			(2) 25		25		25			
Accum. Deprec.-Store Fix.				(2) 25		25				25
Supplies Used			(3) 150		150		150			
			8,195	8,195	18,970	18,970	9,770	11,620	9,200	7,350
Net profit for month (before income taxes)							1,850			1,850
							11,620	11,620	9,200	9,200

Figure 24-1 *A completed worksheet.*

Adjusting Entries

Adjusting entries are necessary to update trial balance figures. For example, the Merchandise Inventory account shows a balance of $10,620. But we have an inventory, taken as of October 31, which tells us that the merchandise actually on hand is $3,000. The difference in these two figures must be the cost of the merchandise sold. Therefore, we make an adjusting entry in the second set of columns to take $7,620 out of the merchandise account and put in a new account, Cost of Goods Sold. This new account, and any others needed for the other adjustments, is opened at the bottom of the worksheet, below the Trial Balance totals. It is a debit to Cost of Goods Sold because such expense accounts are increased by debits, and a credit to Merchandise Inventory because assets are decreased with credits. The Merchandise Inventory account now shows a debit balance of $3,000, which is the value of the current inventory. This amount will be carried over to the Adjusted Trial Balance. This adjustment is marked (1) in the Adjustments column.

The second adjusting entry is to record $25 of depreciation expense on the store fixtures. We open a new account, Depreciation Expense—Store Fixtures, and debit it for $25. The credit is to an account entitled Accumulated Depreciation—Store Fixtures for $25. This is technically known as a minus asset account and is deducted from the Store Fixtures account on the balance sheet. It is carried across the worksheet as a balance sheet account with a credit balance. This entry is marked (2) in the Adjustments column.

Adjustment (3) is necessary to bring the asset account Supplies up to date. On the trial balance it shows a balance of $550. But we have taken an inventory and know that only $400 of these supplies are still on hand. The difference of $150 represents the supplies used up during the month. Therefore, we credit Supplies on Hand $150 and debit a new expense account, Supplies Used, for $150. This entry reduces the balance of the Supplies on Hand account to $400, which is the value of supplies still in inventory.

Adjustment (4) is to close the owner's withdrawal account into his capital account. Withdrawals are not operating expenses but capital reductions. We therefore credit H. Jones, Withdrawals $400, and debit H. Jones, Capital $400. This removes any balance from the Withdrawals account so that no figures need to be carried across the sheet. The debits and credits in the adjustments column are added.

Adjusted Trial Balance

This set of columns is only a total of the first two sets of columns. Unless a debit or credit has been added in the Adjustments column, the same trial balance figure will be carried across to the Adjusted Trial Balance, as illustrated in the case of Cash, Accounts Receivable, and Sales. Merchandise Inventory has a debit in the trial balance for $10,620, but a credit in the Adjustments column for $7,620. The debit balance of $3,000 is accordingly carried over to the Adjusted Trial Balance column. Supplies on Hand has a $550 debit in the trial balance but a $150 credit in the Adjustments column. The difference of $400 is carried over to the Adjusted Trial Balance. Every account, including the new ones opened at the bottom of the Adjustments column, must be carried to the Adjusted Trial Balance.

INCOME STATEMENT AND BALANCE SHEET COLUMNS

Once the Adjusted Trial Balance is complete, the remainder of the worksheet involves only transferring each account on across the sheet to its appropriate column. All income and expense accounts go into the Income Statement column, and asset, liability, and Net Worth (capital) accounts go to the appropriate side of the Balance Sheet columns. When each account has been transferred, the columns should again be added.

Now notice that the difference between the debits and credits in the Income Statement column ($11,620 less $9,770) is the same as in the Balance Sheet columns ($9,200 less $7,350). This difference ($1,850) is the net profit from operations for the month. Another entry is made below these totals to transfer this profit from the Income Statement to the Balance Sheet, where it will appear as part of the owner's new Capital account balance.

We can now prepare formal statements. Items needed are on the worksheet. Samples taken from the worksheet are shown in Tables 24-1 and 24-2.

To prepare the journal-ledger for the next month's operations, insert the balance sheet account balances under the date of November 1.

CASH FLOW STATEMENTS

Because any firm's cash position is important to its economic health, firm managers should use all tools available to keep abreast of cash flow and current cash position. One of the best of these tools is the cash flow chart. It is designed to estimate future cash receipts, outlays, and balances and then compare actual results with the estimate at the end of each month of operations. Careful preparation and use of the chart provides a schedule of cash flow and a ready device for ascertaining if the schedule is being met.

TABLE 24-1
H. JONES COMPANY
INCOME STATEMENT
OCTOBER 1-31, 1978

Gross sales			$12,000
Less sales returns			400
Net sales income			$11,600
Cost of goods sold:			
Inventory, October 1		$2,000	
Purchases during month	$8,620		
Less purchase discounts	20	8,600	
Goods available for sale		$10,600	
Less inventory, October 31		3,000	
Cost of goods sold during month			7,600
Gross margin			$4,000
Operating expenses:			
Rent		$ 200	
Employee salaries		1,400	
Supplies used		150	
Advertising		200	
Delivery charges		50	
Depreciation expense		25	
Insurance expense		75	
Miscellaneous expenses		50	
Total operating expenses			2,150
Net profit from operations before income taxes			$1,850

TABLE 24-2
H. JONES COMPANY
BALANCE SHEET
OCTOBER 31, 1978

ASSETS			LIABILITIES	
Current assets:			Current liabilities:	
Cash		$2,800	Accounts payable	$1,925
Accounts receivable		1,100	Contract payable	300
Merchandise inventory		3,000	Total current liabilities	$2,225
Prepaid expenses		400	Fixed liabilities:	
Total current assets		$7,300	None	0
Fixed assets:			Total liabilities	$2,225
Store fixtures	$1,500		NET WORTH	
Less accumulated depreciation	25	1,475	H. Jones, Capital	$6,950
Showcases		400		
Total fixed assets		$1,875		
TOTAL ASSETS		$9,175	TOTAL LIABILITIES AND NET WORTH	$9,175

CASH FLOW STATEMENTS
(THE ESTIMATED FIGURES (TYPED) ARE PROJECTED FOR A FULL YEAR; THE ACTUAL FIGURES HAVE BEEN INSERTED FOR 3 MONTHS ONLY.)

CASH FLOW STATEMENT - MILLER'S AUTO SUPPLY - 1978

	JANUARY		FEBRUARY		MARCH		APRIL		DECEMBER		YEARLY TOTALS	
	Estimated	Actual	Estimated	Actual	Estimated	Actual	Estimated	Actual	Estimated	Actual	Estimated	Actual
1. Cash on Hand, 1st of Month	$5000	$5,000	$3400	$4,025	$2400	$2,625	$1975	$1,900	$3700			
2. Cash Receipts During Month												
a. Cash Sales	3000	3,800	3500	4,000	4000	4,200	4000		8000		72,600	
b. Payments on Accounts Receivable	1800	2,000	2000	2,000	2400	2,200	2400		4000		32,000	
c. Bank Loans	0	0	0	0	0	0	0		0		6,000	
d. Other Sources (list)	0	0	0	0	0	0	0		0		0	
3. Total Cash Receipts	4800	5,800	5500	6,000	6400	6,400	6400		12000		110,600	
4. Cash Available During Month	9800	10,800	8900	10,025	8800	9,025	8375		15700			
5. Cash Outlays for Month												
a. For Merchandise	1200	1,500	1200	2,000	1500	1,800	1500		4500		49,000	
b. For Wages & Salaries	3600	3,600	3600	3,600	3600	3,600	3600		4600		31,000	
c. Payroll Expenses	100	100	100	100	100	100	100		150		1,800	
d. Rent	400	400	400	400	400	400	400		400		4,800	
e. Utilities	100	125	100	150	100	150	100		200		1,600	
f. Insurance	50	50	50	50	50	50	50		50		600	
g. Interest	0	0	0	0	0	0	0		0		100	
h. Repairs & Mtce.	0	50	0	100	100	50	100		100		1,000	
i. Advertising	100	200	100	200	100	100	100		200		2,000	
j. Supplies	75	75	75	200	100	200	100		200		2,100	
k. Delivery Expenses	150	150	150	150	150	150	150		250		2,200	
l. Taxes	25	25	25	25	25	25	25		25		300	
m. Misc. Expenses	100	150	200	125	100	200	100		200		1,800	
n. Other Expenses (list)	0	50	0	0	0	0	0		0		300	
Total Mdse. & Opr. Exp.	5900	6,475	6000	7,100	6325	6,825	6325		10875		98,500	
Loan Repayments	0	0	0	0	0	0	0		0			
Withdrawals	500	300	500	300	500	300	500		500		6,000	
Equipment Purchases	0	0	0	0	0	0	0		0			
6. Total Cash Paid Out	6400	6,775	6500	7,400	6825	7,125	6825		11375		104,600	
7. Cash Balance End of Month	3400	4,025	2400	2,625	1975	1,900	1550		4325		6,000	

OMITTED MONTHS

If cash shortages are anticipated, arrangements can be made to meet these shortages. Periods needing expanded credit from the bank, for example, can be anticipated and planned for. If surplus funds are anticipated, arrangements can be made for profitably investing such funds. An estimated cash balance and an actual cash balance at the end of each month is provided.

The cash flow chart provides two columns for each month. One is the planned or estimated cash receipts, outlays, and balances. The second column provides for inserting at the end of each month the actual receipts, outlays, and balances. Disparities between the estimated and actual amounts merit close attention. Adverse trends can be detected early and management decisions can be influenced by studying the results.

The estimated columns should preferably be completed for a year in advance. Great care should be exercised in completing the estimates in each area. Many discrepancies between estimates and actual results are caused by failure to recognize lags in collecting accounts receivable and by failure to recognize all cash outlays.

It should be emphasized that we are dealing here only with actual cash flow. Credit sales are not cash receipts. Payments received against accounts receivable are. Bank loans represent cash received. Repayment of such loans are anticipated as a cash outlay. Starting from cash on hand at the beginning of the month, we add all cash received to find cash available during the month. From this amount all cash paid out is deducted to arrive at cash position at end of the month.

Improving cash position by ignoring liabilities and purchase discounts is not to be recommended. When all liabilities are paid as due and cash flow shows a healthy cash position, the firm has a healthy all-around condition.

QUESTIONS FOR CLASS DISCUSSION

Q24-1 How would you describe the worksheet?

Q24-2 Do you think the worksheet can be called "the bookkeeper's best friend"?

Q24-3 Where do the figures for the trial balance columns come from?

Q24-4 Why are adjusting entries necessary? Give some examples of necessary adjusting entries.

Q24-5 Once the adjusted trial balance columns are complete, how does the worksheet proceed?

Q24-6 Can you explain why the difference between the debits and credits in the income statement columns and the balance sheet columns is the same?

Q24-7 How did Mr. Jones's capital account go from $5,500 to $6,950?

Q24-8 On what amount will Mr. Jones pay income taxes for October?

Q24-9 Is the entire $1,850 of profits for October still in the business?

Q24-10 Can you find every item on the formal income statement and balance sheet in the columns of the worksheet?

REFERENCES FOR FURTHER READING

Meigs *et al.*, *Accounting: The Basis for Business Decisions*, 2d Can. ed., revised, McGraw-Hill Ryerson Ltd., Toronto, 1976, chap. 22.

"Planning and Budgeting," Your Business Matters No. 7, The Royal Bank of Canada, 1976.

Preshing, W. A., *Business Management in Canada*, Wiley Publishers of Canada Ltd., Toronto, 1974, chap. 33.

"The Three-Way Budget: A Businessman's Guide to Cash Control," The Royal Bank of Canada, 1975.

CHAPTER 25

Day-to-Day Management of the Ongoing Business Firm

Why should I worry about all those facts of past months? I know that all I have to do to increase profits is sell more merchandise.

The Late Learner

It is appropriate in this final chapter that we take a look at the small firm owner's activities as daily decisions are made governing the total operations of the business. The dynamics of the business world call for decisions almost every day. Problems arise, priorities change, policies are questioned, market developments arise, and countless other things call for the exercise of judgment in arriving at sound management decisions. The "management of change" is often a daily process.

Experience is a great developer of wisdom. Experienced owners carry many facts in their heads, facts which help them make decisions on new developments, as well as facts governing daily operations. Owners with less experience should seek to learn key facts relative to the firm and the industry or to the total business scene in which operations exist. Better judgment will follow.

If each step in a good planning procedure has been thoroughly completed, much time and effort has been expended. After the firm has begun operations, the owner cannot rely upon any automatic fulfilling of the firm's objectives. Management must keep itself aware of key items which affect or may affect the firm's best welfare. The basic management function of control demands regular analysis of operational results and facts for all phases of the total activities of the firm, as well as analysis of outside factors which may have an influence on operations.

The individual small firm owner must normally assume a wider responsibility in giving the firm this management control than does the head of a particular division of a very large firm. In fact, this difference in total responsibility has caused many learned business authorities to say that more ability is needed to manage a substantial small firm than to be a specialized vice president of a very large firm. For example, the vice president for finance of a large automobile manufacturing firm is charged only with keeping advised on matters of finance. These would include cash flow, current cash position, advice on security markets, capital structures of the firm, financial ratios, dividend capability and policy, anticipated cash demands, and so on. The vice president for marketing is charged with decisions and recommendations only in the area of marketing and distribution activities of the firm. The vice president for manufacturing handles problems of production and production schedules. Each of these senior executives carries heavy responsibilities, but each is concerned with only one general area of the total firm activities.

These duties and many more must all be the responsibility of the small firm owner. Every phase of the business is the owner's responsibility. He or she must be concerned with matters of daily sales, personnel, inventory control, supply sources, credit policies, new products, policy changes, market studies, public relations, advertising, location and site reviews, balance sheet data, income statement relationships, economic trends, all of the financial details, and many other issues. The owner's duties call for the management of change as well as the effective control of established procedures.

It is a long-established truism in management that early detection of adverse developments provides speedier correction thereof and thus a minimum loss of efficiency. With so many areas to control, it is obvious that the demands upon the small firm owner are most significant and time-consuming. Yet key control is most essential.

TIME DEMANDS VERSUS ACHIEVING MANAGEMENT CONTROL

It should be recognized that the time demands upon the owner in conducting normal operations may be so great that time for gathering data and analyzing key controls may necessarily become overtime hours. We have all seen many small firms where the presence of the owner is a key part of having the firm open for business. Fine restaurants often build their image around a well-known proprietor. Customers come to see the owner, to be greeted by the owner, and perhaps to have a visit with the owner at their table. If the owner is not available, the customers lose a good deal of the image they have of the firm and lose part of their desire to patronize the restaurant.

If this owner is also one who wants to be at the produce markets at five in the morning to pick out the freshest vegetables and fruits for the kitchen, even more time is consumed in normal operations. All these demands mean that analysis time to study controls of the firm is further limited. Analysis must be performed when the business is not open to customers, probably very late in the evening.

Small firm owners have another problem in that most small firms cannot afford to hire personnel purely to study operational results. As firms grow larger, more delegation of authority becomes essential. If department heads have been appointed or a full-time bookkeeper employed, these people can be most helpful in getting information to the owner to assist in control analyses. The drugstore organization chart studied in Chapter 20 shows that the owner-manager could call upon three department managers and an accountant to supply much data on current operations. Many small drugstores do not have this degree of organization because the volume of business is too small to allow it. In such cases the entire responsibility for accumulating data for analysis falls upon the owner.

ESSENTIAL DATA FOR EFFECTIVE ONGOING CONTROL

Interviews with many successful small firm owners reveals that they usually divide their management information into two categories:

A Data which they analyze daily, weekly, or monthly

B Long-range data which they check less often or whenever the occasion presents itself

In the first category they include:

1 Sales data and trends.
2 Production records.
3 Cash position and cash flow outlook.
4 Inventory data and need for adjustments.
5 Analysis of the accounts receivable ledger.
6 Policy violations and need for change.
7 Price policy questions which may have arisen.

8 Effectiveness of shoplifting and theft-prevention procedures.
9 Suggested new products or new lines.
10 Weekly results compared with weekly break-even chart.
11 Public-relations effectiveness.

In the second category they include:

1 Adequacy of accounting data.
2 Personnel policies.
3 Outlook for expanding or contracting operations. (These aspects of planning and forecasting are a continuing concern at all times.)
4 Effective measures in adjusting to seasonal variations.
5 Review of lease arrangements.
6 Review of location and site values.
7 Possible changes in legal form of organization.
8 Additional asset needs which might improve efficiency.
9 Adequacy of risk coverage.
10 Efficiency in purchasing and possible new sources of supply.
11 Study of broader economic data and local developments which might affect expectations for the firm.

The priorities given to the various items on any owner's list will vary with the other demands upon his or her time and the circumstances surrounding the particular firm. For example, a small private water company would have less need for checking income records so often. A restaurant would need this data almost daily. A small department store would need regular data, at least weekly, on a new department just opened. Owners would be more concerned with inventory movement and inventory control in style goods departments.

USE OF DATA

It is one thing to gather the management data to which we have referred in the preceding paragraphs; it is quite another to use that data in making day-to-day decisions for the firm. It took considerable time for the authors to recover from the shock of hearing a small firm proprietor say, "Why collect all of those facts? They are history and you can't change them now." He was exactly like The Late Learner quoted at the beginning of this chapter. Many college students and experienced operators realize that business history is studied to make improvements in efficiency for the future. We can take a brief look here at each of the items on our data lists to indicate when a management decision might be appropriate.

CATEGORY A ITEMS

Sales Data and Trends If sales are increasing steadily and are in accordance with budgeted income statement plans, they can be looked upon with pleasure. If they are increasing faster than had been expected, that fact may call for a look at inventory adequacy to support the increased sales volume. If sales are dropping below expectations, the owner should find out why, in what departments, in what lines, or if the decline is general. Decisions to be made would involve how to reverse the trend. Would more advertising help? Has advertising been effective? Have we measured that effectiveness? Is the market changing so that total purchasing power in our market will remain lower? When did this trend start? Are there any other reasons for it?

Production Records If the factory was expected to produce 5,000 units of the product in September and only 4,000 were finished, management should ask why. When the reasons are found, decisions must be made to correct the problems. This may involve new machines, inefficient employees, faulty maintenance, absenteeism, labour turnover, training methods, or other things. Management must find the reasons and make decisions to prevent repetition. Perhaps it was only a matter of poor timing of employee vacations.

Cash Position and Cash Flow Outlook Management's concern here is with providing assurance that obligations of the firm can be paid on time—within the discount period if discounts are offered. We have seen the trouble which can result when the cash position is inadequate. Very few small firms have complete cash flow statements (Chapter 24), but experienced small firm owners have a pretty good idea of what cash receipts to expect in the immediate future. If it is found that the cash position is really hurting, the reasons for it must be found. Perhaps it is slow collection of receivables. Is a campaign to collect delinquent accounts appropriate? It may be the purchase of enlarged inventories to take advantage of special buys. If so, should we arrange an additional line of credit to carry the firm until that inventory is sold and funds replenished?

Inventory Data and Need for Adjustments Where departmentalization of a firm is established, inventories must be checked by departments and/or particular lines of merchandise. If sales are up, is the inventory adequate to support sales in each department and in each line? If sales are down, is the decline general or confined to specific departments? It is dangerous to order general inventory reductions if the sales variations are limited to certain departments. When sales are off for a particular department, the inventory of that department may need reduction. When requests for items not carried in the inventory have been received a few times, a decision to add such items to the inventory may be appropriate.

Analysis of Accounts Receivable Ledger Even if the firm does not have a cash position problem, it should still make a regular analysis of its total accounts receivable. This will reveal which customers are getting behind in their payments and suggest caution in further credit to some customers. An aging of accounts receivable (Chapter 18) is a regularly used current management device. Decisions which may result from its analysis may include a new campaign to collect delinquent accounts, cutting off credit for certain customers, a policy of expanding credit more widely if the accounts receivable turnover is more than 12 times a year on 30-day credit, terminating open accounts, and resorting only to cash and credit-card sales. Without the facts, any needed corrective action cannot be taken.

Policy Violations and Need for Change If it is found that there is public objection to some of the policies of the firm, a management decision to change certain policies may be called for. For example, a grocer has a policy of selling all soft drinks only in non-returnable bottles. Public resentment is great, and some customers actually change their patronage to other stores for this single reason. Decision: Bring back returnable bottles to the shelves and change the policy decision against their use. Advertise the new policy change. (In Ontario it is the law now to stock returnable bottles if non-returnables are sold in the store.)

Price Policy Questions Which May Have Arisen It may be found that customers are being driven away because our firm is selling one or two specific items a few cents higher than our competitor down the street. Should we lower those prices? Do we value that type of customer? Is the item purchased in isolation or as part of larger orders? A decision is important. Another possible decision could be on the desirability of cleaning out that slow-moving inventory of certain items via obstacle-course displays, at special prices, or even as loss leaders.

Effectiveness of Shoplifting and Theft Procedures This problem never ends, and the alert merchant is always looking for evidence of the effectiveness of present procedures to combat both shoplifting by outsiders and employee thefts. Whenever an incident of this nature is discovered, a new look at established procedures is appropriate to see if greater effectiveness can be achieved.

Suggested New Products or New Lines Most merchants keep a record of calls for merchandise which they do not carry. Not all such calls merit adding the item involved. But if such requests are repeated, a decision is appropriate on the advisability of adding those goods to the inventory. If the firm sells dresses in two price lines or in two brands and receives numbers of requests for another price line or another brand which is available, this may suggest that the inventory should be expanded to include them. This could again be a recognition that an original policy was not suited to the particular market and that the facts suggest it be changed.

Coincidence of Weekly Results with the Break-Even Chart If an accurate break-even chart has been divided into weekly, monthly, and quarterly periods as well as the annual measure of income-expense relationships, the manager-owner will always have in mind a sales total which will reveal whether sales for any period have placed the operation in the profit area. Many small firm owners have such a figure in mind even without formal break-even charts. This is why they can tell you, "This was a good week," or a good month, or even a good day.

Public Relations Effectiveness Measures of good or bad public relations may appear at any time during any business day, or even at a social gathering. Compliments may be received over participation in a community project, a special service rendered, support of a good cause, or innumerable other things. Likewise, complaints may be received. A manager notes both compliments and complaints to measure total effectiveness and govern future decisions on public-relations activities.

We have taken this brief look at some of the key data managers must have at their fingertips to help in the many decisions they are regularly called upon to make. These were the items in category A as we described priorities here. Not all owners will agree with this division of priorities, but none will disagree with the importance of each item on the list. Any owner having all this key information readily available will make better decisions for the welfare of the firm.

CATEGORY B ITEMS

Adequacy of Accounting Data If an owner is often faced with a decision requiring accounting data which is not readily available, the decision to add financial analysis to the present accounting records will usually be forthcoming. A decision to request a bank loan which demands supporting data on cash flow would be an example. Total accounting value is more than routinely recording operations and preparing the basic statements at the end of a fiscal period. Daily decisions on matters such as ability to make an attractive purchase may be dependent upon basic accounting facts. Expansion plans cannot be properly judged without detailed accounting data. Daily decisions are enhanced with analytical accounting information. There is no uniformity of accounting adequacy for all firms. Each owner must decide the extent to which he or she needs details to govern daily operations.

Personnel Policies Excessive absenteeism and labour turnover are usually signs that something is wrong with the personnel policies of the firm. If unskilled labour requiring little training is being utilized, labour turnover is not as serious as absenteeism, as long as replacements are always available. The public image of the firm, however, is adversely affected by either excessive absenteeism or labour turnover. When these are facts of the firm, a serious look at policies in effect is called for. Excessive absenteeism needs investigation concerning its reasons, its legitimacy, and its incidence for particular employees. Small firms are usually less able than larger firms to absorb absenteeism because of greater dependence upon fewer employees. Ability for one employee to fill in for an absent employee is usually severely limited in the small firm. For example, if two sales persons are handling the retail counter, one person would find it extremely difficult to serve all the customers. It is true that good organization should always anticipate replacements in any position, but opportunities to do so successfully are fewer in a small firm. After reviewing the facts, it may be decided that certain persons must be terminated, salaries may justify review to cope with the problem, personal conflicts between employees may be uncovered, or other corrective measures may be necessary. The important thing is that the manager know the facts and speedily apply corrective action.

Outlook for Expansion or Contraction of Operations Not all small firm owners want to expand, even if the possibilities of profitably doing so exist. Many are satisfied just to keep the business at its present level. The optimists and true entrepreneurs (venture managers) are always looking for profitable ways to expand the firm to become an ever-enlarging part of the total scene in their industry. Basic planning and forecasting are continuous activities. Contracting operations is sometimes dictated by the facts of recent firm history. Market changes and market opportunities represent the kinds of facts needed to make the proper decisions in this area. That is why the efficient manager wants to keep informed on total markets, competition, available locations, detailed costs, and financing possibilities to support any necessary decisions. These are truly long-range considerations, yet they can be of utmost importance to the eventual welfare of the firm.

Adjusting to Seasonal Variations It is most important to have a clear picture of just how important seasonal variations have been in the firm's recent history. Management decisions must then be made concerning the inevitability of these variations and whether they can be evened out through special sales, production policies, or other devices. Changes in buying policies, employee vacation schedules, part-time employment, and even inventory control may be dictated. Nothing can be done authoritatively without detailed facts upon which to base those decisions.

Review of Lease Arrangements Most retailers and many manufacturers lease their business facilities. As a result, the continuation of the business at a particular location is dependent upon renewal of the rental lease. It is very sad to see a successful small firm forced to move only because of its inability to renew its lease at prices the firm can stand. Options for renewal may be written into an existing lease. Percentage leases (a flat rental charge plus a percentage of sales over a stated amount) provide additional rental income for landlords if business sales exceed normally expected totals. Effective management always has one eye on this matter, looks for options, and tries to ensure continued favourable locations for the firm's operations.

Review of Location and Site Values Just as the lease terms are important, so is a review of the value of an existing location and site. Those firms which rent their facilities have the advantage of not being forced to remain in an unfavourable location if that location is losing its true value. When the current lease expires, the owners may not want to renew it because they have found a more favourable location at the right price.

Possible Change in Legal Form of the Firm With all the new legislation by the federal government designed to assist small firms, it is important that the owner know of these opportunities. We covered the details in Chapter 11.

Additional Asset Needs Experience in operations may often suggest that a new piece of equipment, a new showcase, a different type of cash register, or other assets would materially improve the efficiency of the firm. Daily observation of procedures will clarify such needs and indicate which acquisitions are necessary.

Adequacy of Risk Coverage The eternal problem of risks and how best to cope with them must be continually under review. New types of insurance protection appear often. The manager may see that the incidence of loss from certain types of risk has increased and now demands insurance coverage, whereas in the past the firm had relied upon good management to absorb that risk. The limits of public liability insurance that the firm carries may be found to be inadequate, and a decision to increase such coverage may be in order. New features are often written into some insurance policies, such as those which cover inventory losses. Costs and protection may be affected. Fidelity and surety bonds may become appropriate, even though they had previously been deemed completely unnecessary. Minimum losses in some areas of risk may suggest that they be coped with only by good management in the future. The facts of current operations will supply details to justify any appropriate decisions.

Efficiency in Purchasing and Need for New Sources Study of results may reveal lapsed discounts, availability of new sources at better prices and improved quality, better transportation arrangements, or better terms of sale. These matters must also be carefully noted by managers as they make decisions for the ongoing firm.

Economic Data and Local Developments All the information available about general business trends nationally, regionally, and locally should be a concern of management. Trade associations, chambers of commerce, daily newspapers, and business periodicals are all sources of such information. A manager's ability to make decisions on the basis of such data may have a great effect on the firm's welfare. Changing styles, lessened purchasing power in the area, new plant developments and new payrolls, trends in population growth, and changes in buying habits are some of the items falling in this category. It behooves efficient managers to keep themselves apprised of as much information as possible on these matters.

We have approached the subject of managing the ongoing firm from the standpoint of the key data which must be readily available to the manager and how the manager should use that information. It is hoped that this approach has given the student an appreciation of the many duties which fall upon managers' shoulders and how they prepare themselves to make the proper decisions. With all the planning and operating details we have covered in this text, we feel sure that new small firm owners who have studied with us will be better qualified as successful managers. Good luck.

Part 7

CASE STUDIES

CASE 1

Inadequate Investor Capital

ALL THAT GLITTERS IS NOT GOLD

Maxie Stein was a personable young man who graduated from a good business school with a major in management. He always felt that the principles of conservative financing he learned about in his business courses were just too restrictive.

Maxie was particularly critical of such ratios in an opening day balance sheet as a 50 percent proprietorship ratio; he didn't believe in paying a credit-card company 5 percent of his credit sales, even if doing so guaranteed him full payment of the balances by the fifth of the following month; and he had been told that it is foolish to invest too much of your own money in your business because it is difficult for owners to withdraw money from the business.

After working for another firm for five years to gain business experience, Maxie opened his own small department store. He didn't think it wise to pay incorporation fees, so he decided to operate as a proprietorship. Following his convictions about business, he prepared the opening day balance sheet shown on page 328.

Maxie was smart enough to employ an accounting firm to keep his records and give him annual financial statements, but he instructed the accountant not to charge off any depreciation on the fixed assets

STEIN'S DEPARTMENT STORE
OPENING DAY BALANCE SHEET
JANUARY 1, 1975

Current assets:			Current liabilities:		
Cash	$ 5,000		Accounts payable		
Merchandise inventory	10,000		(for inventory)	$ 8,000	
Prepaid supplies	1,000				
Total current assets		$16,000	Fixed liabilities		
			Notes payable	16,500	
Fixed assets:			Total liabilities		$24,500
Store equipment	$ 8,000				
Office furniture and fixtures	2,000		Net worth		
Delivery truck	3,500		M. Stein, proprietorship		5,000
Total fixed assets		13,500			
Total assets		$29,500	Total liabilities and net worth		$29,500

STEIN'S DEPARTMENT STORE
BALANCE SHEET
JANUARY 1, 1979

Current assets:			Current liabilities:		
Cash	$ 200		Accounts payable	$17,000	
Accounts receivable	23,500		Note payable, bank	5,000	
Merchandise inventory	6,000				
Supplies on hand	200		Fixed liabilities:		
Total current assets		$29,900	Note payable (original loan)	10,000	
Fixed assets:			Note payable (father)	5,000	
Store equipment	$ 8,000		Total liabilities		$37,000
Office furniture and fixtures	2,000				
Delivery truck	3,500		Net worth:		
Total fixed assets		13,500	M. Stein, proprietorship		6,400
Total assets		$43,400	Total liabilities and net worth		$43,400

because "after all, we don't write checks to anyone for that kind of expense."

From the day he opened the business, sales exceeded his planned sales volume. Maxie was careful about taking money from the business for himself and restricted himself to $100 per week to cover his own expenses.

The accountant prepared the annual income statement and balance sheet each year. In his optimism that he had proved his points about financing, Maxie looked only at the net profits from operation figure at the bottom of the income statement. During the first four years of operation the income statement showed that he had averaged net profits from operations somewhat in excess of $16,000 per year.

Maxie became conscious of an inability to take advantage of good inventory purchase deals in the third and fourth years. He borrowed $5,000 from the local bank to improve his cash position. He made regular payments on the long-term note with which he had started the business, but he was later forced to borrow $5,000 from his father to meet current obligations.

When he received his annual statements at the end of the fourth year, Maxie was furious. His balance sheet is shown on page 329.

Maxie made an appointment with his accountant the next morning. He questioned the accountant's ability and accused him of being responsible for the fact that Maxie's vendors now sold him C.O.D. only and were pressing him for payments on his outstanding balances to them, for the fact that the bank was pressing him for payments on the bank loan, and for the fact that he was not able to keep his inventory up to date or large enough to support his declining sales volume.

Some of Maxie's specific questions included the following:

1 How is it possible that the firm could have earned more than $64,000 in four years and still be in such poor financial condition?

2 Where are those profits now? I only took out $100 per week.

3 Can I get a refund on the income taxes I paid due to my financial situation now? After all, I paid my income taxes with company checks.

4 Are those income statements correct for the first four years of operation? How can they be?

If you were the accountant, how would you explain the situation to Maxie? Can you explain where most of the profits have gone?

CASE 2

Administrative Problems — Personnel Management

A GOOD MARKET DOES NOT ASSURE SUCCESS

Three young men were looking for a business in which to invest their savings and at the same time give themselves good jobs. All had good business experience and some college training. One was a personable sales type, one a factory supervisor type, and the third a good accountant and office manager. They greatly desired to own a business and preferred to make a product rather than own a retailing outlet.

While investigating possibilities in the Niagara Peninsula, they had a meeting with several growers of grapes and other fruits and vegetables. The growers liked the three young men and indicated the great need in their area for a factory which would manufacture crates in which to ship produce. They offered assistance in making a market survey of the reasonable demand for crates and even showed them a small warehouse which could be used for setting up such a plant. The building was available on a long-term lease at a price which seemed reasonable.

The three men liked the idea, investigated the total costs, and found they could finance the business with their joint savings and a small amount of help from their families. They then went to work to get the business going.

The market survey, the growers practically assured them, showed that a total of 1,200,000 crates annually was a minimum they could sell. Only two types of crates were involved. Of the total, 75 percent would be one type, 25 percent the second type. But the seasonal variation in the demand for the crates was immediately noticed by the factory man. The total demand was broken down into months as follows:

January	40,000 crates
February	50,000
March	50,000
April	60,000
May	70,000
June	90,000
July	200,000
August	200,000
September	250,000
October	80,000
November	60,000
December	50,000
Total	1,200,000 crates

Obviously the demand called for five times as many crates in September as in the slack months of the winter. The proportion between the two types of crates stayed the same throughout the year.

When they purchased the necessary machines, work tables, and tools, they found that their building could only handle enough of this production equipment to produce an average of 4,600 boxes per day, or a total of 1,150,000 in the 250-day work year. To cope with this shortage from the 1,200,000 sales expected, the owners decided that they would request all factory employees to work on Saturdays and Sundays for seven weekends in April and May to provide the extra crates needed to meet anticipated sales. This would produce the extra 50,000 crates with an average of only 3,571 crates per day.

Fortunately the factory opened in February during the lighter demand season. The owners hired 8 supervisors and 24 bench workers from local employment agencies. Some workers needed training, which the owners were able to provide as on-the-job training. Hirees with the most experience were made supervisors when first employed.

Things went very well, profits were good, and the employees increased their efficiency to the point that the planned average daily production was approached. Each owner applied his special talent in selling, factory operations, and general management.

They easily filled orders and built up an inventory of crates on hand.

This inventory began to be a problem almost immediately because of the lack of warehouse space.

When the seven overtime weekends were announced, the owners had no idea the supervisors would not cooperate 100 percent. The bench workers were to receive time and a half, but the supervisors were expected to work without extra pay because they were management employees. This meant that for those 14 days the bench workers earned just about as much as the supervisors. Supervisors received monthly salaries, the workers hourly rates.

The first weekend only four supervisors showed up for work, and production fell off significantly. The owners talked to each supervisor the next week and advised them that strict action would be taken if they failed to show up the next weekend. The next weekend five supervisors showed up, but two who had been there before didn't report. Inventory was also very high by this time in anticipation of the heavy July, August, and September demand. Crates were stored in every available spot. Even the loading docks and empty truck bodies were filled with crates. Rafter space was used. No other warehouse space was available in the town.

The three owners decided on Saturday afternoon to have a meeting to solve the two problems of employee dissatisfaction and storage space.

How would you advise them to solve these problems?

CASE 3

Operating Expense Analysis

HOW FAR DO YOU GO WITH STATISTICS?

Ms. Lucille Schwartz and Ms. Olga Olsen started a beauty supply business 8 years ago. Ms. Olsen handled public relations and concentrated on the sales end of the business. Ms. Schwartz was the business person who watched after the profits and losses and internal management of the firm. From the beginning they were very successful. They incorporated the firm and charged generous salaries for themselves to corporate expense. They equally divided the outstanding stock. Their commercial bank held a line of credit open for them, but they rarely used it. They paid their bills promptly and took advantage of all sales discounts offered by their suppliers.

Their income statement for the eighth year of operation was in line with the previous years and was as follows:

SCHWARTZ AND OLSEN
CONDENSED
INCOME STATEMENT
YEAR ENDED DECEMBER 31, 1978

Net sales	$936,000
Cost of goods sold	702,000
Gross margin	$234,000
Operating expenses	171,600
Net profits from operations	$ 62,400

Ms. Olsen was delighted when the accountant delivered the report for the year. Ms. Schwartz, however, felt that profits should be higher, even though she recognized that both owners had been paid good salaries, which were included in the expenses.

She asked the accountant to prepare a break-even chart for the firm. It showed that their break-even sales volume was far below their present sales volume. But Ms. Schwartz didn't like making deductions from those lines of the chart, so she set about to study the operational figures with good, plain seventh-grade arithmetic.

She took each figure on the annual income statement and divided it by 52 to find the weekly results. She then divided those weekly figures by 6 to find the average daily results. She produced the following table to show Ms. Olsen.

	YEARLY	WEEKLY	DAILY AVERAGE
Sales	$936,000	$18,000	$3,000
Cost of goods sold	702,000	13,500	2,250
Gross margin	$234,000	$ 4,500	$ 750
Operating expenses	171,600	3,300	$ 550
Net profit from operations	$ 62,400	$ 1,200	$ 200

She showed this table to Ms. Olsen whose reaction was, "Isn't that nice. We're making an average of $200 per day over and above our salaries. What an excellent return on our modest investment."

Ms. Schwartz wasn't satisfied yet. She decided to compare average daily sales with average daily margin and average daily expenses. She spent hours on the past records to find the daily average sales for each day of the week. She then computed the 25 percent markup on average daily sales and compared these figures with the average daily expenses. She then produced the following table.

	AVERAGE DAILY SALES	AVERAGE DAILY GROSS MARGIN @ 25%	AVERAGE DAILY EXPENSES
Monday	$ 1,800	$ 450	$ 550
Tuesday	1,200	300	550
Wednesday	1,800	450	550
Thursday	3,600	900	550
Friday	4,200	1,050	550
Saturday	5,400	1,350	550
Weekly totals	$18,000	$4,500	$3,300

Ms. Schwartz was very pleased now. She suddenly realized why she and Ms. Olsen had been able to play golf, enjoy the theatre, and spend more time with their families on Monday, Tuesday, and Wednesday. She triumphantly showed her figures to Ms. Olsen. She insisted that she had proved that the business was losing money on Monday, Tuesday, and Wednesday and that the only way to avoid this loss was to close the business on those days.

Ms. Olsen was shocked. The idea of staying closed three days a week just didn't sound right to her. She asks you to evaluate the situation.

CASE 4

Layout for Factories

SAMMY'S JAM AND JELLIES, INC.

When Sammy Westhoff started making jams and jellies in the kitchen of his home to sell to the public, he never expected that his products would be in such great demand. His success forced him to find larger and larger facilities to produce his excellent products. After 8 years he was determined to find a factory building which would make his production more efficient. The problems he currently faced included much cross hauling of raw materials, inadequate storage space, poor loading and unloading areas, and inability to use conveyor belts or horizontal escalators in the manufacturing process. He knew that his labour cost was higher than that of his competitors because of the inefficiency of his factory operations.

He found an available building which he believed would be ideal for his operations. The building was 150 by 250 feet and had a railroad sidetrack on the north side. It was set back 100 feet from the south side of a busy industrial street. On the east it reached to within 6 feet of a side street. On the west the property had open ground space of 200 feet by 250 feet. The north, west, and south sides of the building had a 10-foot loading platform covered with a roof which reached 4 feet beyond the platform. Ceilings in the building were 40 feet high and sliding partitions reached across the entire floor space from east to west at 50-foot intervals. Some doors were in those partitions, and others could be added.

His manufacturing operations consisted of cooking the fruit, cooling, adding sugar and other ingredients, filling the jars, packing the cases, storing the finished cases, and getting shipments out to buyers. The labelling of jars was done by machine on the production line and the printing on the cases was done before purchase. Most of the fruit, sugar, and other materials were received in carload or truckload lots. Trucks could enter the loading platform area on the three sides of the building with loading docks. The jams and jellies were cooked in 100-gallon steel drums, which had to be moved from the gas stoves in the process of adding other ingredients to the fruit. Each operation required a maximum of 50 feet of operation area in width and varied in length down the line from 15 to 30 feet.

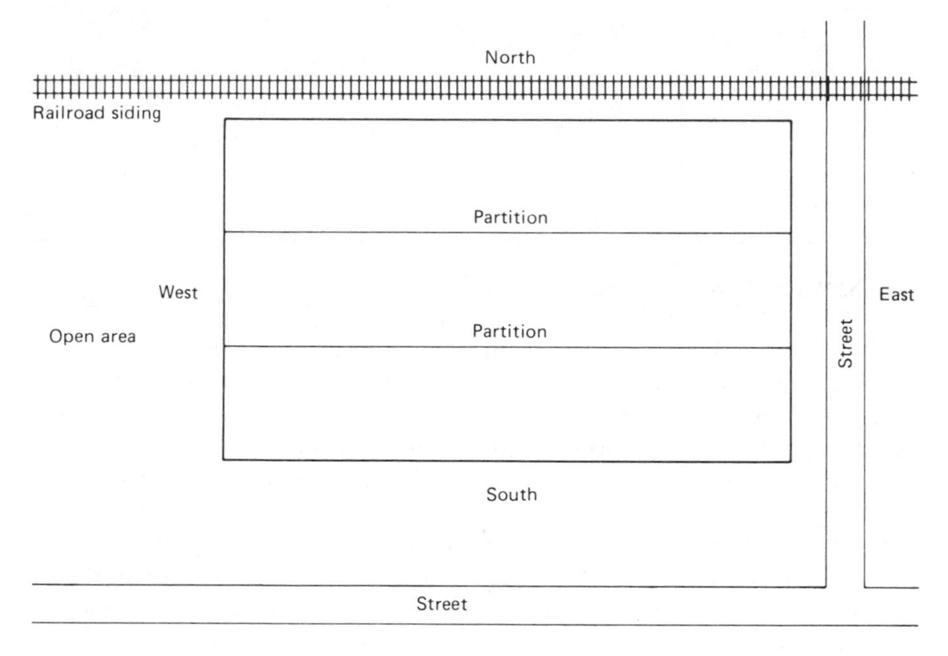

Sammy was satisfied that he could easily meet his production schedule of 600 cases of jam per day and still have space to expand if his demand continued to grow.

He provides you with the above sketch of the building and surrounding area and requests that you make a layout for his new factory.

CASE 5

Inventory Management

SIMILAR FIRMS MAY HAVE GREAT DISSIMILARITIES

Barbara Bowens and Mary Hopkins each operated small business firms of the same type. Each had hired the same firm to make a market survey before they opened their respective businesses. The market surveys revealed that each was located in an area which should produce about the same sales volume at the same prices to similar customers. Because the women were fellow members of the Chamber of Commerce, they had occasion to meet quite frequently. They enjoyed comparing notes on their operations. They were not in direct competition, since their stores were in different parts of town, but they felt that their discussion of operations could be mutually beneficial.

Their discussions led them to the matter of their inventories. They were amazed to find a large discrepancy in the inventories each maintained in her store. They decided to compare income statements for the past year and see if they could account for the variations. Condensed income statements were as follows:

		BARBARA BOWENS' STORE		MARY HOPKINS' STORE
Sales		$200,000		$190,000
Cost of goods sold:				
Inventory, Jan. 1	$ 75,000		$ 15,000	
Purchases	150,000		150,000	
Goods available	$225,000		$165,000	
Inventory, Dec. 31	75,000		15,000	
Cost of goods sold		150,000		150,000
Gross margin		$ 50,000		$ 40,000
Operating expenses		20,000		25,000
Net profits from operations		$ 30,000		$ 15,000

The women knew how to compute average markups, inventory turnovers, and operating expenses as a percentage of sales. They compared all three. When they concentrated on the problem of why they had such different inventories, they turned to their trade association for comparative statistics. They found that the average inventory turnover for their type of firm was five times a year.

When they saw how far they each varied from this average inventory turnover, they decided to see if they could do something about the variations.

Barbara admitted that she had always figured it was better to have plenty of merchandise on hand than to lose a sale due to "stockouts." Mary admitted her dislike for having too much working capital tied up in inventory. She was located close to a wholesale house, which made it easier to send one of her employees there or to drive there herself to get merchandise quickly. She paid for the gas for employee automobiles on such trips. She admitted that she had frequent "stockouts" and that, despite assurances to customers that the item would be available in a short time, those customers often did not come back.

Mary and Barbara decided to resolve their discussions around the following questions, and they ask you to comment on each.

1 What was the average markup, inventory turnover, and profits as a percentage of sales for each store?

2 What are the disadvantages of having too much inventory on hand?

3 What are the disadvantages of having too little inventory on hand?

4 What is the ideal inventory?

5 In what ways can the profitability of the firm be affected by its inventory policy?

6 What recommendations would you make to each woman?

CASE 6

The Overaggressive Sales Rep

The Specialty Shoe Store was a prosperous retail business in a large mid-western city. It sold both men's and women's shoes. Jack Jones, the owner, prided himself on the capabilities of his six sales persons, many of whom had been with him for several years. The three women and three men sales persons averaged 34 years of age, were not unionized, and often gave extra time to their work without extra pay when busy periods occurred. Jones instituted a profit-sharing plan, which was based on the earnings for the year and distributed at Christmas.

In June he was forced to replace one of the salesmen, who moved to another city to open his own store. Jones hired Byron Smith, who had just graduated from the local community college. Smith was clean-cut, 23, had some previous selling experience, and appeared very personable. He was interviewed by the other 5 sales people, as well as by Jones, before he was employed. All gave their approvals.

Within two weeks Jones started receiving complaints from the other sales people about Smith's overaggressive tactics on the sales floor, especially when Jones was not around. Young Smith rudely interrupted the others when they were making sales or considering choices of shoes with customers. He offered his positive opinions to the point that customers resented them. He sometimes took customers away from the other staff members. His favourite comment to the other was "Stick with me! Some day I will own this store." He interrupted the person assigned to balance the cash register at closing time. He insisted he could improve the established procedures because "After all, I've been to college."

At first the other sales people tried to make kind suggestions to Smith, but they failed to change his method of operation. When Jones first became aware of the situation, he talked to Smith. He pointed out that Smith's sales record was good but that customer complaints and the complaints of his fellow sales people had to stop. Smith said he would try to change his behaviour. Jones felt particularly concerned about this situation because Smith's father was a personal friend and a fellow golfer at the local country club. As a result, he put off any final disciplinary action as long as possible.

In December Jones received a memorandum signed by the five senior staff members. It indicated that unless this aggravating situation were corrected immediately, they would not attend the Christmas party and would look for other jobs because they all planned to resign as of January 1. They also said that they would like an opportunity to have a full staff meeting to air their grievances. Jones knew he could no longer postpone positive action. He decided, in view of the total situation and his friendship with Smith's father, that he should have the requested meeting with the entire staff.

If you were Mr. Jones, how would you conduct the meeting and what decisions would you make?

CASE 7

The Heartaches of Credit Management

Mrs. Alice Billings is the credit manager for the ABC Department Store in Halifax. Her duties include making the final decisions on applications for credit after her staff has concluded the regular investigation of formal applications. The ABC Department Store encourages open credit accounts for qualified applicants. It has maintained a good record of efficiency in administering its credit program. Losses on bad debts have been minimal. Few accounts get more than 90 days past due because of the store's effective program for handling delinquent accounts.

One morning Mrs. Billings found an application from Mr. Ned Albers on her desk. She knew Mr. Albers as a fellow church member, a regular contributor to charity, and a very kind and considerate person. He had four children in the public schools. His wife made most of the children's clothing and was also active in the church. They were known as people of modest means and limited income. None of these facts were known to the staff member who investigated the information and references on the application for credit.

The staff member had attached a long, handwritten note for Mrs. Billings to the application. It said that the application should never be approved, that the information given was inaccurate, the income was overstated, and the prior references reported that their credit experience was most unsatisfactory.

It was company policy that the credit manager must have a personal meeting with all credit applicants to advise them of the firm's decision to approve or reject credit and the limits placed on credit extended. Before setting up the appointment, Mrs. Billings learned from a mutual friend that the Albers application was made in the hope of buying a badly needed kitchen stove.

If you were Mrs. Billings, how would you handle the required meeting with Mr. Albers?

CASE 8

If There Is a Will, There May Be a Way—to Get Started

Bill Jacobs was attending university in Regina. His best friend was Jack Evers, who operated a small sporting goods store in Bill's home town. Both young men had always hoped and planned to move to Winnipeg and establish a larger sporting goods store as partners. They planned their move for next June when Bill would graduate with a degree in business administration. When Bill came home for his last spring vacation, he found Jack very downhearted. When he inquired, he found that Jack had figured out the investment they would need to open their Winnipeg store. Jack saw no way they could arrange for sufficient capital. Together they went over the asset needs and came up with the statement of assets to be used which follows:

STATEMENTS OF ASSETS TO BE USED

Cash	$ 3,000
Funds to invest in accounts receivable	3,000
Merchandise inventory	20,000
Prepaid insurance and supplies	1,000
Land and building	65,000
Store equipment	10,000
Office furniture and fixtures	2,000
Delivery truck	3,000
Total assets required	$107,000

Jack figured that he could net $15,000 from the sale of his present store. Bill had $10,000 available to invest. Bill had studied small business management in college. He knew that with certain constraints or decisions on providing needed assets they could open the business with their $25,000.

1 Set up your own constraints (decisions) and make an opening day balance sheet for the new Winnipeg firm.

2 What are your four basic ratios on the balance sheet? Can they be improved? How?

CASE 9

The Unknown Percent of Capacity

When Harry Wong graduated from the university, he was employed as assistant office manager by the Supreme Auto Parts Company. Harry was a keen young man and was anxious to show in practice the many things he had learned in his college study. His first assignment was to establish a combined journal-ledger bookkeeping system for the young but fast-growing business. The owner was so pleased with the resulting saving in bookkeeping time and the efficiency of the system that Harry received his first raise after only 2 months with the firm. His next assignment was to establish a better system of inventory control. Again he did a good job; he installed a perpetual inventory system for the parts department which included signed receipts for every part issued, every part returned, and every part received from vendors. The system gave management a better control of the inventory and seemed to eliminate the unknown losses in inventory which had occurred in the past.

Over coffee one morning Harry asked the owner, Ms. Kadish, is she had ever considered the use of a break-even chart to analyze the results of operations. He pointed out the many uses that could be made of such a chart by showing the relationship of expenses and income at all levels of income of the business. Ms. Kadish replied that she would love to have such data available. She said the reason it had not been done in the past was that no one could establish a percentage of capacity at which the firm operated.

Harry saw a chance to further prove his value to the firm. He promised to make a break-even chart for the firm for the past year. Sales were $300,000; total expenses were $250,000, of which $50,000 was fixed. The percent of capacity was not known.

1 Can you prepare the break-even chart in a 5-inch grid?

2 How does your chart vary from one in which the percent of capacity is known?

CASE 10

Overall Personnel Policy

Mr. Baker, Mr. Carter, Ms. Johnson, and Ms. Garcia are the equal owners, the board directors, and the officers of the Bild Manufacturing Company. The company manufactures dishware and pottery products of various types, including a very popular line of dinnerware. The firm has been in business for 17 years and was started by the present owners and their relatives. It has 75 employees, including 50 factory workers, 12 sales people who travel the sales territory, and 13 office employees. Profits are modest but steady.

One day the owners were called to a special emergency meeting to evaluate possible changes in their personnel policies. The day before, the Provincial Labour Relations Board had conducted an election in the plant to decide upon a collective bargaining agent for the employees. The vote was close, but a 55 percent majority voted for no unionization and no formal collective bargaining.

The directors were shocked and saddened that the vote was so close. They had always prided themselves in the loyalty of their employees. They felt they always rewarded their employees well and that surely they were happy and satisfied people who valued their jobs.

In a meeting with the employees this morning the directors requested information on the complaints which had motivated the election and its close results. They were pleased to learn that a chief complaint was not wages, although they did pay slightly less than their bigger competitors. The complaints revolve around fringe benefits. They can be summarized as follows:

1 Present vacation policy is 1 week after 1 year, 2 weeks after 5 years, and 3 weeks after 10 years' employment. The employees want 2 weeks after 1 year, 3 weeks after 5 years, and 1 month's vacation after 10 years' employment.

2 Employees want a guaranteed annual salary. They are willing to do other jobs, such as maintenance painting, if the factory does not have enough orders to maintain year-round full employment — which has rarely happened in the past.

3 Employees resented it when the management placed much routine accounting and inventory control on a terminal computer service. This eliminated two bookkeepers, who were later given other jobs. Net saving was $12,000 yearly.

4 Employees feel that the sales people make too much money compared with factory workers. Sales people work on a straight commission basis.

5 Employees complain that the company does not follow through on its policy of dismissing new employees whose work is not satisfactory after a three-month trial period. They want a voice in the retention or dismissal decision. They feel that keeping weak employees is hurting plant efficiency.

6 Because a group life insurance policy for employees is a tax-deductible expense for the company, employees want their group policy increased to $25,000 for each employee. This is the legal maximum under the Income Tax Act without it being deemed a taxable benefit in the hands of the employees.

7 It is felt that some supervisors are not enforcing company work rules uniformly for all people under them.

Some of the employees who are known to have agitated for the union frankly indicated that their agitation will cease if acceptable answers can be found to these complaints. They indicated that the rank-and-file employees do not like a plan of union dues writeoff from their salaries, and that they believe in the right-to-work laws, which remove the necessity of being a union member in order to work in their state.

In tomorrow's meeting the directors must recover from their disappointment and shock and take positive action on each of the employee complaints.

If you were a member of the board of directors, what would your recommendation be on each complaint? Can you defend your recommendations? How?

CASE 11

Inventory Valuation

The grand piano department of Rizzo's Music Store showed the following purchases in 1978 after being completely sold out in the Christmas trade of 1977.

January — 5 pianos at $2,000 each
February — 8 pianos at $2,100 each
March — 6 pianos at $2,000 each
April — 5 pianos at $2,200 each
May — 5 pianos at $2,200 each
June — 5 pianos at $2,300 each
July — 5 pianos at $2,300 each
August — 6 pianos at $2,400 each
September — 8 pianos at $2,400 each
October — 10 pianos at $2,500 each
November — 10 pianos at $2,500 each
December — 15 pianos at $2,500 each

On December 31, 1978 the department had an inventory of 12 pianos on hand. The selling price then was $2,500. Of the 12 pianos on hand, 2 were purchased in January, 3 in May, 5 in November, and 2 in December.

How would the remaining 12 pianos be valued under LIFO, FIFO, weighted average cost, and lower of cost or market methods?

On December 31, 1978 the department had an inventory of 12 pianos on hand. The selling price then was $2,500. Of the 12 pianos on hand, 2 were purchased in January, 3 in May, 5 in November, and 2 in December.

How would the remaining 12 pianos be valued under LIFO, FIFO, weighted average cost, and lower of cost or market methods?

CASE 12

An Existing Firm versus a New One

Everett and Jeanie were childhood sweethearts who married after they graduated from high school. Jobs were scarce in their home town so they opened a small restaurant of their own "on a shoestring." They were such a good team that they prospered from the beginning. As their finances improved, despite raising four children, their thoughts turned to their lifetime desire to move to the West Coast. When a chain restaurant offered them $75,000 for their restaurant, they decided the time had come to move West. They settled in New Westminster, British Columbia, and immediately set about finding the location for a new restaurant.

They found an attractive suburban location and proceeded to plan the financing necessary to get underway. The building they planned to rent was new, and no equipment of any kind was available from the landlord. With careful planning they determined that they could equip the place and get underway with a minimum investment of $40,000. The market survey suggested a profit of $20,000 per year.

Jeanie came home from shopping a short time later and reported to Everett that she had found a "for sale" sign on "that cute little restaurant" they had visited some time before. She visited the owner and found that the business could be purchased for $35,000. The owner even showed her his bank deposits and income tax returns to prove that he had averaged between $18,000 and $21,000 net profit each year for the past 10 years. His desire to sell was explained as a wish to retire.

The ensuing discussion between Everett and Jeanie was the bitterest of their entire married life. Everett was screaming the disadvantages of buying an established business and praising the advantages of starting a new firm in the fine location they had found. Jeanie favoured buying the restaurant which had been established for years and was a proven moneymaker. She cautioned Everett about the additional risks undertaken in starting a new firm.

1 Can you help them resolve the dispute?

2 What specific factors should enter into their discussion?

CASE 13

Ethics versus Sharp Practice

Bill and Mary Davis have operated their small cosmetic factory for 5 years. Growth has been slow but steady. They were overjoyed in January of last year to have finally received a large order from the biggest department store in town.

The store's buyer was a shrewd negotiator who got the price for the order down to well below normal. The final requested feature of the order was sales terms of 2/10, n/30. Though this cut the small remaining profit on the order still more, Bill and Mary agreed. They convinced themselves that their working capital would be replaced within 10 days and the exposure of their products in the large store would result in more large orders in the future. The invoice totalled $2,000.

When they failed to receive a cheque within the next 30 days the Davises sent a duplicate statement to the department store. No response was received.

Three months later they received a cheque for $1,960 from the store. It was marked "invoice of January 10, paid in full." Obviously the 2 percent discount ($40) had been deducted from the original amount of the invoice.

Bill and Mary sat in their office pondering what action they should take, if any. What would you advise?

APPENDIX ONE

Management Consultant's Checklist

The following pages give the student or small firm owner a basis upon which to evaluate an existing firm's effectiveness.

The last section shows some of the causes of business failure. The checklists show:

1 What an outside consultant looks for in evaluating an existing firm
2 What owners should check in evaluating their own business

The subjects covered are:

1 The firm's market
2 Asset adequacy
3 Adequacy and use of accounting records
4 Financial condition
5 Location analysis
6 Layout analysis
7 Proper legal form of organization
8 Sales development program
9 Pricing policies
10 Merchandising of lines of goods
11 Seasonal variations and their implications
12 Purchasing and inventory control

13 Expense analysis and break-even chart
14 Credit policies in effect for sales and purchases
15 Risks and protection provided
16 Personnel policies

1 FOR EVALUATING MARKETS

1 Is the firm's major problem a lack of sales?
2 What has been the trend of sales in recent years?
3 What factors can be determined as responsible for the trend of sales?
4 Was a proper market survey made when the firm started?
5 If so, what were the predicted results in sales volume?
6 If not, should such a survey be made now?
7 Have the basic sources of market survey data been studied?
8 Does population growth, new competition, or competitor change in methods justify new ways of serving this market?
9 Has the character of the population in the trading area changed, aside from general growth or decline? Has this affected sales?
10 Has the ratio of population to number of firms in this trading area changed since the firm was established? If so, what has been done by management to keep current with these changes?
11 Does the future look good, medium, or bad for this firm in this market?

2 FOR EVALUATING ASSET ADEQUACY

1 Does the firm lack any assets which would improve its capacity for service, its image, or its profitability?
2 Are its store fixtures, office fixtures, and/or machines modern? Would newer ones improve image, service, or profitability?
3 Are present fixed assets consistent with the floor plan, available additional space, and customer comfort?
4 Does the firm have the necessary capital to finance its own receivables? Should this be done?
5 Are cash balances and working capital adequate for the volume of business being done?
6 Do growth requirements of the immediate future suggest the need of any other current or fixed assets? If so, are plans satisfactory for their acquisition?
7 Could the firm expand sales and profits with more assets in its present operation? How?

3 FOR EVALUATING ADEQUACY OF ACCOUNTING RECORDS

1 Does the proprietor have monthly statements easily available?
2 Does a complete accounting system exist?
3 Does the present system involve excessive posting?
4 Would a combined journal-ledger system reduce the work of the system?
5 Can the owner tell quickly the amounts owed by credit customers? (Is there an accounts receivable ledger of some kind?)
6 Can the owner quickly ascertain the balances due to creditors? (Is there an accounts payable ledger of some kind?)
7 Can sales easily be broken down into departments, chief lines of merchandise, or special items?
8 Does the system in effect provide a means of telling the profitability of individual departments or lines of merchandise?
9 Do the monthly adjustments include properly the charges for depreciation, amortization, and new inventories?
10 What types of information, not now easily available, does an owner need?
11 Does the firm take advantage of purchase discounts? Do the records provide adequate notice of discount periods?
12 Do procedures include a regular aging of accounts receivable?

4 FOR EVALUATING FINANCIAL CONDITION

1 What is the relationship of assets and liabilities?
2 What is the relationship of current assets and current liabilities?
3 Are the current assets truly current?
4 Are the liabilities properly classified?
5 What is the working capital? Is it adequate?
6 What is the current ratio? What is the quick ratio? What is the proprietorship ratio?
7 Is the firm trading on too thin an equity?
8 Does it have trouble paying its current bills? Why?
9 Have the accounts receivable been aged recently? What is the firm's policy on charging off uncollectible accounts?
10 How much of current profits is going to pay for fixed assets?
11 Are any creditors withholding credit because of the company's debt-paying habits or its other financial problems?
12 Does the firm need additional investment capital? Are any sources available?
13 Is the inventory turnover a cause of financial stress? Has it been

reviewed for slow-moving merchandise lately? Are there other problems?

14 Is the gross margin consistent with that of comparable firms? If not, why not?

15 Are operating expenses in line? If not, why not?

16 Do company policies indicate that the financial condition will be improved? How?

17 Are any other financial weaknesses apparent?

5 FOR EVALUATING LOCATION

A For Retailers

1 Is the firm located in a high-rent or a low-rent area? Should it be? Is the rent paid by the firm competitive?

2 If in a low-rent area and competing with firms in high-rent areas, how does it compensate in attracting customers?

3 Is the location good from the standpoint of meeting competition?

4 Is the total traffic in the area adequate?

5 Do neighbouring stores draw potential customers?

6 Is there a parking problem for customers? Would it be worthwhile to pay for customer parking?

7 Is the location good for development of sales via promotion?

8 Is this location appropriate to the principles of location for convenience, shopping, and specialty stores?

9 Is there a better site available in the area?

10 Is the going-home side of the street or the sunny side of the street important to this firm? Does it have that advantage?

11 Do the community and general area suggest adequate payrolls, population trends, living habits, and attitudes to encourage firm development here?

12 Are any other disadvantages of this location observed?

B For Wholesalers

1 Is the location economically accessible to its market?

2 Are shipping costs in receiving inventory the lowest available? Would additional rail, truck, or air facilities improve efficiency and reduce costs?

3 Do competitors have advantages in costs of delivery to customers due to better location?

4 Do customers visit the plant in person or call in orders by phone?

If they visit, is the accessibility and customer convenience satisfactory?

5 Does this location make possible the best layout of merchandise to expedite order filling and minimize labour costs?

C For Factories

1 Should this type of factory be close to its markets or to its raw materials? Is it?
2 Do the facilities at this location make possible the best use of the appropriate production layout?
3 Is the location appropriate to hiring the types of labour required? Is adequate labour of the desired type available?
4 Are utility costs consistent with those available at other potential locations?
5 Are adequate shipping facilities available at competitive costs? Would additional competition by shippers be helpful?
6 Are government attitudes and community facilities encouraging?
7 Do alternative locations offer reduced costs or better profits? Why?

D For Service Firms

1 Is customer visitation an important part of the business? If so, are facilities for customer comfort adequate?
2 Is the location consistent with the type of clientele sought and its habits in buying this service?
3 Does the firm need a high-rent location? Is it in one?
4 If efficient working conditions for employees are important, do they exist?
5 Is the firm paying an expensive rental for space when most of its business comes via telephone? Is this necessary?
6 Is drop-in business important? Does it exist in adequate quantity? Can it be developed by advertising?

6 FOR EVALUATING LAYOUT

A For Retailers

1 Is the present layout encouraging to sales because it reflects buying habits of customers?
2 Could it better reflect a good "selling machine"? How?

3 Is merchandise attractively displayed?
4 Is merchandise displayed to facilitate easy comparisons and easy examination?
5 Is customer comfort properly provided to meet the particular shopping habits of the firm's customers?
6 Arc associated lines of merchandise displayed adjacently?
7 Does the layout reflect maximum use of light, ventilation, and heat?
8 Is maximum view of store space by customers, employees, and managers desirable? If so, is this view now possible?
9 Are selling and nonselling activities properly separated?
10 Are convenience, shopping, and specialty goods properly located in the floor plan?
11 Does the image of the store reflect colours, fixtures, and displays which are compatible with the type of customers sought?

B For Wholesalers

1 Does the layout make order filling easy?
2 Are most popular lines of merchandise located adjacently?
3 Is maximum use made of rolling equipment in filling orders?
4 Do customers visit the firm often? Is so, is the image proper?
5 Are receiving doors convenient to inventory stacks? Are more doors needed?
6 Is the line of travel from merchandise collection for orders to location of loading deliveries direct? Could it be shortened to reduce costs of order filling?
7 Are aisles wide enough for efficient operation?
8 Can the height of merchandise stacks be reduced in the present space?

C For Factories

1 Does the firm now use a process or a product layout?
2 Is maximum use made of the advantages of the present layout?
3 Can the unproductive movement of raw materials, goods in process, or finished products be reduced?
4 Are testing and quality-control stations located in the best spots on the production line? Should there be more quality-control locations?
5 Are materials to be placed in production located close to the point of introduction into production?

6 Are material-receiving areas located as close to storerooms as possible?
7 Are luncheon areas, rest rooms, drinking fountains, and other employee areas located for maximum efficiency?

7 FOR EVALUATING LEGAL FORMS OF ORGANIZATION

1 Under what legal form of organization is the firm now operating?
2 What are the major risks to which the firm is subjected?
3 Does the legal form of organization give the firm proper protection against these risks?
4 Does the firm supplement its legal form of protection with public liability insurance? Is the amount adequate?
5 Is unlimited liability a serious potential problem for the owner(s)?
6 Has the present form limited financial needs in any way?
7 Has the owner considered changing the legal form?
8 What is the relative incidence of the major risks of the firm?
9 Are there tax advantages available by changing the legal form of organization?
10 Is the owner fully aware of the management advantages of the alternative legal forms available for the firm?
11 Is the firm utilizing all the advantages of the present legal form of organization?

8 FOR EVALUATING SALES DEVELOPMENT

1 Has the firm properly distinguished between established demand and promoted or created demand for its goods?
2 Has the owner considered all the direct and indirect sales promotion methods?
3 Are the applicable sales promotion methods being used in effective quantities?
4 Is the present advertising program being checked for its effectiveness?
5 Is the present sales volume consistent with the potential for the firm in this trading area? If not, how could it be increased?
6 Do customers generally reflect a feeling of satisfaction in doing business with the firm?
7 What is the firm's image in the community which it serves?
8 How could it be improved if deficiencies are found?

9 Is personal selling by employees consistent with the best practices?
10 Do any suggestions seem apparent for improving sales promotion?

9 FOR EVALUATING PRICING POLICIES

1 Do prices now produce an average gross margin consistent with the sales volume for this type of firm? If not, why?
2 Is the firm's pricing policy influenced by fair trade laws, nationally advertised prices, or competitor prices?
3 Is market strategy employed in setting prices?
4 Is the owner reluctant to adopt less-than-average markup prices when good judgment dictates their use?
5 Do prices reflect attempts to sell slow-moving merchandise?
6 Are proper methods used in moving slow merchandise?
7 Is style merchandise a factor in markups and markdowns?
8 Does original markup policy reflect normal markdowns, employee discounts, damaged merchandise, and shortages?
9 Does the firm use adequate markups to produce desired results?
10 Are markups based on cost or retail prices?
11 Have loss leaders ever been used? Were they necessary or productive?
12 Does the firm's overall pricing policy reflect a dynamic management?
13 Do above-average markup sales cover the sales in less-than-average markup items?

10 FOR EVALUATING MERCHANDISING

1 Does the owner recognize the differences in convenience, shopping, and specialty goods?
2 Is the merchandise inventory arranged to reflect these categories?
3 If sales effort is primarily in one category, does the merchandising policy properly reflect this fact?
4 Is the merchandising policy generally in line with the majority of customers in the trading area?
5 Are selling policies and services in line with the products (credit plans, delivery services, etc.)?
6 If selling industrial goods, does the firm recognize the differences in merchandising its goods and consumer goods?
7 Is the location consistent with the type of merchandise sold and the price policies in effect?
8 Is employee capability consistent with the needs of the type of merchandise being sold?

11 FOR EVALUATING SEASONAL VARIATIONS

1 Does the firm have distinct variations in sales in different months and/or seasons of the year?
2 Is the management using accepted methods of adjusting operating expenses to these variations?
3 Is purchasing policy consistent with the noted variations?
4 Would the addition of different lines of merchandise or different products help to even out the seasonal variation in sales?
5 If seasonal variations are drastic, would it be better to close the business entirely for some period in the year?
6 If a manufacturing firm, would it be more profitable to use the slack periods to build up inventory and to cut down factory overtime in the busy seasons?

12 FOR EVALUATING PURCHASING AND INVENTORY CONTROL

1 Are the proper sources of supply now being used?
2 Is the firm taking advantage of all purchase discounts?
3 How are minimum inventories and ordering points determined?
4 Has the firm suffered from stockouts of finished merchandise or raw materials?
5 What is the record for quality, service, and price of its present suppliers? How about dependability and assistance in periods of sellers' markets?
6 How does the firm set its minimum ordering quantities?
7 Has buying policy been guilty of buying too large quantities which were not justified by carrying costs?
8 What is the cost of carrying inventories in stock until needed?
9 Does the firm owner know what the best average inventory is and use it to guide purchasing policy?
10 Could more effective purchasing contribute profits to the present results of operation? How?

13 FOR EVALUATING EXPENSES AND A BREAK-EVEN CHART

1 Have fixed and variable expenses been thoroughly determined?
2 Are there advantages to altering the present relationship of fixed and variable expenses? Is this possible?
3 Has the firm produced a break-even chart for annual operations?
4 Has this chart been reduced to monthly periods?
5 Could the break-even point in sales be lowered? How?

6 Can any fixed expenses be made variable in order to reduce risks?
7 How would profits change with a 10 percent increase in sales?
8 How would profits change with a 10 percent reduction in fixed expenses?
9 Is the firm approaching 100 percent of capacity in its present quarters?
10 Is the present percentage of capacity known? Can it be increased?
11 Is each expense dollar providing a productive return to the firm?
12 Can semi-variable expenses be controlled any better?

14 FOR EVALUATING CREDIT POLICIES

1 Is the firm financially equipped to carry its own accounts receivable?
2 What types of credit accounts are available to customers now?
3 Should other types of accounts be made available?
4 What is the cost of administering the present credit program?
5 Would it be better for this firm at this time to discount all its receivables with a finance company or bank?
6 Are credit-card sales being collected efficiently? What is their cost?
7 Should the firm issue its own credit cards?
8 Does its credit policy reflect the fact that the company has both small and large credit sales?
9 Has an aging of accounts receivable been made lately? What does it show?
10 Has the write-off of bad debts been realistic, too low, or too high?
11 If the firm sells to business firms, has a sales discount been offered? Should it be?
12 Has the firm taken advantage of purchase discounts offered to it?

15 FOR EVALUATING PROTECTION AGAINST RISKS

1 Has the ownership truly analyzed all the major risks to which the firm is subject?
2 What protection has been provided against each of these risks?
3 Is the incidence of risk properly considered in the protective action taken?
4 Is self-insurance appropriate for this firm?
5 How many risks are being absorbed? Should they be?

6 Is coinsurance appropriate for this firm? How?
7 Are there any recommendations for reducing risks or getting protection more economically?

16 FOR EVALUATING PERSONNEL POLICIES

1 What has been the turnover of desirable employees?
2 Are any outstanding reasons for resignations to be observed?
3 Does the company provide training for new employees?
4 Are company policies regarding personnel known to all new and old employees?
5 Are there incentives in the personnel policy for employees to seek advancement?
6 Does the policy reflect the generally agreed-upon objectives of all employees?
7 Do opportunities exist for employees to work at different types of positions?
8 Is the company image one that suggests this is a good firm to work with?
9 Are pay scales and/or other advantages consistent with larger firms in the area?
10 Is there any problem of employees being overtrained or undertrained?
11 Are there any recommendations for changes in the present policies?

DIVISION DES RECHERCHES

Dun & Bradstreet Canada Limited/Limitée

TORONTO

Classification of Causes of Business Failures in Canada, Total Year 1977

Based on Opinions of Informed Creditors and Information in Dun & Bradstreet's Credit Reports

LINE OF BUSINESS—ALL				METHOD OF OPERATION—ALL		
Number	Per Cent	UNDERLYING CAUSES		APPARENT CAUSES	Number	Per Cent
				Bad Habits	18	0.4
93	2.2	NEGLECT	Due to:	Poor Health	42	1.0
				Marital Difficulties	20	0.5
				Other	13	0.3
				Misleading Name	—	—
				False Financial Statement	2	0.1
7	0.2	FRAUD	On the part of the principals, reflected by:	Premeditated Overbuy	—	—
				Irregular Disposal of Assets	4	0.1
				Other	1	0.0
475	11.5	LACK OF EXPERIENCE IN THE LINE		Inadequate Sales	1,510	36.6
				Heavy Operating Expenses	1,913	46.3
879	21.3	LACK OF MANAGERIAL EXPERIENCE		Receivables Difficulties	135	3.3
			Evidenced by inability to avoid conditions which result in:	Inventory Difficulties	216	5.2
319	7.7	UNBALANCED EXPERIENCE*		Excessive Fixed Assets	96	2.3
				Poor Location	39	1.0
2,287	55.4	INCOMPETENCE		Competitive Weakness	172	4.2
				Other	6	0.1
				Fire	10	0.2
				Flood	—	—
38	0.9	DISASTER	Some of these occurrences could have been provided against through insurance.	Burglary	4	0.1
				Employees' Fraud	4	0.1
				Strike	3	0.1
				Other	17	0.4
33	0.8	REASON UNKNOWN				
4,131	100.0	TOTAL				

Because some failures are attributed to a combination of apparent causes, the totals of these columns exceed the totals of the corresponding columns on the left.

*Experience not well rounded in sales, finance, purchasing, and production on the part of an individual in case of a proprietorship, or of two or more partners or officer constituting a management unit.

What caused 4,131 businesses to fail in one year?

APPENDIX TWO

Government Publications to Aid Small Businesses

Everybody should know the extent to which governments try to assist those who are planning a new firm and those operating a small firm. Federal and provincial government departments charged with industrial and commercial development have staff available to help small firms in arranging financial assistance, in dealing with management problems, and in getting government contracts. The Federal Business Development Bank has also issued several small publications in pamphlet form which are free. All small firm owners and planners should be familiar with these publications. They should also know the address of the closest Department of Industry, Trade, and Commerce and Federal Business Development Bank field office to which they can write to obtain without charge any of the publications listed below. Addresses are given in the last section of Appendix Two.

FEDERAL BUSINESS DEVELOPMENT BANK PUBLICATIONS

No. 1 Reference booklets for small business
No. 2 Giving credit to your customers
No. 3 Presenting your case for a term loan
No. 4 Forecasting for an existing business

No. 5 Managing your current assets
No. 6 Forecasting for a new business
No. 7 Managing your fixed assets
No. 8 Managing your cash
No. 9 Working capital
No. 10 Changes of ownership
No. 11 Planning a motel
No. 12 Equity capital for small companies
No. 13 Paying your employees
No. 14 Personnel records
No. 15 Planning the start of your retail business

DEPARTMENT OF INDUSTRY, TRADE, AND COMMERCE PUBLICATIONS

AGRICULTURE AND FOOD

Canadian Export Trade Development Agriculture and Food — English and French (1976)

BUSINESS AND FINANCE

Doing Business in Canada

Series published in English, French, and German — outlining basic legislation and regulations affecting the conduct of business in Canada.

1) Business Environment
2) Forms of Business Organization
3) Canadian Customs Duties
4) Taxation — Income, Business, Property
5) Taxation — Sales, Excise and Commodity
6) Labour Legislation
7) Construction Equipment Standards
8) Federal Incentives to Industry
9) Patents, Trademarks, Industrial Designs and Copyrights

Financing Canadian Industries — English and French (1977)
Sources of Venture Capital — English and French (1977)
Federal Export Programs and Services — Bilingual (1976)

CHEMICALS

Statistical Profile of the Plastics Processing Industry in Canada — English and French (1976)
A Report on the Plastics Processing Industry in Canada — English and French (1977)

CONSTRUCTION

Computer Uses in the Construction Industry — English and French (1976)
Export Opportunity for Canadian Manufactured Homes — English and French (1974)

DESIGN

Design Education in Canada, List of Institutions — Bilingual (1977)

ECONOMY

Sector Profiles Series: English and French (1978)

- Aerospace Manufacturing
- Automotive
- Cement and Concrete
- Clothing
- Commercial Printing
- Construction
- Electrical Products
- Electronics
- Fertilizer
- Footwear
- Forest Products
- Processed Fruits and Vegetables
- Furniture
- Primary Iron and Steel
- Machinery
- Non-Ferrous Metals
- Ocean Industry
- Petrochemical
- Plastic Processing
- Primary Textiles
- Shipbuilding and Repair
- Urban Transportation Equipment
- Tourism

EXPORTS

Markets for Canadian Exporters — Series of bilingual booklets on export opportunities for the following countries:

— Australia (1974)
— Central America (1976)
— Chile (1977)
— Mexico (1975)
— Mid-Atlantic (1973)
— New England States (1977)

- — China (1976)
- — Colombia, Ecuador (1977)
- — Cuba (1975)
- — Detroit (1973)
- — Eastern Caribbean (1976)
- — Haiti, Puerto Rico, Dominican Republic (1976)
- — Hong Kong (1977)
- — Japan (1976)
- — Korea (1977)
- — Malaysia (1975)
- — New York (1976)
- — New Zealand (1976)
- — Nigeria (1974)
- — Pakistan (1977)
- — Peru, Bolivia (1977)
- — Philippines (1976)
- — Singapore (1976)
- — Thailand (1975)
- — Upstate New York (1972)
- — Venezuela (1977)

World Market Opportunities Series — English and French (1977)

- — Agriculture and Food Products
- — Capital Projects
- — Chemicals
- — Defence
- — Electrical and Electronics
- — Fisheries
- — Grains
- — Machinery
- — Resource Industries
- — Textile and Consumer Products
- — Transportation

Guide to Kwangchow — English and French (1975)

Market Profiles of Eastern Europe

Markets in Brief — Latin American Countries

GENERAL INFORMATION

Annual Report — English and French
Canadian Federal Services to Business — English and French (1977)
Small Business in Canada: Perspectives — Bilingual (1977)
Computer-Aided Design and Manufacturing in Canada — English and French (1977)
Cad/Cam and Canada — English (1977)

RESOURCE INDUSTRY

Report on the 1976 Survey on the Canadian Ferrous Foundry Industry — English and French 1976
Terminology of the Copper Industry — Glossary English-French/French-English (1976)

TEXTILES AND CONSUMER PRODUCTS

Report of the Anti-Dumping Tribunal Respecting the Effects of Imports on the Canadian Footwear Industry — Bilingual (1977)

TRANSPORTATION

Review of the North American Automotive Industry — English and French (1977)

STATISTICS CANADA

Statistics Canada, as Canada's central statistical agency, has a national responsibility for collecting and publishing the statistical information needed by governments, industry, and the general public to understand the social and economic conditions of the country.

Information is available at minimum cost on almost every business, industrial, economic, and social activity in the country. While the bureau prints an average of nine publications each working day, only some of the available information is released in this fashion. Much more is available upon request or is released in microform, as a computer print-out or on a computer tape, or is available on-line through CANSIM, the bureau's machine-readable database. A free catalogue summarizes information available in the publications and gives references to the unpublished information, the microform products, and the important CANSIM program.

Specialized services are available to the public from the various subject areas, for example, trade statistics, price statistics, and manufacturing statistics. The quinquennial Census of Population is the bureau's largest single program and the Census Information Service can provide a wide variety of socio-economic information on individuals and households for large or small geographic areas. In addition to the published data for almost all Census variables and some basic cross-tabulations of variables, more information is available in microform, on computer tapes and maps, and custom-tabulations can also be provided for special geographical areas at a reasonable cost.

Free publications are available to help the businessman find out more about the products and services of Statistics Canada and how to use statistics. In addition to the Catalogue, there are, for example, "Infomat," a weekly bulletin which summarizes highlights of bureau releases and lists titles of publications released each week: "Your Guide to thc Consumer Price Index"; and "How a Manufacturer Can Profit from Facts."

The bureau has a User Advisory Services Division whose primary task is to help people identify, obtain, and effectively use statistical information. The Division has statistical reference centres in nine major cities and toll-free telephone access is available in several other areas.

These centres are the easiest point of entry to Statistics Canada. They are staffed by inquiries officers who each year answer over 140,000 requests for statistics or advice on the meaning and use of data. Most requests are received by telephone but many are by letter or from visitors to the libraries, which are open during normal working hours and provide study areas and permit limited photocopying. Arrangements to purchase publications can be made through the centres or directly from Ottawa. Computer terminals are available in each centre to access information directly from CANSIM.

Each local office has one or more Regional Advisers who promote the use of statistics through visits, talks, and meetings; assist both experienced and inexperienced users with data problems and, if necessary, help people get in touch with the appropriate specialists in Ottawa; and feed back to Ottawa users' views, comments, criticisms, etc., to help Statistics Canada improve its products and services.

STATISTICS CANADA REGIONAL USER ADVISORY SERVICES

Central Inquiries Service	Statistics Canada Ottawa, Ont. K1A 0T6 (613) 992-2959 (613) 992-4734
St. John's	Statistics Canada P.O. Box 8556 3rd Floor, Viking Building Crosbie Road St. John's, Nfld. A1B 3P2 (709) 726-0713
Halifax	Statistics Canada 1256 Barrington Street Halifax, N.S. B3J 1Y6 (902) 426-5331
Montreal	Statistics Canada Alexis Nihon Plaza 1500 Atwater Avenue Montreal, Que. H3Z 1Y2 (514) 283-5725

Toronto	Statistics Canada 25 St. Clair Avenue East Toronto, Ont. M4T 1M4 (416) 966-6586
Winnipeg	Statistics Canada Room 500, General Post Office 266 Graham Avenue Winnipeg, Man. R3C 0K4 (204) 985-4020
Regina	Statistics Canada 530 Midtown Centre Regina, Sask. S4P 2B6 (306) 569-5405
Edmonton	Statistics Canada 10th Floor, Baker Centre Building 10025 — 106th Street Edmonton, Alta. T5J 1G9 (403) 425-5052
Vancouver	Statistics Canada 16 East Hastings Street Vancouver, B.C. V6A 1N1 (604) 666-3695

Toll-free access to the Halifax office is available from Charlottetown, Moncton, Saint John, and Sydney by calling the operator and asking for ZENITH 22066. Throughout Saskatchewan, the Regina office can be reached by dialing 1-(800)-667-3524, and in Alberta, the Edmonton office can be reached by dialing 1-(800)-222-6400.

To subscribe to publications, write to:

Publications Distribution
Statistics Canada
Room 1045, Statistics Canada Bldg.
Tunney's Pasture
Ottawa, Ont. K1A 0T6

PROVINCIAL AND TERRITORIAL STATISTICAL AGENCIES

Alberta	Alberta Bureau of Statistics Room 480, Terrace Bldg. Edmonton, Alta. T5K 2C3
British Columbia	Economic Plans and Statistics Department of Economic Development Parliament Bldgs. Victoria, B.C. V8V 1X4
Manitoba	Manitoba Bureau of Statistics Room 202, 323 Portage Ave. Winnipeg, Man. R3B 2C1
New Brunswick	Office of the Economic Advisor P.O. Box 6000 Fredericton, N.B. E3B 5H1
Newfoundland	Central Statistical Services Executive Council Confederation Bldg. St. John's, Nfld. A1C 5T7
Nova Scotia	Economics and Statistics Division Department of Development P.O. Box 519 Halifax, N.S. B3J 2R7
Ontario	Central Statistical Services 10th Floor, 56 Wellesley St. West Toronto, Ont. M7A 1Y9
Prince Edward Island	Treasury Board P.O. Box 2000 Charlottetown, P.E.I. C1A 7N8
Québec	Bureau de la statistique Ministère de l'industrie et du commerce Chambre 710, Place d'Youville Québec, Qué. G1R 4Y4

Saskatchewan	Planning and Research Executive Council Room 137, Legislative Bldg. Regina, Sask. S4S 0B3
Northwest Territories	Financial Adviser Government of the Northwest Territories Yellowknife, N.W.T.
Yukon Territory	Statistical and Planning Advisor P.O. Box 2703 Whitehorse, Y.T.

DEPARTMENT OF INDUSTRY, TRADE, AND COMMERCE REGIONAL OFFICES

Across Canada, whenever and wherever a businessman or industrialist wants help or advice on how to improve his operation, there is a federal Department of Industry, Trade, and Commerce Regional Office within easy reach. Offices are located in Vancouver, Edmonton, Regina, Winnipeg, Toronto, Montreal, Quebec, Halifax, Charlottetown, St. John's, and Fredericton.

The Regional Offices are part of the department's Field Operations, which include the Trade Commissioner Service.

Informed and competent staff members in each of the 11 offices are well prepared to provide information and guidance on industrial incentive programs, export opportunities, and many other ways of improving productivity.

REGIONAL OFFICES IN CANADA

NEWFOUNDLAND REGION
210 Water Street
St. John's, Newfoundland
A1C 1A9
Tel: (709) 737-5511
Telex: 016-4749

NOVA SCOTIA REGION
Suite 1124, Duke Tower
5251 Duke Street
Scotia Square
Halifax, Nova Scotia
B3J 1N9
Tel: (902) 426-7540
Telex: 019-21829

PRINCE EDWARD ISLAND REGION
Dominion Building
97 Queen St, P.O. Box 2289
Charlottetown, P.E.I.
C1A 8C1
Tel: (902) 892-1211
Telex: 014-44129

NEW BRUNSWICK REGION
Suite 642
440 King Street
Fredericton, New Brunswick
E3B 5H8
Tel: (506) 454-9707
Telex: 014-46140

QUEBEC CITY
Suite 620
2 Place Quebec
Quebec, Quebec
G1R 2N5
Tel: (418) 694-4726
Telex: 011-3312

QUEBEC REGION
Room 2124, Place Victoria
P.O. Box 257, Tour de la Bourse
Montreal, Quebec
H4Z 1J5
Tel:(514) 283-6254
Telex: 012-0280

ONTARIO REGION
Commerce Court West
51st Floor, P.O. Box 325
Toronto, Ontario
M5L 1G1
Tel: (416) 369-3711
Telex: 022-1691

MANITOBA REGION
Suite 1104, Royal Bank Bldg.
220 Portage Avenue
Winnipeg, Manitoba
R3C 0A5
Tel: (204) 985-2381
Telex: 075-7624

SASKATCHEWAN REGION
980-2002 Victoria Avenue
Regina, Saskatchewan
S4P 0R7
Tel: (306) 569-5020
Telex: 071-2745

ALBERTA & NORTHWEST TERRITORIES REGION
500 Macdonald Place
9939 Jasper Avenue
Edmonton, Alberta
T5J 2W8
Tel: (403) 425-6330
Telex: 037-2762

BRITISH COLUMBIA & YUKON REGION
Suite 2743, P.O. Box 49178
Bentall Centre, Tower "III"
595 Burrard Street
Vancouver, British Columbia
N7X 1K8
Tel: (604) 666-1434
Telex: 045-1191

DEPT. OF REGIONAL ECONOMIC EXPANSION OFFICES

ATLANTIC (REGIONAL OFFICE)
Director of Incentives
Department of Regional Economic Expansion
14th Floor, Assumption Place
770 Main Street
P.O. Box 1210
Moncton, New Brunswick E1C 8P9
Tel: (506) 858-2851

NEW BRUNSWICK
Manager, Incentives
Department of Regional Economic Expansion
Armstrong Building
590 Brunswick Street
P.O. Box 578
Fredericton, New Brunswick E3B 5A6
Tel: (506) 454-9751

NEWFOUNDLAND
Manager, Incentives
Department of Regional Economic Expansion
Ashley Building
Peet Street
P.O. Box 8950
St. John's, Newfoundland A1B 3R9
Tel: (709) 722-7200

NOVA SCOTIA
Manager, Incentives
Department of Regional Economic Expansion
Centennial Building
1645 Granville Street
Halifax, Nova Scotia B3J 1X3
Tel: (902) 426-6360

PRINCE EDWARD ISLAND
Manager, Incentives
Department of Regional Economic Expansion
Dominion Building
97 Queen Street
P.O. Box 1115
Charlottetown, Prince Edward Island C1A 7M8
Tel: (902) 892-8551

QUEBEC (BUREAU REGIONAL)
Directeur des subventions
Ministère de l'expansion économique régionale
Pièce 4328
Tour de la Bourse
800, Place Victoria
C.P. 247
Montréal (Québec) H4Z 1E8
Tél: (514) 283-7813

Administrateur des subventions
Ministère de l'expansion économique régionale
Edifice Le Claridge
220, Grande Allée est
Pièce 820
Québec (Québec) G1R 2J1
Tél: (418) 694-4451

ONTARIO (REGIONAL OFFICE)
Director of Incentives
Department of Regional Economic Expansion
6th Floor, Niagara Building
1300 Yonge Street
Toronto, Ontario M4T 1X3
Tel: (416) 996-6006

Manager, Incentives
Department of Regional Economic Expansion
Court Holding Building
233 Court Street South
P.O. Box 3348, Station "P"
Thunder Bay, Ontario P7B 2X9
Tel: (807) 345-1161

WESTERN (REGIONAL OFFICE)
Director of Incentives
Department of Regional Economic Expansion
814 Bessborough Tower
601 Spadina Crescent
Saskatoon, Saskatchewan S7K 0E9
Tel: (306) 242-7681

REPRESENTATIVES OF THE EXPORT DEVELOPMENT CORPORATION

HEAD OFFICE
Corporate Communications Department
Export Development Corporation
P.O. Box 655
Ottawa, Canada K1P 5T9
Tel: (613) 237-2570
Telex: 053-4136
Cable: Excrecorp

IN THE EASTERN PROVINCES
Eastern Region Manager
Export Development Corporation
Lock Box 124
Tour de la Bourse Postal Station
Montreal, Quebec H4Z 1C3
Tel: (514) 866-4796

IN THE PROVINCE OF ONTARIO
Ontario Region Manager
Export Development Corporation
Suite 2011, 145 King Street West
Toronto, Ontario M5H 1J8
Tel: (416) 364-0135

Toll free from Belleville, Kingston, London, Kitchener-Waterloo, North Bay, Peterborough, Sault Ste. Marie, Sudbury, Thunder Bay, and Windsor — call operator and ask for Zenith 85920.

IN THE WESTERN PROVINCES
Western Region Manager
Export Development Corporation
P.O. Box 49024, The Bentall Centre
Vancouver, British Columbia V7X 1C4
Tel: (604) 688-8658
Telex: 053-4284

Toll free from Winnipeg, Regina, Saskatoon, Edmonton, Calgary, and Victoria — call operator and ask for Zenith 08659.

PROVINCIAL GOVERNMENT OFFICES AND AGENCIES

Province	Government Department	Industrial Development Agency
Alberta	Department of Business Development and Tourism Centennial Building Edmonton, Alta. T5J 0H4	Alberta Opportunity Company 1710 Centennial Building 1015-103 Avenue Edmonton, Alta. T5J 0H4
British Columbia	Ministry of Economic Development Parliament Buildings Victoria, B.C. V8V 1X4	British Columbia Development Coporation Suite 272, Granville Square 200 Granville Street Vancouver, B.C. V6C 1S4
Manitoba	Department of Industry and Commerce 358 Legislative Building Winnipeg, Man. R3C 0V8	Manitoba Development Corporation 600 Power Building 428 Portage Avenue Winnipeg, Man. R3C 0E4
New Brunswick	Department of Commerce and Development P.O. Box 6000 Fredericton, N.B. E3B 5H1	New Brunswick Industrial Development Corporation P.O. Box 6000 Fredericton, N.B. E3B 5H1
Newfoundland	Department of Industrial Development Confederation Building St. John's, Nfld. A1C 5T7	Newfoundland and Labrador Development Corporation Confederation Building St. John's, Nfld. A1C 5T7

Nova Scotia	Department of Development P.O. Box 519 5151 George Street Halifax, N.S. B3J 2R7	Industrial Estates Limited Suite 700 5151 George Street Halifax, N.S. B3J 2R7
Ontario	Ministry of Industry and Tourism 900 Bay Street Toronto, Ont. M7A 2E4	Ontario Development Corporation Mowat Block 900 Bay Street Toronto, Ont. M7A 2E7
Prince Edward Island	Department of Industry and Commerce P.O. Box 2000 Charlottetown, P.E.I. C1A 7N8	Industrial Enterprises Incorporated West Royalty Industrial Park West Royalty, P.E.I. C1A 1B0
Québec	Ministère de l'industrie et du commerce 710 Place d'Youville Québec, P.Q. G1A 1K9	Société de développement industriel du Québec Edifice Tour de la Base Bureau 4203 Montreal, P.Q. H4Z 1E8 Société générale de financement du Québec 680 ouest, rue Sherbrooke Bureau 800 Montréal, P.Q. H3A 2M7
Saskatchewan	Department of Industry and Commerce Power Building Regina, Sask. S4P 2Y9	Saskatchewan Economic Development Corporation 1106 Winnipeg Street Regina, Sask. S4R 6N9

FEDERAL BUSINESS DEVELOPMENT BANK OFFICES

ATLANTIC REGIONAL OFFICE:
1400 Cogswell Tower, Scotia Square, Halifax, N.S. B3J 3K1
Tel.: (902) 426-7860

Branch Office	Address	Telephone
ST. JOHN'S	Viking Bldg., Crosbie Rd. St. John's, Nfld. A1B 3K4	(709) 737-5505
GRAND FALLS	42 High Street Grand Falls, Nfld. A2A 1C6	(709) 489-2181
CORNER BROOK	Corner Brook Plaza Trans Canada Highway Corner Brook, Nfld.	(709) 639-9186
HALIFAX	Trade Mart 2021 Brunswick St. Halifax, N.S. B3K 2Y5	(902) 426-7850
SYDNEY	48-50 Dorchester St. Sydney, N.S. B1P 5Z1	(902) 539-4556
BRIDGEWATER	655 King Street Bridgewater, N.S. B4V 1B5	(902) 543-7821
TRURO	CN Commercial Centre 34 Esplanade St. Truro, N.S. B2N 2K3	(902) 895-6377
SAINT JOHN	75 Prince William Street Saint John, N.B. E2L 2B2	(506) 658-4751
FREDERICTON	Kings Place Complex 440 King Street Fredericton, N.B. E3B 5H8	(506) 455-7745
MONCTON	860 Main Street Moncton, N.B. E1C 1G2	(506) 858-2370
BATHURST	270 Douglas Ave. Bathurst, N.B. E2A 1M9	(506) 548-3345
CHARLOTTE- TOWN	137 Kent Street Charlottetown, P.E.I. C1A 1N3	(902) 892-9151

QUEBEC REGIONAL OFFICE:

4600 Place Victoria, 800 Victoria Square, Montreal, P.Q. H4Z 1C8
Tel.: (514) 283-3657

SEPT-ILES	690 Laure Blvd. Sept-Iles, P.Q. G4R 1X9	(418) 968-1420
RIMOUSKI	320 St. Germain Street, East Rimouski, P.Q. G5L 1C2	(418) 724-4461
CHICOUTIMI	475 des Champs Elysées Street Chicoutimi, P.Q. G7H 5V7	(418) 545-1580
QUÉBEC	925 Chemin St. Louis Quebec, P.Q. G1S 1C1	(418) 681-6341
LÉVIS	113 St. Georges Street West Lévis, P.Q. G6V 4L2	(418) 837-0282
TROIS-RIVIÈRES	1410 Des Cyprès Street Trois-Rivières, P.Q. G8Y 4S3	(819) 375-1621
DRUMMOND-VILLE	228 Hériot St. Drummondville, P.Q. J2C 1K1	(819) 478-4951
SHERBROOKE	2532 ouest, rue King Sherbrooke, P.Q. J1J 2E8	(819) 565-4740
GRANBY	161 rue Principale Granby, P.Q. J2G 2V5	(514) 372-5202
LONGUEUIL	Complexe Blenville 1000 de Sérigny Street Longueuil, P.Q. J4K 5B1	(514) 670-9550

VALLEYFIELD	85 Champlain St. Valleyfield, P.Q. J6T 1W4	(514) 371-0611
MONTRÉAL	1008 Place Victoria 800 Victoria Square Montreal, P.Q. H4Z 1C8	(514) 878-9571
	205 Place Frontenac 2600 Ontario Street, East Montreal, P.Q. H2K 4K4	(514) 524-1188
LASALLE	1550 Dollard Avenue LaSalle, P.Q. H8N 1T6	(514) 364-4410
ST. LAURENT	750 Laurentien Blvd. St. Laurent, P.Q. H4M 2M4	(514) 748-7323
ST. LÉONARD	5960 Jean-Talon Street East, St. Léonard, P.Q. H1S 1M2	(514) 254-6073
LAVAL	2525 Marois Blvd. Chomedey, Laval, P.Q. H7T 1S9	(514) 681-9289
ST. JÉRÓME	Galeries dos Laurentides St. Antoine des Laurentides P.Q.	(514) 436-6441
ROUYN-NORANDA	147 Mercier Ave. Rouyn, P.Q. J9X 4X4	(819) 764-6701
HULL	Plaza Val Téireau 400 Alexandre Taché Blvd. Hull, P.Q. J9A 1M5	(819) 997-4434

ONTARIO REGIONAL OFFICE:
250 University Avenue, Toronto, Ont. M5H 3E5
Tel.: (416) 368-4874

OTTAWA	151 Sparks Street Ottawa, Ont. K1P 5E3	(613) 237-8430

KINGSTON	797 Princess Street Kingston, Ont. K7L 1G1	(613) 549-1531
PETERBOROUGH	340 George St. N. Peterborough, Ont. K9H 7E8	(705) 748-3241
OSHAWA	22 King Street, West Oshawa, Ont. L1H 1A3	(416) 576-6800
TORONTO	204 Richmond St. W. Toronto, Ont. M5V 1V6	(416) 598-0341
ETOBICOKE	Valhalla Executive Centre 302 The East Mall Islington, Ont. M9B 6C7	(416) 239-4804
SCARBOROUGH	2978 Eglinton Ave., East Scarborough, Ont. M1J 2E7	(416) 431-5410
TORONTO-NORTH	4430 Bathurst Street Downsview, Ont. M3H 3S3	(416) 638-0823
BARRIE	70 Collier Street Barrie, Ont. L4M 1G8	(705) 728-6072
OAKVILLE	345 Lakeshore Road, East Oakville, Ont. L6J 1J5	(416) 844-0911
HAMILTON	8 Main Street, East Hamilton, Ont. L8N 1E8	(416) 528-0471
ST. CATHARINES	71 King Street St. Catharines, Ont. L2R 3H6	(416) 684-1153
KITCHENER-WATERLOO	305 King Street, West Kitchener, Ont. N2G 1B9	(519) 744-4186
OWEN SOUND	1139 Second Avenue, East Owen Sound, Ont. N4K 2J1	(519) 376-4431
LONDON	197 York Street London, Ont. N6A 1B2	(519) 434-2144

WOODSTOCK	430 Dundas Street Woodstock, Ont.	(519) 537-5846
STRATFORD	1036 Ontario Street Stratford, Ont. N5A 6Z3	(519) 271-5650
CHATHAM	59 Adelaide Street, South Chatham, Ont. N7M 4R1	(519) 354-8833
WINDSOR	500 Ouellette Avenue, Windsor, Ont. N9A 1B3	(519) 254-8626

Northern Ontario District Office:
421 Bay Street, Sault Ste. Marie, Ont. P6A 5N7
Tel.: (705) 949-1983

SUDBURY	96 Larch Street Sudbury, Ont. P3E 1C1	(705) 674-8347
TIMMINS	83 Algonquin Blvd., West Timmins, Ont. P4N 2R4	(705) 264-9432
SAULT STE. MARIE	452 Albert Street, East Sault Ste. Marie, Ont. P6A 2J8	(705) 949-3680
THUNDER BAY	106 Centennial Square Thunder Bay, Ont. P7E 1H3	(807) 623-2745
KENORA	20 Main Street, South Kenora, Ont. P9N 1S7	(807) 468-5575

PRAIRIE AND NORTHERN REGIONAL OFFICE:
161 Portage Avenue, Winnipeg, Man. R3B 0Y4
Tel.: (204) 943-8581

WINNIPEG	386 Broadway Avenue Winnipeg, Man. R3C 3R6	(204) 944-9991
ST. BONIFACE	851 Lagimodiere Blvd. Winnipeg, Man. R2J 3K4	(204) 233-6791

BRANDON	136-11th Street Brandon, Man. R7A 4J4	(204) 727-8415
REGINA	2220-12th Avenue Regina, Sask. S4P 0M8	(306) 569-6478
SASKATOON	1102 CN Towers Midtown Plaza Saskatoon, Sask. S7K 1J5	(306) 665-4822
PRINCE ALBERT	1100-1st Avenue East Prince Albert, Sask. S6V 2A7	(306) 764-6448
LETHBRIDGE	740-4th Avenue South Lethbridge, Alta. T1J 0N9	(403) 328-9681
CALGARY	404 Sixth Avenue, S.W. Calgary, Alta. T2P 0R9	(403) 269-6981
CALGARY-SOUTH	5940 Macleod Trail, S.W. Calgary, Alta. T2H 2G4	(403) 253-6501
RED DEER	4909 Gaetz Avenue Red Deer, Alta. T4N 4A7	(403) 346-8821
EDMONTON	10150-100th Street Edmonton, Alta. T5J 0P6	(403) 429-4926
EDMONTON SOUTH	11044-51st Avenue Edmonton, Alta. T6H 5B4	(403) 436-6533
EDMONTON WEST	11574-149th Street Edmonton, Alta. T5M 1W7	(403) 452-3232
YELLOWKNIFE	5010-50th Avenue Yellowknife, N.W.T.	(403) 873-3566
GRANDE PRAIRIE	10135-101st Avenue Grande Prairie, Alta. T8V 0Y4	(403) 532-8875
WHITEHORSE	Travelodge Commercial Mall Whitehorse, Y.T.	(403) 667-7333

BRITISH COLUMBIA REGIONAL OFFICE:
900 West Hastings Street, Vancouver, B.C. V6C 1E7
Tel.: (604) 666-8631

CRANBROOK	30 South 11th Avenue Cranbrook, B.C. V1C 2P1	(604) 426-7241
KELOWNA	260 Harvey Avenue Kelowna, B.C. V1Y 7S5	(604) 762-2035
VERNON	3303 Coldstream Ave. Vernon, B.C. V1T 1Y1	(604) 545-7215
KAMLOOPS	235 First Avenue Kamloops, B.C. V2C 3J4	(604) 374-2121
WILLIAMS LAKE	30A North, Third Avenue Williams Lake, B.C. V2G 2A2	(604) 398-8233
PRINCE GEORGE	1320 Fifth Avenue Prince George, B.C. V2L 3L5	(604) 563-0641
TERRACE	4548 Lakelse Avenue Terrace, B.C. V8G 1P8	(604) 635-4951
CHILLIWACK	Kamar Plaza 45850 Yale Road West Chilliwack, B.C. V2P 2N9	(604) 792-8621
ABBOTSFORD	2467 Pauline St. Abbotsford, B.C. V2S 3S1	(604) 853-5561
LANGLEY	20316-56th Ave. Langley, B.C. V3A 3Y7	(604) 533-1221
NEW WESTMINSTER	227-6th Street New Westminster, B.C. V3L 3A5	(604) 525-1011
BURNABY	4240 Manor Street Burnaby, B.C. V5G 3X5	(604) 438-3581
RICHMOND	3751 Shell Road Richmond, B.C. V6X 2W2	(604) 273-8611

VANCOUVER	885 Dunsmuir Street Vancouver, B.C. V6C 1N7	(604) 681-7484
VANCOUVER EAST	3369 Fraser Street Vancouver, B.C. V5V 4C2	(604) 873-6391
NORTH VANCOUVER	145 West 15th Street North Vancouver, B.C. V7M 1R9	(604) 980-6571
VICTORIA	850 Fort Street Victoria, B.C. V8W 1H8	(604) 385-3375
NANAIMO	190 Wallace St. Nanaimo, B.C. V9R 5B1	(604) 753-2471
COURTNEY	497 Fitzgerald Ave. Courtney, B.C. V9N 2R1	(604) 338-6232
CAMPBELL RIVER	906 Island Highway Campbell River, B.C. V9W 2C3	(604) 287-9236
DUNCAN	394 Duncan Street Duncan, B.C. V9L 3W4	(604) 748-5202

DEPOSITORY LIBRARIES FOR CANADIAN GOVERNMENT PUBLICATIONS

This is a list of libraries recognized by the Publishing Centre, Department of Supply and Services, Ottawa, as full depositories for Canadian federal government publications. The libraries receive publications listed in the Daily Checklist of Government Publications automatically and without charge. Libraries marked with an asterisk (*) receive both English and French editions.

Alberta

Calgary	Calgary Public Library 616 Macleod Trail S.E. Calgary, Alta. T2G 2M2 (403) 268-2880
	University of Calgary Library 2920 24th Avenue N.W. Calgary, Alta. T2N 1N4 (403) 284-5954

Edmonton	Edmonton Public Library No. 7 Sir Winston Churchill Sq. Edmonton, Alta. T5J 2V4 (403) 423-2331
	Legislature Library of Alberta 216 Legislature Bldg. Edmonton, Alta. T5K 2B6 (403) 229-4313
British Columbia Burnaby	Simon Fraser University Library Burnaby, B.C. V5A 1S6 (604) 291-3261
Vancouver	University of British Columbia Library 2075 Wesbrook Place Vancouver, B.C. V6T 1W5 (604) 228-3871
	Vancouver Public Library 750 Burrard Street Vancouver, B.C. V6Z 1X5 (604) 682-5911
Victoria	Legislative Library of British Columbia Parliament Bldgs. Victoria, B.C. V8V 1X4 (604) 387-6500
	McPherson Library University of Victoria Victoria, B.C. V8W 2Y3 (604) 477-6911
Manitoba Winnipeg	Elizabeth Dafoe Library University of Manitoba Winnipeg, Man. R3T 2N2 (204) 474-9881
	Legislative Library of Manitoba 257 Legislative Bldg. 200 Vaughan Street Winnipeg, Man. R3C 0P8 (204) 946-7214

New Brunswick

Fredericton	Harriet Irving Library University of New Brunswick Fredericton, N.B. E3B 5H5 (506) 453-4740
	New Brunswick Legislative Library Legislative Bldg. Queen Street Fredericton, N.B. E3B 5H1 (506) 453-2338
Moncton	Bibliothèque Champlain Université de Moncton Moncton, N.B. E1A 3E9 (506) 858-4012
Sackville	Ralph Pickard Bell Library Mount Allison University Sackville, N.B. E0A 3C0 (506) 536-2040
Saint John	Saint John Regional Library 20 Hazen Avenue Saint John, N.B. E2L 3G8 (506) 693-1191

Newfoundland

St. John's	Provincial Reference Library Arts and Culture Centre Allendale Road St. John's, Nfld. A1B 3A3 (709) 722-2500
	Memorial University of Newfoundland Library Elizabeth Avenue St. John's, Nfld. A1C 5O7 (709) 753-1200

Nova Scotia

Halifax	Izaak Killam Memorial Library Dalhousie University Halifax, N.S. B3H 4H8 (902) 424-3601

	Legislative Library of Nova Scotia Nova Scotia Provincial Library Province House, Hollis Street Halifax, N.S. B3H 3J5 (902) 424-5932
Wolfville	Harold Campbell Vaughan Memorial Library Acadia University Acadia Street Wolfville, N.S. B0P 1X0 (902) 542-2201
Ontario Hamilton	Hamilton Public Library 55 Main Street West Hamilton, Ont. L8P 1H5 (416) 529-8111
	Mills Memorial Library McMaster University 1280 Main Street West Hamilton, Ont. L8S 4L6 (416) 525-9140
Kingston	Douglas Library Queen's University at Kingston Kingston, Ont. K7L 5C4 (613) 547-5950
London	D.B. Weldon Library University of Western Ontario 1151 Richmond Street North London, Ont. N6A 3K7 (519) 679-3165
Ottawa	*Library of Parliament Parliament Bldgs. Ottawa, Ont. K1A 0A9 (613) 995-7113
	*National Library of Canada 395 Wellington Street Ottawa, Ont. K1A 0N4 (613) 995-9481

	*Morisset Library University of Ottawa 65 Hastey Ottawa, Ont. K1N 6N5 (613) 213-6880
Sudbury	*Laurentian University Library Ramsey Lake Road Sudbury, Ont. P3E 2C6 (705) 675-1151
Thunder Bay	Lakehead University Library Thunder Bay, Ont. P7B 5E1 (807) 345-2121
	Thunder Bay Public Library 285 Arthur Street Thunder Bay, Ont. P7B 1A9 (807) 344-3585
Toronto	Legislative Library of Ontario Parliament Bldgs. Queen's Park Toronto, Ont. M7A 1A3 (416) 965-5261
	Metropolitan Toronto Central Library 789 Yonge Street Toronto, Ont. M4W 2G8 (416) 928-5150
	Robarts Library University of Toronto 130 St. George Street Toronto, Ont. M5S 1A1 (416) 978-2294
	Toronto Public Library 40 Orchard View Blvd. Toronto, Ont. (416) 484-6087

Scott Library
York University
4700 Keele Street
Downsview, Ont. M3J 2R2
(416) 667-2235

Windsor

Windsor Public Library
850 Ouellette Avenue
Windsor, Ont. N9A 4M9
(519) 258-8111

Prince Edward Island
Charlottetown

Planning Library
Government Reference Library
Charlottetown, P.E.I. C1A 7N8

Quebec
Montreal

*La Bibliothèque Municipale
1210 Sherbrooke St. East
Montréal, Qué. H2L 1L9
(514) 872-2908

Concordia University Library
1455 de Maisonneuve Blvd. West
Montreal, Que. H3G 1M8
(514) 879-7261

*La Bibliothèque
Ecole des Hautes Etudes Commerciales
5255 Ave Decelles
Montréal, Qué. H3T 1V6
(514) 343-4480

*McGill University Libraries
3459 McTavish Street
Montréal, Qué. H3A 1Y1
(514) 392-4948

*Centrale des bibliothèques
Ministère de l'Education du Québec
1685 est, rue Fleury
Montréal, Qué.

	*Bibliothèque Sciences Humaines et Sociales Université de Montréal Montréal, Qué. H3T 1J4 (514) 343-6899
Quebec City	*Bibliothèque de l'Université Laval Cité Universitaire Ste- Foy, Québec, Qué. G1K 7P4 (418) 656-2043
	*Bibliothèque de la Législature Hôtel du Gouvernement Québec, Qué. (418) 643-2896
Saskatchewan Regina	Regina Public Library 2311-12th Avenue Regina, Sask. S4P 0N3 (306) 523-7621
	Saskatchewan Legislative Library 234 Legislative Bldg. Regina, Sask. S4S 0B3 (306) 565-2277
	Murray Memorial Library University of Saskatchewan Saskatoon, Sask. S7N 0W0 (306) 343-4216

Although not published by government, the following publications by the Royal Bank are specifically directed to small businesses. The series is called, "Your Business Matters — A Guide for Independent Business."

No. 1 How to Finance Your Business
2 Pointers to Profit
3 Good Management — Your Key to Survival
4 Exporting — Importing, An Open Door to Additional Profit
5 Financial Reporting and Analysis
6 Control Over Direct Costs and Pricing

7 Planning and Budgeting
8 Control Over Inventory Investment
9 Taxation and Independent Business
10 Credit Management and Fixed Assets
12 Management of Liabilities and Equities
13 Management Audit for Independent Business
14 Market Planning
15 Advertising and Sales Promotion
16 Managing the Future Sales

These excellent booklets are available from the local branches of the Royal Bank free of charge.

Another aid of note to small businesses is "Three-Way Budget, A Businessman's Guide to Cash Control," prepared by the partners of Coopers & Lybrand, a major accounting firm. You can obtain a complimentary copy of this booklet from the local branches of the Bank of Montreal and the Royal Bank or from the local office of Coopers & Lybrand.

Index